revised fourth edition

SPARKS

a reader to energize writing

DONA BARNARD

Orange Coast College

Kendall Hunt
publishing company

Cover image © Shutterstock, Inc.

Kendall Hunt
publishing company

www.kendallhunt.com
Send all inquiries to:
4050 Westmark Drive
Dubuque, IA 52004-1840

PAK ISBN: 978-1-5249-5997-5
Text Alone ISBN: 978-1-5249-5998-2

Published in the United States of America

Dedicated to

Barbara Underwood

in admiration of her courage; and

Bonnie Garcia;

I miss you both.

Brief Contents

Detailed Contents

Essays by Rhetorical Mode

NARRATION

"A Voice for the Lonely" by Stephen Corey

"Mortality" by Bailey White

"Turbulence" by David Sedaris

"Burl's" by Bernard Cooper

"Learning to Read and Write" by Frederick Douglas

"Meat" by Brian Doyle

"Reading the River" by Mark Twain

DESCRIPTION

"Museum Piece" by David Huddle

"Joyas Voladoras" by Brian Doyle

Burl's" by Bernard Cooper

"A Tree Beyond Imagining" by Reg Sanger

"The Courage of Turtles" by Edward Hoagland

"American Children" by John Updike

ILLUSTRATION/EXEMPLIFICATION

"The Little Mermaid" by Pauline Kael

"Joyas Voladoras" by Brian Doyle

"Roll Over Bach, Too!" by Jack Kroll

"Monster Mash" by Jack Kroll

"Musical Awakenings" by Clayton Collins

"Black Widow" by Gordon Grice

"The Content of Our Character" by Shelby Steele

"Disposable Rocket" by John Updike

"The Courage of Turtles" by Edward Hoagland

"The Chemist's War" by Deborah Blum

"Somebody's Baby" by Barbara Kingsolver

"A Dark and Stormy Knight: Why Batman?" by Travis Langley

Preface From *The Dumbest Generation: How the Digital Age Stupefies Young Americans and Jeopardizes Our Future* by Mark Bauerlein.

DEFINITION

"On the Uncertainty of the Future" by Yoshida Kenko

"Joyas Voladoras" by Brian Doyle

"The Content of Our Character" by Shelby Steele

"The Culture of Celebrity" by Joseph Epstein

"Truth" by J. Ruth Gendler

"The Surfing Savant" by Paul Solotaroff

PROCESS

"Disposable Rocket" by John Updike

"Black Widow" by Gordon Grice

"Learning to Read and Write" by Frederick Douglass

Essays by Subject and Theme

SUBTEXT AND FIGURATIVE LANGUAGE

HUMOR AND SATIRE

Style Guide

See specific page numbers in the index for exercises on these style techniques. For brief explanations—including common errors such as fragments, comma splices, and run-on sentences—see the glossary.

ALLITERATION: "Prince."

APPOSITIVES: "Modern Times."

CONCLUSIONS: "Joyas Voladoras."

COLONS: "American Children," "Drugs," "The Content of Our Character," "The Writing Life: The Point of the Long and Winding Sentence."

DASHES: "Modern Times," "Museum Piece," "How to Drive Fast," "Black Widow."

DESCRIPTION AND SENSORY WRITING: "A Voice for the Lonely," "Burl's."

DETAILS AND WORD CHOICE: "Joyas Voladoras," "American Children," "The Little Mermaid," "Mortality."

DIALOGUE: "Turbulence."

EXAMPLES: "The Little Mermaid."

INTRODUCTIONS: "Roll Over Bach, Too!" "Truth," "The Chemist's War," "Somebody's Baby."

LISTING: "American Children," "Disposable Rocket," "The Content of Our Character," "A Dark and Stormy Knight: Why Batman?" Preface From *The Dumbest Generation: How the Digital Age Stupefies Young Americans and Jeopardizes Our Future*, "Community College."

QUESTIONS: "Nourishing Awareness in Each Moment," "Roll Over Bach, Too."

PERIODIC AND LOOSE SENTENCES:

PERIODIC—"A Dark and Stormy Knight: Why Batman?"

LOOSE—"Meat," "Letter to His Master," "How to Drive Fast," "Advice to Youth," "A Voice for the Lonely," Preface From *The Dumbest Generation: How the Digital Age Stupefies Young Americans and Jeopardizes Our Future.*

TITLES: "Monster Mash."

TRANSITIONS: "About Men."

WORD PLAY (SIMILE, METAPHOR, PERSONIFICATION, HYPHENATED WORDS): "The Courage of Turtles," "Joyas Voladoras" (Teaming Up #2), "Musical Awakenings," "The Culture of Celebrity," "A Tree Beyond Imagining," "Truth," "Reading the River."

Assignment Guide

Refer to specific readings under "Writing Ideas" for writing assignments using one or more of these rhetorical modes.

ANALYZING AND EXPLAINING: "A Voice for the Lonely," "Modern Times," "Burl's," "The Courage of Turtles," "Museum Piece," "Roll Over Bach, Too," "Monster Mash," "Musical Awakenings," "Disposable Rocket," "Black Widow," "The Culture of Celebrity," "Fiddling While Africa Starves," "About Men," "How to Drive Fast," "Turbulence," "Somebody's Baby," Preface From *The Dumbest Generation: How the Digital Age Stupefies Young Americans and Jeopardizes Our Futures*, "A Dark and Stormy Knight: Why Batman?" "Community College."

ARGUMENTATION: "Black Widow," "The Little Mermaid," "Drugs," "The Content of Our Character," "Letter to His Master," "The Chemist's War," "The Writing Life: The Point of the Long and Winding," "A Dark and Stormy Knight: Why Batman?" Preface From *The Dumbest Generation: How the Digital Age Stupefies Young Americans and Jeopardizes Our Future.*

CAUSE/EFFECT: "Nourishing Awareness in Each Moment," "How to Drive Fast," "Advice to Youth," Preface From *The Dumbest Generation: How the Digital Age Stupefies Young Americans and Jeopardizes Our Future.*

COMPARISON/CONTRAST: "On the Uncertainty of the Future," "Museum Piece," "Nourishing Awareness in Each Moment," "Roll Over Bach, Too!" "Prince," "Monster Mash," "Joyas Voladoras," "American Children," "Disposable Rocket," "The Little Mermaid," "Letter to His Master," "The Tree Beyond Imagining," "Meat," "Drugs,""Reading the River," "Somebody's Baby," "A Dark and Stormy Knight: Why Batman?"

CLASSIFICATION: "Mortality," "Turbulence."

DEFINITION: "The Culture of Celebrity," "About Men," "The Content of Our Character," "Truth."

DESCRIPTION: "Museum Piece," "Toys," "Prince," "Monster Mash," "American Children," "About Men," "How to Drive Fast," "Mortality," "Turbulence," "Burl's."

NARRATION: "A Voice for the Lonely," "Burl's," "The Courage of Turtles," "On the Uncertainty of the Future," "American Children," "On the Content of Our Character," "Turbulence," "Advice to Youth," "Meat."

PROCESS ANALYSIS: "Advice to Youth."

RESEARCH: "A Voice for the Lonely," "Modern Times," "Burl's," "The Courage of Turtles," "Musical Awakenings," "Black Widow," "Drugs," "Fiddling While Africa Starves," "The Content of Our Character," "Advice to Youth," Preface From *The Dumbest Generation: How the Digital Age Stupefies Young Americans and Jeopardizes Our Future*, "A Dark and Stormy Knight: Why Batman?"

Acknowledgments

A special thanks to those extraordinary professors Alice Brekke and Eileen Lothamer—colleagues, friends, mentors—for setting me on my life's path, helping me achieve my goals, and encouraging me throughout this endeavor. You changed my life.

Muchas gracias to Gary and Glynis Hoffman and their book *Adios, Strunk and White* for helping me find my writer's voice and transforming my writing. A gal couldn't have better office mates or friends. Thank you for always being there.

And what would I have done without fellow writer, friend, track buddy, and idea man Gene Garofolo? Thanks for those brainstorming sessions during painful workouts but pleasant coffee sessions.

Once again, a big thanks to Lara Sanders for her continued guidance on this fourth edition. You're a rock star.

Thank you, Bev Kraus, for saving the day. You have been incredible.

To all of you at Kendall Hunt, you are the best in the business.

My dear sister, Professor Sherry Williams, thank you for your expertise and help on the reading section. Most of all, thank you for being a friend, for always having my back, for all the things you taught me growing up. I wouldn't be the person I am today without your lifelong strength, encouragement, and friendship.

Preface

WHY THIS BOOK?

Today's students are, in general, technology savvy with social media and searching online for material, though academic research needed for college often seems outdated to them. They view print as obsolete. In their social media-saturated world of quick sound bites, college level reading and writing can seem unnecessary and even bewildering. Increasingly, a majority of students have never seen the inside of an academic library—or even a public library. Impressing upon them the importance of using valid online data bases, and yes, even the occasional book, instead of relying solely on a google search is a challenge.

Reading and writing levels have fallen, and the beginning writing classroom has become more demanding than ever. In this fourth edition, I've attempted to address some of these issues. The reading tips have been expanded to include more techniques to improve comprehension. The new "Sweating the Small Stuff" includes exercises aimed at cleaning up bad habits students have acquired through texting and use of emoticons instead of complete sentences and correct word choices. "Punctuation is Style" strives to help students see that punctuation can help them write in more creative ways and find their writer's voice while attempting to help control common errors like fragments, run-ons, and comma splices.

Sparks stresses the importance of style, using the essays as jump-off points for writing. Each essay includes a blurb on the author, cultural and historical references in the "Dustbin of History and Culture," and vocabulary definitions with ideas for usage in "Exploring Language." "Thinking and Talking Points" are designed to guide students toward better comprehension as they read. "Styling" focuses on one technique from each essay and instructs students how to model the author's approach and then incorporate it into their own writing assignments. "Teaming Up" activities often contain more style ideas from the essays students can work on in small groups. "Writing Ideas" and "Essay Connections" help spark ideas for prompts.

The writing strategies section outlines rhetorical modes while emphasizing the necessity of combining them for college level writing. Traditional prewriting, ideas for generating snappier titles, introduction styles—riddles, personification, mythology, symbolism and other not-often-thought-of strategies—conclusion solutions, body paragraph structure, steps for creating thesis statements, transitions, tips for writing summaries, paraphrasing, avoiding plagiarism—all can be found in section four.

"Research" provides the basics beginning writers need to document their sources, written to lessen the intimidation factor of MLA format, breaking down each type of source into parenthetical references and untangling the complications of a works cited page, complete with works cited and first page examples.

Professor Mark Bauerlein's preface from his book *The Dumbest Generation: How the Digital Age Stupefies Young Americans and Jeopardizes Our Future* sums up the problems teachers and students face in the technology age:

> Once youths enter the digital realm, the race for attention begins, and it doesn't like to stop for a half-hour with a novel or a trip to the museum. Digital offerings don't like to share, and tales of Founding Fathers and ancient battles and Gothic churches can't compete with a message from a boyfriend, photos from the party, and a new device in the Apple store window. Parents and teachers have a new rival in the lives of kids: not just a circle of friends, but a spreading glossy marketplace of communications technology with a certified youth meaning. Put them together—the e-tools and the collective will of teens—and they look invincible."

Perhaps Bauerlein's preface will lead students to think about what they're missing when they ignore opportunities to be mentored by professors, hone skills needed to succeed in college and throughout life, and miss out on important intellectual experiences or developing friendships that can turn into life-long contacts. Bauerlein's essay is the first one I have students read. So far the response has been positive and triggered engaging discussion. Some even put down their cell phones during the break and talk to each other. It's a hopeful beginning.

User's Guide

HOW TO USE THIS BOOK

Because most essays are hybrids, blending various modes, *Sparks* is not organized in the strictly traditional rhetorical or thematic arrangement (though alternative tables of contents are included as a helpful tool for the reader). A narrative can present an argument and almost always contains description; an exemplification essay might also define; a classification essay may explain and so forth, so I've divided the book into four sections: In "Remembering Personal Voices," you'll find a diversity of voices telling their stories, relating their experiences, making their points through memories. "Contemplations: Essays that Explain and Explore" contains essays that attempt to make sense of the world, of history, nature, art, and the human mind. Section Three, "Essays Argue and Define," while containing some traditional arguments, also presents viewpoints in a variety of forms, offering narration, satire, process analysis, and other styles. Within each section, I've attempted to arrange the essays, questions, and assignments from simpler to more complex, an arrangement I owe to my students; they've illustrated to me through their writing, questions, and class discussion which assignments and readings present more challenges.

Because I cover style as it relates to the essays, you might find a technique covered in different spots in the book, which might seem repetitive, but techniques need practice for mastery, and it's possible to read many of the essays and not run across a particular technique even though it's offered several times in the book. The **periodic** and **loose** sentences might accompany several essays because the sentences themselves take on many forms. Colons and semicolons can be used in a variety of ways. I've focused on these styles because students often come to college without some of the tools that spark writing—or haven't practiced them since early high school. Modeling good writers improves writing.

If you're working from a rhetorical mode perspective, the assignment arrangement, too, may be unfamiliar because you might find narrative assignments, for example, in every section. The Assignment Guide at the beginning of the book will tell you where to find writing ideas compatible with narration, description, argumentation, cause/effect, and so forth.

Two other features attempt to help students understand the essays: the "Dustbin of History and Culture" (meant ironically) preceding each essay explains references to history, culture, mythology, literature, and others that might be unfamiliar to some students (The "Dustbin of History" is a phrase Greil Marcus borrowed from Leon Trotsky for his book of the same title; Greil argues that history does not belong only to the past, relegated to the dustbin). Though some of the references may seem obvious to some, they may not to others, and the allusions are there because my students have asked me, "What's that mean?" While a feather quill might seem obvious to most, I've had several students ask me about it, students unfamiliar with cultures or historical periods where feather quills might be common, and some students might be embarrassed to ask about a reference that the rest of the class takes for granted. At other times, I list cultural references that might be familiar but detail and context of time and place might be elusive.

The second feature, the "Exploring Language" section, defines words and gives ideas for usage. The more words students add to their vocabulary arsenal, the more complex their reading, thinking, and writing skills develop.

Survival Kit

NAVIGATING THE COLLEGE QUAGMIRE

Many students have a tough time adjusting to college. Others glide. Even the best students fumble at times, so consider these tips to help navigate the system.

TIPS FOR SUCCESS

First, find out what resources your college has to help. Is there a tutoring center? A writing lab? Learning disabled center? Financial aid? Make use of these resources. Students might not know that schools often offer free health care on campus. If reading skills need polish, find out if the college offers reading courses. See if there's a spelling course or computer lab with a spelling tutorial. The same goes for weaknesses in grammar, math, or any area. Seek and ye shall find.

Consider the workload. Talk to a counselor about your schedule and whether it's too much. Working full time and taking five or six classes may be overdoing it; if you're struggling in classes, it may be time to reconsider.

Get organized. Some schools have classes in surviving college, often offered through counseling. Be sure to have a good notebook with a section for each class, and take notes. Unless you have a photographic mind, you can't possibly remember everything important the teacher says. Write it down, especially if it's on the board, PowerPoint, document cam, or other electronic source. Though using a cell phone to photograph the board has become more popular than taking notes, writing material down helps with retention; a photograph does not. If a teacher repeats an idea, write it down. If you must be absent, get someone in class to take notes for you. Offer to return the favor. While this may seem obvious, I often see students neglect note taking and then wonder why their grades suffer.

Homework can be overwhelming. Set aside time each day to study. Budget your time: study, work, play. We all need time away from work to do the things we enjoy. The word *recreation* means to re-create, so budget time to recreate yourself. The general rule for studying is to budget two hours of study time for each hour spent in class, so a three-hour class requires six hours a week of studying.

Don't be afraid to ask questions. Raise your hand. If the teacher has an office and office hours, make use of them. Be sure you understand the homework assignments. If not, get clarification. If you miss class, find out what you missed. Assume you missed something.

Read the syllabus and know the teacher's rules. Know how many absences each teacher allows, and keep track. Don't assume a teacher will take late homework because of illness. If you must miss class, get your homework to school somehow, by friend, relative, courier.

Turn off all electronics unless instructed otherwise. Buy the books or find out if the library has them or if the teacher has placed them on reserve. Don't sit in silence, not understanding lectures and failing tests because you don't have the books. Find out what help is available. You might be eligible for financial aid.

Many students don't realize the abundance of resources available on campus, often for free. Surviving college means balancing your time, staying organized, and seeking help when you need it. Ask. Your college wants to help.

READING TIPS

In a visual culture where most of our stories come in the form of movies or television and our news from the Internet and television, where films make it easy for us to avoid reading difficult classic literature like Shakespeare and Homer why, then, should we bother to read, other than learning basic communications skills so we can surf the net, play online games, catch up with friend on social networks, and fill out job applications?

Reading does more than provide information. It hones intelligence, forces interaction with the text, teaches vocabulary through context, sharpens critical thinking skills, improves verbal and written communication, and illustrates punctuation and difficult sentence structure. You think in language. The more you read, the more language you learn, and the more sophisticated your thinking and analysis become. What you get from reading versus viewing is incalculable.

To be a successful college student, read actively. When you sit down to read, do so with a highlighter, notepad, and dictionary, paper or electronic. Looking up words in a dictionary can be tedious—but to learn, to improve reading, to be able to think more complexly, then a dictionary is a must. Don't stop to look up every unfamiliar word; mark the words and reach for the dictionary later. Don't just find the words and jot down their meanings; figure out the context and match the proper definitions. Practice using the words in daily conversations and writings. If you look up the meaning but never use the word, you probably won't remember it.

Highlight meaningful or unclear passages the teacher points out. Try to figure out the writer's main idea and key supporting points. Write questions about difficult passages in the margin as they occur to you.

Here are some points to consider when **annotating** (see the glossary) the text:

1. Ask a question about a difficult concept, and then attempt to answer it.
2. Compliment the writer on style: strong word choices, description, specific detail, **metaphor and simile**, **personification**, use of punctuation, sentence structure (for example, **loose** and **periodic** sentences), a hook in the introduction, a snazzy title or complain about any of these techniques.
3. Point out the main idea or thesis of the essay and the supporting evidence.
4. Comment on the strength of the argument or point. Agree or disagree.
5. Look for smooth transitions between paragraphs or ideas within paragraphs.
6. Pinpoint the tone or mood of the essay: academic/analytical, casual, melancholy, contemplative, humorous, cynical, joyful, poignant, and so on.
7. Mention the essay's organization. Is it chronological (order of events), point-by-point (one point in each paragraph), or some other method?

Sometimes you read a passage only to find you have no idea what you just read. It's normal for the mind to drift, but make every effort to get back on task. Read the passage again, highlighter and pencil ready. If you're highlighting and making notes, looking up words and thinking about definitions, you'll be an active reader, more likely to absorb material.

Textbooks usually suggest reading an assignment or essay at least three times: once through quickly to survey, a second time to question the content, and a third time to review. Although that's the best approach, crowded schedules don't always permit this type of diligence, but you should at least highlight, question, and look up words. Try to read a difficult piece at least twice.

Professor Sherry Williams, in "Reading Recovery," from *Success Strategies: Accelerating Academic Progress by Addressing the Affective Domain* has developed strategies for students to follow before, during, and after reading to help with comprehension.

Before reading (or pre-reading), scan the essay or chapter, browsing the title, any section headings, photographs, charts, bolded words or phrases, anything that might help determine the content. For example, in *Sparks*, pre-reading for the essays would include the title, the author blurb below the title that often hints at the essay's purpose, reading the "Dustbin of History and Culture," perusing the "Exploring Language" to identify unfamiliar vocabulary words, and finally studying the "Thinking and Talking Points" to help with predictions, and then write down predictions, what you think the essay will be about.

During reading, use the pre-reading material to locate important information. Write down your reactions to the reading as well as any questions that come to mind. In *Sparks*, also focus on style as well as meaning, and use the tips for annotating to guide comprehension.

After reading, immediately reread your annotations and predictions, to either "confirm or reject" predictions and clarify annotations. Summarize key information and the author's purpose (or thesis) and supporting evidence, as well as any writing strategies (see the "Summarizing" and "Paraphrasing" sections for help writing summaries).

If you're not convinced as to the benefits of reading, think about what it would be like to be denied the privilege. Frederick Douglass, an American slave, tells his story in the following essay, "Learning to Read and Write," from his famous work, *Narrative of the Life of Frederick Douglass.*

LEARNING TO READ AND WRITE

Frederick Douglass—an American slave—escaped from captivity to Massachusetts, becoming a famous writer and lecturer, speaking out against the evils of slavery, and advising Abraham Lincoln. In this essay, he recounts how he learned to read and write despite laws forbidding slaves an education.

1   I lived in Master Hugh's family about seven years. During this time, I succeeded in learning to read and write. In accomplishing this, I was compelled to resort to various stratagems. I had no regular teacher. My mistress, who had kindly commenced to instruct me, had, in compliance with the advice and direction of her husband, not only ceased to instruct, but had set her face against my being instructed by any one else. It is due, however, to my mistress to say of her, that she did not adopt this course of treatment immediately. She at first lacked the depravity indispensable to shutting me up in mental darkness. It was at least necessary for her to have some training in the exercise of irresponsible power, to make her equal to the task of treating me as though I were a brute.

2   My mistress was, as I have said, a kind and tender-hearted woman; and in the simplicity of her soul she commenced, when I first went to live with her, to treat me as she supposed one human being ought to treat another. In entering upon the duties of a slave-holder, she did not seem to perceive that I sustained to her the relation of a mere chattel, and that for her to treat me as a human being was not only wrong, but dangerously so. Slavery proved as injurious to her as it did to me. When I went there, she was a pious, warm, and tender-hearted woman. There was no sorrow or suffering for which she had not a tear. She had bread for the hungry, clothes for the naked, and comfort for every mourner that came within her reach. Slavery soon proved its ability to divest her of these heavenly qualities. Under its influence, the tender heart became stone, and the lamblike disposition gave way to one of tiger-like fierceness. The first step in her downward course was in her ceasing to instruct me. She now commenced to practise her husband's precepts. She finally became even more violent in her opposition than her husband himself. She was not satisfied with simply doing as well as he had commanded; she seemed anxious to do better. Nothing seemed to make her more angry

than to see me with a newspaper. She seemed to think that here lay the danger. I have had her rush at me with a face made all up of fury, and snatch from me a newspaper, in a manner that fully revealed her apprehension. She was an apt woman; and a little experience soon demonstrated, to her satisfaction, that education and slavery were incompatible with each other.

3   From this time I was most narrowly watched. If I was in a separate room any considerable length of time, I was sure to be suspected of having a book, and was at once called to give an account of myself. All this, however, was too late. The first step had been taken. Mistress, in teaching me the alphabet, had given me the *inch*, and no precaution could prevent me from taking the *ell*.

4   The plan which I adopted, and the one by which I was most successful, was that of making friends of all the little white boys whom I met in the street. As many of these as I could, I converted into teachers. With their kindly aid, obtained at different times and in different places, I finally succeeded in learning to read. When I was sent on errands, I always took my book with me, and by going one part of my errand quickly, I found time to get a lesson before my return. I used also to carry bread with me, enough of which was always in the house, and to which I was always welcome; for I was much better off in this regard than many of the poor white children in our neighborhood. This bread I used to bestow upon the hungry little urchins, who, in return, would give me that more valuable bread of knowledge. I am strongly tempted to give the names of two or three of those little boys, as a testimonial of the gratitude and affection I bear them; but prudence forbids;—not that it would injure me, but it might embarrass them; for it is almost an unpardonable offence to teach slaves to read in this Christian country. It is enough to say of the dear little fellows, that they lived on Philpot Street, very near Durgin and Bailey's shipyard. I used to talk this matter of slavery over with them. I would sometimes say to them, I wished I could be as free as they would be when they got to be men. "You will be free as soon as you are twenty-one, *but I am a slave for life!* Have not I as good a right to be free as you have?" These words used to trouble them; they would express for me the liveliest sympathy, and console me with the hope that something would occur by which I might be free.

5   I was now about twelve years old, and the thought of being *a slave for life* began to bear heavily upon my heart. Just about this time, I got hold of a book entitled "The Columbian Orator." Every opportunity I got, I used to read this book. Among much of other interesting

matter, I found in it a dialogue between a master and his slave. The slave was represented as having run away from his master three times. The dialogue represented the conversation which took place between them, when the slave was retaken the third time. In this dialogue, the whole argument in behalf of slavery was brought forward by the master, all of which was disposed of by the slave. The slave was made to say some very smart as well as impressive things in reply to his master—things which had the desired though unexpected effect; for the conversation resulted in the voluntary emancipation of the slave on the part of the master.

6   In the same book, I met with one of Sheridan's mighty speeches on and in behalf of Catholic emancipation. These were choice documents to me. I read them over and over again with unabated interest. They gave tongue to interesting thoughts of my own soul, which had frequently flashed through my mind, and died away for want of utterance. The moral which I gained from the dialogue was the power of truth over the conscience of even a slaveholder. What I got from Sheridan was a bold denunciation of slavery, and a powerful vindication of human rights. The reading of these documents enabled me to utter my thoughts, and to meet the arguments brought forward to sustain slavery; but while they relieved me of one difficulty, they brought on another even more painful than the one of which I was relieved. The more I read, the more I was led to abhor and detest my enslavers. I could regard them in no other light than a band of successful robbers, who had left their homes, and gone to Africa, and stolen us from our homes, and in a strange land reduced us to slavery. I loathed them as being the meanest as well as the most wicked of men. As I read and contemplated the subject, behold! that very discontentment which Master Hugh had predicted would follow my learning to read had already come, to torment and sting my soul to unutterable anguish. As I writhed under it, I would at times feel that learning to read had been a curse rather than a blessing. It had given me a view of my wretched condition, without the remedy. It opened my eyes to the horrible pit, but to no ladder upon which to get out. In moments of agony, I envied my fellow-slaves for their stupidity. I have often wished myself a beast. I preferred the condition of the meanest reptile to my own. Any thing, no matter what, to get rid of thinking! It was this everlasting thinking of my condition that tormented me. There was no getting rid of it. It was pressed upon me by every object within sight or hearing, animate or inanimate. The silver trump of freedom had roused my soul to eternal wakefulness. Freedom

now appeared, to disappear no more forever. It was heard in every sound, and seen in every thing. It was ever present to torment me with a sense of my wretched condition. I saw nothing without seeing it, I heard nothing without hearing it, and felt nothing without feeling it. It looked from every star, it smiled in every calm, breathed in every wind, and moved in every storm.

7   I often found myself regretting my own existence, and wishing myself dead; and but for the hope of being free, I have no doubt but that I should have killed myself, or done something for which I should have been killed. While in this state of mind, I was eager to hear any one speak of slavery. I was a ready listener. Every little while, I could hear something about the abolitionists. It was some time before I found what the word meant. It was always used in such connections as to make it an interesting word to me. If a slave ran away and succeeded in getting clear, or if a slave killed his master, set fire to a barn, or did any thing very wrong in the mind of a slaveholder, it was spoken of as the fruit of *abolition*. Hearing the word in this connection very often, I set about learning what it meant. The dictionary afforded me little or no help. I found it was "the act of abolishing"; but then I did not know what was to be abolished. Here I was perplexed. I did not dare to ask any one about its meaning, for I was satisfied that it was something they wanted me to know very little about. After a patient waiting, I got one of our city papers, containing an account of the number of petitions from the north, praying for the abolition of slavery in the District of Columbia, and of the slave trade between the States. From this time I understood the words *abolition* and *abolitionist,* and always drew near when that word was spoken, expecting to hear something of importance to myself and fellow-slaves. The light broke in upon me by degrees. I went one day down on the wharf of Mr. Waters; and seeing two Irishmen unloading a scow of stone, I went, unasked, and helped them. When we had finished, one of them came to me and asked me if I were a slave. I told him I was. He asked, "Are ye a slave for life?" I told him that I was. The good Irishman seemed to be deeply affected by the statement. He said to the other that it was a pity so fine a little fellow as myself should be a slave for life. He said it was a shame to hold me. They both advised me to run away to the north; that I should find friends there, and that I should be free. I pretended not to be interested in what they said, and treated them as if I did not understand them; for I feared they might be treacherous. White men have been known to encourage slaves to escape, and then, to get the reward, catch them and return them to their mas-

ters. I was afraid that these seemingly good men might use me so; but I nevertheless remembered their advice, and from that time I resolved to run away. I looked forward to a time at which it would be safe for me to escape. I was too young to think of doing so immediately; besides, I wished to learn how to write, as I might have occasion to write my own pass. I consoled myself with the hope that I should one day find a good chance. Meanwhile, I would learn to write.

8   The idea as to how I might learn to write was suggested to me by being in Durgin and Bailey's ship-yard, and frequently seeing the ship carpenters, after hewing, and getting a piece of timber ready for use, write on the timber the name of that part of the ship for which it was intended. When a piece of timber was intended for the larboard side, it would be marked thus—"L." When a piece was for the starboard side, it would be marked thus—"S." A piece for the larboard side forward, would be marked thus—"L.F." When a piece was for starboard side forward, it would be marked thus—"S.F." For larboard aft, it would be marked thus—"L.A." For starboard aft, it would be marked thus—"S. A." I soon learned the names of these letters, and for what they were intended when placed upon a piece of timber in the ship-yard. I immediately commenced copying them, and in a short time was able to make the four letters named. After that, when I met with any boy who I knew could write, I would tell him I could write as well as he. The next word would be, "I don't believe you. Let me see you try it." I would then make the letters which I had been so fortunate as to learn, and ask him to beat that. In this way I got a good many lessons in writing, which it is quite possible I should never have gotten in any other way. During this time, my copy-book was the board fence, brick wall, and pavement; my pen and ink was a lump of chalk. With these, I learned mainly how to write. I then commenced and continued copying the Italics in Webster's Spelling Book, until I could make them all without looking on the book. By this time, my little Master Thomas had gone to school, and learned how to write, and had written over a number of copy-books. These had been brought home, and shown to some of our near neighbors, and then laid aside. My mistress used to go to class meeting at the Wilk Street meeting-house every Monday afternoon, and leave me to take care of the house. When left thus, I used to spend the time in writing in the spaces left in Master Thomas's copy-book, copying what he had written. I continued to do this until I could write a hand very similar to that of Master Thomas. Thus, after a long, tedious effort for years, I finally succeeded in learning how to write.

ADVICE FOR WORKING IN GROUPS

Your instructor has just asked you to break into groups to work together on a project—perhaps one of the Teaming Up exercises in this book—or for peer evaluations or discussion. You may dislike this idea, feeling that you always get stuck with the bulk of the work, or perhaps you just prefer to work alone; or you might relish the idea, enjoying the group interaction and break from routine (regardless of your viewpoint, many instructors and businesses consider group work essential practice for the work place). Whether you love or loathe it, you may be asked to participate, so here are a few guidelines to help your group get along, split up the work fairly, stay focused on the task, and get the most out of the session.

1. Introduce yourselves and perhaps exchange phone numbers in case you have questions later.
2. Draw up some rules of civility. How will you handle discussion to ensure that each member gets a chance to speak? What will you do about an unruly or rude student? What will you do if a member of the group doesn't show up with a crucial part of the project? What happens if a team member slacks off, bringing shoddy work or none at all?
3. Consider assigning each member a daily task: discussion director, note taker, reader (someone to read passages or directions to the group), typist, spokesperson. You can alternate the jobs each time you split into groups or keep the same tasks.
4. Split up the work fairly. If the project involves research, be sure that each person is responsible for a portion. If you're writing a group essay, assign each person a paragraph to work on at home.
5. Stay focused. If you notice your group deteriorating into discussion of the latest football score or concert attended, try to steer the members back to work. It's natural to get sidetracked, but if it happens too frequently, you're in danger of not completing the work, irritating the teacher, and embarrassing yourselves in front of the rest of the class.
6. Keep noise to a minimum.
7. If you give it a good try and feel you just can't work with your group, it's okay to ask the teacher if you can switch teams, but do it diplomatically. Tell your group that you plan to ask for a transfer, citing philosophical differences. Or say something polite like "I've really enjoyed working with you but would like to try another group, get to know some new people." Don't leave the group with ill feelings.

8. To minimize distractions, check all cell phones and other electronic devices to be sure they're in the "Off" mode and won't buzz and interrupt the group.

In general, be courteous to your group and the rest of the class. Follow that golden rule to treat others as you would like to be treated.

PEER EVALUATIONS: RESPONDING TO YOUR CLASSMATES' WORK

Reading and responding honestly to your peer's writing can be difficult. Afraid to offend, you offer only positive remarks, ignoring the flaws, sending the poor soul home with the mistaken impression he or she has written a masterpiece. Or perhaps you're the critical type, finding fault with everything, not offering a kind word, demoralizing your classmate into giving up. Neither response is ideal, but perhaps a balance between the two will help the student discover the positive aspects of his or her work as well as what might need revision. Following are some questions that might help you evaluate another's work kindly but constructively. You'll need a separate sheet of paper, a pen, and a highlighter.

Note: Do not edit another student's work by correcting grammar, punctuation, and spelling. That's the student's job. It's all right to point out that an essay contains several **comma splices** or other errors, but leave the detective work to your peer.

1. Start out positive. What do you like best about the paper? Be specific. Instead of "I really like how you describe things," write "The line in your essay *A thick layer of snow covers the road, and the leafless trees impose a sinister feel; our steps on the crunchy snow break the silence* is so vivid I feel like I'm there. Well done!"

2. Does the essay have a title that grabs your interest? If not, make suggestions or refer the student to the index of this book to look up strategies for creating snappy titles.

3. Does the introduction hook the reader? If not, again refer the student to the index to look up strategies for writing introductions.

4. Does the essay have a thesis or make a point? What is the point? If you are not sure, ask the writer. Does the thesis address the prompt?

5. Does the writer use vivid detail so that you see, hear, smell, feel, taste the experience? If not, tell the writer where you think more detail or description is needed.

6. Is the writing specific, using strong verbs and nouns? ("Joe ambled along the rocky shore" is stronger than "The boy walked along the beach.") Point out sentences that could be more specific.

7. Does the writer provide enough examples to support his or her point? Are the examples appropriate, or would others be stronger?

8. Is the paper well organized? Does the writer make clear paragraph breaks with **transitions** (see the glossary)? Is each paragraph organized around a central idea, or do details wander away from the topic? Does each paragraph support the main idea of the essay?

9. Are there any mechanical errors that detract from the paper, like frequent misspellings, punctuation problems, fragments, run-on sentences, shifts in tense or person, or other errors?

10. How is the writing style? Are the sentence patterns varied (short, medium, long sentences)? Can some sentences be combined? Does the writer use **figurative language** (see the glossary)? Does the writer rely on too many "to be" verbs (is, are, was, were, be, being, been, am)? Use your highlighter to highlight each "to be" verb. More than three or four per page signals weak verb use. Is the writing clear? Are there spots where you're not sure of the meaning?

Remembering: Personal Voices

INTRODUCTION

Sharing personal experiences motivates some of the finest writing; many writers use the first person point of view to explain, to argue, to reflect, to analyze. The narrative voice, once considered the lightweight of academia, has gained acceptance as a legitimate form of expression for argument, research, and other essay strategies. Whether writing about nature, science, medicine, history, psychology, education, or any topic, writers know that engaging the reader with personal experience, description, figurative language, and other style techniques make otherwise dry material digestible.

Most of the essays in this book rely in part on the personal voice, even if it isn't the primary mode of expression, whether an introduction, an anecdote, or a conclusion: Shelby Steele's personal experiences growing up black and middle class in "On the Content of Our Character" strengthen his argument and help define the dilemma; Gretel Ehrlich's stories of growing up around cowboys in Wyoming help bust a stereotype; and so on.

The essays in this section lean on narration more than others, though their arguments and analysis are just as strong and convincing: Bernard Cooper's beautifully written struggle with sexual identity; Edward Hoagland's fable-like stories of turtles and their plight; Brian Doyle's tribute to a fallen friend in the 9/11 attacks and its subtext; "We all churn inside" as Doyle writes before the conclusion of "Joyas Voladoras."

A VOICE FOR THE LONELY

Stephen Corey

Stephen Corey is an editor and author of poetry and essays. In this piece, he reminisces about the death of singer Roy Orbison of "Pretty Woman" fame, speculating on friendship, the impact of music, and "forces of circumstance and the fate of inches."

DUSTBIN OF HISTORY AND CULTURE

TRANSISTOR RADIO: a small, often pocket-sized, portable radio receiver developed in 1954, becoming popular in the 1960's and 1970's, especially with teenagers, not unlike today's IPods and other devices with portable music.

1   The right silence can be a savior, especially in these days of motor-cycles, leaf blowers, and malls that thrum with a thousand voices and dozens of sundry machines. Five or six days a week, I get up pretty early—generally around 4 A.M.—and one of the things I like most about those last hours of darkness is their stillness. The house is quiet, the streets are quiet, and (except on weekends, when some of the serious drunks are hanging on) the all-night restaurants are quiet. Reading and writing and thinking come more easily when you know you won't be interrupted, and over the past 20 years I've never found a better mental bodyguard than the hours before dawn.

2   I got my first serious training as an early riser when I acquired a newspaper delivery route in seventh grade: three miles of widely scat-tered houses on the edge of Jamestown, New York, and beyond—just me, the moon, darkness, and the various faces of silence. I recall stop-ping my brisk walk sometimes, especially in winter when every step squeaked and crunched on the snow that nearly always covered the ground, and marveling at how there were no sounds except those of my own making. But just as often, that quiet made me nervous, even though my hometown was awfully safe in those days. I learned to offset the urge to look over my shoulder by carrying a pocket-sized transistor radio.

3   The music helped me to cope with more than just the empty morning streets—I was, as I said, in seventh (and then eighth, and finally ninth) grade during those lone marches. In short, I was just

learning something of what much of that music was about: love—lost, found, hoped for, and despaired of.

4   Most habits die hard, and old ones can seem immortal. Last week, I was up as usual at 4 A.M., and I headed out in the car toward the nearest newspaper box. As always during these quick runs, I flipped on the radio for some wake-up rhythms to jolt my system for the solitary work time soon to come back at the house.

5   Instead of music, I caught the voice of the all-night deejay just as she was saying, "We have tragic news in over the wire: singer Roy Orbison is dead . . ." She gave a quick flurry of details (heart attack, Hendersonville, North Carolina, hospital), repeated the central fact— "Roy Orbison, dead at 52"—and then (my heart applauds her still for this) said not a word but cut straight into "Only the Lonely."

6   There I was, cruising down the abandoned city street with the radio now up as loud as I could stand it, mouthing the rising and falling words, rocking side to side as I held the wheel, and riding Orbison's wailing, nearly-cracking voice back 24 years to the passenger seat of Jon Cresanti's Volkswagen beetle.

7   We're told these days that the hottest and fastest wire into memory is our sense of smell, but music must run a close second. Some songs carry us into a certain mood, some to a general region of our past lives, and some to a very particular moment and situation in time. Jon and I were brought together by chance and loneliness for a couple of months during our sophomore year in high school. The alphabetical seating in our homeroom put us next to each other in the back row, and Jon was a talker. We hadn't known each other before: we came from different parts of town, had different friends, and moved through different sequences of classes. But for a while we found a bond: my girlfriend had recently dropped me after more than a year of going steady, and Jon had eyes for a girl who had none for him.

8   I had time—all the time I was no longer spending with my girl. John had a car and was old enough to drive it, having failed a grade and thereby become a crucial year older than the typical sophomore. I signed on board, and we cruised day after day, weekend after weekend, killing time and eating at the wondrous new "fast food restaurant" that had just opened. We sat in his car eating 15-cent hamburgers and 12-cent french fries near the real golden arches, the kind that curved up and over the entire little structure (no inside seating, no bathrooms)—and, naturally, listening to the radio. The Four Seasons were with us, as were The Beach Boys, Nat King Cole, The Supremes.

9   But in those two desperate months of shotgunning for Jon, there was only one song that really mattered, one song we waited for, hoped for, and even called the radio station and asked for: Roy Orbison's "Pretty Woman."

10   That opening handful of heavy guitar notes (a lovesick teenager's equivalent of Beethoven's Fifth) carried us into a world of possibility, a world where a moment's fancy could generate love, where losers could be winners just by wishing for success. The pretty woman walks on by, and another failure has occurred—but suddenly, the downward sweep of the wheel is reversed as the woman turns to walk back; and there is nothing in the world but fulfillment of one's dreams.

11   Pop songs are full of such stuff, of course, and have been for as long as the phonograph record and the radio have been with us; we get all kinds of talk about the importance of television in modern life, but I think we need more examination of the ways we have been encompassed by music. I'm not talking about ranting "discussions" of the immorality of certain strains of pop music, but some real studies of the much wider and deeper implications of growing up in a world awash with radio waves.

12   Needless to say, I wasn't concerned about such matters there in the McDonald's parking lot. I wouldn't even have thought about what it was in Orbison's singing that made him so important to me. I took the words of the song's story for their relevance to my own emotional state, and I floated with those words inside a musical accompaniment that both soothed and roused my fifteen-year-old body.

13   When I heard of Orbison's death, I found myself wanting to figure out just what it was in that strange voice that might have been so compelling for me and others across the years. I think it might be in the way the voice itself often seems about to fail: in Orbison's strange and constant modulations, from gravelly bass-like sounds to strong tenor-like passages to piercing falsetto cries, there is the feeling for the listener that the singer is always about to lose control, about to break down under the weight of what he is trying to sing. Never mind that this is not true, that Orbison's style was one carefully achieved; what we are talking about here is emotional effect, the true stuff of pop and country music.

14   If Roy could make it, we could make it. And if Roy could stand failing, so could we.

15   This feeling of camaraderie with the faraway record star increased for me, I think, the first time I saw him. He was so ordinary-looking— no, he was so *homely,* so very contrary to what one expects romantic musical heroes to look like. He was *us.*

16   The right singer, the right sadness, the right silence. The way I heard the story of the death of Orbison's wife in 1966 (and the way I'll keep believing it) was that the two of them were out motorcycling when an errant car or truck hit them from an angle. She was riding just a few feet to the side of and behind him, so the other vehicle clipped the back of his cycle but caught hers full force. I've never gotten over this chilling illustration of the forces of circumstance and the fate of inches, so much so that over the years I have regularly found the story called to mind for retelling in classrooms or at parties.

17   I graduated from high school the year of the accident, and Orbison disappeared from the national music scene. (It wasn't until recently that I heard how the death of two sons by fire in 1967 compounded Orbison's private tragedies.) Oddly, there is a way in which the disappearance or the death of a singer these days doesn't really matter to his or her listeners, since that person is still present in exactly the same way as before. All the songs take on a slightly new cast, but the singer still lives in a way that one's own deceased relatives and friends cannot.

18   When my girl wanted me back, I dropped Jon's friendship and never tried to regain it—a not-very-commendable way to be. But we were glued for a while by those banging Orbison notes and those erratic vocals, and maybe that was enough, or at least all that one could hope for.

19   Music can block out silence, on dark scary roads and in moments of loneliness. But there's also a sense or two in which a song can create silence: when we're "lost in a song" the rest of the world around us makes, for all practical purposes, no sound. And in an even more strange way, a song we love goes silent as we "listen" to it, leaving us in that rather primitive place where all the sounds are interior ones—sounds which can't be distinguished from feelings, from pulsings and shiverings, from that gut need to make life stronger than death for at least a few moments.

20   When "Only the Lonely" faded, that wonderful deejay still knew enough not to say a word. She threw us straight forward, 4:15 A.M., into "Pretty Woman."

A VOICE FOR THE LONELY

Exploring Language

camaraderie: a feeling of getting along, friendship, or kinship.
erratic: irregular or unpredictable.
falsetto: a high-pitched voice, usually referring to a male.
modulations: changes in tone or pitch.
sundry: various or miscellaneous.
tenor: in this context , a music term referring to an adult male voice
   whose pitch falls between the bass (low pitch) and alto (high pitch).
thrum: strum, as in playing a stringed musical instrument.
Note: For pronunciation, go to dictionary.com, search the word, and
click on the speaker icon.

USAGE   Notice how Corey uses *thrum* in his opening paragraph to describe
noises not related to music. Consider other words connected to music
that might be used in unusual ways.

Thinking and Talking Points

1. Corey writes, "We're told these days that the hottest and fastest wire
   into memory is our sense of smell, but music must run a close second." Find examples of how music helps Corey wire into his memory. Think about the other senses like smell, touch, taste, sight and
   discuss whether they have a similar ability to conjure up memory.
   Rate them as to their effectiveness. Why do you think music has been
   proven to be such a powerful memory invoker?
2. Reread paragraph #17. What does Corey mean by "the songs take on
   a slightly new cast"?
3. Reread paragraph #19. How does a song create silence for Corey? Explain
   how music leaves the listener in a "primitive" place of "pulsings and shiverings." What other entertainment might create this type of silence?
4. What is the purpose of Corey's essay? Is it just a tribute to Roy
   Orbison, or does he have another purpose?
5. Corey writes, "I've never gotten over this chilling illustration of the
   forces of circumstance and the fate of inches." Look up fate and destiny. Though used as synonyms, there are some subtle differences

between these two words. What do you discover when comparing the definitions? In your own words, describe the differences. What is your definition of fate and destiny?

Styling

A **loose sentence** begins with a main (complete) sentence followed with a series of add-ons—using commas to separate them—all describing or providing more information about the same subject in the main sentence, similar to items or actions in a series but more detailed.

In "A Voice for the Lonely," Stephen Corey uses this style to write about music transporting him back in time:

> There I was, *cruising* down the abandoned city street with the radio now up as loud as I could stand it, *mouthing* the rising and falling words, *rocking* side to side as I held the wheel, and *riding* Orbison's waiting, nearly-cracking voice back 24 years to the passenger seat of Jon Cresanti's Volkswagen Beetle.

The sentence breaks down into a main clause plus three add-ons:

> (Main) There I was, cruising down the abandoned city street with the radio now up as loud as I could stand it,
> (Add-on) mouthing the rising and falling words,
> (Add-on) rocking side to side as I held the wheel,
> (Add-on) and riding Orbison's waiting, nearly-cracking voice back 24 years to the passenger seat of Jon Cresanti's Volkswagen Beetle.

Notice that the add-ons cannot stand alone as complete sentences. They depend on the main sentence to make them complete. All three describe Corey's action, staying on the same subject. Each add-on begins with an "ing" action word.

Note: See "Commas with Add-Ons" in the "Punctuation is Style" section.

PRACTICE   Add-on three dependent word groups beginning with "ing" to the main sentence below. Try to be detailed and specific so that your sentence doesn't look like a simple list. Strive for the same length as Corey's sentence. Use a comma after each "ing" group.

Maria sat under the oak tree,

YOU TRY IT   Write five sentences of your own based on the above model, making sure that each one begins with a complete sentence (the main sentence) followed by three or four "ing" add-ons.

Warning: Edit your sentences for run-on, comma splice, and fragment errors (see the glossary or the rules in the "Punctuation is Style: Basic Rules and Practice" section if you are not familiar with these terms).

Teaming Up

1. **Warm-up for Writing Idea #3.** Bring in an article on a favorite singer, alive or dead. Before you come to class, write a summary of the article. In your group, do a **freewrite** on why you like this particular singer or group. Read your freewrites aloud in your group. Who has the most convincing freewrite? You can use your summary and freewrite for Writing Idea #3.

2. **Warm-up for Writing Idea #2.** At home, freewrite on the idea of fate. To what degree do you think fate controls our lives? Why? What's your experience with fate? Read your freewrites in your group, comparing responses, debating the issue.

Writing Ideas

(For more writing ideas on music, see "Prince," "Musical Awakenings," and "Roll Over Bach, Too").
1. Write an essay about a friend who was once very close to you. Explain what made the friendship special and why the friendship broke off. If music played a role in the memories, describe it, modeling Corey when he writes about his memories of John, making use of the sense of sound.
2. Corey writes about the death of Roy Orbison's wife, stating, "I've never gotten over this chilling illustration of the forces of circumstance and the fate of inches." Write an essay about a time when you first realized you were—to some degree—at the mercy of fate. Use at least one of the senses in your essay: sight, sound, smell, touch, taste.
3. Use your school or local library's online periodicals database and find an article on a singer you admire. Use the information to write a tribute, as Corey does, to this singer. Write about the music's impact on you, either emotionally or as a memory link. If the singer has died, write about where you were when you heard the news and your reaction.

Essay Connections

In "Musical Awakenings," Clayton Collins writes about music's ability to heal, and Jack Kroll, in "Roll Over Bach, Too," writes an essay about the Beatles and their tremendous impact on music and culture. "Prince" by Chuck Klosterman expresses the author's admiration of Prince as a genius.

COMMUNITY COLLEGE

Professor Tim Bascom

Professor Bascom is the Director of Creative Writing at Waldorf University in northern Iowa. He has been published in numerous magazines, including The Missouri Review, Florida Review, and Dynasty: InFlight Magazine of China Airlines. Books include Chameleon Days: An American Boyhood in Ethiopia and Running to the Fire: An American Missionary Comes of Age in Revolutionary Ethiopia. The essay "Community College" was published in a 2007 issue of Witness Journal and chosen for The Best Creative Nonfiction, Third Edition, 2009. This factual list-style essay compiles a sixteen week log of students' excuses for missing class, but along the way, it creates a wrenching portrait of his student's lives.

Week 1

1   Larry can't come because he went to his dad's place and found him on the floor, facedown, dead. Dwayne can't come because he's got black lung from smoking cigarettes. Mindy can't come because Wal-Mart changed her schedule; it's either eat or learn.

Week 2

2   Dwayne and Mindy are back, but Larry still can't come because of his dad's funeral.

3   Amanda is here, and she wants to talk. She's upset because, well, it's embarrassing, but after Blake asked her out and she said no, he sent her a nasty e-mail saying he had seen her on the Internet having sex. He's telling other people. She knows because a friend told her. She doesn't want people talking. Even if she did do that stuff, it's none of his business.

Week 3

4   Larry is back, but he may have to miss class once more so he can talk to the lawyer about his father's estate. His dad owned Larry's house. Now the sister wants to sell it. For her it's money; for him, it's where he lives.

5   Amanda is here, along with Blake, but they keep mouthing messages across the room.

First appearing in *Witness*, Vol. XXI, 2007. Copyright © 2007 by Timothy Bascom. Reprinted by permission.

6   Jane is here, as well, even though her daughter is struggling and her husband, a trucker, is away. She wants to write about the guy who came around selling insurance, the one who thought she shouldn't have painted her hallway like a U.S. flag. Where does he get off telling her what might upset people? If he doesn't like it, he can go back to India, or wherever he came from.

Week 4

7   Arlene can't come because she's attending a one-week course for beauticians. Nikki can't come because she's cutting herself, at least according to her friend. And John can't make it because he's in the psych ward.

8   Dwayne's gone, too—in the hospital—because the black lung turned to pneumonia. He'll be back, he whispers on the phone. He knows he's here for a reason; otherwise, he'd be dead. He's been stabbed and shot, and almost died from the bad lungs, but God won't let him go. Jesus has a plan.

9   Oh, and Sara can't make it because she's got a migraine. They dilated her eyes, so it hurts to read.

Week 5

10   Jane is on time, as usual, but she looks frustrated. She isn't going to write about that guy who criticized her hallway walls. Who cares? She's going to write about her first husband—because he was an addict and she didn't think her kids knew until she was at a pizza place and the littlest one got scared by a man at the next table. Her daughter said the man was a druggie. "How can you tell?" Jane asked. "Cause he has eyes like Daddy."

Week 6

11   Larry is back. He argued with his sister in the parking lot, so the estate isn't settled.

12   John is back, too, released from the psych ward. He says in high school he was a star on the football team and got good grades—before the army put him in a morgue where he had to look at bodies from Iraq. He says he can make up all the work now, if he can find his books.

Week 7

13   Dan's been coming every day, despite his diabetes. His sight is getting worse, but he can still use the computer. He types his notes

big—about two inches tall—and if he pulls at the corners of his eyes, he can read.

14   Jimmy is here all the time, too, and he smiles. He says he didn't used to be so easygoing, not until the skull fracture. His parents aren't so sure about the change, but he's happy. He thinks he used to cause too much trouble. He grins when he describes the extreme kickboxing that he does to make money on the side. The best way to win, he explains, is to hurt the other guy in a leg.

Week 8—Midterm

15   Arlene has disappeared, never to return from the beautician's course. And Chase is gone, even though his first paper (about body piercing) was beautiful. Mindy is AWOL as well, after coming back long enough to explain that she's not sure if she's a lesbian—which, along with the Wal-Mart work schedule, is making it hard for her to get anything done.

16   Amanda is back, but she doesn't want to press Blake on the Internet thing. There's something she should have explained—because actually she is on the Internet. It was one of those webcam things, and there's lots of others involved. She didn't think anyone here would see it.

17   Dwayne is back, too. The pneumonia is over, but now he doesn't care about anything. His woman friend says she can't see him since she isn't divorced. It doesn't make sense; if she loves him, then why doesn't she want to see him? He can feel himself going hard inside like he used to get before he went to prison. He wants to feel that way again so it doesn't hurt. If God gave him this woman, then why take her away?

Week 9

18   Sara has another migraine, so she can't make it. Heather can't be here because her fiancé is returning from Iraq for the wedding. Nikki can't be here because she has been cutting herself again, according to her friend, who says that once, in grade school, Nikki convinced a boy to break her arm.

19   Clarissa isn't coming either. She won't say why, but her brother, Ronnie, thinks she's depressed. As for Ronnie, he comes all the time, despite the fact that he was born with spina bifida and had fifteen surgeries on his legs and has to use a wheelchair.

Week 10

20   Dan is on time as usual, with his cane in hand and his bad eyes up to the computer. He is applying for a scholarship for the blind, so he can get into computer programming at the university. He wants to know if he will get his paper back. Last year the woman in charge never gave papers back. Not even on the last day. He doesn't want an A if he didn't earn it.

21   Larry is coming regularly, too, although his dad's estate is in stalemate. He says he will have to miss class once more when he goes to court with his ex. He doesn't like the essay about how women get marked—Miss, Mrs., and Ms. "Men get marked, too," he says. "Men are always at fault. Go to court and you'll see."

22   Dwayne is still coming, but he doesn't know why. His woman friend won't see him, and he can't stand the apartment. It reminds him of the way his dad used to put him in the garage and make him sleep there.

Week 11

23   For the first time, Jane is absent. She drops by to apologize. She has discovered that her junior high-age daughter stole $1,000 out of the ATM machine to give to a girl who keeps kicking her after school. There was a note in her daughter's drawer explaining why she might kill herself. Jane's sorry to be late, but she had to talk to the principal. If he won't do anything, she's going to press charges.

24   John hasn't made up any of his missed work, and he is not answering emails. Mindy isn't answering e-mails either. And now William is missing because he has rehearsal for the community play, *Julius Caesar.* He's playing a commoner, he says in his message. "Hey, like real life!" he adds.

Week 12

25   Dan is here as usual, but he says he will have to leave halfway through. He's still putting together the scholarship application—the one for blind students—but he can't stay because there's been some trouble at home. Family first, you know.

26   Nikki is back, too, and she wants to write about people who cut themselves.

27   Jimmy is smiling like usual, but he announces that he will take next semester off. He's going to stop the extreme kickboxing. They don't pay enough to cover the injuries. Instead, he's going to be a

bounty hunter in Chicago, going after guys who skip bail. There's a device to help him see into a room. That's the main thing—to see inside before you knock down the door.

28   Amanda hasn't come for weeks. She sends e-mails to explain. She's sorry about the whole Blake-Internet-sex thing. But she's got her act together now—because she has joined the army. After a year at a fort in Texas, she'll ship out to Iraq. It will be tough on her family, she knows. Especially her two-year-old. But she's not worried because the girl will be in good hands.

Week 13

29   Sara is back. The migraines are over. She wants to write about mules because she has one at home. They're not stubborn, she says. They're smart.

30   Mindy is back, too, after two weeks AWOL. She says she doesn't want to talk about it, but then she does it anyway. A guy friend raped her, and she couldn't come to class because she had a black eye. She hasn't told her parents because her dad might do something stupid. She says this isn't helping with the whole lesbian deal, or the job at Wal-Mart.

Week 14

31   Jane has turned in her paper about the ex-husband who's an addict, and she's proud of it. She says her junior high daughter is doing much better now that the other girl isn't kicking her.

32   Blake has turned in his paper also (about hunting for turkeys), but it's word-for-word from a site on the Internet. So's Amanda's paper, which she e-mailed from where she is getting trained as a soldier. After she learns that she has been caught, she e-mails back to say she's sorry. She feels just terrible. Since she doesn't deserve to take classes, she's going to drop them all.

33   Sara turns in her paper about mules, and she's right: they're smart.

Week 15

34   Maxine will have to miss the last two weeks because she's getting her stomach stapled.

35   John, who has been released from the psych ward for the second time, says he is going to let this semester ride. He'll try again after the meds are adjusted.

36   Mindy wants an extension, so she can make up the missing paper after she works through the rape and the whole lesbian issue.

37   Nikki turns in her paper late—the one about people who cut themselves—and it's a fine bit of writing. Still, she says, she's not going to take classes anymore. Her friend explains: "She's pregnant. The guy's a jerk.

38   Larry gets his paper in late, too. He says it's okay to dock it. He understands. Anyway, he doesn't know if he'll be back. The lawyer told him he might have to sell his house. How's he going to finish his degree if he's homeless?

Week 16—Finals Week

39   Jimmy comes by on the last day of the semester, just to say bye. He says he learned a lot. He says he'll be back if the bounty hunter deal doesn't pan out.

40   Dan drops by, too, when everyone else has gone. He holds out a letter from the university. It says he got the scholarship. He is full of thanks. Thanks for the letter of reference and the advice about the application. Thanks for helping to make it happen. His eyes are pale. They focus on nothing. He shifts the cane to his left hand and reaches with his right. He doesn't want to hear about how he did all the work himself, or how he deserves the money. His grip is firm.

COMMUNITY
COLLEGE

Exploring the Language

spina bifida: a birth defect that means "split spine"; babies with this defect are born with their spines not closed all the way.

stalemate: a deadlock; any position in which no progress can be made; in chess, a position where a player cannot move any piece except the king but cannot move the king without putting it in check.

Thinking and Talking Points

1. This list style essay appears at first to be factual and objective, a catalogue of student excuses for missing class. A closer reading, though, does show emotion, a portrait of his students' lives, along with a little frustration on the professor's part. Pick out passages that illustrate the author's attitudes and feelings for his students. Focus on word choices and punctuation that emphasize the writer's emotions.

2. Which excuses appear to be legitimate? Do any seem fabricated or overblown? How do students differ in their handling of adversity in their lives?

3. How does Bascom develop his students' characters? Do you get distinct impressions of their personalities? Give specific examples and explain.

4. What student triumphs and failures does the writer uncover by the end of the essay?

5. How does the writer use repetition to emphasize his point? Make a list of the repetitions in the essay and discuss how well they work to achieve the writer's objectives.

6. What is Bascom's purpose in writing this essay?

Styling

Because this type of essay is a style that uses mostly basic and compound sentences, the focus is on brevity, using lists of facts that in the end, show the writer's feelings about the topic. Though Bascom breaks his list into sixteen weeks, any time frame will suit the purpose—twenty four hours, a week, a month, a year.

PRACTICE Compile a list similar to Bascom's. Ideas include all the things a parent says to a child, a teenager to a parent, a husband to a wife, an owner to a pet, a teacher to students, or a boss to an employee; the excuses a student makes for not doing homework; what people say to someone when they want to break up; a list of mean-spirited behavior; dreams; what you'd like to say to other drivers on the road; excuses to politely get out of a date.

Choose a timeframe and beak it into three or four components, either by hours, days, weeks, or years.

Write in complete sentences, but keep them short and compound. This type of writing also lends itself to repetition, as Bascom does: he is, he has, Arelene is, can't come, etc.

The tone should be clear without using emotionally charged words. The tone can be ironic, sarcastic, despairing, humorous, angry, disgusted, joyful, or mix of these and others.

YOU TRY IT Organize the list in some logical way, either chronologically or items that go together for some reason: for example, a list of a mother's clichés might be grouped according to whether she's encouraging, scolding, or warning and broken down into the stages child, teen, and adult. Overall, the piece should illustrate a slice of time about a single topic.

Proofread and create a title (see "Titles, Introductions, and Conclusions" for ideas).

Teaming Up

1. **Warm-up for Writing Ideas #1 and #2:** In groups of three or four, work together on the "Styling," brainstorming ideas and then dividing the work evenly so that each student is responsible for one listing paragraph and its tone. When finished with individual sections, collaboratively organize, proofread, and title the work.
2. In groups of three or four, individually make a list of phony excuses you use either to miss class or to get out of some kind of work. Be brutally honest. If you are the perfect student and son or daughter, list excuses you've heard others use. Share your lists. Compile a master list, editing out repeated excuses. Organize the list from trivial fibs to outrageous lies. Discuss the morality of this behavior—is it sometimes okay or never okay to make such excuses?

Writing Ideas

1. Write an essay that mocks, condemns, or applauds a specific behavior. Use the "Styling" or first "Teaming Up," and insert at least two lists from the exercise as concrete evidence. Modify the list as needed.
2. Read the "Writing Strategies for Classification." Use these strategies and the list technique in the "Styling" or first "Teaming Up" to write a list essay.

Essay Connections

P.J. O'Rourke's "How to Drive Fast" satirizes another teen behavior, drinking and driving. In the preface from *The Dumbest Generation*, Mark Bauerlein bemoans technology's negative influence on the current generation of young people. "Turbulence" by David Sedaris humorously recounts an incident of bad behavior on an airplane. In "Somebody's Baby," Barbara Kingsolver points out how Americans treat children like "toxic waste," especially when contrasted with other cultures like Spain.

TURBULENCE

David Sedaris

Essayist and funny man David Sedaris has several collections to his credit: Me Talk Pretty One Day, Naked, Holidays on Ice, and Dress Your Family in Corduroy and Denim (a grammy winner for best spoken-word album). He's also a frequent contributor to The New Yorker magazine, where "Turbulence" appeared.

For a copy of this essay, visit the Links tab on the companion website: www.grtep.com

TURBULENCE

Thinking and Talking Points

1. Analyze the behavior of both people. Should he have moved his seat? Why or why not? If the woman were to tell the story, how would she tell it? Outline both points of view.
2. Though not everyone has the same sense of humor, the essay has intended humor. Whether or not you think the essay is funny, discuss strategies Sedaris uses to convey humor.
3. What is the main point of the story?
4. Much of the story is told using dialogue. Rewrite a section of the dialogue into prose. What does the story lose by this change?
5. What is the purpose of the example of how he resolves conflicts with Hugh?

Styling

You might come across a writing situation where dialogue is appropriate or necessary to get across your point, tone, or characterization. Dialogue can liven up a section of otherwise dull prose.

Notice that in Sedaris's essay, whenever the speaker changes, a new paragraph begins (the proper format for dialogue). Punctuation goes inside the quotation marks:

> "Well," I said, "ordinarily I'd be happy to move, but he's in the bulkhead, and I just hate the bulkhead."
> "He's in the what?"
> "The bulkhead," I explained. "That's what you call that front row."

Also note that when an interruption like "I said" or "said Rob" occurs in the middle of the sentence being quoted, a comma goes after it, and you would not capitalize "ordinarily" because it's part of the sentence containing the word "well."

PRACTICE Put the following exchange between Alice and the Caterpillar —from *Alice 's Adventures in Wonderland* by Lewis Carroll—in dialogue form, using correct punctuation, quotation marks, and a new line when the speaker changes.

What do you mean by that? said the Caterpillar, sternly. Explain yourself! I can't explain myself, I'm afraid Sir, said Alice because I'm not myself, you see. I don't see said the Caterpillar. I'm afraid I can't put it more clearly Alice replied, very politely for I can't understand it myself, to begin with; and being so many different sizes in a day is very confusing. It isn't said the Caterpillar.

You can see how confusing it is when each speaker is not clarified with punctuation, quotation marks, and a new paragraph.

YOU TRY IT   In dialogue form, write down a recent conversation, or rewrite a section of your last essay to include dialogue. You can also write down an exchange from a favorite film.

Teaming Up

1. **Warmup for Writing Idea #1.** Discuss the situation in the essay, and how you think the woman, Becky, would tell her side of the story. After brainstorming, rewrite the situation from Becky's point of view. Use proper dialogue form. Be prepared to read your paper to the rest of the class.

2. Individually, make a list of Pet Peeves (minor, annoying things that other people do that bother you). Next share your list. Chances are that at least one item on someone else's list is something that you're guilty of doing. Discuss ways to resolve such conflicts or control the behavior in ways acceptable to all in the group.

Writing Ideas

1. Write a narrative essay about a ridiculous, embarrassing, or otherwise unpleasant encounter you've experienced. Describe the situation and use dialogue. Explain how you resolved—or wish you had resolved—the conflict.

2. Write an essay about everyday annoyances, social niceties that people sometimes ignore, and the conflicts or misunderstandings they can cause. Give advice on how these situations might be peaceably resolved. Consider splitting types of annoyances into classifications (see Writing Strategies for Classification in Section Five), perhaps from minor offenses to more major ones.

3. Think of something to which you attach a significance (for Sedaris, it's the *New York Times* crossword puzzle); it can be an object, a rit-

ual, anything that has meaning for you in some small way. Avoid major social rituals like attending church or getting married. Find something that you do on a regular basis that has significance. Write an essay describing the object or ritual and explain its significance and perhaps analyze whether or not there's anything absurd in your attachment.

Essay Connections

P. J. O'Rourke's "How to Drive Fast" and Mark Twain's "Advice to Youth," both have themes of bad behavior. "Somebody's Baby" by Barbara Kingsolver also recounts a rude encounter on an airplane.

MODERN TIMES

Lawrence Weschler

Lawrence Weschler, on the first day after Desert Storm, is both fascinated and repelled by a war fought with technology. He recounts the coldness of the news media, which celebrates the clean aerial strikes, but ignores the carnage left behind. He connects the tragedy in San Francisco to the tragedy of war.

DUSTBIN OF HISTORY AND CULTURE

DESERT STORM: The Persian Gulf War between the United States and Iraq in 1991. MODERN TIMES: a 1936 film by Charlie Chaplin, a social protest against the dehumanization caused by the Industrial Age with its assembly lines and machines.

1   The morning after the launching of Desert Storm, a group of us at my office were talking about this awesome new thing that has entered the world, these awesome new things: this unprecedented kind of warfare with its truly precision, pinpoint aerial bombing; this unprecedented kind of war where, thanks to the various satellite technologies, you get to hear the results of that bombing instantaneously, as it's happening. Modern, we said, high-tech, uncanny, eerie, futuristic. And yet, of course, at another level, there's nothing new here. On the ground, the carnage of war, the gore, the frantically desperate attempts at rescue, the bitterly expiring hopes—they're all the same as they've ever been.

2   One of my friends there at the office that day commented on the way he'd been haunted all morning by the memory of an article he'd read last year—he couldn't remember where—about the San Francisco earthquake. About this young couple who'd been buried alive together in a small room in their collapsed apartment, their bones crushed in debris up to their waists, the two of them huddled together in this narrow air pocket. And of how the rescuers finally got to them—but at that very moment the wreckage caught fire; they were able to free up the husband, but he was forced to leave his wife behind and she perished in the flames.

3   We were all silent for a moment—CNN in the background was cross-cutting between the latest Pentagon briefing and live coverage of a speech by the Turkish prime minister in Ankara.

4   "Wait a second," my friend said. "I remember: it was in the *Whole Earth Review*. In fact, I bet we can even access it over Nexus." Our office is tied into one of those computerized data bases which offers continuously updated access to the complete back-contents of hundreds of newspapers and periodicals. My friend set himself down before the system's console, revved up the machine, punched in a few key words—*earthquake* and *fire* and *rescue* and *couple*—and instantaneously that very article appeared on the screen. He punched a few more buttons and the console's neighboring printer revved up and began spewing out a copy. The whole process didn't take more than a few moments.

5   The account, by Stewart Brand, was every bit as compelling as our colleague had remembered it. It turned out that Brand himself had happened to be visiting the neighborhood at the moment the earthquake struck and that he'd played an impromptu part in the volunteer rescue attempts: he'd been one of those on the outside, scrambling through the wreckage. "Of course, it wasn't as direct and purposeful as this brief account makes it seem," he records. "A real rescue is dreamy and hesitant, full of false starts and conflicting ideas, at times frantic and focused, at times diffuse. It is a self-organizing process, neither quick nor tidy. . . ." Much later, weeks after the disaster, he'd gone back and interviewed several of the principals from that evening's incident, including Bill Ray, the husband, who was still recovering at a hospital. In his article, Brand interwove their stories, and his account climaxed as the firemen were being driven back by the flames:

> "I told Janet," [this is Ray talking] "I told her 'I'm going to get free, and we're both going to get free.' I assumed that I was binding her and that if I could get loose, then she could get loose. You just start pulling with everything you've got. You reach up and you pull on the lathe and the plaster, and it's breaking off in your hand. . . . Janet was screaming because it was a lot of pain and her arms were trapped, and a picture frame of glass was cutting her.
>
> "Then I got free, but she still wasn't. I tried to pull her out. Smoke was coming in. You could hear the flames cracking and popping. She couldn't pull herself loose, and I couldn't get to her."
>
> What they said to each other then, Bill Ray prefers to keep private. "Then I left," [Ray recalls] "I crawled out that hole. . . ."

6   And so forth. That terrible lacuna—the private moment, what they possibly could have said to each other—has haunted me, too, ever since I read it. And, of course, I've been imagining the hundreds of variations of that scene being played out half a globe away; the fact that accidental strikes on civilian targets are purportedly being kept to a minimum doesn't comfort me in the least. I envision seventeen-year-old boys scrambling desperately to rescue their buddies, having to abandon the attempt in the face of further bombardments, and the image is in no way softened by the allegedly mitigating circumstance that the boys in question may be wearing uniforms.

7   But, strangely, the image that really haunts me, and the one I just can't shake, is that of my colleague in the eerie glow of his Nexus console, calmly punching that set of keys, activating the machine—the machine silently humming away, surveying the veritable continents of information before it, instantaneously targeting its quarry, yanking it out of the endless field and delivering it up to us whole. The surgical precision of the whole process. For a moment that morning, my colleague seemed to me like one of those amazing young officers strapped to his battle station aboard the AWACs control planes circling high above Saudi Arabia—coolly surveying his console, punching in the coordinates, splaying out the information, directing the entire battle.

8   CNN, Nexus, AWACs—they're all of a piece. And the carnage on the ground is something entirely else, almost infinitely removed.

MODERN TIMES

Exploring Language

camaraderie: a feeling of getting along; friendship or kinship.

carnage: the leftovers from slaughter, usually referring to dead people, especially after a battle.

diffuse: to scatter or spread.

eerie: ghostly or spooky.

impromptu: spontaneous or unrehearsed.

lacuna: break or interruption; cavity.

mitigating circumstances: special situations that allow for tolerance when leniency might not otherwise be permitted.

quarry: the victim or prey that one is hunting or focusing on.

splaying: spreading out.

uncanny: strange, weird, extraordinary.

unprecedented: never seen before; new, unrivaled.

Note: For pronunciation, visit dictionary.com, search the word, and click on the speaker icon.

USAGE   Examine the author's use of *mitigating* and *eerie*. Why do you think he made these particular choices? Here's a vocabulary challenge: use *uncanny, eerie,* and *quarry* in the same sentence.

Thinking and Talking Points

1. Why do you think the piece is called "Modern Times"? Give examples from the essay.

2. Explain the connection between the war and the earthquake. Why is Weschler's friend "haunted all morning" by the memory of an earthquake incident? What's significant about the friends' silence after hearing the earthquake story in paragraph #2 and the CNN coverage in the background?

3. What is Weschler's point? Do you think he's saying that war is not justified? Or is he just lamenting the need for war? Find evidence in the article to support your response.

4. Why is Weschler haunted by the image of his colleague at the console of the computer?
5. How do you think this highly technological war differs from previous wars like Vietnam and War World II? What does Weschler indicate he thinks? What's the emotional or psychological difference for the soldiers? Can you relate his ideas on war and technology to the Iraq war or the war in Afghanistan?

Styling

Weschler uses variations of **loose** and **periodic** sentence styles and dashes for writing spice (for more on using dashes, see the Styling section with David Huddle's "Museum Piece"). But let's take a look at a sentence with dashes that set off an **interrupting clause** called an **appositive**. Appositives rename, describe, or give more information about **nouns** (subjects) and help eliminate clunky clauses using *who* and *which*. Here's Weschler's sentence:

> My friend set himself down before the system's console, revved up the machine, punched in a few key words—*earthquake* and *fire* and *rescue* and *couple*—and instantaneously that very article appeared on the screen.

The group of words set off by dashes is an appositive because it renames *key words*. Notice that Weschler's sentence would be complete without the appositive:

> My friend set himself down before the system's console, revved up the machine, punched in a few key words, and instantaneously that very article appeared on the screen.

You have a choice of setting off interrupters with commas, dashes, or parentheses. When interrupting a sentence with a list, as Weschler does, it's a good idea to use dashes, especially when the list contains commas. Dashes will help avoid misreading. If Weschler had used commas instead of the dashes and conjunctions, and if the key words had not been italicized, the sentence would be confusing:

> My friend set himself down before the system's console, revved up the machine, punched in a few key words, earthquake, fire, rescue, couple, and instantaneously that very article appeared on the screen.

Weschler also uses appositives with commas to rename nouns:

Much later, weeks after the disaster, he'd gone back and interviewed several of the principals from that evening's incident, including Bill Ray, the husband, who was still recovering at a hospital.

The husband renames the noun *Bill Ray*.

Identity the appositives in the following sentences; notice which ones require dashes for clarity.

Her acupuncturist, Jerry, moved to Thailand.

The orchids—dendrobiums, oncidiums, cymbidiums, and cattleyas—bloomed a riot of colors.

My dog, a lazy Golden Retriever, is loveable but useless.

PRACTICE   Fill in the blanks below with words or phrases that describe, rename, or give extra information about the nouns.

My college, _____, changes to a sixteen-week semester next spring.

Her car, _____, sat crumpled in the corner of the police impound yard.

The band, _____, drew a large crowd at the county fair.

The vegetable garden—_____—grew despite neglect.

YOU TRY IT   Create five sentences of your own with appositives, using dashes and a list in at least two of them. Use this technique in one of the Writing Ideas below.

Teaming Up

1. Have each group member bring in some information about the reasons behind the Persian Gulf War (or another war), half of the group finding arguments justifying the war, half against it. Discuss these reasons and whether or not you think the war was justified.

2. **Warm-up for Writing Idea #2.** In your group, make a list of technological advances that have had an impact on people's lives. Discuss the positive and negative aspects of these technologies. Compare your results with those of the other groups in your class.

Writing Ideas

1. Using a list from "Teaming Up" activity #2, choose one technological advance to explore. Write an essay that discusses the advantages and disadvantages of the technology, proposing a solution to minimize the disadvantages.

2. Research the public's reaction to the Persian Gulf War; then research the reaction to the Vietnam War or Iraq. Write an essay describing these reactions and the reasons behind them. What has changed culturally or socially to cause a change in attitude?

3. Watch the silent Charlie Chaplin film *Modern Times* and discuss its relevance to Weschler's ideas in his essay. How is Weschler's essay a social protest? What is he protesting? How might his point, and Charlie Chaplin's, be relevant today? Draw direct parallels between the film, the essay, and current events.

MORTALITY

Bailey White

In this excerpt from her book Mama Makes Up Her Mind and Other Dangers of Southern Living, Bailey White—a first grade teacher, writer, radio commentator—writes about her life in the South, where she lives with her eccentric mother. Here, with gentle humor, she compares her aging car to her new car as well as her aging body.

DUSTBIN OF HISTORY AND CULTURE

GRACIE ALLEN: (1906–1964) American film and TV comedian, married to comedian George Burns.

VIVALDI: (1678–1741) Italian composer and violinist.

1   It really makes you feel your age when you get a letter from your insurance agent telling you that the car you bought, only slightly used, the year you got out of college, is now an antique. "Beginning with your next payment, your insurance premiums will reflect this change in classification," the letter said.

2   I went out and looked at the car. I thought back over the years. I could almost hear my uncle's disapproving voice. "You should never buy a used car," he had told me the day I brought it home. Ten years later I drove that used car to his funeral. I drove my sister, Louise, to the hospital in that car to have her first baby, and I drove to Atlanta in that car when the baby graduated from Georgia Tech with a degree in physics.

3   "When are you going to get a new car?" my friends asked me.

4   "I don't need a new car," I said. "This car runs fine."

5   I changed the oil often, and I kept good tires on it. It always got me where I wanted to go. But the stuffing came out of the backseat and the springs poked through, and the dashboard disintegrated. At 300,000 miles the odometer quit turning, but I didn't really care to know how far I had driven.

6   A hole wore in the floor where my heel rested in front of the accelerator, and the insulation all peeled off the fire wall. "Old piece of

junk," my friends whispered. The seat-belt catch wore out, and I tied on a huge bronze hook with a fireman's knot.

7   Big flashy cars would zoom past me. People would shake their fists out the windows. "Get that clunker off the road!" they would shout.

8   Then one day on my way to work, the car coughed, sputtered, and stopped. "This is it," I thought, and I gave it a pat. "It's been a good car."

9   I called the mechanic. "Tow it in," I said. "I'll have to decide what to do." After work I went over there. I was feeling very glum. The mechanic laughed at me. "It's not funny," I said. "I've had that car a long time."

10   "You know what's wrong with that car?" he said. "That car was out of gas." So I slopped a gallon of gas in the tank and drove ten more years. The gas gauge never worked again after that day, but I got to where I could tell when the gas was low by the smell. I think it was the smell of the bottom of the tank.

11   There was also a little smell of brake fluid, a little smell of exhaust, a little smell of oil, and after all the years a little smell of me. Car smells. And sounds. The wonderful sound when the engine finally catches on a cold day, and an ominous tick tick in July when the radiator is working too hard. The windshield wipers said "Gracie Allen Gracie Allen Gracie Allen." I didn't like a lot of conversation in the car because I had to keep listening for a little skip that meant I needed to jump out and adjust the carburetor.

12   I kept a screwdriver close to hand—and a pint of brake fluid, and a new roter, just in case. "She's strange," my friends whispered. "And she drives so slow."

13   I don't know how fast I drove. The speedometer had quit working years ago. But when I would look down through the hole in the floor and see the pavement, a gray blur, whizzing by just inches away from my feet, and feel the tremendous heat of internal combustion pouring back through the fire wall into my lap, and hear each barely contained explosion just as a heart attack victim is able to hear his own heartbeat, it didn't feel like slow to me. A whiff of brake fluid would remind me just what a tiny thing I was relying on to stop myself from hurtling along the surface of the earth at an unnatural speed, and when I finally arrived at my destination, I would slump back, unfasten the seat-belt hook with trembling hands, and stagger out. I would gather up my things and give the car a last look. "Thank you, sir," I would say. "We got here one more time."

14   But after I got that letter, I began thinking about getting a new car. I read the newspaper every night. Finally I found one that sounded good. It was the same make as my car, but almost new. "Call Steve," the ad said.

15   I went to see the car. It was parked in Steve's driveway. It was a fashionable wheat color. There was carpet on the floor, and the seats were covered with a soft, velvety-feeling stuff. It smelled like acrylic and vinyl and Steve. The instrument panel looked like what you would need to run a jet plane. I turned a knob. Mozart's Concerto for Flute and Harp poured out of four speakers. "But how can you listen to the engine, with music playing?" I asked Steve.

16   I turned the key. The car started instantly. No desperate pleadings, no wild hopes, no exquisitely paired maneuvers with the accelerator and the choke. Just instant ignition. I turned off the radio. I could barely hear the engine running, a low, steady hum. I fastened my seat belt. Nothing but a click.

17   Steve got in the passenger seat, and we went for a test drive. We floated down the road. I couldn't hear a sound, but I decided it must be time to shift gears. I stomped around on the floor and grabbed Steve's knee before I remembered it had automatic transmission. "You mean you just put it in 'Drive' and drive?" I asked.

18   Steve scrunched himself way over against his door and clamped his knees together. He tested his seat belt. "Have you ever driven a car before?" he asked.

19   I bought it for two thousand dollars. I rolled all the windows up by mashing a button beside my elbow, set the air-conditioning on "Recirc," and listened to Vivaldi all the way home.

20   So now I have two cars. I call them my new car and my real car. Most of the time I drive my new car. But on some days I go out to the barn and get in my real car. I shoo the rats out of the backseat and crank it up. Even without daily practice my hands and feet know just what to do. My ears perk up, and I sniff the air. I add a little brake fluid, a little water. I sniff again. It'll need gas next week, and an oil change.

21   I back it out and we roll down the road. People stop and look. They smile. "Neat car!" they say.

22   When I pull into the parking lot, my friends shake their heads and chuckle. They amble into the building. They're already thinking about their day's work. But I take one last look at the car and think what an amazing thing it is, internal combustion. And how wonderful to be still alive!

MORTALITY

Thinking and Talking Points

1. Why does White title her essay "Mortality"?
2. Find sensory details in the essay. How do these details enhance the humor?
3. Most people are excited about the prospect of owning a new car. Why is White so reluctant to relinquish her old clunker?
4. How is White's old car a metaphor? What clues are there in the essay to support a metaphorical subtext?
5. Is White simply trying to entertain her reader or is she making a point?

Styling

In Thinking and Talking Points #2, you located sensory details, a strong tool writers use to enhance writing, to make the reader feel, hear, taste, smell, and see the experience.

PRACTICE Sit in your car or another spot and **freewrite** on each of the senses for five minutes.

YOU TRY IT Use the best details from your freewrite above to write a paragraph describing your car or other spot. You can use your description in Writing Idea #1.

Teaming Up

1. **Warm-up for Writing Idea #2.** Bring in photos of various styles of cars. In your group, co-write a paragraph describing and comparing each car and the type of person who would drive each vehicle. Make a list of the stereotypes you created about each person. Then debunk each stereotype (noting how each stereotype might be refuted).

2. Before class, write a paragraph describing an object or place—your car or perhaps your room—and what it reveals about your personality. In class—without yet revealing your writing—team up with another person and tell each other what object you chose. Now write what you think the other person's choice reveals about his or her personality. Compare. Did your speculations match?

Writing Ideas

1. What you drive—like hairstyle and clothing—can reveal personality. Write an essay describing your car—or dream car—and what it says about your identity.
2. Observe several people and their cars, and write an essay that classifies people and the types of cars they drive, illustrating how what we drive can reveal something about our personalities. Admit that you are generalizing and there are always exceptions to your classification; otherwise, you might get accused of committing a logic error.
3. Write an essay that discusses what the automobile says about American culture. If you like, you can restrict your discussion to the culture of a particular region like New York or California.

Note: See Writing Idea #3 with "Disposable Rocket."

Essay Connections

Joseph Epstein explores America's obsession with celebrities in "The Culture of Celebrity." Other essays that have subtext or overriding metaphors include "Disposable Rocket" by John Updike, and Brian Doyle's "Meat" and "Joyas Voladoras."

READING THE RIVER

From Life on the Mississippi, Mark Twain

Mark Twain (Samuel L. Clemens, 1835-1910, born in Florida, Missouri), best known for his novels The Adventures of Huckleberry Finn *and* Tom Sawyer—*as well as his tall tales— grew up in Hannibal, Missouri, along the Mississippi River, and worked as steamboat pilot for five years, where he heard the riverboat term "mark twain," meaning two fathoms (12 feet deep), a safe depth for navigation. In this excerpt from his book* Life on the Mississippi, *he recounts his experiences learning to navigate the river, lamenting that though a pilot gains knowledge and skill, he loses much of the appreciation of the "beauty and romance," much like a doctor who no longer sees a woman's beauty, only the telltale signs of illness.*

DUSTBIN OF HISTORY AND CULTURE

MISSISSIPPI RIVER: The third longest river in North America, flowing approximately 2,350 miles from Lake Itasca in Minnesota to the Gulf of Mexico.

1   It turned out to be true. The face of the water, in time, became a wonderful book—a book that was a dead language to the uneducated passenger, but which told its mind to me without reserve, delivering its most cherished secrets as clearly as if it uttered them with a voice. And it was not a book to be read once and thrown aside, for it had a new story to tell every day. Throughout the long twelve hundred miles there was never a page that was void of interest, never one that you could leave unread without loss, never one that you would want to skip, thinking you could find higher enjoyment in some other thing. There never was so wonderful a book written by man; never one whose interest was so absorbing, so unflagging, so sparklingly renewed with every reperusal. The passenger who could not read it was charmed with a peculiar sort of faint dimple on its surface (on the rare occasions when he did not overlook it altogether); but to the pilot that was an italicized passage; indeed, it was more than that, it was a legend of the largest capitals, with a string of shouting exclamation points at the end of it, for it meant that a wreck or a rock was buried there that could tear the life out of the strongest vessel that ever floated. It is the faintest and simplest expression the water ever makes, and the most hideous to a pilot's eye. In truth, the passenger who could not read this book saw nothing but all manner of pretty pictures in it, painted by the sun and shaded by the clouds, whereas

to the trained eye these were not pictures at all, but the grimmest and most dread-earnest of reading matter.

2   Now when I had mastered the language of this water, and had come to know every trifling feature that bordered the great river as familiarly as I knew the letters of the alphabet, I had made a valuable acquisition. But I had lost something, too. I had lost something which could never be restored to me while I lived. All the grace, the beauty, the poetry, had gone out of the majestic river! I still kept in mind a certain wonderful sunset which I witnessed when steamboating was new to me. A broad expanse of the river was turned to blood; in the middle distance the red hue brightened into gold, through which a solitary log came floating, black and conspicuous; in one place a long, slanting mark was broken by boiling, tumbling rings, that were as many-tinted as an opal; where the ruddy flesh was faintest, was a smooth spot that was covered with graceful circles and radiating lines, ever so delicately traced; the shore on our left was densely wooded, and the somber shadow that fell from this forest was broken in one place by a long, ruffled trail that shone like silver; and high above the forest wall a clean-stemmed dead tree waved a single leafy bough that glowed like a flame in the unobstructed splendor that was flowing from the sun. There were graceful curves, reflected images, woody heights, soft distances; and over the whole scene, far and near, the dissolving lights drifted steadily, enriching it every passing moment with new marvels of coloring.

3   I stood like one bewitched. I drank it in, in a speechless rapture. The world was new to me, and I had never seen anything like this at home. But as I have said, a day came when I began to cease from noting the glories and the charms which the moon and the sun and the twilight wrought upon the river's face; another day came when I ceased altogether to note them. Then, if that sunset scene had been repeated, I should have looked upon it without rapture, and should have commented upon it, inwardly, after this fashion: "This sun means that we are going to have wind tomorrow; that floating log means that the river is rising, small thanks to it; that slanting mark on the water refers to a bluff reef which is going to kill somebody's steamboat one of these nights, if it keeps on stretching out like that; those tumbling 'boils' show a dissolving bar and a changing channel there, the lines and circles in the slick water over yonder are a warning that troublesome place is shoaling up dangerously; that silver streak in the shadow of the forest is the 'break' from a new snag, and

he has located himself in the very best place he could have found to fish for steamboats; that tall dead tree, with a single living branch, is not going to last long, and then how is a body ever going to get through this blind place at night without the friendly old landmark?

4   No, the romance and the beauty were all gone from the river. All the value any feature of it had for me now was the amount of usefulness it could furnish toward compassing the safe piloting of a steamboat. Since those days, I have pitied doctors from my heart. What does the lovely flush in a beauty's cheek mean to a doctor but a 'break' that ripples above some deadly disease? Are not all her visible charms sown thick with what are to him the signs and symbols of hidden decay? Does he ever see her beauty at all, or doesn't he simply view her professionally, and comment upon her unwholesome condition all to himself? And doesn't he sometimes wonder whether he has gained most or lost most by learning his trade?

READING
THE RIVER

Exploring Language

acquisition: something acquired or gained.
bewitch: to enchant or charm; to cast a spell over someone as in witchcraft.
conspicuous: easily seen or noticed.
opal: a gem that comes in a variety of colors.
ruddy: a healthy red, as in a ruddy complexion.
rapture: ecstatic joy or delight.
reperusal: perusal means to survey or read; reperusal means to survey or read again.
shoaling: shoals are shallow places in a body of water.
somber: dark, gloomy; dimly lit.
trifling: insignificant; of very little importance.
void: empty; without content.
wrought: worked or embellished.
yonder: over there; the thing more distant, or farther.
Note: For pronunciation, visit dictionary.com, search the word, and click on the speaker icon.

USAGE Look up other forms of the word *rapture* (rapturous, enraptured) and use each in a sentence. Use *somber* to describe the tone or mood of an inanimate object, perhaps a particular artwork like a film, painting, or novel. Look up the words *further* and *farther*, noting the differences and using each in a sentence.

Thinking and Talking Points

1. Discuss the implications of the title, the many ways Twain reads the river.
2. Study the repetition of the word "never" in paragraph #1. How does repetition work in his favor? How does it underscore his point? When would a writer avoid such repetition? (See **"Teaming Up" #1** for practice using this technique.) Also study the first line of the introduction. How does this simple declarative sentence hook the reader?
3. List—from paragraph #1—each comparison of the river to reading and writing, explaining the meaning. For example, he compares "faint

dimples" on the river's surface to italicized passages. What do italics signal to the reader?

4. In paragraphs #2 and #3, Twain describes the river before and after he learned to pilot a riverboat. Study the word choices and phrases he uses to create **tone**. Discuss the tone in each paragraph and how Twain achieves the desired contrast.

5. Twain combines two techniques in his conclusion: extended comparison and the question style paragraph. Why is the analogy appropriate to his subject? How do the questions build up to a concluding thought? Rewrite the questions into statements. Is anything lost in the translation? (See **Teaming Up #2** for practice with the question paragraph.)

Styling

In his conclusion, Mark Twain uses an extended comparison, or **metaphor**, of a doctor examining a beautiful woman to a riverboat pilot navigating the river. Notice that he breaks down different aspects of the features considered beautiful in a woman and directly compares them to what the doctor might see, moving from specific to general:

Beautiful Features	**Doctor's View**
lovely blush in a beauty's cheek	break that ripples above some deadly disease
visible charms	signs and symbols of decay
beauty	unwholesome condition

Joyce Carol Oates, in her essay "On Boxing," uses this technique, comparing the boxing match to a story: the dialogue is the unspoken language between the boxers; the setting is the ring, lights, ropes, and stained canvas; the spectators are the audience; ringside announcers are narrators. By breaking down both the elements of the boxing ring and the elements of story, she matches them up, creating an extended metaphor.

PRACTICE List the qualities and activities associated with the seasons of the year. For example, under winter the list might contain bleak, cold, hibernation, snow, rain, bare trees, storms, death, warm fires, snow skiing, ice skating, short days and long nights.

Next, list the qualities of particular people in your life: family members, friends, spouses, or co-workers. Pick one to match up with one of the seasons you listed. For example, a brother might be compared to winter:

has a temper, doesn't care for your feelings, is sharp-tongued, but in the right mood, perhaps he's warm and fun loving.

YOU TRY IT   Write an extended metaphor using your practice list. Begin the comparison mentioning the person and the season: "My brother is a cold winter day, bleak and barren." Then go on to match up items from your list in the season with the qualities of the person.

Note: If the season activity doesn't result in a good extended comparison, try breaking down other items or activities like cooking, a zoo, baseball, a clock, state of mind, and so on.

Teaming Up

1. The style activity works well in groups with small adjustments: brainstorm the qualities of the seasons together, help each other with word choices for the people-in-your-life lists, write paragraphs separately, and peer review the finished products. Revise and edit at home.
2. Most paragraphs with statements can be turned into strong questions, creating a thought-provoking introduction or conclusion. A paragraph of questions—like Mark Twain's conclusion—stands out. Read the following question style paragraphs:

From an introduction to an essay titled "No Wonder They Call Me a Bitch" by Ann Hodgman:

"I've always wondered about dog food. Is a Gaines-burger really like a hamburger? Can you fry it? Does dog food 'cheese' taste like real cheese? Does Gravy Train actually make gravy in the dog's bowl, or is that brown liquid just dissolved crumbs? And exactly what are by-products?"

From *An Almanac for Moderns* by Donald Culross Peattie:

"But of what use, pray, is man? Would anybody, besides his dog, miss him if he were gone? Would the sun cease to shed its light because there were not human beings here to sing the praises of sunlight? Would there be sorrow among the little hiding creatures of underwood, or loneliness in the hearts of the proud and noble beasts? Would the other simians feel that their king was gone? Would God, Jehovah, Zeus, Allah, miss the sound of hymns and psalms, the odor of frankincense and flattery?"

Rewrite each paragraph into statements and discuss whether or not the paragraphs work better as questions or statements. What do the questions imply about the writer's attitude toward the topic?

Choose one of the styles to imitate. For the first example, think of a product to target, and begin "I've always wondered about _____." Some topics to consider for the second example: lawyers, CEO's, vice-presidents, politicians, infomercials, reality television. You might begin your writing, "Of what use is _____."

Note: Adjust the verb as needed for singular or plural subjects. "Of what use are politicians?"

Writing Ideas

1. Write an essay contrasting and/or comparing the style (word choice, sentence structure, figurative language, organization, description, and other techniques) in "Reading the River" and Ken Chen's "City Out of Breath." Consider the two cultures and time periods and how they may or may not impact the writer's viewpoint. Express an opinion.
2. Describe a place or activity from two points in time and how your perspective changed. You might describe it first as you knew it as a child and how, as an adult, your view has changed. Often, a place or activity we enjoy when young loses its charm as we mature. Describe each view of the place in detail. Try using an extended comparison in one of the paragraphs. Use the senses—sight, sound, smell, touch, taste—in both descriptive sections and zoom in on details.

Essay Connections

Parts of "The Courage of Turtles" by Edward Hoagland (the pond before and after) provide contrast for the second writing idea. Reg Saner's "The Tree Beyond Imagining" uses extended comparison to describe Utah conifers.

MEAT

Brian Doyle

Brian Doyle's work—short stories, poems, essays—have appeared in numerous publications, including Best American Essays, The American Scholar, The Atlantic Monthly, Harper's, *and many anthologies. He's also written several essay collections and a novel,* Mink River. *"Meat" appeared in* The Sun Magazine, *March 2012. Like "Joyas Voladoras," his essay surprises the reader with its not-what-it-appears-on-the-surface conclusion.*

DUSTBIN OF HISTORY AND CULTURE

ABBOTABAD: a city in Pakistan.

1   My friend Tommy Crotty, who was a terrific basketball player in New York and went on to play college ball and be a cheerful husband and excellent dad before the idiot who just died in Abbottabad murdered him and thousands of people on September Eleventh, used to call every big guy he ever played with *Meat.*

2   Hey, Meat, he would say to the lumbering earnest centers he played with, and hey, Meat, he would say to his tree-trunk power forwards, and even his high-strung small forwards were all leaner Meat to Tommy, except in cases like mine; I started at small forward because guys who were bigger than me couldn't score if you locked them in the gym for a week, and guys who could shoot better wouldn't go into the lane to rebound without a helmet and crowbar, and I could at least convert easy shots and grab uncontested rebounds. So I started up front alongside two Meats, and Tommy ran the point with a succession of reckless gunners at shooting guard, which was a misnamed position on any team Tommy ran unless he trusted the other guard to take decent shots and hit half of them, in which case he would deliver the ball to him like a cake on a silver platter.

3   He was a most amazing point guard, Tommy Crotty, his name often all one word in the mouths of the coaches and refs and parents and fans who came to watch him slide like a grinning knife through what seemed like every Catholic-school team in the greater New York

metropolitan area: *tommycrotty!* You would even hear this odd word in churches and bars and one time at a police station, where there was a misunderstanding about an automobile until the sergeant realized that we played with *tommycrotty*, the word reverential in his mouth like he was talking about one of the lesser Apostles. It turned out one of his kids was a ballplayer, and his kid's team had gone up against our team, and, total respect for you other guys, said the sergeant, but our guys had your number except for that kid at the point, that kid is a magician, I never seen a kid do things like that with a basketball, and he is not the most athletic kid I ever seen either, which was true, Tommy was never going to be six feet tall, not in this life, and he was what even his mom called husky.

4   One time I asked Tommy why he called all the big guys Meat and he said it was just easier that way, learning their names was pointless because they all responded to the same simple stimuli. They want the ball early, you know, said Tommy. I think to reassure themselves that they exist. So I get each Meat a basket early, and then they're *happy,* man. They are not the brightest bulbs in the galaxy. Once they score they are good for long stretches. Meat has short memory. Later in the half I get them another bucket or two each, just to be sure they're awake. Otherwise I want them *working,* you know? Not worrying about scoring. I'll take care of the score, but I need work done out there, and *you're* not going to do it, prancing around like a hairy ballerina. At least *you* don't yell for the ball, which is why I give it to you when you're open. Some guys actually *yell at me* for the ball, can you imagine? Once in a while a Meat will set up his tent in the hole and wave for the ball. I wave back, man. Can you imagine signaling *me* to give *you* the ball? You don't think *I* know where the ball should go? Jesus. I had a Meat once who was waving for the ball, and I waved back, and his face lit up, and he says *hey Tommy!* This is why I call them Meat, man. They are not the brightest bulbs who ever lived.

5   This was how Tommy talked to us in the gym and the playground, but when he was talking to the coaches and refs and parents and fans who called him *tommycrotty* he used his Altar Boy Voice, all polite and reasonable and thanking the Madonna for what small gifts he had been given, and stuff like that. You could melt butter in the mouth that otherwise pretty much had only the words *meat* and *good game* in it. He didn't talk on the floor at all during the game but afterwards he was one of the few guys I ever knew who made a point of shaking every guy's hand on both teams and saying *good game* and actually

meaning it, which is rare, most guys don't mean it at all and they would give you the finger if people weren't watching.

6   But what I really want to tell you about Tommy isn't how he called all big guys Meat; it's about the time I absolutely hammered a guy on a blind pick in a game, and Tommy said something to me afterwards that I've thought about a lot since he was murdered by the idiot in Abbottabad. The guy I clocked had been fouling Tommy the whole game, because basically Tommy was killing his team and the rest of us weren't and this guy figured he would cut the head off the snake, you know? So he bashed Tommy every chance he got, setting mean picks, cracking Tommy's hands and arms while supposedly going for the ball, really dropping the hammer on him twice when he drove to the basket, and one time accidentally on purpose whipping a pass right in Tommy's face like the ball slipped but it didn't. Finally the rest of us had had enough, and me and the Meat set up a blind back pick, which is an evil basketball way to exact vengeance on a guy. The guy you are trying to nail comes flying around the Meat pick, a standard high pick he expects and has seen all game, and then runs smack into a second vicious pick which he did *not* expect, the second pick being me with an elbow aimed at his eye. Well, the guy went down in a heap, and there was a ruckus with coaches and dads yelling, but the ref had seen the way the guy was bashing Tommy, and he figured an eye for an eye, so that was that.

7   But that *wasn't* that, as it turned out, because after the game Tommy read me the riot act, and told me never to do that again, not on his floor, or I would never see the ball again except in the windows of sports stores. He said he understood why we had done it, and he appreciated the thought, but there was a right way and a wrong way to play, and he would be damned if anyone on his team played the wrong way. I asked what about the other guy hammering him and he said screw the other guy, with a guy like that you just play harder and show him the error of his ways. I said that was stupid, that guys like that were idiots, and would never see the error of their ways, and the best way to deliver a message to guys like that was with your elbow in his eyeball, maybe both elbows. You are not listening to me, said Tommy patiently, which is disappointing, you are not Meat, try to pay attention, and remember I have the ball and you do not. There is a right way and a wrong way to play. We play the right way. Guys who play the wrong way will lose in the end. Are you listening to me? Do I have to write this down? The way to teach a guy who plays the

wrong way is to play the right way. *They want you to play the wrong way.* Get it? They are not the brightest bulbs in the galaxy. So the way to really drive them bonkers and make them go home and punch the wall is to play the right way. Firstly it is the only way to play, and secondly it gives them a chance to wake up, although personally I would not bet the house on that. Are you listening to me?

8   Yes, I was. Yes.

MEAT

Exploring Language

reverential: to show reverence (respect, awe).
ruckus: commotion, uproar.
Note: For pronunciation, visit dictionary.com, search the word, and click on the speaker icon.

USAGE   For practice with different forms of words, write one sentence using the word *reverence* and one using *reverent.*

Thinking and Talking Points

1. Doyle begins his essay with a long sentence, clauses connected with the conjunction "and." The main sentence is "My friend Tommy Crotty used to call every big guy he ever played with *Meat*." The rest of the material interrupts the main sentence. Most students have been taught not to connect a series of clauses or phrases with too many conjunctions. Why would an award-winning author like Doyle break this so-called rule?

2. Look for other casual writing elements or rule-breaking (comma splices, clichés, word choices, sentence structures) in "Meat" and discuss their use. How do they work in the author's favor?

3. Make a list of the similes and identify the ones that do not fall into the **cliché** category.

4. What is the essay's **subtext** (underlying message), Doyle's real purpose? How does that purpose relate to the opening of the essay? How do Tommy's thoughts on the right and wrong way to play—especially since Tommy's death—hint at this subtext, especially when related to the opening lines of the essay and Doyle's last line?

5. In the beginning of paragraph #6, Doyle writes that it isn't Tommy calling all the big guys Meat that he wants to share, but something he's thought a lot about since Tommy was murdered. How do the first five paragraphs set the reader up for his real topic?

Styling

This **loose sentence** conveys a sense of action that would be lost if broken into a series of sentences:

> So he bashed Tommy every chance he got, setting mean picks, cracking Tommy's hands and arms while supposedly going for the ball, really dropping the hammer on him twice when he drove to the basket, and one time accidentally on purpose whipping a pass right in Tommy's face like the ball slipped but it didn't.

The main sentence, "So he bashed Tommy every chance he got," functions independently and could end with a period but continues with a series of actions using commas:

> *setting* mean picks,
> *cracking* Tommy's hands and arms while supposedly going for the ball,
> really *dropping* the hammer on him twice when he drove to the basket,
> and one time accidentally on purpose *whipping* a pass right in
> Tommy's face like the ball slipped but it didn't.

Commas separate each action; these actions cannot function alone, relying on the first main sentence to be complete. Notice that turning these actions into complete, separate sentences sounds stilted and simplistic:

> So he bashed Tommy every chance he got. He set mean picks. He cracked Tommy's hands and arms while supposedly going for the ball. He really dropped the hammer on him twice when he drove to the basket. One time he accidentally on purpose whipped a pass right in Tommy's face like the ball slipped but it didn't.

By simply turning the verbs (set, cracked, dropped, whipped) into the "ing" form (setting, cracking, dropping, whipping) and omitting the subject "he," the writer creates a sentence packed with action that flows, underscoring the abuse heaped upon Tommy by the other basketball player.

PRACTICE   Combine the following sentences into one by changing the verbs (in italics) to the "ing" form, omitting the subject, connecting them to the first sentence with commas, but leaving the first sentence as it is to avoid writing a long fragment:

The boxer jabbed at his opponent. He hit him with a vicious right hook. He slammed him with a mind-numbing left. He backed him into the corner of the ropes. He pummeled him with a series of unforgiving blows. He finished him with an uppercut for the win.

YOU TRY IT   Write five loose sentences with a series of at least four actions using the "ing" form.

Teaming Up

1. Brainstorm a list of five social issues. Discuss ideas that might be used as narrative (story) to imply or illustrate each issue. Use one of the ideas—or one of your own—for Writing Idea #2.

Writing Ideas

1. Drawing on the answers to Thinking and Talking Points 1-3, write an essay analyzing Brian Doyle's style, perhaps comparing/contrasting it to other essays with casual style like "Prince" by Chuck Klosterman; or compare/contrast "Meat" to an essay with more traditional style like "The Chemist's War" by Deborah Blum.
2. After reading other essays that are metaphor or contain subtext for a larger point—"Disposable Rocket" by John Updike, "Mortality" by Bailey White, "The Tree Beyond Imagining" by Reg Sanger—write an essay that uses a narrative (like Doyle) or metaphor to make a point about a larger issue.

Essay Connections

For essays with subtext or metaphor, see the list in Writing Idea #2. "The Surfing Savant" by Paul Solotaroff is about a famous surfer, Clay Marzo, and his struggle with Asperger syndrome.

BURL'S

Bernard Cooper

Bernard Cooper is a writing teacher whose work has been published in Harper's Magazine, The Paris Review, and Best American Essays. "Burl's" appeared in the Los Angeles Times Magazine and Best American Essays. In this essay, a young Bernard Cooper discovers that things aren't always as they appear: life is more complex and ambiguous than he thought. He ponders this idea using a series of incidents that contribute to or lead up to this realization, as well as an epiphany about his own sexual identity and "the hazy border between the sexes."

DUSTBIN OF HISTORY AND CULTURE

MUSES: Greek goddesses of inspiration—prompted memory and presided over the arts and sciences; calling on the muse was a standard literary convention in epic poetry like Milton's *Paradise Lost*.

1   I loved the restaurant's name, a compact curve of a word. Its sign, five big letters rimmed in neon, hovered above the roof. I almost never saw the sign with its neon lit; my parents took me there for early summer dinners, and even by the time we left—father cleaning his teeth with a toothpick, mother carrying steak bones in a doggie bag—the sky was still bright. Heat rippled off the cars parked along Hollywood Boulevard, the asphalt gummy from hours of sun.

2   With its sleek architecture, chrome appliances, and arctic temperature, Burl's offered a refuge from the street. We usually sat at one of the booths in front of the plate-glass windows. During our dinner, people came to a halt before the news-vending machine on the corner and burrowed in their pockets and purses for change.

3   The waitresses at Burl's wore brown uniforms edged in checked gingham. From their breast pockets frothed white lace handkerchiefs. In between reconnaissance missions to the table, they busied themselves behind the counter and shouted "Tuna to travel" or "Scorch that patty" to a harried short-order cook who manned the grill. Miniature pitchers of cream and individual pats of butter were extracted from an industrial refrigerator. Coca-Cola shot from a glinting spigot. Waitresses dodged and bumped one another, frantic as atoms.

4   My parents usually lingered after the meal, nursing cups of coffee while I played with the beads of condensation on my glass of ice
water, tasted Tabasco sauce, or twisted pieces of my paper napkin
into mangled animals. One evening, annoyed with my restlessness,
my father gave me a dime and asked me to buy him a *Herald Examiner*
from the vending machine in front of the restaurant.

5   Shouldering open the heavy glass door, I was seared by a sudden
gust of heat. Traffic roared past me and stirred the air. Walking toward
the newspaper machine, I held the dime so tightly it seemed to melt
in my palm. Duty made me feel large and important. I inserted the
dime and opened the box, yanking a *Herald* from the spring contrap-
tion that held it as tight as a mousetrap. When I turned around, paper
in hand, I saw two women walking toward me.

6   Their high heels clicked on the sun-baked pavement. They were
tall, broad-shouldered women who moved with a mixture of haste
and defiance. They'd teased their hair into nearly identical black bee-
hives. Dangling earrings flashed in the sun, brilliant as prisms. Each
of them wore the kind of clinging, strapless outfit my mother referred
to as a cocktail dress. The silky fabric—one dress was purple, the other
pink—accentuated their breasts and hips and rippled with insolent
highlights. The dresses exposed their bare arms, the slope of their
shoulders, and the smooth, powdered plane of flesh where their cleav-
age began.

7   I owned at the time a book called *Things for Boys and Girls to Do.*
There were pages to color, intricate mazes, and connect-the-dots. But
another type of puzzle came to mind as I watched those women walking
toward me: What's Wrong With This Picture? Say the drawing of a dining
room looked normal at first glance; on closer inspection, a chair was
missing its leg and the man who sat atop it wore half a pair of glasses.

8   The women had Adam's apples.

9   The closer they came, the shallower my breathing was. I blocked
the sidewalk, an incredulous child stalled in their path. When they
saw me staring, they shifted their purses and linked their arms. There
was something sisterly and conspiratorial about their sudden close-
ness. Though their mouths didn't move, I thought they might have
been communicating without moving their lips, so telepathic did they
seem as they joined arms and pressed together, synchronizing their
heavy steps. The pages of the *Herald* fluttered in the wind. I felt them
against my arm, light as batted lashes.

10   The woman in pink shot me a haughty glance and yet she seemed
pleased that I'd taken notice, hungry to be admired by a man, or even

an awestruck eight-year-old boy. She tried to stifle a grin, her red lipstick more voluptuous than the lips it painted. Rouge deepened her cheekbones. Eye shadow dusted her lids, a clumsy abundance of blue. Her face was like a page in *Things for Boys and Girls to Do,* colored by a kid who went outside the lines.

11   At close range, I saw that her wig was slightly askew. I was certain it was a wig because my mother owned several; three Styrofoam heads lined a shelf in my mother's closet; upon them were perched a Page-Boy, an Empress, and a Baby-Doll, all in shades of auburn. The woman in the pink dress wore her wig like a crown of glory.

12   But it was the woman in the purple dress who passed nearest me, and I saw that her jaw was heavily powdered, a half-successful attempt to disguise the telltale shadow of a beard. Just as I noticed this, her heel caught on a crack in the pavement and she reeled on her stilettos. It was then that I witnessed a rift in her composure, a window through which I could glimpse the shades of maleness that her dress and wig and makeup obscured. She shifted her shoulders and threw out her hands like a surfer riding a curl. The instant she regained her balance, she smoothed her dress, patted her hair, and sauntered onward.

13   Any woman might be a man. The fact of it clanged through the chambers of my brain. In broad day, in the midst of traffic, with my parents drinking coffee a few feet away, I felt as if everything I understood, everything I had taken for granted up to that moment—the curve of the earth, the heat of the sun, the reliability of my own eyes—had been squeezed out of me. Who were those men? Did they help each other get inside those dresses? How many other people and things were not what they seemed? From the back, the impostors looked like women once again, slinky and curvaceous, purple and pink. I watched them disappear into the distance, their disguises so convincing that other people on the street seemed to take no notice, and for a moment I wondered if I had imagined the whole encounter, a visitation by two unlikely muses.

14   Frozen in the middle of the sidewalk, I caught my reflection in the window of Burl's, a silhouette floating between his parents. They faced one another across a table. Once the solid embodiments of woman and man, pedestrians and traffic appeared to pass through them.

15   There were some mornings, seconds before my eyes opened and my senses gathered into consciousness, that the child I was seemed to hover above the bed, and I couldn't tell what form my waking would take—the body of a boy or the body of a girl. Finally stirring, I'd blink

against the early light and greet each incarnation as a male with mild surprise. My sex, in other words, didn't seem to be an absolute fact so much as a pleasant, recurring accident.

16   By the age of eight, I'd experienced this groggy phenomenon several times. Those ethereal moments above my bed made waking up in the tangled blankets, a boy steeped in body heat, all the more astonishing. That this might be an unusual experience never occurred to me; it was one among a flood of sensations I could neither name nor ignore.

17   And so, shocked as I was when those transvestites passed me in front of Burl's, they confirmed something about which I already had an inkling: the hazy border between the sexes. My father, after all, raised his pinky when he drank from a teacup, and my mother looked as faded and plain as my father until she fixed her hair and painted her face.

18   Like most children, I once thought it possible to divide the world into male and female columns. Blue/Pink. Rooster/Hens. Trousers/Skirts. Such divisions were easy, not to mention comforting, for they simplified matter into compatible pairs. But there also existed a vast range of things that didn't fit neatly into either camp: clocks, milk, telephones, grass. There were nights I fell into a fitful sleep while trying to sex the world correctly.

19   Nothing typified the realms of male and female as clearly as my parents' walk-in closets. Home alone for any length of time, I always found my way inside them. I could stare at my parents' clothes for hours, grateful for the stillness and silence, haunting the very heart of their privacy.

20   The overhead light in my father's closet was a bare bulb. Whenever I groped for the chain in the dark, it wagged back and forth and resisted my grasp. Once the light clicked on, I saw dozens of ties hanging like stalactites. A monogrammed silk bathrobe sagged from a hook, a gift my father had received on a long-ago birthday and, thinking it fussy, rarely wore. Shirts were cramped together along the length of an aluminum pole, their starched sleeves sticking out as if in a halfhearted gesture of greeting. The medicinal odor of mothballs permeated the boxer shorts that were folded and stacked in a built-in drawer. Immaculate underwear was proof of a tenderness my mother couldn't otherwise express; she may not have touched my father often, but she laundered his boxers with infinite care. Even back then, I suspected that a sense of duty was the final erotic link between them.

21   Sitting in a neat row on the closet floor were my father's boots and slippers and dress shoes. I'd try on his wingtips and clomp around, slipping out of them with every step. My wary, unnatural stride made me all the more desperate to effect some authority. I'd whisper orders to imagined lackeys and take my invisible wife in my arms. But no matter how much I wanted them to fit, those shoes were as cold and hard as marble.

22   My mother's shoes were just as uncomfortable, but a lot more fun. From a brightly colored array of pumps and slingbacks, I'd pick a pair with the glee and deliberation of someone choosing a chocolate. Whatever embarrassment I felt was overwhelmed by the exhilaration of being taller in a pair of high heels. Things will look like this someday, I said to myself, gazing out from my new and improved vantage point as if from a crow's nest. Calves elongated, arms akimbo, I gauged each step so that I didn't fall over and moved with what might have passed for grace had someone seen me, a possibility I scrupulously avoided by locking the door.

23   Back and forth I went. The longer I wore a pair of heels, the better my balance. In the periphery of my vision, the shelf of wigs looked like a throng of kindly bystanders. Light streamed down from a high window, causing crystal bottles to glitter, the air ripe with perfume. A makeup mirror above the dressing table invited my self-absorption. Sound was muffled. Time slowed. It seemed as if nothing bad could happen as long as I stayed within those walls.

24   Though I'd never been discovered in my mother's closet, my parents knew that I was drawn toward girlish things—dolls and jump rope and jewelry—as well as to the games and preoccupations that were expected of a boy. I'm not sure now if it was my effeminacy itself that bothered them as much as my ability to slide back and forth, without the slightest warning, between male and female mannerisms. After I'd finished building the model of an F-17 bomber, say, I'd sit back to examine my handiwork, pursing my lips in concentration and crossing my legs at the knee.

25   One day my mother caught me standing in the middle of my bedroom doing an imitation of Mary Injijikian, a dark, overeager Armenian girl with whom I believed myself to be in love, not only because she was pretty but because I wanted to be like her. Collector of effortless A's, Mary seemed to know all the answers in class. Before the teacher had even finished asking a question, Mary would let out a little grunt and practically levitate out of her seat, as if her hand were filled with helium. "Could we please hear from someone else today besides Miss

Injijikian," the teacher would say. *Miss Injijikian.* Those were the words I was repeating over and over to myself when my mother caught me. To utter them was rhythmic, delicious, and under their spell I raised my hand and wiggled like Mary. I heard a cough and spun around. My mother froze in the doorway. She clutched the folded sheets to her stomach and turned without saying a word. My sudden flush of shame confused me. Weren't boys supposed to swoon over girls? Hadn't I seen babbling, heartsick men in a dozen movies?

26   Shortly after the Injijikian incident, my parents decided to send me to gymnastics class at the Los Angeles Athletic Club, a brick relic of a building on Olive Street. One of the oldest establishments of its kind in Los Angeles, the club prohibited women from the premises. My parents didn't have to say it aloud: they hoped a fraternal atmosphere would toughen me up and tilt me toward the male side of my nature.

27   My father drove me downtown so I could sign up for the class, meet the instructor, and get a tour of the place. On the way there, he reminisced about sports. Since he'd grown up in a rough Philadelphia neighborhood, sports consisted of kick-the-can or rolling a hoop down the street with a stick. The more he talked about his physical prowess, the more convinced I became that my daydreams and shyness were a disappointment to him.

28   The hushed lobby of the athletic club was paneled in dark wood. A few solitary figures were hidden in wing chairs. My father and I introduced ourselves to a man at the front desk who seemed unimpressed by our presence. His aloofness unnerved me, which wasn't hard considering that no matter how my parents put it, I knew their sending me here was a form of disapproval, a way of banishing the part of me they didn't care to know.

29   A call went out over the intercom for someone to show us around. While we waited, I noticed that the sand in the standing ashtrays had been raked into perfect furrows. The glossy leaves of the potted plants looked as if they'd been polished by hand. The place seemed more like a well-tended hotel than an athletic club. Finally, a stoop-shouldered old man hobbled toward us, his head shrouded in a cloud of white hair. He wore a T-shirt that said "Instructor"; his arms were so wrinkled and anemic, I thought I might have misread it. While we followed him to the elevator, I readjusted my expectations, which had involved fantasies of a hulking drill sergeant barking orders at a flock of scrawny boys.

30   The instructor, mumbling to himself and never turning around to see if we were behind him, showed us where the gymnastics class took place. I'm certain the building was big, but the size of the room

must be exaggerated by a trick of memory, because when I envision it, I picture a vast and windowless warehouse. Mats covered the wooden floor. Here and there, in remote and lonely pools of light, stood a pommel horse, a balance beam, and parallel bars. Tiers of bleachers rose into darkness. Unlike the cloistered air of a closet, the room seemed incomplete without a crowd.

31   Next we visited the dressing room, empty except for a naked middle-aged man. He sat on a narrow bench and clipped his formidable toenails. Moles clotted his back. He glistened like a fish.

32   We continued to follow the instructor down an aisle lined with numbered lockers. At the far end, steam billowed from the doorway that led to the showers. Fresh towels stacked on a nearby table made me think of my mother; I knew she liked to have me at home with her—I was often her only companion—and I resented her complicity in the plan to send me here.

33   The tour ended when the instructor gave me a sign-up sheet. Only a few names preceded mine. They were signatures, or so I imagined, of other soft and wayward sons.

34   When the day of the first gymnastics class arrived, my mother gave me money and a gym bag and sent me to the corner of Hollywood and Western to wait for a bus. The sun was bright, the traffic heavy. While I sat there, an argument raged inside my head, the familiar, battering debate between the wish to be like other boys and the wish to be like myself. Why shouldn't I simply get up and go back home, where I'd be left alone to read and think? On the other hand, wouldn't life be easier if I liked athletics, or learned to like them?

35   No sooner did I steel my resolve to get on the bus than I thought of something better: I could spend the morning wandering through Woolworth's, then tell my parents I'd gone to the class. But would my lie stand up to scrutiny? As I practiced describing phantom gymnastics, I became aware of a car circling the block. It was a large car in whose shaded interior I could barely make out the driver, but I thought it might be the man who owned the local pet store. I'd often gone there on the pretext of looking at the cocker spaniel puppies huddled together in their pen, but I really went to gawk at the owner, whose tan chest, in the V of his shirt, was the place I most wanted to rest my head. Every time the man moved, counting stock or writing a receipt, his shirt parted, my mouth went dry, and I smelled the musk of sawdust and dogs.

36   I found myself hoping that the driver was the man who ran the pet store. I was thrilled by the unlikely possibility that the sight of

me, slumped on a bus bench in my T-shirt and shorts, had caused such a man to circle the block. Up to that point in my life, lovemaking hovered somewhere in the future, an impulse a boy might aspire to but didn't indulge. And there I was, sitting on a bus bench in the middle of the city, dreaming I could seduce an adult. I showered the owner of the pet store with kisses and, as aquariums bubbled, birds sang, and mice raced in a wire wheel, slipped my hand beneath his shirt. The roar of traffic brought me to my senses. I breathed deeply and blinked against the sun. I crossed my legs at the knee in order to hide an erection. My fantasy left me both drained and changed. The continent of sex had drifted closer.

37   The car made another round. This time the driver leaned across the passenger seat and peered at me through the window. He was a complete stranger, whose gaze filled me with fear. It wasn't the surprise of not recognizing him that frightened me, it was what I did recognize—the unmistakable shame in his expression, and the weary temptation that drove him in circles. Before the car behind him honked, he mouthed "hello" and cocked his head. What now, he seemed to be asking. A bold, unbearable question.

38   I bolted to my feet, slung the gym bag over my shoulder, and hurried toward home. Now and then I turned around to make sure he wasn't trailing me, both relieved and disappointed when I didn't see his car. Even after I became convinced that he wasn't at my back—my sudden flight had scared him off—I kept turning around to see what was making me so nervous, as if I might spot the source of my discomfort somewhere on the street. I walked faster and faster, trying to outrace myself. Eventually, the bus I was supposed to have taken roared past. Turning the corner, I watched it bob eastward.

39   Closing the kitchen door behind me, I vowed never to leave home again. I was resolute in this decision without fully understanding why, or what it was I hoped to avoid; I was only aware of the need to hide and a vague notion, fading fast, that my trouble had something to do with sex. Already the mechanism of self-deception was at work. By the time my mother rushed into the kitchen to see why I'd returned so early, the thrill I'd felt while waiting for the bus had given way to indignation.

40   I poured out the story of the man circling the block and protested, with perhaps too great a passion, my own innocence. "I was just sitting there," I said again and again. I was so determined to deflect suspicion away from myself, and to justify my missing the class, that I portrayed the man as a grizzled pervert who drunkenly veered from lane to lane as he followed me halfway home.

41   My mother cinched her housecoat. She seemed moved and shocked by what I told her, if a bit incredulous, which prompted me to be more dramatic. "It wouldn't be safe," I insisted, "for me to wait at the bus stop again."

42   No matter how overwrought my story, I knew my mother wouldn't question it, wouldn't bring the subject up again; sex of any kind, especially sex between a man and a boy, was simply not discussed in our house. The gymnastics class, my parents agreed, was something I could do another time.

43   And so I spent the remainder of that summer at home with my mother, stirring cake batter, holding the dustpan, helping her fold the sheets. For a while I was proud of myself for engineering a reprieve from the athletic club. But as the days wore on, I began to see that my mother had wanted me with her all along, and forcing that to happen wasn't such a feat. Soon a sense of compromise set in; by expressing disgust for the man in the car, I'd expressed disgust for an aspect of myself. Now I had all the time in the world to sit around and contemplate my desire for men. The days grew long and stifling and hot, an endless sentence of self-examination.

44   Only trips to the pet store offered any respite. Every time I went there, I was too electrified with longing to think about longing in the abstract. The bell tinkled above the door, animals stirred within their cages, and the handsome owner glanced up from his work.

45   I handed my father the *Herald.* He opened the paper and disappeared behind it. My mother stirred her coffee and sighed. She gazed at the sweltering passersby and probably thought herself lucky. I slid into the vinyl booth and took my place beside my parents.

46   For a moment, I considered asking them about what had happened on the street, but they would have reacted with censure and alarm, and I sensed there was more to the story than they'd ever be willing to tell me. Men in dresses were only the tip of the iceberg. Who knew what other wonders existed—a boy, for example, who wanted to kiss a man—exceptions the world did its best to keep hidden.

47   It would be years before I heard the word "transvestite," so I struggled to find a word for what I'd seen. "He-she" came to mind, as lilting as "Injijikian." "Burl's" would have been perfect, like "boys" and "girls" spliced together, but I can't claim to have thought of this back then.

48   I must have looked stricken as I tried to figure it all out, because my mother put down her coffee cup and asked if I was O.K. She

stopped just short of feeling my forehead. I assured her I was fine, but something within me had shifted, had given way to a heady doubt. When the waitress came and slapped down our check—"Thank You," it read, "Dine out more often"—I wondered if her lofty hairdo or the breasts on which her nametag quaked were real. Wax carnations bloomed at every table. Phony wood paneled the walls. Plastic food sat in a display case: fried eggs, a hamburger sandwich, a sundae topped with a garish cherry.

BURL'S

Exploring Language

akimbo: hands on the hips and elbows turned outward.

askew: in this context, crooked or out of line.

cloistered: secluded or sheltered from the world.

conspiratorial: suggestive of having a conspiracy, which means having a secret or plot.

elongated: stretched out or lengthened.

ethereal: delicate or rare; otherworldly.

fraternal: in this context, brotherly union or affection.

frothed: bubbled or foamed.

garish: tasteless and/or flashy; excessively ornate.

haughty: arrogant or scornful.

incredulous: astounded, shaken, shocked, surprised.

insolent: bold, rude, discourteous.

periphery: on the edge or border.

pretext: misleading behavior or appearance, intentionally to conceal a true purpose.

reconnaissance: an information-gathering mission. The military often sends reconnaissance missions made up of a few people (sometimes only one) into enemy territory to gather information about the other side.

scrupulously: carefully, exactly, meticulously; honestly.

stalactite: an icicle-shaped deposit of calcium carbonate hanging from the roof of a cave.

synchronizing: happening at the same time.

telepathic: being able to communicate through the mind rather than words or gestures.

transvestite: a person, usually a male, who adopts the clothing and manner of the opposite sex for emotional or sexual gratification.

voluptuous: suggesting fullness of form and beauty; sensual.

USAGE Create **personification** using the words *insolent* and *haughty* to describe an object. For example, Cooper writes, "The silky fabric—one dress was purple, the other pink—accentuated their breasts and hips and rippled with insolent highlights." The word *insolent* is a human quality, but he uses it to describe the highlights in their dresses. Make a list of as many objects as you can, and then try *insolent* and *haughty* in front of each one. Choose your best combination and write a sentence.

Thinking and Talking Points

1. Examine Cooper's word choices, particularly how he uses strong **verbs** like *hovered* and *rippled*. What other style techniques does Cooper use in his essay? Find *similes* and *metaphors* and explain what they add to the essay.

2. At what point in the essay did you first suspect Cooper is leading up to a realization about his own sexual identity? What clues can you find early in the essay?

3. Discuss Cooper's parents and their reaction to their son's not-so-masculine qualities. How do they cope with the situation? Is their reaction typical of many parents? Do you think they ever accept young Bernard's sexual orientation? What clues in the essay lead you to this conclusion?

4. Cooper writes, "Like most children, I once thought it possible to divide the world into male and female columns." What blurs this line for young Bernard? To what extent do you divide the world along gender lines? What other situations can you think of where things aren't always what they appear?

5. Analyze the structure of this essay. Why does Cooper begin and end with the restaurant? In what way are the series of events he describes related? Why does he put them in the order he does? What conclusion do they lead to about the world?

Styling

Slowing down time like a slow motion camera, Cooper takes a slice of time—a few seconds—and describes it in minute detail, stretching a few seconds onto a canvas, creating a vivid portrait of the two women who walk by him on the sidewalk outside of Burl's. He could have written, "Two women dressed as men walked by me on the sidewalk." We wouldn't be nearly as intrigued nor surprised. He teases the reader, leading up to realization that these two women are men, recreating the experience he had as a young boy, puzzling over it, finally astounding himself and the reader with the line—set off by itself—"The women had Adam's apples." His slow motion technique creates a sense of reality, pulling the readers into the piece, making them see the event through young Bernard's eyes.

PRACTICE   Reread the section where Cooper describes seeing the two women on the sidewalk. Examine how he slows down time, zooming in on the details. Make a lists of word choices and phrases he uses to accomplish this goal. Underline or list strong verb choices and **figurative language** (see the glossary).

Next, think of a meaningful event in your life, perhaps one that led you to some realization about the world. Choose something that happened in a short period of time so you can zoom in close on the details. If you can't recreate a scene, sit in a public place and people-watch until you see an interesting person or event to describe. Make a list of details. Pay close attention. If you're writing about a person, you might list things like this: frayed collar, cracked toenails, lipstick-smeared mouth. Think about fabrics, accessories, expressions. If you get stuck, reread Cooper's piece for ideas.

YOU TRY IT   Using your list of details, write a paragraph or two describing a person or event. If it's a person, he or she should be in motion. Use slow-motion-camera writing to zoom the reader in on the action. Use at least one *simile* or *metaphor*, strong *verbs,* and lots of details. Make use of the senses: touch, taste, smell, sound, sight.

Teaming Up

1. In your group, make a list of big things (a whale, for example). Think of at least ten items. Next, replace the word *continent* in Cooper's sentence, "The continent of sex had moved closer." Try out each word on the list. Do any of them work as well as Cooper's metaphor? Discuss Cooper's use of *continent* to describe sex. Why does it work so well? What word choices on your list flopped?

2. **Warm-up for Writing Idea #2.** Before class, brainstorm and do a **freewrite** about a time you had a child-to-adult epiphany, a time when you realized that appearances can be deceiving. Now share your freewrites.

Writing Ideas

1. Write an essay about an awareness you had as a child that things aren't always what they seem. Think of several events that led to, contributed to, or confirmed this epiphany (a sudden, illuminating discovery), and use them to lead the reader to your realization.

2. Visit an online database that subscribes to periodicals, such as Infotrac, available at your public, college, or university library. Do some research on the controversy surrounding the genetic link to sexual orientation. Look at both sides of the issue. Write an essay explaining the controversy.

Essay Connections

"Oranges and Sweet Sister Boy" by Judy Ruiz—not in this text, but in *Best American Essays* college edition—makes a good companion essay to "Burl's." For other companion essays, consult the Identity/Growing Up section in the front material, "Essays by Subject and Theme."

THE COURAGE OF TURTLES

Edward Hoagland

Edward Hoagland is best known for his nature and travel essays, with several collections to his credit, among them Walking the Dead Diamond River, The Final Fate of Alligators, and The Courage of Turtles. In this essay from the book of the same title, Hoagland expresses his admiration of these creatures through anthropomorphizing and a series of stories resembling fables.

DUSTBIN OF HISTORY AND CULTURE

BERET: French, a cap with no visor, usually made of wool.

BON MOTS: French, literally meaning "good word"; clever remark or witticism.

IDÉE FIXE: French meaning fixed idea; obsession.

MARGAY CAT: A small, spotted, forest-dwelling cat of Central and South America, closely resembling the ocelot.

1   Turtles are a kind of bird with the governor turned low. With the same attitude of removal, they cock a glance at what is going on, as if they need only to fly away. Until recently they were also a case of virtue rewarded, at least in the town where I grew up, because, being humble creatures, there were plenty of them. Even when we still had a few bobcats in the woods the local snapping turtles, growing up to forty pounds, were the largest carnivores. You would see them through the amber water, as big as greeny wash basins at the bottom of the pond, until they faded into the inscrutable mud as if they hadn't existed at all.

2   When I was ten I went to Dr. Green's Pond, a two-acre pond across the road. When I was twelve I walked a mile or so to Taggart's Pond, which was lusher, had big water snakes and a waterfall; and shortly after that I was bicycling way up to the adventuresome vastness of Mud Pond, a lake-sized body of water in the reservoir system of a Connecticut city, possessed of cat-backed little islands and empty shacks and a forest of pines and hardwoods along the shore. Otters, foxes, and mink left their prints on the bank; there were pike and perch. As I got older, the estates and forgotten back lots in town were parceled out and sold for nice prices, yet, though the woods had shrunk, it seemed that fewer people walked in the woods. The new

residents didn't know how to find them. Eventually, exploring, they did find them, and it required some ingenuity and doubling around on my part to go for eight miles without meeting someone. I was grown by now, I lived in New York, and that's what I wanted to do on the occasional weekends when I came out.

3   Since Mud Pond contained drinking water I had felt confident nothing untoward would happen there. For a long while the developers stayed away, until the drought of the mid-1960s. This event, squeezing the edges in, convinced the local water company that the pond really wasn't a necessity as a catch basin, however; so they bulldozed a hole in the earthen dam, bulldozed the banks to fill in the bottom, and landscaped the flow of water that remained to wind like an English brook and provide a domestic view for the houses which were planned. Most of the painted turtles of Mud Pond, who had been inaccessible as they sunned on their rocks, wound up in boxes in boys' closets within a matter of days. Their footsteps in the dry leaves gave them away as they wandered forlornly. The snappers and the little musk turtles, neither of whom leave the water except once a year to lay their eggs, dug into the drying mud for another siege of hot weather, which they were accustomed to doing whenever the pond got low. But this time it was low for good; the mud baked over them and slowly entombed them. As for the ducks, I couldn't stroll in the woods and not feel guilty, because they were crouched beside every stagnant pothole, or were slinking between the bushes with their heads tucked into their shoulders so that I wouldn't see them. If they decided I had, they beat their way up through the screen of trees, striking their wings dangerously, and wheeled about with that headlong, magnificent velocity to locate another poor puddle.

4   I used to catch possums and black snakes as well as turtles, and I kept dogs and goats. Some summers I worked in a menagerie with the big personalities of the animal kingdom, like elephants and rhinoceroses. I was twenty before these enthusiasms began to wane, and it was then that I picked turtles as the particular animal I wanted to keep in touch with. I was allergic to fur, for one thing, and turtles need minimal care and not much in the way of quarters. They're personable beasts. They see the same colors we do and they seem to see just as well, as one discovers in trying to sneak up on them. In the laboratory they unravel the twists of a maze with the hot-blooded rapidity of a mammal. Though they can't run as fast as a rat, they improve on their errors just as quickly, pausing at each crossroads to look left and right. And they rock rhythmically in place, as we often

do, although they are hatched from eggs, not the womb. (A common explanation psychologists give for our pleasure in rocking quietly is that it recapitulates our mother's heartbeat *in utero.*)

5   Snakes, by contrast, are dryly silent and priapic. They are smooth movers, legalistic, unblinking, and they afford the humor which the humorless do. But they make challenging captives; sometimes they don't eat for months on a point of order—if the light isn't right, for instance. Alligators are sticklers too. They're like war-horses, or German shepherds, and with their bar-shaped, vertical pupils adding emphasis, they have the *idée fixe* of eating, eating, even when they choose to refuse all food and stubbornly die. They delight in tossing a salamander up towards the sky and grabbing him in their long mouths as he comes down. They're so eager that they get the jitters, and they're too much of a proposition for a casual aquarium like mine. Frogs are depressingly defenseless: that moist, extensive back, with the bones almost sticking through. Hold a frog and you're holding its skeleton. Frogs' tasty legs are the staff of life to many animals— herons, raccoons, ribbon snakes—though they themselves are hard to feed. It's not an enviable role to be the staff of life, and after frogs you descend down the evolutionary ladder a big step to fish.

6   Turtles cough, burp, whistle, grunt and hiss, and produce social judgments. They put their heads together amicably enough, but then one drives the other back with the suddenness of two dogs who have been conversing in tones too low for an onlooker to hear. They pee in fear when they're first caught, but exercise both pluck and optimism in trying to escape, walking for hundreds of yards within the confines of their pen, carrying the weight of that cumbersome box on legs which are cruelly positioned for walking. They don't feel that the contest is unfair; they keep plugging, rolling like sailorly souls—a bobbing, infirm gait, a brave, sea-legged momentum—stopping occasionally to study the lay of the land. For me, anyway, they manage to contain the rest of the animal world. They can stretch out their necks like a giraffe, or loom under-water like an apocryphal hippo. They browse on lettuce thrown on the water like a cow moose which is partly submerged. They have a penguin's alertness, combined with a build like a brontosaurus when they rise up on tiptoe. Then they hunch and ponderously lunge like a grizzly going forward.

7   Baby turtles in a turtle bowl are a puzzle in geometrics. They're as decorative as pansy petals, but they are also self-directed building blocks, propping themselves on one another in different arrangements, before up-ending the tower. The timid individuals turn fear-

less, or vice versa. If one gets a bit arrogant he will push the others off the rock and afterwards climb down into the water and cling to the back of one of those he has bullied, tickling him with his hind feet until he bucks like a bronco. On the other hand, when this same milder-mannered fellow isn't exerting himself, he will stare right into the face of the sun for hours. What could be more lionlike? And he's at home in or out of the water and does lots of metaphysical tilting. He sinks and rises, with an infinity of levels to choose from; or, elongating himself, he climbs out on the land again to perambulate, sits boxed in his box, and finally slides back in the water, submerging into dreams.

8   I have five of these babies in a kidney-shaped bowl. The hatchling, who is a painted turtle, is not as large as the top joint of my thumb. He eats chicken gladly. Other foods he will attempt to eat but not with sufficient perseverance to succeed because he's so little. The yellow-bellied terrapin is probably a yearling, and he eats salad voraciously, but no meat, fish, or fowl. The Cumberland terrapin won't touch salad or chicken but eats fish and all of the meats except for bacon. The little snapper, with a black crenelated shell, feasts on any kind of meat, but rejects greens and fish. The fifth of the turtles is African. I acquired him only recently and don't know him well. A mottled brown, he unnerves the greener turtles, dragging their food off to his lairs. He doesn't seem to want to be green—he bites the algae off his shell, hanging meanwhile at daring, steep, head-first angles.

The snapper was a Ferdinand until I provided him with deeper water.

9   Now he snaps at my pencil with his downturned and fearsome mouth, his swollen face like a napalm victim's. The Cumberland has an elliptical red mark on the side of his green-and-yellow head. He is benign by nature and ought to be as elegant as his scientific name (*Pseudemys scripta elegans*), except he has contracted a disease of the air bladder which has permanently inflated it; he floats high in the water at an undignified slant and can't go under. There may have been internal bleeding, too, because his carapace is stained along its ridge. Unfortunately, like flowers, baby turtles often die. Their mouths fill up with a white fungus and their lungs with pneumonia. Their organs clog up from the rust in the water, or diet troubles, and, like a dying man's, their eyes and heads become too prominent. Toward the end, the edge of the shell becomes flabby as felt and folds around them like a shroud.

10   While they live they're like puppies. Although they're vivacious, they would be a bore to be with all the time, so I also have an adult

wood turtle about six inches long. Her top shell is the equal of any seashell for sculpturing, even a Cellini shell; it's like an old, dusty, richly engraved medallion dug out of a hillside. Her legs are salmon-orange bordered with black and protected by canted, heroic scales. Her plastron—the bottom shell—is splotched like a margay cat's coat, with black ocelli on a yellow back-ground. It is convex to make room for the female organs inside, whereas a male's would be concave to help him fit tightly on top of her. Altogether, she exhibits every camouflage color on her limbs and shells. She has a turtleneck neck, a tail like an elephant's, wise old pachydermous hind legs, and the face of a turkey—except that when I carry her she gazes at the passing ground with a hawk's eyes and mouth. Her feet fit to the fingers of my hand, one to each one, and she rides looking down. She can walk on the floor in perfect silence, but usually she lets her plastron knock portentously, like a footstep, so that she resembles some grand, concise, slow-moving id. But if an earthworm is presented, she jerks swiftly ahead, poises above it, and strikes like a mongoose, consuming it with wild vigor. Yet she will climb on my lap to eat bread or boiled eggs.

11   If put into a creek, she swims like a cutter, nosing forward to intercept a strange turtle and smell him. She drifts with the current to go downstream, maneuvering behind a rock when she wants to take stock, or sinking to the nether levels, while bubbles float up. Getting out, choosing her path, she will proceed a distance and dig into a pile of humus, thrusting herself to the coolest layer at the bottom. The hole closes over her until it's as small as a mouse's hole. She's not as aquatic as a musk turtle, not quite as terrestrial as the box turtles in the same woods, but because of her versatility she's marvelous, she's everywhere. And though she breathes the way we breathe, with scarcely perceptible movements of her chest, sometimes instead she pumps her throat ruminatively, like a pipe smoker sucking and puffing. She waits and blinks, pumping her throat, turning her head, then sets off like a loping tiger in slow motion, hurdling the jungly lumber, the pea vine and twigs. She estimates angles so well that when she rides over the rocks, sliding down a drop-off with her rugged front legs extended, she has the grace of a rodeo mare.

12   But she's well off to be with me rather than at Mud Pond. The other turtles have fled—those that aren't baked into the bottom. Creeping up the brooks to sad, constricted marshes, burdened as they are with that box on their backs, they're walking into a setup where all their enemies move thirty times faster than they. It's like the nightmare most of us have whimpered through, where we are weighted

down disastrously while trying to flee; fleeing our home ground, we try to run.

13   I've seen turtles in still worse straits. On Broadway, in New York, there is a penny arcade which used to sell baby terrapins that were scrawled with bon mots in enamel paint, such as KISS ME BABY. The manager turned out to be a wholesaler as well, and once I asked him whether he had any larger turtles to sell. He took me upstairs to a loft room devoted to the turtle business. There were desks for the paper work and a series of racks that held shallow tin bins atop one another, each with several hundred babies crawling around in it. He was a smudgy-complexioned, bespectacled, serious fellow and he did have a few adult terrapins, but I was going to school and wasn't actually planning to buy; I'd only wanted to see them. They were aquatic turtles, but here they went without water, presumably for weeks, lurching about in those dry bins like handicapped citizens, living on gumption. An easel where the artist worked stood in the middle of the floor. She had a palette and a clip attachment for fastening the babies in place. She wore a smock and a beret, and was homely, short, and eccentric-looking, with funny black hair, like some of the ladies who show their paintings in Washington Square in May. She had a cold, she was smoking, and her hand wasn't very steady, although she worked quickly enough. The smile that she produced for me would have looked giddy if she had been happier, or drunk. Of course the turtles' doom was sealed when she painted them, because their bodies inside would continue to grow but their shells would not. Gradually, invisibly, they would be crushed. Around us their bellies—two thousand belly shells—rubbed on the bins with a mournful, momentous hiss.

14   Somehow there were so many of them I didn't rescue one. Years later, however, I was walking on First Avenue when I noticed a basket of living turtles in front of a fish store. They were as dry as a heap of old bones in the sun; nevertheless, they were creeping over one another gimpily, doing their best to escape. I looked and was touched to discover that they appeared to be wood turtles, my favorites, so I bought one. In my apartment I looked closer and realized that in fact this was a diamondback terrapin, which was bad news. Diamondbacks are tidewater turtles from brackish estuaries, and I had no seawater to keep him in. He spent his days thumping interminably against the baseboards, pushing for an opening through the wall. He drank thirstily but would not eat and had none of the hearty, accepting qualities of wood turtles. He was morose, paler in color, sleeker and more Oriental in the carved ridges and rings that formed his shell. Though

I felt sorry for him, finally I found his unrelenting presence exasperating. I carried him, struggling in a paper bag, across town to the Morton Street Pier on the Hudson River. It was August but gray and windy. He was very surprised when I tossed him in; for the first time in our association, I think, he was afraid. He looked afraid as he bobbed about on top of the water, looking up at me from ten feet below. Though we were both accustomed to his resistance and rigidity, seeing him still pitiful, I recognized that I must have done the wrong thing. At least the river was salty, but it was also bottomless; the waves were too rough for him, and the tide was coming in, bumping him against the pilings underneath the pier. Too late, I realized that he wouldn't be able to swim to a peaceful inlet in New Jersey, even if he could figure out which way to swim. But since, short of diving in after him, there was nothing I could do, I walked away.

THE COURAGE OF TURTLES

Exploring Language

amicably: friendly, peaceable.

apocryphal: doubtful, false; can also imply mythical.

benign: gentle, gracious; of mild character.

brackish: salty or not appealing to the taste; repulsive.

canted: slanted or tilted.

carapace: protective shell or shell-like covering.

convex: a surface that curves outward; concave curves inward.

crenelated: dented or notched.

elongating: lengthening or extending.

estuaries: where rivers—fresh water—meet the sea.

forlorn: in despair or depressed.

giddy: light-hearted or silly.

gimpy: with a limp; handicapped.

governor: in this context, an attachment to a machine or engine to regulate or control speed, like on a car.

id: psychological term referring to the part of the unconscious that embodies the instinctual need and desires, like pleasure.

humus: decomposed animal or vegetable material in soil.

ingenuity: inventive or skillful.

inscrutable: in this context—inscrutable mud—not able to see through it; unfathomable.

interminably: seemingly unending.

lush: luxuriant, abundant vegetation.

metaphysical: abstract thought; sometimes refers to the supernatural.

menagerie: a collection of varied and usually unusual animals, though can refer to people or things.

morose: gloomy, sullen.

napalm: a jellylike, inflammable substance used in bombs.

nether: lower or under; below the surface.

ocelli: a simple eye or an eye-like spot as on a peacock's feathers.

parceled: a quantity or unit of something bundled or packaged up for sale.

portentous: ominous or threatening; momentous.

priapic: phallic, or penis-like.
perambulate: walk or stroll about.
rapidity: quickness.
recapitulate: to repeat in a summarized form.
ruminatively: to meditate or ponder.
stickler: perfectionist; an unyielding person.
untoward: improper; unfavorable or unfortunate.
vivacious: lively, spirited.
voracious: consuming large quantities, as in "voracious appetite" or "voracious reader."
wane: to fade or come near an ending; the moon wanes when it is past its full part.
wax: the period between the new and full moon.
Note: For pronunciation, go to dictionary.com, search the word, and click on the speaker icon.

USAGE   Use three of the words from the list to describe an animal in one of the Writing Ideas or in Teaming Up #3.

Thinking and Talking Points

1. Hoagland uses **anthropomorphizing** (assigning human characteristics or personality traits to animals) of turtles throughout the essay. An example would be the quality of courage, a trait generally associated with humans. How do the turtles display courage? Locate other human characteristics like courage and then discuss why you think he relies so heavily on this technique.

2. Examine where Hoagland compares turtles to other animals. What is his purpose with these comparisons?

3. In addition to anthropomorphizing, Hoagland uses other style devices: simile, metaphor, vivid description, sentence variety—long, medium, and short sentences—and punctuation marks such as dashes and semicolons. Choose at least one of each style and discuss how the style enhances the essay.

4. Several stories—often compared to fables—concerning turtles connect to make a point in this essay. What do you think is the overall purpose? Identify the moral of each story and the order in which he arranges them. Discuss why he chooses to end the essay with the story of the Diamondback turtle.

5. What does the essay imply about human interference with animal habitat? Is there an environmental commentary embedded here?

Styling

Adding comparisons in the form of **simile** and **metaphor** to your essay helps your reader envision size, shape, swiftness, slowness, facial features— almost anything. It goes beyond mere description, elevating your writing to sharpness and clarity. Edward Hoagland, instead of using boring measurements for size, describes snapping turtles "as big as greeny wash basins" and a hatchling as "not as large as the top joint of my thumb." For other details, he describes baby turtles "as decorative as pansy petals," for movement "rolling like sailorly souls" and "hunch and ponderously lunge like a grizzly going forward." Students sometimes complain that they're not creative enough to write **figurative language**, but you can learn to write strong comparisons by using simple techniques and remembering a golden rule—if you've heard it before, don't use it. It has become a **cliché**. Strive for originality.

Here is how to get started. To describe, for example, how fast an animal moves, think of all the things that move swiftly and make a list: shooting stars, a magician's sleight of hand, bottle rockets, a jet fighter. The list could go on and on, but when choosing which comparison to use, think about the tone, the feeling you want the reader to experience about the animal. A shooting star might imply fading-into-the-background; a magician's sleight of hand may lend mystery; a jet fighter a fierce or battle-like tone; a bottle rocket, a sudden burst of speed. Then pick the best one and write a sentence about it. One student wrote about dolphins riding in the wake of the boat, "Suddenly, they were off like bottle rockets."

Practice

Think of an animal or person to write about. Make a list of features you'd like to describe. Following the instructions above, brainstorm a list for each feature. Then create a fill-in-the-blank comparison, something like the following:

As fast as (or as slow as) _____

A nose like _____

As big as (or as small as) _____

A body like (choose a shape to compare, for example a football)

_____

Don't limit yourself to these examples. Try to come up with some of your own.

YOU TRY IT Create sentences for each of your best comparisons. You might also try dropping *like* or *as* for a more direct metaphor.

Teaming Up

1. **Anthropomorphizing: Warm-up for Writing Idea #1:** In small groups (or as a class with the teacher writing suggestions on the board), brainstorm a list of human character—or personality—traits like humility, patience, greed. Write down at least twenty. Next, individually write a type of animal at the top of a sheet of paper. Take three minutes to write down any human character traits (you can use them from the list or create your own) that might be associated with that animal. At the end of three minutes, pass the paper to the right. Each person must then continue the list they have received. For the second round, work for two minutes. Repeat this process a third time, working for one minute. Give the list back to its original owner. Now each person has a brainstorming list to use for Writing Idea #1.

2. **Warm-up for Writing Ideas #2 and #3:** Each student brings one of *Aesop 's Fables* to class (available online with a Google search. Edu sites are best). In small groups, read each fable and choose one to present to the class. Identify and discuss the elements of fables listed in Writing Idea #3 and summarize and outline the chosen fable. Decide who will present which element to the class (each student should be responsible for at least one of the elements). For the presentation, each team member explains to the class how one element functions in the story. You might choose one student to summarize the story.

Writing Ideas

1. Research a wild animal you admire and write an essay that uses **anthropomorphizing** to humanize the creature. The essay can be humorous, mourn the plight of the animal, argue whether or not the animal should be kept as a pet (no giraffes, rhinos, or other animals that would not make reasonable pet choices; consider ferrets, snakes, racoons, wild birds, or other small creatures), or admire the animal's

ability to survive, either in the wild or in an environment encroached on by development.

2. Write an essay that uses a series of stories (from your own experience) with morals. Before writing, find a copy of *Aesop's Fables* (some available online) and read a few stories to help you understand the format. All stories should connect to illustrate an overall point. Be sure to use proper **transition**.

3. Write your own **fable** (a story where animals represent humans to teach lessons or morals concerning humans; "The Ant and the Grasshopper" in *Aesop's Fables* is a good example). Involve at least two animals using the elements of fables: characters and setting, action/dialogue, conflict, events that result from the conflict, and a moral. Read several fables—some available online—to warm-up.

Essay Connections

Other animal essays in *Sparks* include "Black Widow" by Gordon Grice and "Joyas Voladoras" by Brian Doyle.

Contemplations: Essays that Explain and Explore

INTRODUCTION

Visit an art museum and gaze at a Jan Vermeer painting through David Huddle's eyes. Discover Music's healing power with Clayton Collins. Explore the psychology of Batman with Travis Langley. Get a new perspective on truth in Ruth Gendler's personification. Analyze two painter's views of children with John Updike. Crawl into the world of the black widow spider with Gordon Grice. In this section, writers attempt to explain some aspect of the world, from art to hearts, naps to meditation.

These essays—like most—are hybrids, often blending rhetorical modes, not always fitting into a classic argument, narrative, definition, or other organizational box. Some contemplate, like Brian Doyle in "Joyas Voladoras," a seemingly on-the-surface meditation of animal facts, but the heartbreaks in the conclusion give the piece another subtext to consider; others marvel at the wonder of nature while explaining its inner workings, as does Reg Saner in "A Tree Beyond Imagining;" John Updike amuses with his exploration of the male body, but at the end sobers with its allusions to death; Jack Kroll looks at our darker motivations for watching horror films in "Monster Mash" while Travis Langley explores the dark side of the human psyche in "A Dark and Stormy Knight: Why Batman?"

Trying to light some aspect of the complex world invites critical thinking, research, and rumination. Analysis, an important skill in college and throughout life, explores the many facets of a subject.

As you read, study how these writers organize their essays, but also pay attention to the thinking process evident in the writing. How do they arrive at their conclusions? What evidence do they use for support? *How* writers write is as important as *what*, so examine style—figurative language (metaphor, simile, personification), sentence variety, punctuation, transition. Studying others' writings teaches us by example how to become better writers and thinkers.

ON THE UNCERTAINTY
OF THE FUTURE

Yoshida Kenko

In this short essay, Japanese poet, essayist, and Buddhist priest Yoshida Kenko (approximately 1283–1350) ruminates on how uncertainty, to some extent, controls our lives. Kenko, a prominent literary figure in his day, is still an important part of Japanese education.

1   You may intend to do something today, only for pressing business to come up unexpectedly and take up all of your attention the rest of the day. Or a person you have been expecting is prevented from coming, or someone you hadn't expected comes calling. The thing you have counted on goes amiss, and the thing you had no hopes for is the only one to succeed. A matter which promised to be a nuisance passes off smoothly, and a matter which should have been easy proves a great hardship. Our daily experiences bear no resemblance to what we had anticipated. This is true throughout the year, and equally true for our entire lives. But if we decide that everything is bound to go contrary to our anticipations, we discover that naturally there are also some things which do not contradict expectations. This makes it all the harder to be definite about anything. The one thing you can be certain of is the truth that all is uncertainty.

ON THE UNCERTAINTY OF THE FUTURE

Thinking and Talking Points

1. Summarize Kenko's purpose in this short meditation. What support does he use?
2. To what extent does the author think uncertainty plays a role in our lives?
3. How relevant is this essay to modern life? Give examples to support your view.
4. What point does the essay make about contrary expectations (expecting things will go wrong)?
5. What tone does Kenko take when addressing his readers? Study his **point of view** for help discerning his tone.

Teaming Up

1. Each member of the group make a list of expectations—things that you are reasonably certain will go smoothly. The list can be composed of anything from technology expectations (cell phones, computers, DVRs) to more meaningful expectations (medical test results, a job interview, a marriage proposal). Hand your list to the person on your right. Each person, on a scale of one to ten (ten being absolutely certain, one being will never happen) rate each item on the list. Discuss the results. Are the results in favor of optimism or pessimism?

2. **Warm-up for Writing Idea #1:** Individually, write a paragraph about a time you had an expectation that turned out the opposite, something you thought would happen but didn't (you can brainstorm ideas first with the group). After writing your paragraph, read them aloud and decide who has the best one to read to the class.

Writing Ideas

1. Write an essay about a time you had an expectation that turned out to be a disappointment (or a time you had a negative expectation that turned out positive). Describe the anticipation leading up to the expectation, the event itself, and your feelings afterward.

2. Compare the writing style and philosophy of Yoshida Kenko's essay to Thich Nhat Hanh's piece "Nourishing Awareness in Each Moment." Is there a similarity in the thought of these two Buddhists from very different time periods?

3. Write your own meditation on something from your daily life: an emotion (anger, joy, depression, grief, humility), a philosophy or belief (destiny, solitude, death), an institution (marriage, education, medicine), nature (many essays in the book provide examples of reflections on nature, and pair well with Thich Nhat Hanh's essay, "Nourishing Awareness in Each Moment").

Essay Connections

Thich Nhat Hanh's "Nourishing Awareness in Each Moment" (a rumination on television and mood by a modern Vietnamese monk) pairs up with Kenko's essay. Joseph Epstein's "The Culture of Celebrity" comments on our obsession with famous people, connecting to Hanh's piece. Many reflective nature essays appear in this book, teaming up with Hanh's ideas of solitude and meditation rather than noisy television that can affect mood.

MUSEUM PIECE

David Huddle

David Huddle is a university professor and writer of fiction and nonfiction. He's written a collection of essays titled "The Writing Habit" as well as a novella, three collections of poetry, and four collections of short stories. In this short piece, he describes three paintings by Jan Vermeer, focusing on "A Lady Writing," proclaiming, "All those art history courses, all these visits to the museum, attending lectures, reading catalogs: nothing teaches you just to look the way you're doing it now!"

DUSTBIN OF HISTORY AND CULTURE

JAN VERMEER: Dutch painter who lived from 1632–1675.
FEATHER QUILL: A feather with a hollow reed used as a pen.

1   Jan Vermeer's *The Girl with the Red Hat* always appealed to you because of that hat. Incredible scarlet aura spinning around her head like pure energy. Mouth open. Delicate coating of light that makes you think she's just licked her lips. Got to appreciate the composition. Lively and precise at the same time. The face of the girl isn't much. You like the look of her hat. You know it excites her to be wearing that hat. But there's nothing about the actual person. What she has to say wouldn't be much. Features are crude. Common girl all dressed up.

2   Another Vermeer here you've gotten to know. *Maiden with a Flute.* Little sister of *The Girl with the Red Hat.* Not nearly as flamboyant, but it's another composition that makes you smile. They're both paintings that have some wit.

3   This one day, instead of passing with a quick pause-and-look, the way you always have before—maybe because the room is empty, and you have plenty of time—you take one step closer to the third of those Vermeers: *A Lady Writing.* One step closer to a picture you've seen dozens of times before.

4   The lady of the picture isn't really writing. She's stopped writing. Her pen—it's a small feather quill—is still in place on the paper. Her other hand is holding the page down. She's just looked up. You've

interrupted her. Her face has this expression that is warm and so complex. But that expression is not for you—it's left over from the moment before she saw you. She looks that way because of whatever it was she was writing. It has to be a letter: this lady is writing to her good friend—or maybe to her sister—about something that really pleases her. You wonder what it could be. You can almost sense the pleasure flying away from her as she stops her writing.

5   She isn't beautiful. The way her hair is fixed, it looks like she's put it up in curlers. But you get her whole life out of this picture. All those art history courses, all these visits to the museum, attending lectures, reading catalogs: nothing teaches you just to look the way you're doing it now! Thousands of days of this lady's living click into this single instant. Across three hundred years of time, she looks you straight in the eyes. *Look,* she says. *Go ahead and look. My life feels to me the same as yours feels to you—so full I could burst with it. Please let me get back to my letter. You go on with whatever you're doing out there in the twentieth century.*

MUSEUM PIECE

Thinking and Talking Points

1. Study the painting of *A Lady Writing* (available online), and then reread Huddle's description. What is your reaction? Is it similar to Huddle's or do you have a different response?
2. As a student, you've probably been told to avoid "you" when writing essays. Why do you think Huddle uses "you" to address the reader? In what situations might it be acceptable to address the reader so casually?
3. Huddle breaks another general writing rule: don't use sentence **fragments**. Sometimes, though, fragments can work to the writer's advantage. Examine the fragments. Why do you think Huddle uses them?
4. In the last paragraph, what point does Huddle make about enjoying versus studying paintings? Rewrite his point in your own words. What other subjects might apply to his point?

CAUTION While writers often use **fragments** for a particular effect, I caution beginning writers against using them until they have mastered **complete sentences**.

Styling

This short essay pops with style, making it difficult to focus on just one technique. In addition to breaking writing rules in favor of style, Huddle also uses **simile**: "Incredible scarlet aura spinning around her head like pure energy." His detailed descriptions and lively word choices draw you into the essay. But look more closely at how he uses dashes (—), a writing tool that students aren't often taught. Dashes can be used in place of commas around groups of words called **interrupters** because they interrupt the main sentence to add information or detail:

> Her pen—it's a small feather quill—is still in place on the paper.

Huddle could write, "Her pen is still in place on the paper." The clause "it's a small feather quill" interrupts the main sentence with extra information. The writer could use commas or parentheses instead of dashes, but he chose the stronger dashes to draw attention to the feather quill. Study the other dashes in the essay. Notice that dashes can also be used to set off a phrase, clause, or another sentence at the end of a sentence.

SAMPLE SENTENCE WITH DASHES The Okapi—like a creature out of a fairy tale—is an animal that looks half giraffe, half zebra.

PRACTICE Fill in the blank between the dashes with a descriptive or informational phrase.

The child—_____—shoved cake into her mouth.

YOU TRY IT Create three sentences of your own using dashes. It might help to write a simple sentence first, inserting the interrupting words and dashes later.
  Tip: parentheses whisper, commas talk, dashes shout.

Teaming Up

1. Bring to class a picture of a painting or other artwork that appeals to you. One place to look is the Metropolitan Museum website—you can visit almost any museum online and print pictures. Before coming to class, **freewrite** about the picture. What does the picture make you think about? What feeling do you get from looking at it? What details stand out the most? Group up in teams of three to five members. Pass the pictures to the right. Study the picture and freewrite about it. Pass pictures to the right and freewrite two more times so that each person has written about three pictures plus his or her own. Pull out the freewrite written at home. Group all of the freewrites with the picture they are about. Read the freewrites and discuss the reactions. What details or reactions seem to be the same in the majority of freewrites? Did feelings differ significantly on the same picture? Which picture got the most varied reactions?

2. Go to the library (or search the online databases) and find art criticism on some of Jan Vermeer's paintings. You'll find books on art criticism in the reference section as well as the regular book stacks. Sister Wendy's criticisms of art are a good place to start—her writing is not muddled with overblown language. If you have trouble finding an article, ask the librarian. In groups, read the criticisms and compare them to Huddle's essay. Which piece did you enjoy the most? Which one gives the most insight into the painting? Study the style in each

article. Do the writers of these articles use strong style, as Huddle did?

CAUTION   Avoid the Web when looking for criticism. The Web is full of dubious articles. You can search for hours without finding anything. You're better off visiting the library at your college or in your community or accessing a reputable library's online databases.

Wrting Ideas

1. Find a painting or photograph of an historical event: *Third of May* by Francisco Goya; *Washington Crossing the Delaware* by Emanuel Gottlieb Leutze; *Death of Socrates* by Jacques-Louis David. You can also use photographs—try visiting an online photography exhibit or a book like the *History of Rock and Roll;* possibilities are endless. Next, study the picture and imagine yourself there: sights, sounds, smells, feelings, tastes. Choose a point of view: who will you be, an observer of the scene or one of the characters in the picture? Be sure to look up the historical facts. Facts must be accurate, but you can invent the sensory details. Now, write an essay narrating the event. Stick to the picture as much as possible. Practice using dashes.

2. Browse through some art books and choose an artist who interests you. Choose three paintings by the same artist. Following Huddle's model, write an essay discussing the three paintings. Notice that Huddle saves the painting that he most strongly reacts to discuss last, spending two full paragraphs on it. Use **simile** and strong description.

3. Find a painting—a portrait—of a person who seems to be speaking to you. You can use the website or visit the library. After studying the portrait, write an essay using details to describe the painting and what you imagine the person is thinking. Write in the present tense and address the reader as "you."

Essay Connections

John Updike's essay "American Children," like Huddle's essay, analyzes art in an easy-to-understand manner.

NOURISHING AWARENESS
IN EACH MOMENT

Thich Nhat Hanh

Spiritual leader and Zen monk Thich Nhat Hanh has many achievements: he founded a Buddhist university in Vietnam and a social services school for youth, taught at the Sorbonne and Columbia University, chaired the Buddhist delegation in the Paris Peace Talks, was nominated by Martin Luther King Jr. for the Nobel Peace Price, has helped refugees all over the world, founded a meditation in south of France (where he lives as an exile from his native country), and written many books on Buddhist thought and meditation, including The Art of Power, Anger, The Miracle of Mindfulness, and Peace is Every Step, where "Nourishing Awareness in Each Moment" appears. In this essay, he wonders why people will watch bad television programs rather than cherish solitude, believing that when we watch bad television, "we become the TV program."

1   One cold, winter evening I returned home from a walk in the hills, and I found that all the doors and windows in my hermitage had blown open. When I had left earlier, I hadn't secured them, and a cold wind had blown through the house, opened the windows, and scattered the papers from my desk all over the room. Immediately, I closed the doors and windows, lit a lamp, picked up the papers, and arranged them neatly on my desk. Then I started a fire in the fireplace, and soon the crackling logs brought warmth back to the room.

2   Sometimes in a crowd we feel tired, cold, and lonely. We may wish to withdraw to be by ourselves and become warm again, as I did when I closed the windows and sat by the fire, protected from the damp, cold wind. Our senses are our windows to the world, and sometimes the wind blows through them and disturbs everything within us. Some of us leave our windows open all the time, allowing the sights and sounds of the world to invade us, penetrate us, and expose our sad, troubled selves. We feel so cold, lonely, and afraid. Do you ever find yourself watching an awful TV program, unable to turn it off? The raucous noises, explosions of gunfire, are upsetting. Yet you don't get up and turn it off. Why do you torture yourself in this way? Don't you want to close your windows? Are you frightened of soli-

tude—the emptiness and the loneliness you may find when you face yourself alone?

3   Watching a bad TV program, we *become* the TV program. We are what we feel and perceive. If we are angry, we are the anger. If we are in love, we are love. If we look at a snow-covered mountain peak, we are the mountain. We can be anything we want, so why do we open our windows to bad TV programs made by sensationalist producers in search of easy money, programs that make our hearts pound, our fists tighten, and leave us exhausted? Who allows such TV programs to be made and seen by even the very young? We do! We are too undemanding, too ready to watch whatever is on the screen, too lonely, lazy, or bored to create our own lives. We turn on the TV and leave it on, allowing someone else to guide us, shape us, and destroy us. Losing ourselves in this way is leaving our fate in the hands of others who may not be acting responsibly. We must be aware of which programs do harm to our nervous systems, minds, and hearts, and which programs benefit us.

4   Of course, I am not talking only about television. All around us, how many lures are set by our fellows and ourselves? In a single day, how many times do we become lost and scattered because of them? We must be very careful to protect our fate and our peace. I am not suggesting that we just shut all our windows, for there are many miracles in the world we call "outside." We can open our windows to these miracles and look at any one of them with awareness. This way, even while sitting beside a clear, flowing stream, listening to beautiful music, or watching an excellent movie, we need not lose ourselves entirely in the stream, the music, or the film. We can continue to be aware of ourselves and our breathing. With the sun of awareness shining in us, we can avoid most dangers. The stream will be purer, the music more harmonious, and the soul of the filmmaker completely visible.

5   As beginning meditators, we may want to leave the city and go off to the countryside to help close those windows that trouble our spirit. There we can become one with the quiet forest, and rediscover and restore ourselves, without being swept away by the chaos of the "outside world." The fresh and silent woods help us remain in awareness, and when our awareness is well-rooted and we can maintain it without faltering, we may wish to return to the city and remain there, less troubled. But sometimes we cannot leave the city, and we have to find the refreshing and peaceful elements that can heal us right in

the midst of our busy lives. We may wish to visit a good friend who can comfort us, or go for a walk in a park and enjoy the trees and the cool breeze. Whether we are in the city, the countryside, or the wilderness, we need to sustain ourselves by choosing our surroundings carefully and nourishing our awareness in each moment.

NOURISHING AWARENESS IN EACH MOMENT

Exploring Language

hermitage: a place where one can live in solitude; a retreat.
raucous: rough-sounding, harsh.
Note: For pronunciation, go to dictionary.com, search the word, and click on the speaker icon.

USAGE Use *raucous* in a sentence to describe one of the following: laughter, sporting event, specific television program, particular music or song, or something mechanical (for example, a machine, tool, or musical instrument).

Thinking and Talking Points

1. Hanh writes, "Sometimes in a crowd we feel tired, cold, and lonely." What evidence does he give for this statement? How do you interpret his statement?
2. Another statement Hanh writes, "Our senses are our windows to the world, and sometimes the wind blows through them and disturbs everything within us," is a **metaphor** (see the glossary). Explain the comparison. What other metaphors does he use?
3. What connection does he make between our fear of solitude and bad television programs? Do you agree that bad television programs affect our mood? How might it negatively "guide us, shape us, and destroy us"? Are some people afraid of being alone and need noise to distract them? What do you think they fear?
4. Bad television, according to Hanh, is not the only thing that affects our mood. What other "lures" do you think pull us away from "ourselves"? What examples does he mention?
5. What solution does Hanh propose to the problem he presents? Do you agree or disagree with his ideas? Provide evidence to support your view.

Styling

This essay uses several thought-provoking questions that speak directly to the reader. Though often students are taught not to use questions, this style—when done well—can create moments of hesitation, causing the reader to think and attempt to answer.

In paragraph #2, Hanh writes, "Do you ever find yourself watching an awful TV program, unable to turn it off?" and, "Why do you torture yourself this way? Don't you want to close your windows? Are you frightened of solitude—the emptiness and loneliness you may find when you face yourself alone?"

Hanh asks questions that he believes most people will—if they're honest with themselves—have to answer yes. Notice that the first question asks something that most of us have found ourselves doing, so we nod, almost smiling in agreement. But the second question catches us off guard: we've probably not thought of it as torturing ourselves. The question stops us momentarily, making us wonder why we watch such bad programs. It's a gentle reprimand. The third question, "Don't you want to close your windows?" applies to an earlier metaphor of the senses being windows to the world; in other words, he's asking, "Don't you want to stop the torture?" The final question gets to the heart of his point: we're afraid of solitude, of being alone with ourselves, so we'll use any device to distract us from ourselves. These statements wear a costume, disguised as questions.

PRACTICE Make a list of other negative behaviors people participate in to ward off loneliness or to procrastinate.

YOU TRY IT Take one behavior from your list and create a series of thought-provoking questions that are really statements in disguise. Follow the above example, building your questions to a conclusion about the behavior.

Teaming Up

1. **Warm-up for Writing Idea #1:** The Styling makes a good Teaming Up activity. Make a group brainstorming list; select one item and have each member of the team write as many questions as possible in five minutes. Next, read all of the questions and decide which ones to use to create the Styling paragraph. Build your questions to a conclusion about the behavior.

2. **Warm-up for Writing Idea #2:** As a group, brainstorm a list of television programs that you consider bad by Hanh's standards. Next to each one, write why you think each program has a negative impact. Co-write a paragraph about these programs, describing the programs and their effects, and attempt to explain why you watch them.

Writing Ideas

1. Write an essay that explores another distraction people use as an avoidance technique. Examine the causes (what, how, and why people are avoiding) and effects (what long-term harm this behavior does to the individual or to others). Some examples might be the boss who never delegates (or delegates too much), a sibling who avoids family confrontations, or the spouse or partner who always agrees or backs down to avoid conflict.

2. Write an essay about the effect of bad television programs on our minds and moods. Explore and explain why people watch such programs and how they're harmful (or write a defense of such programs).

3. Compare the style and Buddhist thought in Hanh's essay to Yoshida Kenko's "On the Uncertainty of the Future." Though of vastly different centuries, what do these two essays have in common?

Essay Connections

Yoshida Kenko's "On the Uncertainty of the Future" is an obvious choice. Another commentary on modern life is Joseph Epstein's "The Culture of Celebrity."

TRUTH

J. Ruth Gendler

Multifaceted—artist, teacher, author—J. Ruth Gendler, in addition to her numerous poems, essays, and nationally exhibited artwork, has written three books: Notes on the Need for Beauty, Changing Light: The Eternal Cycle of Night and Day, *and* The Book of Qualities *where she personifies 100 human emotions in sometimes humorous and often close-to-the-bone ways.*

1   Truth is tall and rather unconventional looking. He has golden hair and a short beard. He does not like statistics and is not particularly concerned about fact, but he loves a good story. He chronicled the contemporary film scene for a while. He quit when his reviews started being quoted out of context. Though he never hides what he feels, by nature he is gentle and not at all sarcastic. However, he does have a fierce temper. He has observed that people who only listen with one ear when he says something in a kind way are always impressed by his anger.

2   Truth has been employed as a thief stealing illusions. He can climb over any security fence we have constructed to keep out disturbing influences. Although he can unlock any window or door, he is no longer interested in breaking in or getting away. No longer thrilled by the chase nor by defying authorities, he has given up on the challenge of trying to find new ways to escape.

3   X-rays, photographs of cells, and the history of plants fascinate Truth. When Truth's fingers touch my shoulder, I hear bone touching bone. Truth has set down his bundle of needs, and his shoulders are soft and spacious, outlined by light.

4   Truth learned to act in the theater of qualities, and his studies in mime continue. He lingers in the long pauses between the questions and the answers. He has made an altar to his loneliness. Certainty and Uncertainty are both welcome at his table. Truth is willing to wait for a long time with little attentions or visible encouragement. Truth is not willing to live without Love.

TRUTH

Thinking and Talking Points

1. Gendler writes that Truth is unconventional looking, isn't concerned much with facts, but "he loves a good story." How do these details make the reader think about truth in a new way? Explain the implications of these details.

2. Examine Truth's jobs—reviewing contemporary film, a thief stealing illusions, and acting and studying mime: how are these jobs appropriate for this quality? Reread the paragraphs that include his employment and then explain the implied meaning.

3. Why might Truth be fascinated by "X-rays, photographs of cells, and the history of plants"?

4. Why might people construct a security fence to keep out a "disturbing influence" like Truth?

5. Why would Truth make "an altar to his loneliness" and welcome Certainty and Uncertainty at his table?

Styling

Gendler's *personification* of truth shows the many sides of this quality, the ways we twist it, often not welcoming it for forcing reality. In other personifications in her book, Gendler has Rage as Depression's only friend, and Confusion is Patience's nephew; Doubt camps out in the living room; Patience "carries sacks of peace and purses filled with small treasures." She develops each quality into a mini story, revealing often-not-thought-about aspects of the word.

PRACTICE   Choose an emotion or human personality trait to personify and freewrite for five minutes, focusing on other feelings that might occur with the trait like depression with anger, fear and anxiety, or guilt with manipulation. Decide on gender, what the word might look like, what jobs or hobbies it might have, what its favorite food might be, where it hangs out. Use the other qualities as friends or relatives (see the "Introductions" section of your text for a list to get started).

YOU TRY IT Write a one to two paragraph personification using your ideas from the practice. Capitalize each of the qualities used as characters, like a proper name, and avoid using the word to describe itself (for example, don't write that Depression is depressed).

Teaming Up

1. Each person in the group answers the "Thinking and Talking Points." Compare answers and discuss differing opinions.

2. Do the Styling as a group, choosing one quality to develop together. Brainstorm ideas and decide which ones to use. Co-write a paragraph.

Writing Ideas

1. Use the Styling as an introduction to a larger definition essay. The rest of the essay should use the "Strategies for Defining Terms," perhaps building a paragraph around each strategy.
2. Use personification to write an essay defining a human quality or emotion. Sustain the personification throughout, but try to blend the "Strategies for Defining Terms" into the personification.

Essay Connections

Joseph Epstein's "The Culture of Celebrity" clarifies the difference between fame and celebrity, a good essay for modeling definition strategies, as does "On the Content of Our Character" by Shelby Steele. "A Tree Beyond Imagining" uses personification, and "The Courage of Turtles" **anthropomorphizes**.

FROM "THE SURFING SAVANT"

Paul Solotaroff

Paul Solotaroff is a contributing editor to Rolling Stone and Men's Journal, with articles appearing in Vanity Fair, GQ, Vogue, and The New York Times Magazine. Books include The House of Purple Hearts (1995), Group (1999), and his latest, The Body Shop (2010), a memoir chronicling his use of steroids in the 1970's. His writing has also appeared several times in Best American Sports Writing. "The Surfing Savant," first published in Rolling Stone in 2010 and the 2011 edition of Best American Sports Writing, tells the story of surfing champion Clay Marzo and his struggle with Asperger's syndrome, a high-functioning form of autism.

DUSTBIN OF HISTORY AND CULTURE

CHA CHA: a Latin ballroom dance with a quick three-step movement.

SHAUN WHITE: American champion snowboarder and two-time Olympic gold medalist.

1   Put him in the water and Clay Marzo is magic, a kid with so much grace and daring that you laugh in disbelief to watch him surf. Every day he's out there in the South Pacific, shredding huge swells till he's faint with hunger and near the verge of dehydration. He doesn't really ride waves as much as fly them, soaring above the sea foam upside down and spinning the nose of his board in whiplash twists. Just two years out of high school, Marzo is remaking a sport held hostage by rules and hack judges, turning it into a cross between aquatic parkour and X Games stunt work. Call it what you want, it's a sight to behold. *Sorry, but humans can't do that,* you keep thinking. Then he goes and does it all morning long.

2   But if you sit and list the things that Marzo has trouble doing, they quickly outrun the things he finds easy. He's unable, for instance, to eat a simple meal without much of it ending up on his shirt or the floor. Out of water, he has trouble interacting with other people, either staring in bafflement at their grins and jokes or avoiding casual contact altogether. He blurts things out, chants rap songs to himself, and pulls out clumps of his hair when anxious. When he speaks, which isn't often, he seems younger than his 20 years, mumbling like a bash-

ful eighth-grader. For years, the rap on Marzo has been that, for all his talents, he's a pothead who chokes in competitions. And then there are the even-nastier names he's had to deal with, slurs that burned deep: retard, moron, slacker, zombie. In middle school, Marzo was treated so badly that his mother, Jill, had to pull him out and teach him at home, where he wouldn't be punched for staring at wannabe thugs. His agonizing shyness has fractured his family and sparked ugly set-tos with his father, Gino, an old-school hard-hat striver who accused him of flaking off and screwing up his shot at stardom. That charge hurts Clay more than the others combined: when your own .father misconceives you so badly, how can you hope that strangers will understand?

3   Now, pushing back from lunch at a Maui fish stand, bits of ahi po'boy dotting his face and lap, Marzo wears the grin of a birthday boy who gets to eat as much cake as he wants. To see him like this, hands clasped across his belly, is to encounter a kid whose first and last directive is pure, physical joy. But the facts are more complex and less happy. Marzo has Asperger's syndrome, a form of high-functioning autism that causes no end of social confusion and anguish, and that commonly burdens those afflicted with a single, smothering obsession: bird songs or train routes or the history of naval warfare. "Though Asberger's teens are typically bright and verbal, they can't connect with kids their age or with people they don't know well," says Dr. Michael Linden, an autism specialist who diagnosed Marzo at the age of 18, after a dozen years of botched assessments. "Feelings are a foreign language to them, and they're unable to pick up social cues. A lot of them retreat from relationships and get stuck in a special activity or interest that they devote themselves to intensely."

4   Like a lot of adult Aspies, as some with the diagnosis have taken to calling themselves, Marzo is a baffling mix of powers and deficits. He has no interest in the written word (and has read few of the dozens of stories about him in sports magazines, which regularly anoint him one of surfing's saviors) but is brilliant, even clairvoyant, in the water. Looking at the horizon, Marzo can read waves that others can't and intuit where they'll break before they crest. Traveling fills him with such dread that he's sick with nausea days before boarding a plane, but he gets up each day and surfs lethal points on Maui's western shore. The kinds of waves he lives on don't crash near sandy beaches; instead, he climbs down lava cliffs to reach breaks rife with boulders and a seafloor of spear-tipped coral reefs that can turn a surfer's chest

to chum. His body is a travelogue of scars and welts, but it bores him to talk about the dangers he courts—the boards he routinely snaps taking hellish falls; the waves that hold him down till his lungs scream, half a minute or more during really heavy sets. Only once, he says, has he been afraid of the surf. "There were tiger sharks behind me," he says, wiping a quarter-size splotch of mayo off his cheek. "They were pretty big, so I bailed quick."

5   After lunch, Marzo pays a visit to Adam Klevin, a muscular, bald-shaved man who's seen more of Clay in water than anyone besides his mother. For the past five years, Klevin has risen at dawn to film every wave that Marzo catches and compile the highlights. Today, on one of the flatscreens in the unkempt room that Klevin uses as an editing suite, Marzo is up and riding a 12-foot swell. Dancing on the wave front with cha-cha turns that brace him for a bigger move, he whips the back of the board into a savage 360 that surfers call a throw-tail reverse. It's a common trick, but there are few people on the planet who can successfully nail it in Maui after a recent storm has raised waves the size of houses. Marzo is barely upright as he exits the spin, his mouth a perfect O of exaltation. He bangs a hard left into the next section of wave and throws a front-side snap that lifts him clean out of the water, arms and knees in vehement opposition. He can't possibily make it—his rear end's gone, and God knows what he's looking at over his shoulder as he grabs the rail of the board for dear life. The wave collapses on the jagged floor, blowing up a squall of white-capped spray in which the boy and board go missing. For a moment there's nothing, just the chaos of foam. Then the chop parts, and here he somehow comes, half off the board but still in charge. This isn't surfing, this is sorcery, a kid so alive and electrically good that he makes this look like the world's one true religion.

6   But when I turn to say as much, Marzo is somewhere else, head down and eyes fixed on some inner shore. He has everything he needs to be his sport's Shaun White—the face, the body, the game-changing skill—and a chance to be a beacon for the 1.5 million kids in this country with autism-related disorders. But Marzo has neither the drive nor the nervous system to handle being famous. No, if it's all the same, he'd rather be alone, paddling back out, through the churn and boulders, to where the big waves break. It's the one place on Earth he feels safe.

7   For an island synonymous with God-sent waves and the goofy-foot cool of surf kitsch, Maui has produced shockingly few riders driven enough to compete with the sport's name-brand stars. "There's

a small-town vibe here that's held guys back when they surfed the bigger stages," says Erik Aeder, a surf photographer and Maui native who has shot every local kid who showed much promise. "Plus, the trade winds make the waves choppy, which made it hard to learn the elegant moves that used to win tournaments."

8   But in the late eighties, a new breed of riders stood the game on end. Inspired by the halfpipe pyrotechnics of skate and snowboarders, surfers like Kelly Slater and Christian Fletcher started to approach waves differently, shooting over the top of the lip, using the wave's speed to do airs and inverts and sudden, violent turns. "Those guys made their style a global phenomenon through videos and photo spreads," says Matt Warshaw, author of the forthcoming *The History of Surfing* and former editor of *Surfer* magazine. "Kids everywhere went to school on their hi-fi moves, and that next generation went bigger and faster, trying for stunt-show things in junior contest."

9   Among that contingent was a brood from Maui of exceptionally gifted boys. Raised within an hour's drive of each other, they came up together through the Pee-Wee ranks and traveled as extended family, becoming stars before they were in their teens. Dusty Payne was the first to join the pro-surfer tour after winning an international juniors competition in 2008. Kai Barger and Granger Larsen are right behind him, and all three, according to an industry insider, "should be solid fixtures" on the top-money list of years to come.

10   But the best of that bunch, from boyhood on, was Marzo. With his bottomless hunger for hugh maneuvers and unsinkable sense of balance and intuition, he looked, to all who saw him, like the future of the sport while he was still in grade school. He was fiercely competitive at tournaments, racked up wins in every age division, and seemed an inevitable heir to Slater, the great soul surfer with nine world titles. "When he showed up for the national championships and put down perfect 10s at age 15, the media declared him the next great icon," says Warshaw. "Other kids could do some of the things he did, but not with his power and naturalness and skill at getting out of tight spots."

11   Though tournaments aren't as crucial to surfing fans as they are in other sports—there's a widespread sense that the rules are too archaic, favoring cautious riders over hellions—the hope was that Marzo and his class of big-air starlings would push the game up the board-sport totem and land it in the mainstream. (Surfing, eclipsed by X Games theatrics, remains virtually invisible on TV.)

12   Marzo seemed made to order for the thresher of pro surfing, which has cut down many kids with outsize talent. It begins with the year-

long World Qualifying Series, a continent-hopping gauntlet of contests against hundreds of amateur riders, all of them vying for 16 slots on the World Tour. Once Marzo turned pro and moved on to the big leagues, he would compete against the world's top 44 surfers in a globe-spanning season that lasts 10 months.

13   But it's one thing to rule the scholastic circuit, where no one's really watching but the families of other surfers, and a kid with Marzo's gifts could crush opponents by going bigger, faster, and braver. It's another to dominate the junior tour, where Marzo encountered battle-tested surfers with three or four years on him, most of them versed in the mind games and sly mechanics of contest strategy. The fake-outs on the waves, the jockeying for position—it was a language his Aspie brain couldn't process, blind as it is to tacit cues. Add in the crowds of fans, the announcers blaring scores over the PA system, and the cameramen in the water shooting action footage, and Marzo was sabotaged by his own senses. Nor did he fully grasp the rudiments of tournament rules, which give riders a half-hour to produce two scoring runs. Often, Marzo would land a hellfire move on an early wave, then bob like a buoy as time ran out, waiting for the perfect swell. "He had a couple of years of brilliance, but then something happened," says Warshaw. "We figured maybe it was the pressure of the travel or—well, no one really knew at the time."

14   Including Clay. Almost from birth, he's had a sizable gift for confounding expectations. Born in San Diego, he moved at nine months to the small town of Lahaina, steps from the sea in Maui; his mom and dad, both avid surfers, wanted to be closer to the waves. "Clay was wading before he could walk, and he walked at seven and a half months," recalls Jill. "At three months, he swam with his head under water, and by one he was on the front of his dad's surfboard, riding waves all the way in." Both parents were fine, if workaday, athletes—Jill, a massage therapist, loved volleyball as a kid; Gino, a carpenter, played baseball in college—and they organized their lives around the care and feeding of not one but two surf prodigies. Clay's half-brother, Cheyne, who is seven years older, was signed by sponsors at the age of 13. "Clay adored Cheyne and wanted to be like him, right up to the stickers on his board," says Jill. "And it went both ways: Cheyne bragged him up to sponsors, saying, "Wait'll you get a load of my younger brother."

15   Clay entered his first contest at the age of five, and took home a trophy for finishing fourth. By seven, he'd joined the kiddie corps of

local prodigies, sharing sleepovers, picnics, and family trips with Payne, Barger, and Larsen. "We were doing bigger, wilder stuff because we always had waves to play with," Clay recalls. "It's the Maui style: trying to top each other and look like we weren't even trying." There'd be half a dozen boys in the back of Jill's van, burping and farting the 15 miles to surf the North Shore breaks. "That was a magical time for Clay, the best years of his life," says Jill. "They were wonderful with him, really treated him like a brother, though even then they could see that he was different."

16   But even with the fact of his diagnosis, the surf world expects things of Marzo. Tierney thinks he should "bite the bullet" and do the Qualifying Series, which can now be completed in a "doable" six months instead of a hellish year. "It would be a tough haul, but he'd get to join the World Tour and surf against his idols in great waves," Tierney insists. "He's one of the five best on the planet in terms of talent, and with focus and a couple of years' experience he could be one of the best who ever did it." Marzo's manager is pinning hopes on a prospective new pro tour for big-air, balls-out riders. "Just 16 guys, the best progressive surfers, and an hour, not a half-hour, for heats. No one knows if it'll go yet—there's no sponsor attached—but it would be perfect for Clay," says Varnes. Even Marzo is prone to grand ambitions, though they change each time you ask him. "The new tour would be cool—I could deal," he says. But the next day he's talking about the free-surf option, in which the great alternative riders—Dane Reynolds, Bruce Irons—command big money to travel the globe for films and photo shoots.

17   Still, as I stand on the rise overlooking the beach in Maui, it's hard to imagine how a kid like Marzo could manage any of those options. I think back on our first—and last—sit-down chat, in which he all but fled the room, screaming. It began well enough, with Marzo talking about his childhood and name-checking his heroes, Bruce Irons and Kalani Robb. "Those guys invented the moves," he says. "We were just trying to take them farther." Then, out of the blue, he announces that surfing is the thing that "saved" him. "It's the best drug ever," he says, "and I'm lucky to have it."

18   I gently ask what it saved him from. He stares out the window and starts to yank his forelock. "I just...see things different, from the back of my brain," he says. "Other people see'em from the front, I guess. It's not good or bad, just how I am. Sort of makes it harder, though, you know?"

19   "How so?"

20   His free hand paws the side of his trunks, damp in the air-chilled room. "Well, I need people's help to get stuff done. Telling me where to go and what to say, and sometimes I don't like that, or I'm tired and don't want..."

21   The sentence just hangs there, whirring in space. I hold off, giving him room to work through the tangle of half-formed thoughts. Instead, he tugs his hair so hard that a clump comes off in his fingers. Panicked, I ask about the feeling he gets when he does something splendid on a wave. "I can't describe it," he says, slouching so low that he burrows into his chest. "Just pleasure, I guess. Where you want it over and over, and do anything to get it...Are we almost done?"

22   "Just one more," I say, looking at a poster-size photo on the wall. In it, Marzo is stock-still on his board, raising his arms in benediction as a 20-foot wave hulks above him. In the undepicted instant after the photo was taken, he paddled coolly around the edge of the wave before it smashed him to bits on the rocks. "What do you think when you see that picture?" I ask.

23   He mashes his lower lip, but releases the hair he's wrapped around a clenched index finger. "I was stoked," he says. "That wave was bombing, and there was another, even bigger, right behind it."

24   What he doesn't add is that he had just returned from a nightmare trip and felt blessed to be home again. Marzo is a creature of waves, but of these waves, the rocky, shark-toothed waters of Maui that he knows by heart. Look at him now, out beyond the reef, doing tricks to raise his flagging spirits. In surf no bigger than a picket fence, he's positioned himself above the swell, skimming like a coin from crest to crest. Just as each dies, he spies a new section to carve his name upon, hurling his board up the short-sleeve face to ride the foam again. He's forgotten the guys watching from their pickup trucks, and the small crowd up here with our mouths agape, and the father he can't please, and the brother who cut him dead—all of that's gone now, carried away by the hunchbacked westerly waves. He'll surf until lunchtime, then come back after a nap, and if not for the tiger sharks that hunt these waters once the sun goes down, he might never get out of the bliss machine, which makes no claim, only grants them.

THE SURVING SAVANT

Exploring Language

agape: mouth wide open in surprise or amazement.

archaic: an older form, commonly used in an earlier time, though rare today.

exaltation: in praise; euphoric; elated.

intuit: to know or discover by intuition.

kitsch: tasteless or sentimental junk-art.

parkour: also known as freerunning, running through city streets, jumping or climbing to get around obstacles as quickly as possible.

rife: of common occurrence; plentiful or abundant.

rudiments: the first or basic principles of a subject.

striver: someone who strives (strive meaning to try hard or exert; with much effort).

tacit: understood without being openly address; implied; silent.

thresher: a machine (or flail, a handheld stick-like instrument) that separates grains and seeds from plants like wheat.

vehement: intense or passionate; strongly emotional.

Note: For pronunciation, visit dictionary.com, search the word, and click on the speaker icon.

Thinking and Talking Points

1. In paragraph #11, Solotaroff writes, "Marzo seemed made to order for the thresher of pro surfing, which has cut down many kids with outsize talent." Explain the metaphor (see the definition for "thresher" on the Exploring Language list if unfamiliar with it).

2. List other metaphors and similes in the essay and discuss how the comparisons help the reader visualize or understand the subject.

3. How does the writer gain the reader's empathy for Marzo? Find word choices, sentences, and paragraphs from the essay to illustrate.

4. How is Asperger's syndrome both a help and a hindrance for Marzo? What are the symptoms?

5. In paragraph #4, the author uses contrasts, juxtaposing them with the conjunction "but." Study the paragraph and explain how these contrasts help the reader better understand Marzo.

Styling

Reread paragraph #5, the description of Clay Marzo surfing. Notice how the writer zooms into the scene, breaking down each motion, slowing the action so the reader sees each movement. Study each sentence for word choices and comparisons.

PRACTICE Think of a familiar action—a sport, dance, race, skateboarding, snowboarding, almost anything with action will work—and break it down into smaller parts, focusing on less than a minute of the action, visualizing each movement, making notes on each. The project works better if you can either watch the action live or view on TV or the internet.

YOU TRY IT Write the action into a paragraph using detailed description of each movement. Use at least one comparison. For paragraph structure, see "Writing Strategies."

Teaming Up

1. **Warm-up for Writing Idea #1.** Clay Marzo had been diagnosed with attention deficit disorder as a child, before Dr. Linden correctly confirmed that Clay has Asperger's. Have each group member bring in articles on both disorders, as well as listing Clay's symptoms from the essay. Make a list of similarities and differences of symptoms between attention deficit disorder and Asperger's. Compare your findings. Why did it take until Clay was 18 before he got an accurate diagnosis? How similar/different are the disorders? Are they that easy to mistake?

2. The essay contains numerous dashes. Have each member work on a section of the essay, writing down the sentences with dashes. Using the "Styling" with "Black Widow" by Gordon Grice and the rules for "Dashes" in the "Punctuation is Style: Basic Rules and Practice" section in the text, individually write a sentence for each type of dash usage in the essay. Compare sentences and peer edit for correctness.

Writing Ideas

1. Using the warm-up from "Teaming Up" #1, write a mini-research paper that discusses these two disorders, comparing symptoms. Research statistics as to how many Asperger's children initially get a

misdiagnosis. In the conclusion, make some recommendations to help people more easily recognize Asperger's. **Or** write about two other disorders that often are mistaken, like bi-polar disorder and depression. Use personification as an introduction.

2. Using the "Styling" practice, write an essay that examines in depth another sport, arguing for it as an art form, using artistic terms to describe it. Reread the descriptions of Clay Marzo surfing for ideas. Use figurative language, comparing the sport to an art, like Solotaroff does with describing one of Clay's moves as the Cha Cha. Tip: break down an art like dance, music, painting, or an animal in nature, and so on, listing the movements and actions to find comparisons to the sport.

Essay Connections

Brian Doyle in "Meat" describes basketball, with a surprising subtext to the story.

Jack Kroll

Jack Kroll was an award-winning journalist and drama critic for Newsweek. He died at age 74 on June 8, 2000. This article appeared in a special edition of Newsweek (summer 1998). Kroll explores our fascination with horror, chronicling the development of the genre, lamenting the newer horror films like Scream that "[make] the genre seem to be regressing."

DUSTBIN OF HISTORY AND CULTURE

FREUDIAN: A reference to the ideas of Sigmund Freud (1856–1939), an Austrian psychiatrist and founder of psychoanalysis.

IONIANS: Greeks who lived toward the end of the second millennium B.C., some emigrating to what is now Turkey and the west coast of Asia Minor, giving the region the name Ionia.

1   "Then his teeth flew out; from two sides, blood came to his eyes; the blood that from lips and nostrils he was spilling, open-mouthed; death enveloped him in its black cloud."

2   Is this from the script for *The Texas Chain Saw Massacre? Friday the 13th, Part VIII?* No, it's from Homer's *Iliad,* which opened 3,000 years ago, performed to a preliterate audience by bards who were the ancestors of theater and film. The terror inspired in those ancient Ionians by such passages must have been something to see.

3   Terror may have been the first feeling that human beings ever experienced, in a world that threatened their very survival. The horror genre is a way for humans to revisit that primal fear, to turn it into pleasure, the pleasure of being safely scared. Horror lets us die vicariously, producing an artificial orgasm of mortality. Horror films came in with the very birth of the movies. Thomas Edison couldn't wait to get *Frankenstein* into his newly invented medium, turning out a 16-minute version of Mary Shelley's novel in 1910. Frankenstein's monster, Dracula and the Wolf Man are the unholy three of horror movies. Frankenstein's collage of body parts is the embodiment of

man's arrogant desire to write his own Book of Genesis. The monster has new meaning in our age of genetic splicing and artificial intelligence. Dracula is Death as seducer; he sucks our blood to take us to a perverse immortality. The Wolf Man wrenches us back to our origins in the animal world of pure instinct, reversing evolution with its burden of consciousness and responsibility.

4   Boris Karloffs burlap-suited, screw-necked creature in James Whale's 1931 *Frankenstein* is still the greatest of all incarnations of monsterhood, an amazing blend of bewilderment, despair and savage rage beyond anything human. Bela Lugosi, a much more limited actor, nonetheless achieved vampiric perfection in Tod Browning's *Dracula* (also 1931). The best-dressed of all monsters, Lugosi's Dracula is also the most erotic, surveying the necks of various lily-skinned maidens with a connoisseur's libidinous leer before puncturing them with his miniphalic incisors. Lon Chaney Jr. as the Wolf Man (1941) is such a clumsy galoot of an actor that he is believably hapless in his vulpine transformation, giving his soul-saving death at the hands of his father an affectingly Freudian pathos.

5   The '30s were a golden age for horror movies: Fredric March convulsing between virtue and vice as Dr. Jekyll and Mr. Hyde (1932), mad scientist Charles Laughton turning innocent animals into screwed-up humans in *The Island of Lost Souls* (1932) and, perhaps the most nightmarish of all horror films, Tod Browning's *Freaks,* in which a troupe of real sideshow freaks takes revenge on a beautiful trapeze artist and turns her into a monstrous half-human, half-bird. These films had a special resonance in the Depression, especially *King Kong,* in which the giant ape rampaging in a New York split between bread lines and skyscrapers seemed to symbolize a society at the mercy of Darwinian forces.

6   When men went off to war in the '40s, horror movies gave equal time to the unconscious sado-sexual yearnings of women in Jacques Tourneur's *Cat People* movies, with the enigmatic Simone Simon playing a feline version of the Wolf Man. The postwar '50s closed with a masterpiece, Alfred Hitchcock's *Psycho,* the *Citizen Kane* of horror movies in its far-ranging influence. Hitchcock's ironic genius mixed themes of cross-gendering, straightforward and perverse sexuality, Oedipal conflict and schizophrenia. Janet Leigh's last moments of life in the shower turned a bathtub into a mini-Transylvania of ordinary life. Horror provided a counterpoint to the disruptions of the '60s when George Romero created splatter movies with *Night of the*

Living Dead (1968), in which a militia of corpses left their graves to attack those who dared to live. Splatter pics mutated like killer amoebas, targeting young people as both protagonists and audiences. In endlessly sequeled series like *Halloween* and *Nightmare on Elm Street*, the hockey-masked Jason and razor-gloved Freddy were like demonized parental surrogates punishing kids for their newfound sexual freedom.

7   But the flood of teen horror makes the genre seem to be regressing. In Wes Craven's recent box-office smashes, *Scream* and *Scream 2*, it's as if the horror movie were engaged in autoerotic worship of itself. The kids in *Scream* talk incessantly about horror flicks, with a faux hipness that makes you wish all of them would be killed by some self-respecting monster. Horror movies need to return to good old guilt-ridden grown-up panic. The apocalyptic dangers in our time should give new life to the pure horror film. It's doubtful that the Americanization of Godzilla will do the job.

MONSTER MASH

Exploring Language

autoerotic: self-satisfaction of sexual desire.

connoisseur: an expert or judge of taste, usually in a specific area, like a wine connoisseur.

enigmatic: puzzling or paradoxical (contradictory).

galoot: a clumsy person.

hapless: unfortunate or unlucky.

leer: to look at with lustful intent or in a lewd way; lascivious.

libidinous: lustful.

pathos: arousing pity, sympathy.

preliterate: a culture that hasn't developed writing.

vicariously: through the experience of another. Kroll means that moviegoers experience death through the characters in horror films.

vulpine: resembling a fox; crafty. Which definition do you think Kroll means?

Note: For pronunciation, go to dictionary.com, search the word, and click on the speaker icon.

USAGE Write a sentence or two explaining how you (or someone you know) live vicariously, either through films, reading, or television.

Thinking and Talking Points

1. How does Kroll organize the essay?
2. What point does he make about modern horror films? If you've seen any of the films he mentions, do you agree with him?
3. Kroll comments, "Horror movies need to return to good old guilt-ridden grown-up panic." What does he mean? Why does he think guilt-ridden films offer more to the viewer?
4. "The monster has new meaning in our age of genetic splicing and artificial intelligence." In what way? Can you think of examples from film and life that support Kroll's observation?

5. How is the horror genre "a way for humans to revisit that primal fear, to turn it into pleasure, the pleasure of being safely scared"? How does horror let us "die vicariously"?

Styling

Jack Kroll knew that hooking the reader with a spirited title is a valuable tool, and he often uses lines or titles from old rock and roll songs. His essay "Roll Over, Bach, Too" borrows its title from a Beatles song titled "Roll Over, Beethoven." He lifts "Monster Mash" from another old rock and roll song of the same title. Many writers borrow from music, literature, and pop culture for lively titles.

PRACTICE   Think of a possible essay topic for each of the following song titles (or brainstorm your own list of song titles to practice with):

"Mr. Pitiful" (from the soundtrack of the film *The Commitments*).

"Cupid's Dead" (from the CD *III Sides to Every Story* by Extreme).

"Only the Lonely" (Roy Orbison).

YOU TRY IT   For your next essay, find a title off a CD or a line from a song to use as your essay title.

Note: For more ideas on creating titles, see the titles section in "Writing Basic College Essays."

Teaming Up

1. Brainstorm favorite movie scenes from a **genre** like action/adventure (for example, the Indiana Jones series, *Star Wars,* or *Iron Man*), drama, or science fiction (or other genres), and discuss why you like the films. Have each person in the group choose their favorite from the list and write an individual paragraph explaining how someone lives or dies vicariously through that type of character, perhaps a former jock who relives his or her glory day vicariously through armchair football or sports films. You may use yourself as an example or someone you know.

Writing Ideas

1. Watch two horror films, one old and one new, and write an essay arguing whether or not Kroll's assessment of modern teen horror movies is true: "But the flood of teen horror makes the genre seem to be regressing."

2. Write an essay comparing Dracula—perhaps Bela Lugosi's portrayal (or Bram Stoker's book)—to the modern vampire Edward Cullen in the book (or film) *Twilight*. How has the image of the vampire changed to reflect modern culture?

3. Watch one of the films discussed in "Monster Mash" and write an essay analyzing the film and its "good old guilt-ridden, grown-up panic." Quote from Kroll's essay to make your points. Use strong description of film scenes.

Essay Connections

Pauline Kael's "The Little Mermaid" provides an example of film review writing. Kroll also writes a music analysis of the Beatles' influence on culture.

THE TREE BEYOND IMAGINING

Reg Saner

Nature writer and poet Reg Saner (born in 1931) has won numerous awards for his work, including a National Endowment of the Arts Fellowship, the Walt Whitman Award, and the Colorado's Governor Award. He studied as a Fulbright scholar in Florence, Italy, and has been published in over 140 magazines and 40 anthologies, with several books to his credit, mostly set in the American West: Living Large in Nature, The Dawn Collector: On My Way to the Natural World, Reaching Keel Seel: Ruin's Echo and the Anasazi, *and* The Three-Cornered Falcon: Essays on the Interior West and the Natural Scene.

1   Seeing is not believing. Any tree "acting out" in such hogwild and crazy ways—or so I used to feel—can't be truly arboreal. This one thinks it's a mad dog. Here's another trying to prove chaos might be a conifer. Yet another so riven, so warped, it looks like self-knowledge. Or is it just pretending to summarize World History? During our first acquaintance I ran across examples so willful and creaturely that my glance often boggled at believing what it saw. How could a juniper, I would ask myself, be throwing a fit?

2   Botanically speaking, of course, a juniper can't be perverse. As a dirt-common member of the cypress family it can at worst be only an oddball conifer. Other arboreal species may echo states we recognize in ourselves, but none I've run across seems so moody and emotional. Lifelong, we humans conceal our intimate histories, even while a version of them gets slowly written into our faces. This tree's neurotic past, however, appears at a glance, visible through no matter how many feigned identities. And though cone-bearing species may be tricky to tell, one from another, the one I have in mind is easy.

3   Beneath erstwhile needles that evolution has smoothed like snakeskin, and under cones shrunk to beads, a greyish-brown welter of wood appears. If it looks like tensed muscle and sinew, that illusion and the preceding traits do add up to generic juniper. But if the bark is shaggy as hanks of unbraided sisal; if the absolutely motionless trunk seems to be groveling in frenzy or twisting like smoke; and if in even the best-behaved specimen you see branches that mime

devastation having a temper tantrum, you know you're not only deal-
ing with *Juniperus osteosperma*, Utah juniper. You know the example
before your eyes is a special case: a high-desert strain of that species,
one growing where it ought not to try.

4   If animal, such trees would be camels, and almost are. But what
camel drinks sand? Hence the near-incredulity. On a sun-spattered,
all-but-windless morning in Utah, for example, you stand smack in
front of one, gasping at its self-tormented trunk fed by red sand; or
fed by far less, a crevice in rock which that sand once was. Yet on
naked stone those knotted roots have knuckled down to sipping a
trunk and limbs into life. From a low writhing branch you might strip
off a fibrous dangle of bark the creature seems clad in, all threads and
shreds and tatters, like a beggar's rags. Obviously the bark's stringy
hairs are real. Just as clearly, its tree as *tree* lacks full credibility. The
riven trunk, the gesturing limbs in every style of passion, cannot be
anything Nature approves, much less intended. So you're bound to
wonder about botanical vandalism. Novice-like, you stand there in
south-eastern Utah just staring and shaking your head: "Surely someone has *done* this?"

5   Fact is, among Utah juniper of the high desert, flabbergasting
abnormality is the norm only among individual trees defying limita-
tion. Lots of rock, lots of sand, lots of wind, and very little rain can
make juniper stands growing there, at the far end of possibility, an
outpost of marginalized eccentrics. Not the whole species. No, the
stressed-out examples I'm talking about, the trees you can see without quite believing, grow where they almost can't—at their ecological
edge. We think timberline a question of mountain altitudes beyond
which no conifer can rise. For desert junipers timberline may be a
limit drawn in the sand, not by rarefied air but by rain, lower than
which there is none, or as good as.

6   Thus, it's by taking root at the threshold of impossibility that this
most irrational tree grows against all reason. A Utah juniper at the
edge of its range is either so distraught or far gone in perplexity it
can't make sense of itself. "Do you suppose I'd have grown this way,"
it seems to snort, "if I'd had any idea what I was getting into?"

7   Although the specimens I admire would indeed make more interesting museum pieces than many a prize now under glass, I realize
that bringing just the tree inside wouldn't do. You'd need to bring
along with it the thin air of its Southwestern plateau. You'd need too
that powdery fine sand red as rust, rippled dunes sparsely tufted with

greasewood or Indian rice grass. And skies blue as chicory petals. Floating puffs of cumulus too, their undersides tinted by the red miles beneath them. Birdsong as well; rock wrens, horned larks, mockingbirds, vireos, piñon jays. And scrub jays, cowbirds, towhees. And vultures. Above all, you'd need desert sun with its glare, its incomparable clarities, deep shadows; its refusal to lie.

8   On the Grand Canyon's south rim, I have spent hours of clear weather, more intrigued by its pygmy forest of piñons and junipers than by the view. Happily roving among outcrops of chert and Kaibab limestone, well-content at being scolded by piñon jays, I have come upon deep depression and recovery—both alive in the same tree. How had it grown so depressed, I wondered. Through wrestling for its own affections? Or by being too much a shape-shifter ever to tire of dilemma? And how had recovery and relapse grown from the same trunk? Because its moods, like ours, don't believe in each other? There I found trees giving instructions in bravery. Found them more typical than not. To look at such lives and say "struggle" doesn't touch it.

9   During the same afternoon I stumbled upon a juniper who had once been a witch and couldn't quit practicing; then found countless others its bad example converted. As if they had used witchery to request eternal life and youth, they seemed the picture of what happens when only the first half is granted. The picture of how losers look when they win.

10   There amid the deranged and violent I also discovered "good" trees battening on the same rimrock; witnessed all the living optimism, all the hurt joy that can scuffle upward out of rock and suffer open. In wresting a living from limestone's long famines of rain they must sometimes have felt that enduring there was next to impossible, yet endure they had.

11   We admire most, I suppose, those virtues our souls utterly lack, or need more of. Even after twenty years, therefore, I'm apt to be spellbound by the drama of a particular trunk and limbs. Feeling sympathy and awe before such pure indomitability costs nothing, I know, because I've often stood that way a longish while, unaware that I was; as if hoping a touch of juniper courage might agree to come with me.

THE TREE BEYOND IMAGINING

Exploring Language

arboreal: relating to trees or treelike.

battening: in this context, thriving or prospering.

boggled: overwhelmed or bewildered.

chert: a type of brittle rock primarily made up of microcrystalline quartz.

chicory: a blue-flowered plant, its leaves used in salads and the roots ground as a substitute for coffee.

distraught: agitated, upset, distracted.

eccentric: odd, erratic, or peculiar.

erstwhile: past or previous.

feigned: disguised or faked; pretend.

flabbergasting: astounding, bewildering, astonishing.

frenzy: extreme agitation or excitement; deranged.

groveling: complete submission; fawning in fear.

hank: in this context, a knot, loop, or coil.

incredulity: doubt, disbelief, skepticism.

indomitability: unconquerable.

marginalized: to place in a position of little importance, influence, or power.

novice: beginner or newcomer.

perverse: determined to go against what is right, expected, or desired; persistent or obstinate in what is wrong.

rarified: elevated in nature or style; of rare, high value.

rimrock: rock forming a natural boundary of a plateau or other rise.

riven: split apart (past participle form) or tear.

sinew: another name for tendon.

sisal: a fiber from the agave plant used to make ropes, rugs, and other items.

sparsely: thinly scattered; not thick (as in sparse hair or sparse population).

spattered: scattered or dashed in small particles ("Paint spattered the walls.")

tufted: threads, fibers, feathers, hair, etc. formed into a tight bunch at the bottom but loose at the top.

Note: For pronunciation, go to dictionary.com, search the word, and click on the speaker icon.

USAGE Choose two words from the above list that begin with the same sound and use them in a sentence, creating **alliteration** (see the glossary for definition).

Thinking and Talking Points

1. Make a list of comparisons to humans (personification) Saner uses to describe the Utah juniper; write a paragraph, in your own words, of the overall impression these personifications reveal about the writer's attitude toward these trees.

2. Saner writes, "Other arboreal species may echo states we recognize in ourselves, but none I've run across seems so moody and emotional." What other states of mind does he attribute to the Utah juniper? What other tree species might "echo states we recognize in ourselves"?

3. Explain how this essay's **subtext** contains a metaphor for the human mind and body. Pick out specific descriptive passages to prove the point. Study the conclusion—what is Saner's point?

4. What environment does this tree need to grow the way it does? How might this environment echo human emotional environment?

5. What other style—word choices, punctuation, sentence structure, specific detail, description—does the author use? Write down at least three and discuss how well—or not—the techniques work to improve the essay.

Styling

Personification of an object or state of being can lead to critical thinking about **subtext**: Saner's tree echoing human states; Hoagland's turtles (anthropomorphizing) mustering courage against the odds, the ministories becoming fables about the environment and our relationship with nature; Gendler's "Truth" is a thief stealing illusions.

PRACTICE Make a list of human personality traits (draw on #1 in Thinking and Talking Points or create a list from scratch). A thesaurus with synonyms can help (for example, look up the word happy and write down all of its synonyms, and do the same with other qualities on the list). A list of at least ten will make the project easier.

YOU TRY IT Find pictures of different trees or other plant life. Choose one and read a little about it. Drawing from the list, write a paragraph personifying the plant. When finished, share the writing with others and determine what subtext you might have created.

Teaming Up

1. **Practice for Writing Idea #1:** The style exercise works well as a group activity. Each member of the group brings in a picture of a tree or plant along with a little information. Brainstorm the list of qualities as a group, decide which qualities go with each plant (it's okay if they overlap), and then individually write the paragraphs— modeling Saner—using the human qualities to describe the plant or tree. Share the writing and discuss the subtext.

2. Each group member brings in pictures of the Utah juniper and other junipers. Study the photos and make a list of differences and similarities. Co-write a paragraph that describes the uniqueness of the Utah species in comparison to a more common juniper.

Writing Ideas

1. Research another plant or tree that grows in difficult conditions, perhaps desert flowers or certain types of orchids. Using the research and personification, write an essay that not only describes and personifies, but discusses how the plant or tree solves the problem of living in such an environment. For ideas, review Saner's essay and study where he talks about how the Utah Juniper survives in such a harsh place.

2. Read Brian Doyle's "Joyas Voladoras" and study it for subtext. Compare and/or contrast that essay to Saner's "The Tree Beyond Imagining." Discuss the use of subtext and style.

Essay Connections

Other essays containing subtext, comparisons (metaphor, simile), or personification include Ruth Gendler's "Truth"; Brian Doyle's "Joyas Voladoras"; Brian Doyle's "Meat"; Edward Hoagland's "The Courage of Turtles" (anthropomorphizing and subtext in the fable form); John Updike's "Disposable Rocket"; and Bailey White's "Mortality."

A DARK AND STORMY KNIGHT: WHY BATMAN?

Professor Travis Langley

In his book Batman and Psychology: A Dark and Stormy Knight, *Psychology Professor Travis Langley asks, "Why do we love Batman? Why do we analyze him more than any other superhero?" In these excerpts from his book, he attempts to answer those questions. Professor Langley teaches the psychology of crime, mental illness, and social behavior at Henderson State University. He writes a column for* Psychology Today *titled "Beyond Heroes and Villains" and is published in numerous online journals. Other books include* The Walking Dead: Psychology *and* Star Wars: Psychology.

DUSTBIN OF HISTORY AND CULTURE

JOSEPH CAMPBELL: (1904-1987) An American professor at Sarah Lawrence, Campbell was a writer and anthropologist, best known for his work in mythology. His books on the importance of mythology include *The Power of Myth*, *The Hero with a Thousand Faces*, and *The Masks of God*.

CARL GUSTAV JUNG: (1875-1961) Jung was a Swiss psychologist who worked with Sigmund Freud, but eventually broke from Freud's focus on sex to study dream analysis, the human psyche, and the collective unconscious.

Modern Mythology and Grim Tales

1   Psychiatrists (e.g., Bender, Kambam, & Pozios, 2011; Wertham, 1954) and psychologists (e.g., Daniels, 2008; Dreyer, 2009; Killian, 2007; Langley & Rosenberg, 2011; plus others interviewed in the History Channel documentary *Batman Unmasked: The Psychology of the Dark Knight*) analyze Batman more than any other superhero — the character himself, that is. Looking at Superman psychologically means looking at modern mythology. He's the modern demigod myth. While there's something mythic about Batman too, to be sure, he's more akin to the mortal legends like Robin Hood and pulp heroes like Zorro and the Shadow, extraordinary men but men nonetheless.

2   In bright, shining Superman, Jerry Siegel and Joe Shuster drew inspiration from divine heroes throughout the ages, "like Samson, Hercules, and all the strong men I ever heard of rolled into one — only more so"

(Siegel, quoted by O'Neil, 2008, p. 1), to create not only Superman himself but the very concept of the costumed superhero. They made the meme. Where Superman drew his might from the Earth's sun, Batman found his in a city's darkness. Jerry and Joe played with the bright and impossible. Bob Kane and Bill Finger, in creating Batman, expanded the meme by adding the coin's other side, the dark and improbably possible.

Me and My Shadow

3   Carl Jung (1964) and Joseph Campbell (1949) looked at how archetypes, universal themes we inherit as part of our collective unconscious, symbolically shape myths and legends of heroes in similar ways throughout every culture in the world. According to them, the so-called "Hero's Journey" represents individuals' own psychological growth as they confront features of their personal and collective unconscious in order to grow, mature, and fulfill their potential as human beings.

4   The Shadow archetype represents your own dark side, not necessarily your evil side but the part of you that is hidden, out of the light, the sum of those characteristics you conceal from both the world and yourself. Bruce Wayne confronts his own darkest nature early in life, chooses to work with it, and uses it to instill fear in others. His bright and dark sides work together to fight evil. From a Jungian perspective, therefore, Batman appeals to our own need to face and manage our own Shadow selves. We want Batman in our shadows.

The Bat's Humanity

5   Regardless of possible mythical or archetypal reasons for the Dark Knight's appeal, we like him because he's fully human. Batman's the superhero with no superpowers. He can walk into a room full of people who fly, read minds, and run faster than light, and yet he's the one who intimidates them. His personality defines him, not superpowers.

6   His origin defines him as well, so much so that it's part of his personality. Bruce Wayne doesn't hail from some alien planet or mythical island, and his abilities don't come from any magic ring, secret formula, or radioactive mishap. He was—and in many ways is—a little boy whose parents got gunned down in front of him.

Self-Made Man

7   Spider-Man and Superman are heroes because of their great upbringing, because their adoptive parents taught them through word and deed that with great power comes great responsibility. Bruce Wayne's altruistic

parents similarly taught him to help those who have less than himself. Upbringing helped make heroes of all three, but a radioactive spider and extraterrestrial biology made the first two *super*heroes. Batman made *himself* super. Through years of hard work and sheer determination, he built himself into the person he wanted to become, and that's inspiring. We know we can't become Spider-Man or Superman. Maybe we know we can't become Batman either, but Bruce Wayne nevertheless helps us feel that we can become something great, *something* of our own choosing.

Bats in His Belfry?

8   Because Batman is fully human and because a horrible trauma leads him to wear a mask and wage his war on crime, we can contemplate real psychological issues that drive people to do extreme things. Psychologists can examine how well he does or does not fit the symptoms of a variety of disorders. Nobody thinks it's weird for Superman to apply his natural gifts to help the members of this human race in a manner that keeps him above it all. When a guy runs around dressed like a bat, we have to wonder: Why the mask, the bat, and the underage partner? Why does he really wear a costume to fight crime? Why are his most intimate relationships with "bad girls" he ought to lock up? And why won't he kill that homicidal clown?

9   Is Batman neurotic? Psychotic? Does he have PTSD, OCD, or any other mental illness? Whether Batman has any specific mental disorder is a topic for another time. The point right now is that his characteristics and fictional biography provide plenty for anyone to mull over from a psychological perspective.

Enemies

10   Duality and obsession, his enemies' and his own, fill Batman's stories. His enemies reflect and distort facets of himself. What psychopathologies lurk in the minds of supervillains like the Joker, the Riddler, Two-Face, and Catwoman? Are they really rogues and villains, or simply misunderstood victims of a heartless society? Do Batman and his foes depend on each other?

11   After the arrival of its mysterious hero, Gotham City sees a proliferation of costumed characters, some of them vigilantes but most of them criminals whose theatrics and preoccupations rival the Dark Knight's. Does Batman inspire their histrionics no less than he inspires new heroes, or does he attract creative crooks to his city? The Riddler and *The Dark Knight Rises'* antagonist Bane, for example, each move

to Gotham City specifically because they think Batman offers them each a worthy challenge. Maybe the city itself draws them all.

12   Like the hero who pursues them, most of Gotham City's supervillains are human beings defined by their personalities instead of superpowers. We describe many of Spider-Man's enemies first and foremost by referring to abilities like becoming a lizard, turning into sand, or wielding cybernetic tentacles. We define most of Batman's foes by behaviors like their killer pranks, riddling compulsions, themed obsessions, ruthless environmentalism, or decision making via coin toss to do right or wrong. No other superhero sees an entire mental hospital, Arkham Asylum in this case, become best known for housing his fanciful foes.

Primal Fear

13   When this character's creators decided what must drive this man to dress like a bat and make his city's criminals cower at the sight of him, Bob Kane and Bill Finger tapped into our most primal childhood fears. A father, mother, and son, after a night out at the movies, walk together down the street. A gunman demands the wife's necklace. The husband moves to protect her. Gunshots. A scream. He dies. She dies. Their son stands alone in tears. Within the fictional biography of Bruce Wayne, this page-and-a-half scene from *Detective Comics #33* (1939) is where Batman begins.

14   "Bill and I discussed it," Kane recalled (Daniels, 1999, p. 31), "and we figured there's nothing more traumatic than having your parents murdered before your eyes." Losing one's parent or parents when old enough to know about it ranks as the single most stressful common life event children can experience (e.g., Monaghan, Robinson, & Dodge, 1979). Uncommon traumas like torture or terrorist attacks are not universal experiences, not things most of us can anticipate, but sooner or later we all learn that our parents can and will die.

Justice

15   We want justice. People who believe in a just world suffer less stress and depression, and enjoy life more than people who do not (Lipkus, Dalbert, & Siegler, 1996). Many cultures teach their members from childhood to believe the world operates with natural order and justice — the just-world phenomenon that psychologist Melvin Lerner says comforts us because most of us, even the worst of us, consider ourselves basically good and worthy of fair treatment (Lerner, 1980; Lerner & Miller, 1978). Our need to believe justice will prevail even when the system fails, even when criminals evade arrest or avoid conviction, makes us want there to be somebody out there who can get them anyway.

Conclusion: What Batman Really Is to Us

16   Why don't children fear this hero who dresses like a monster? Because he's their monster. He's ours. Even when children learn that magic will not save them nor will a hero in blue fly out of the sky, so they develop more realistic hopes, they can still hope that when they can't find the strength to stand up to life's bullies, someone who is strong and capable might do the right thing and help. In Batman, they see the wounded boy who makes himself big and strong enough to turn fear against the fearsome. With both brain and brawn, he's the part of us that wants to scare life's bullies away.

17   Why Batman? A child can wish for superpowers. An adult, who may have given up that particular dream, can still wish for strength enough.

A DARK AND STORMY KNIGHT: WHY BATMAN?

Exploring Language

altruistic: unselfishly concerned with the welfare of others.

duality: divided in two; double (as in dual nature, meaning a person has two distinct personalities).

demigod: a mythological being who is part god and part human; Hercules is an example of a demigod, his mother being a human and his father the god Zeus.

facets:: phases or aspects; in this context, Langley claims that Batman's enemies reflect parts of Batman's personality.

histrionics: over-dramatized speech or actions, usually insincere.

meme: a cultural item that is transmitted by repetition and replication: an image, video, or phrase, that is often widespread and sometimes altered in the process.

psychopathologies: in this context, deviations from normal or efficient behavior; psychoses or mental disorders.

proliferation: rapid and often excessive speed or increase.

rogue: a dishonest person; a scoundrel (in the context of this essay).

Note: For pronunciation, visit dictionary.com, search the word, and click on the speaker icon.

Usage: Look up other meanings of rogue and use at least one of them in a sentence.

Thinking and Talking Points

1. Langley has posed the questions "Why do we love Batman? Why do we analyze him more than any other superhero?" Sum up his thesis statement and how he answers these questions in the essay.
2. Discuss Batman's enemies. How might they reflect aspects of Batman's own personality?
3. How does Langley define the Shadow archetype? Why do "we want Batman in our shadows"?
4. What is the author's point concerning justice?
5. How does Batman "tap into our primal fears"?

Styling

Lead-ins (see the "Punctuation is Style" section, "Commas with Lead-ins") to main clauses can function in many ways: as a simple introduction to a main sentence, as a **periodic** sentence—multiple lead-ins that anticipate the main sentence—as multiple verbs for emphatic action, as "ing" words for more lilting action, or as multiple subjects. Langley pairs up multiple subjects for his lead-in:

> Duality and obsession, his enemies' and his own, fill Batman's stories.

The commas separate the **two pairs**: Duality and obsession, his enemies' and his own. The second pair explains whose duality and obsession.

Sentence Breakdown:
Subjects:
> Pair number one: Duality and obsession.
> Pair number two: his enemies' and his own.

Action (verb) and completing the thought:
> *fill* Batman's stories.

In his essay "Children in the Woods," (not in this text) Barry Lopez uses this style to list the types of animals he sees in the woods:

> White-footed mice and mule deer, mink and coyote move through here.

Notice how Lopez breaks down his list of animals into two groups:

> Pair number one: white-footed mice and mule deer
> Pair number two: mink and coyote.

He finishes his thought with the verb clause *move through here.*
    Diane Ackerman, in "Mute Dancers: How to Watch a Hummingbird," (not in this edition of the text) uses a set of actions in the "ing" form to lead into her sentence about how hummingbirds live their lives:

> Feasting and flying, courting and dueling, hummingbirds live life
> at a fever pitch.

Ackerman's slightly different style emphasizes actions that do not function as part of the subject. The main sentence that comes after the lead-ins can function on its own: *Hummingbirds live life at a fever pitch.*

These writers pair up items or actions according to what the two things have in common: Langley's first pair—duality and obsession—are psychological terms (in this context), while the second explains whose duality and obsession; Lopez's *white-footed mice and mule deer* both begin with the letter *m*, creating **alliteration**, while mink and coyote might be considered sly creatures, and coyote prey on mink; Ackerman's *feasting and flying* are not simply alliterative; hummingbirds tend to feast and fly simultaneously, and courting and dueling also occur together, as male hummingbirds duke it out for the attention of the female.

PRACTICE   Fill in the blanks in this first sentence with nouns (perhaps types of people or animals) that might slink through a city at night, pairing up items according to what they have in common:

_____ and _____, _____ and _____ slink through the dark streets of the city.

Fill in the blanks in this sentence with pairs of "ing" actions that describe the subject:

_____ and _____, _____ and _____, dolphins are the acrobats of the ocean.

YOU TRY IT   Write two sentences in each of the practice styles. If you are working on an essay, try at least one of them on the topic of your assignment.

Teaming Up

1. **Warm-up for Writing Idea #1.** Separately, write down one or two names of your favorite superheroes or villains or ones that first come to mind. Next, share the names with the group, and combine any repeats to form a master list of four or five superheroes/villains. Together, brainstorm a list of qualities for each superhero that people might relate to on some level. For example, Spiderman, despite his "Spidey" powers, is an outcast at school who gets bullied.
2. **Warm-up for Writing Idea #2.** Each student in the group brings in an ancient mythological story (a summary will do, readily available

online with a quick search) of a god/goddess or hero, whether Greek, Roman, Nordic, Japanese, or some other group. Before class, each student should read his or her story and highlight the qualities of the character, the skills, powers, and personality traits that set the hero apart from average humans. Share the findings, and then brainstorm each person's mythological character to find a modern superhero that shares some of those same attributes.

Writing Ideas

1. Research a superhero and explore its psychological and sociological influence, why people relate to it (books, PBS videos, and articles are abundant on this topic). Use a riddle introduction (see "Riddles" in the "Hooks, Introductions, and Conclusions" section).
2. Research a mythological hero or god and compare/contrast to a modern superhero. Argue whether or not Langley's and others' assertions that superheroes are the new mythology have validity.

Essay and Film Connections

Other essays in the book that explore popular culture include Joseph Epstein's "The Culture of Celebrity, "The Little Mermaid" by Pauline Kael, Preface From *The Dumbest Generation* by Mark Bauerlein, and "Monster Mash" by Jack Kroll.

JOYAS VOLADORAS

Brian Doyle

Brian Doyle has several books of essays to his credit: Leaping: Revelations and Epiphanies, The Wet Engine: Exploring the Mad Wild Miracle of the Heart (where "Joyas Voladoras" appears), and Spirited Men. This essay also appeared in Best American Essays 2005. His collection of short stories is titled Epiphanies and Elegies.

1   Consider the hummingbird for a long moment. A hummingbird's heart beats ten times a second. A hummingbird's heart is the size of a pencil eraser. A hummingbird's heart is a lot of the hummingbird. *Joyas voladoras,* flying jewels, the first white explorers in the Americas called them, and the white men had never seen such creatures, for hummingbirds came into the world only in the Americas, nowhere else in the universe, more than three hundred species of them whirring and zooming and nectaring in hummer time zones nine times removed from ours, their hearts hammering faster than we could clearly hear if we pressed our elephantine ears to their infinitesimal chests.

2   Each one visits a thousand flowers a day. They can dive at sixty miles an hour. They can fly backward. They can fly more than five hundred miles without pausing to rest. But when they rest they come close to death: on frigid nights, or when they are starving, they retreat into torpor, their metabolic rate slowing to a fifteenth of their normal sleep rate, their hearts sludging nearly to a halt, barely beating, and if they are not soon warmed, if they do not soon find that which is sweet, their hearts grow cold, and they cease to be. Consider for a moment those hummingbirds who did not open their eyes again today, this very day, in the Americas: bearded helmetcrests and booted rackettails, violet-tailed sylphs and violet-capped woodnymphs, crimson topazes and purple-crowned fairies, red-tailed comets and amethyst woodstars, rainbow-bearded thornbills and glittering-bellied emeralds, velvet-purple coronets and golden-bellied star-frontlets, fiery-tailed awlbills and Andean hillstars, spatuletails and pufflegs, each the most amazing thing you have never seen, each thunderous wild

heart the size of an infant's fingernail, each mad heart silent, a brilliant music stilled.

3   Hummingbirds, like all flying birds but more so, have incredible enormous immense ferocious metabolisms. To drive those metabolisms they have racecar hearts that eat oxygen at an eye-popping rate. Their hearts are built of thinner, leaner fibers than ours. Their arteries are stiffer and more taut. They have more mitochondria in their heart muscles—anything to gulp more oxygen. Their hearts are stripped to the skin for the war against gravity and inertia, the mad search for food, the insane idea of flight. The price of their ambition is a life closer to death; they suffer more heart attacks and aneurysms and ruptures than any other living creature. It's expensive to fly. You burn out. You fry the machine. You melt the engine. Every creature on earth has approximately two billion heartbeats to spend in a lifetime. You can spend them slowly, like a tortoise, and live to be two hundred years old, or you can spend them fast, like a hummingbird, and live to be two years old.

4   The biggest heart in the world is inside the blue whale. It weighs more than seven tons. It's as big as a room. It is a room, with four chambers. A child could walk around in it, head high, bending only to step through the valves. The valves are as big as the swinging doors in a saloon. This house of a heart drives a creature a hundred feet long. When this creature is born it is twenty feet long and weighs four tons. It is waaaaay bigger than your car. It drinks a hundred gallons of milk from its mama every day and gains two hundred pounds a day, and when it is seven or eight years old it endures an unimaginable puberty and then it essentially disappears from human ken, for next to nothing is known of the mating habits, travel patterns, diet, social life, language, social structure, diseases, spirituality, wars, stories, despairs, and arts of the blue whale. There are perhaps ten thousand blue whales in the world, living in every ocean on earth, and of the largest mammal who ever lived we know nearly nothing. But we know this: the animals with the largest hearts in the world generally travel in pairs, and their penetrating moaning cries, their piercing yearning tongue, can be heard underwater for miles and miles.

5   Mammals and birds have hearts with four chambers. Reptiles and turtles have hearts with three chambers. Fish have hearts with two chambers. Insects and mollusks have hearts with one chamber. Worms have hearts with one chamber, although they may have as many as eleven single-chambered hearts. Unicellular bacteria have

no hearts at all; but even they have fluid eternally in motion, washing from one side of the cell to the other, swirling and whirling. No living being is without interior liquid motion. We all churn inside.

6   So much held in a heart in a lifetime. So much held in a heart in a day, an hour, a moment. We are utterly open with no one, in the end— not mother and father, not wife or husband, not lover, not child, not friend. We open windows to each but we live alone in the house of the heart. Perhaps we must. Perhaps we could not bear to be so naked, for fear of a constantly harrowed heart. When young we think there will come one person who will savor and sustain us always; when we are older we know this is the dream of a child, that all hearts finally are bruised and scarred, scored and torn, repaired by time and will, patched by force of character, yet fragile and rickety forevermore, no matter how ferocious the defense and how many bricks you bring to the wall. You can brick up your heart as stout and tight and hard and cold and impregnable as you possibly can and down it comes in an instant, felled by a woman's second glance, a child's apple breath, the shatter of glass in the road, the words "I have something to tell you," a cat with a broken spine dragging itself into the forest to die, the brush of your mother's papery ancient hand in the thicket of your hair, the memory of your father's voice early in the morning echoing from the kitchen where he is making pancakes for his children.

JOYAS VOLADORAS

Exploring Language

inertia: resistance to motion, action, or change.
infinitesimal: extremely small; too small to be measured.
ken: knowledge or understanding.
mitochondria: simply put, it's part of the cell.
Note: For pronunciation, go to dictionary.com, search the word, and click on the speaker icon.

Thinking and Talking Points

1. Find several comparisons Doyle makes (like "heart the size of an infant's fingernail"). How do these comparisons help the reader visualize and/or relate to the animals he's describing?
2. How do the examples and points show our relationship to the creatures? What is Doyle's overall point?
3. Is the conclusion unexpected? If so, what is the expectation? How do the examples relate to the conclusion?
4. Usually, beginning writers are told not to repeat words too close together. How does Doyle use repetition to his advantage?
5. Other than comparison, what other style techniques liven up this essay? Examine the length of the sentences. What do you notice? Also consider punctuation in your examination.

Styling

In addition to brilliant and vivid comparisons (see the Styling with Hoagland's "The Courage of Turtles"), this essay's unexpected conclusion—shifting from the physical workings of hearts to the emotional— moves the reader in almost the same way as the specific heartbreaks he mentions. It's these powerhouse **specifics**—a woman's second glance, a child's apple breath, the shatter of glass in the road, the words "I have something to tell you," a cat with a broken spine dragging itself into the forest to die, the brush of your mother's papery ancient hand in the thicket of your hair, the memory of your father's voice early in the morning echoing from the kitchen where he is making pancakes for his children—that make this conclusion so utterly unforgettable.

Notice that these examples are detailed as well as specific: not just a cat with a broken spine, but dragging itself into the forest to die; instead of simply mother's hand, it's papery ancient hand; a child's *apple* breath. These details hammer the heart, right on target.

PRACTICE   Think of an issue that concerns you, whether personal, social, or political. For example, you might be concerned about the plight of abused and neglected children; the unnecessary deaths of pets at a local animal shelter that still kills for space; a politician's views; a relative's health, and so on. Brainstorm a list of at least ten specific, detailed examples.

YOU TRY IT   Make a point about the issue you brainstormed, and write a sentence modeled on Doyle's concluding sentence. Consider livening up the conclusion to your next essay with this technique.

Teaming Up

1. The above Styling technique works well as a group activity. Everyone contribute an idea; then vote on which idea to brainstorm. Decide which examples are the most vivid or memorable, and then co-write the sentence.

2. **Warm-up for Writing Idea #1:** Break down the parts of a machine— an automobile, an oven, washer or dryer, a computer, anything—or the anatomy of a particular animal (bird, insect, mammal). Have one person in the group list each part on a piece of paper. Discuss how each part might be a metaphor for a human emotion or personality trait, something like this:

> beak = nagging
> claws = jealousy
> feathers = mothering

(You can use a particular animal or machine for your brainstorm: duck instead of bird; Volkswagen rather than car). List as many parts and traits as you can. Now examine the list for a tone: are the qualities mostly bitter, joyful, philosophical, sad, mean, humorous? Choose items from the list that seem similar in tone. Now co-write a paragraph comparing the animal parts to human behavior.

Writing Ideas

1. Using the warm-up in Teaming Up #2, write an essay that compares a person to either the parts of a machine or an animal. The person can be someone you know personally (a friend or relative, for example) or a public figure.

2. Compare and/or contrast Doyle's style and tone to Gordon Grice's "Black Widow." You might discuss a different style element—figurative language, sentence variety, word choice, punctuation—in each paragraph. Consider concluding with a contemplation of tone.

Essay Connections

See the Writing Ideas and Essay Connections with Hoagland's "The Courage of Turtles" and Gordon Grice's "Black Widow."

AMERICAN CHILDREN

John Updike

John Updike was an American author of novels, poems, plays, essays, and frequent contributions to The New Yorker magazine. This essay, from his book Just Looking: Essays on Art, analyzes and compares two paintings of children, one by Winslow Homer and the other by John Singer Sargent. John Updike died in January, 2009.

DUSTBIN OF HISTORY AND CULTURE

WINSLOW HOMER: (1836–1910) Often considered one of the best 19th-century American naturalist painters.

JOHN SINGER SARGENT: (1856–1925) Primarily known for his portraits of wealthy and influential American families.

1   The boys and girls depicted here might not mix very well if they were released from their frames, but separately they compose two peaceful groups and two beautiful paintings. Winslow Homer's anonymous lads are taking their ease in a pasture; the daughters of the prosperous Edward Boit are scattered through two fine rooms, and all but one of them gaze with respectful curiosity at the busy bearded intruder into their home, the fashionable painter John Singer Sargent. The dashing impressionism of Sargent's technique carries a generation farther Homer's flickering grasses and dabs of sunny red, and the triangular pose of the little girl in the foreground mirrors the unified shape of the two country idlers. Both painters surround their childish subjects with large margins of environment. The effect is of silence: silent vases, silent sky, silent carpet and turf underfoot. A great hushed world waits around these children to be tasted, explored, grown into.

2   They take themselves seriously, and are taken seriously. Homer gives his little subjects a monumental dignity; there is something of Greek drapery in the color-gouged fold of the sunlit white sleeve, and something angelically graceful in the extended, self-shadowed feet. And Sargent, catching his subjects where they have alighted like white butterflies, displays deep spaces about them, and permits them all

the gravity their young femininity warrants. They recede, from youngest to oldest, toward a dark other room; beyond the toddler with her doll a girl no longer quite childish stands on the edge of shadow while her sister, a little taller and older still, is half-turned into it. The huge vase she leans against suggests a woman's shape. These young ladies are watching, not just the painter, but us, to see what we will do next, and whether what we do will be worthy of their responding. Like butterflies, they will elude us if we startle them.

3   Sargent's painting could have been a mere commission, an expert piece of toadying within the upper classes, but the jaunty eccentricity of its composition, and a daring within its deference, save it for art. Winslow Homer's could have been a bit of calendar art, falsely bucolic, but for the abstract power of a severe and stately composition that locks the barefoot pair as if forever into the center of the canvas and that lends solemn substance to a fleeting summer day. There is a mystery to the faces; the painter has declined all opportunity for easy anecdote within the ruddy shade of those hats.

4   Both artists have attempted honest portraits of children, as perhaps only Americans could have done. Though the Declaration of Independence nowhere promises a better deal for children, the American child does appear freer than his European counterpart and is taken more seriously—as a source of opinion, as a market for sales, and as not just a future inheritor but an independent entity now, while still a child. Childhood and then youth are seen in our democracy as classes that cut across class distinctions. Within their frames these two sets of children are similarly pensive. Responsible but powerless, childhood does not smile; it watches and waits, amid shadows and sun.

AMERICAN CHILDREN

Exploring Language

anecdote: a narrative account or story.
bucolic: relating to rural (country) life.
deference: respect or esteem for an elder or superior.
jaunty: carefree or high spirited.
pensive: thoughtful or meditative, in a dreamy sort of way, sometimes suggesting sadness.
toadying: brownnosing, flattering or, in modern slang, sucking up.
Note: For pronunciation, go to dictionary.com, search the word, and
click on the speaker icon.

USAGE Practice using *pensive;* it's more descriptive than thoughtful.
Look up thoughtful and pensive. What is the difference in meaning? Use
each in a sentence that captures the subtle difference.

Thinking and Talking Points

1. What details in the essay help you understand the paintings or notice
   things you might otherwise have missed? Look up the paintings
   online and study the details.
2. Updike comments that American children "appear freer" than
   European children, and are "taken more seriously—as a source of
   opinion, as a market for sales, and as not just a future inheritor but
   an independent entity now, while still a child." Do you agree or disagree that American children are taken seriously? Be ready to support your response with examples.
3. At the end of his essay Updike writes, "Responsible but powerless,
   childhood does not smile; it watches and waits, amid shadows and
   sun." What do you think he means? In what way is childhood "responsible but powerless"?
4. Updike says of the children in the paintings that "there is a mystery
   to the faces" and "these two sets of children are similarly pensive."
   Study the paintings (available online). What features—facial, pos-
   ture—make them look this way?

Styling

Updike uses a colon to list silent objects in the painting, an effective way to create sentence variety, establish a mood, and gather supporting details. He writes:

> The effect is of silence: silent vases, silent sky, silent carpet and turf underfoot.

Use a colon only after a complete sentence.

Usually, you don't want to repeat a word as Updike does with silent, but sometimes it's an effective tool to make a point. Though we're mostly concerned with practicing using the colon, try his repetition technique as a style bonus. You wouldn't want to do this in a paper too frequently, but one sentence like this can make an impact.

PRACTICE   Fill in the blanks with details that support the sentence. Here's an example:

> The concert radiated noise: *noisy drums, noisy bass,* and *noisy fans.*

> Jerry's bedroom oozed dust: _____ , _____ , and _____ .

> After the storm, the old farmhouse leaked water: _____ , _____ , and _____ .

> The items in the refrigerator were covered in mold: _____ , _____ , and _____ .

YOU TRY IT   Create five sentences of your own that begin with a complete sentence followed by a colon and a list of details. Try expanding your lists beyond three items.

Teaming Up

1. Bring in copies of the photos Updike discusses (available online). Discuss why you think Updike wrote that the children "might not mix very well if they were released from their frames." Co-write a dialogue between the two groups, what you imagine they would say to one another if they did meet.

2. Bring in a photograph of yourself (or someone else if you don't have a photo of yourself) as a child. Trade photos with another member of the group. Write a description of the picture of your classmate,

describing the mood of the child by giving details of facial expression, setting, and clothing, and what you think he or she might have been thinking at the time of the photograph.

Writing Ideas

1. Write an essay about a time you felt powerless but responsible when you were a child.
2. Find a painting that moves you in some way. Write an essay describing the painting and the feelings it evokes.
3. Find two paintings or photographs by different artists of the same subject: two landscapes, two women, two men, two dogs, any subject. Write an essay comparing and/or contrasting the two pieces of art.

Essay Connections

Updike's book *Just Looking: Essays on Art* teems with essays full of style. David Huddle's essay "Museum Piece" journeys into the paintings of Jan Vermeer.

MUSICAL AWAKENINGS

Clayton S. Collins

This essay first appeared in Profiles: The Magazine of Continental Airlines. Clayton Collins discusses the work of neurologist and author Oliver Sacks, a strong believer in the healing power of music, and the essay contains fascinating case studies of people debilitated by stroke or other neurological diseases who are able to move once again when exposed to music.

DUSTBIN OF HISTORY AND CULTURE

FRIEDRICH NIETZSCHE: (1844–1900) A German philosopher, poet, and philologist (one who studies human speech, especially as it pertains to shedding light on culture). He coined the phrase "God is dead."

BIZET: (1838–1875) French composer best known for his operas, especially *Carmen*.

T. S. ELIOT: (1888–1965) British poet and critic. He won the Nobel prize for literature in 1948.

1   Oliver Sacks danced to the Dead. For three solid hours. At sixty. And with "two broken knees."

2   The Oxford-educated neurologist who likes to say, with an impish grin, that he doesn't like any music after Mozart's *Magic Flute,* wasn't particularly taken by the Grateful Dead concert in Friedrich Nietzsche's mnemonic sense, he explains (as only he would), "But in a tonic and dynamic sense they were quite overwhelming. And though I had effusions for a month after, it was worth it."

3   The power of music—not just to get an aging physician with classical tastes up and rocking, but also to "bring back" individuals rendered motionless and mute by neurological damage and disorders—is what's driving Sacks these days. The shyly brilliant and best-selling author of *The Man Who Mistook His Wife for a Hat* and *Awakenings*—the latter of which was made into a 1990 film starring Robin Williams—is working on another case-study book, one that deals in part with the role of music as a stimulus to minds that have thrown up stiff sensory barriers, leaving thousands of victims of stroke, tumors, Parkinson's

disease, Tourette's syndrome, Alzheimer's, and a wide range of less-publicized ailments alone, debilitated, and disoriented.

4   "One sees how robust music is neurologically," Sacks says. "You can lose all sorts of particular powers, but you don't tend to lose music and identity." His conviction regarding the role of music in helping the neurologically afflicted to become mentally "reorganized" runs deep: "Whenever I get out a book on neurology or psychology, the first thing I look up in the index is music," he says. 'And if it's not there, I close the book."

5   Born in London in 1933 and a permanent resident of the United States for the past thirty-four years, Sacks is a frequent public speaker, careening from stories about great composers and poets to a report about goldfish dancing to a Strauss waltz. However, Sacks is a reluctant celebrity. The fourth son (three of them doctors) of two physicians, he preferred solitary research early in his career, far more comfortable extracting myelin from earthworms than working with humans. But when he misplaced a vial of the white fatty substance in 1966, he was banished, in effect, to the less-prestigious realm of clinical medicine. Since then, Sacks has burrowed deep into the illnesses and the lives of persons in his care, a miner in the catacombs of the catatonic, chipping away at the walls around their neurological cores. . . .

6   Much of what he has encountered, particularly in working with patients at Beth Abraham Hospital, in the Bronx, is startling. Much of it relates to music.

7   "One saw patients who couldn't take a single step, who couldn't walk, but who could dance," he says. "There were patients who couldn't speak, but who could sing. The power of music in these patients was instantaneous . . . from a frozen Parkinsonian state to a freely flowing, moving, speaking state."

8   Sacks remembers a woman with Parkinson's who would sit perfectly still until "activated" by the music of Chopin, which she loved and knew by heart. She didn't have to hear a tune played. "It was sometimes sufficient to give her an opus number," Sacks says. "You would just say 'Opus 49,' and the F-minor *Fantasy* would start playing in her mind. And she could move."

9   Music is certainly cultural, acknowledges the doctor, but it is basically biological. "One listens to music with one's muscles," he says, quoting Nietzsche again. "The 'tonic' [the key] is mostly brainstem, an arousal response." The "dynamic"—how loud or forcefully the

music is played—registers in the basal ganglia. And the "mnemonic" aspect of songs speaks to the unique memories of individuals: from tribal chant to the blare of bagpipes to Bizet. The old cliché about music's universality, he says, has merit.

10   "Deeply demented people respond to music, babies respond to music, fetuses *probably* respond to music. Various animals respond to music," Sacks says. "There is something about the animal nervous system . . . which seems to respond to music all the way down.

11   "I don't know how it is with invertebrates. I think it's a desperately needed experiment to see how squids and cuttlefish respond," he says, his grin widening.

12   In 1974, Sacks was able to apply music therapy to himself to speed an orthopedic recovery. Hospitalized after a fall while climbing in Norway, he experienced neural damage and partial paralysis and sensed that he was, as a result, losing his "motor identity"—forgetting how to walk.

13   For weeks, flat on his back, he listened to a recording of a Mendelssohn violin concerto. One morning, awakened by the familiar piece, he got up and walked across the room to turn off the tape. He found that the concerto wasn't playing, except in his head. Then he realized he'd been walking, carried along by the tune. It was, he says, "the most dynamic experience in my life.

14   "I'm not normally all that fond of Mendelssohn," he jokes.

15   "I think the notion of music as being a prosthesis in a way, for neurological dysfunctions, is very fundamental," Sacks says, citing the case of a patient with damage to the frontal lobes of his brain.

16   "When he sings, one almost has the strange feeling that [music] has given him his frontal lobes back, given him back, temporally, some function that has been lost on an organic basis," Sacks says, adding a quote from T. S. Eliot: "You are the music, while the music lasts."

17   The key, says Sacks, is for patients to "learn to be well" again. Music can restore to them, he says, the identity that predates the illness. "There's a health to music, a life to music."

18   Those may not sound like the words of a typical clinician. But don't toss terms like "new age" and "holistic" at the good doctor. "I always tighten up a little bit when I hear the word 'holistic,'" he says, professing disdain for "Californian and Eastern" practices. For Sacks, who's been affiliated with a half-dozen neurological institutes and written dozens of seminal papers, medicine needs to be demonstrable, firmly grounded in physiology. Music's been healing for thousands of years, Sacks says. "It's just being looked at now more systematically and with these special populations."

19   So if the Grateful Dead moved Sacks to dance, it had been in the name of research. Seeking a clinical application, Sacks returned to Beth Abraham the next day and "kidnapped" one of his patients. "Greg" was an amnesiac with a brain tumor and no coherent memories of life since about 1969—but an encyclopedic memory of the years that came before, and a real love of Grateful Dead tunes.

20   Sacks took Greg to that night's show. "In the first half of the concert they were doing early music, and Greg was enchanted by everything," Sacks recalls. "I mean, he was not an amnesiac. He was completely oriented and organized and with it."

21   Between sets Sacks went backstage and introduced Greg to band member Mickey Hart, who was impressed with the depth of Greg's knowledge of the group but quite surprised when Greg asked after Pigpen. When told that the former band member had died twenty years before, "Greg was very upset," Sacks recalls. "And then thirty seconds later he asked, 'How's Pigpen?'"

22   During the second half, the band played its newer songs. And Greg's world began to fall apart. "He was bewildered and enthralled and frightened. Because the music for him—and this is an extremely musical man, who understands the idiom of the Grateful Dead—was both familiar and unfamiliar. . . . He said, 'This is like the music of the future.'"

23   Sacks tried to keep the new memories fresh. But the next day Greg had no memory of the concert. It seemed as if all had been lost. "But—and this is strange—when one played some of the new music, which he had heard for the first time at the concert, he could sing along with it and remember it."

24   It is an encouraging development. Amnesiacs have never been found capable of learning anything new. Children have been found to learn quickly lessons that are embedded in song. Sacks, the one-time quiet researcher, is invigorated by the possibilities. He wonders whether music could carry such information, to give his patient back a missing part of his life. To give Greg "some sense of what's been happening in the last twenty years, where he has no autobiography of his own."

25   That would have Sacks dancing in the aisles.

MUSCIAL AWAKENINGS

Exploring Language

careening: leaning, swaying, or tipping to one side while in motion.
demonstrable: capable of being demonstrated.
effusions: look up this word and decide which context Collins is using.
enthralled: fascinated, absorbed.
holistic: looking at the whole thing rather than its parts; when applied to medicine, it means treating the mind and body as one.
invertebrates: animals with no backbone (no spine).
invigorated: energized; renewed; restored.
mnemonic: assisting memory—like the childhood learning songs mentioned in Thinking and Talking Points #3. Those tools help you remember information.
myelin: a fatty white goo that helps protect nerves.
neurological: having to do with the nervous system.
orthopedic: having to do with the bones, or skeletal system.
prosthesis: artificial limb.
seminal: creative; contributing to later development. In other words, Sacks wrote papers that got people thinking and developing his ideas.
Note: For pronunciation, go to dictionary.com, search the word, and click on the speaker icon.

USAGE Many of the words in the above list are medical and scientific terms which will be useful when reading and writing about those subjects. The words *effusions, invigorated, enthralled* beg to be used; they hop off the page. So in your essay, instead of writing "The song held my interest," write "The song enthralled me."

Thinking and Talking Points

1. According to Oliver Sacks, music is a powerful tool for healing. Go through the essay and list specific examples Sacks gives to support his view. What other powers can you attribute to music?
2. Collins writes that Sacks doesn't approve of "new age" or "holistic" therapies. But music therapy was once considered—and to some still

is—quack medicine. Find examples from the essay that support his point concerning therapy. What other once-considered-hogwash therapies can you think of that have become mainstream? What is your opinion about some of these therapies? Do you base your view on personal experience or what you've read or heard from others?

3. Collins writes that "children have been found to learn quickly lessons that are embedded in song." Do you remember any of these learning songs from childhood? Do you remember song lyrics better than test material? Explain.

4. Study the opening paragraph to this essay. How does it hook the reader's attention? Apply this technique of short, catchy sentences to your paragraph in Teaming Up #2.

Styling

In addition to a catchy opening and intriguing examples for support, Collins uses **metaphor** to spark life into his essay. He writes:

> Since then, Sacks has burrowed deep into the illnesses and the lives of persons in his care, a miner in the catacombs of the catatonic, chipping away at the walls around their neurological cores.

Collins compares Sacks to a miner and his patients' minds to catacombs. Look at this simple example from the Russell Sanders essay "Grub":

> Bloomington is ringed by the usual necklace of fast food shops.

The necklace image gives the reader a clearer picture of the town.

Here's an example based on the Sanders model: *Laguna Beach is the McDonald's of the art world.*

PRACTICE (For another technique for creating figurative language, see Teaming Up #1.) Fill in the blanks below with your town or a nearby community and an appropriate metaphor. Try brainstorming lists of toys, brand name foods, or retail shops to get ideas for metaphors. For example, Barbie Doll becomes this sentence: *Beverly Hills is the Barbie Doll of Southern California.* Your metaphor should convey a recognizable attitude about the city. The Barbie Doll example works because Beverly Hills has a reputation for being full of affluent people who drive expensive cars, drink Evian water, and get a lot of plastic surgery; not everyone in Beverly Hills fits this stereotype, but enough do to make the metaphor appropriate. And let's face it, Barbie must have had breast implants, and she has everything.

_____ is the _____ of

_____ .

YOU TRY IT   Create three more sentences using metaphor. You can try this technique on other towns or cities you're familiar with, or describe friends or family members, your car, whatever sounds like fun: *My 1970 Chevy Vega is the Mr. Potato Head of the car world* (not very popular in our high-tech world, the Vega is seen as an oddity). Don't worry if some of the metaphors sound odd or silly. The idea is to practice creating metaphor.

Teaming Up

1. Here's a trick for creating a type of figurative language called **personification**. Form groups of three to five members and list some basic colors. Then list the various shades of that color. It helps if someone in the group has a set of colored pencils with various shades. Next, make a list of basic emotions. Think of as many words as you can that are similar for each emotion (synonyms). A thesaurus might help. Your lists might look like this:

Blue	*Happy*	*Sad*
navy	glad	unhappy
midnight	ecstatic	depressed
powder	cheerful	forlorn
peacock	delighted	melancholy
aquamarine	joyful	gloomy
royal	pleased	dejected

Brainstorm other emotions. Now replace each shade of color with an emotion that you think describes that color. For example, peacock blue is a shocking color, so you might label it *ecstatic blue*. Midnight blue might become *melancholy blue*. Now attach each emotion/color combination to an object: melancholy blue recliner; forlorn pink ribbon. Finally, build sentences for each emotion/color/object combination:

> The melancholy blue recliner sulked in the corner of the living room.

> My three-year-old sister's forlorn pink ribbon straggled limply through her tangled curls.

2. **Warm-up for Writing Idea #1.** Have your group decide on a song that you all agree you like. I know this may be difficult with the diver-

sity of tastes, but you can also use this activity to convince a dissenting member of the group that your song is worth listening to. Have one member bring in the lyrics, and if possible, have everyone listen to the song before class and write down their reactions. In groups, read and analyze the lyrics. Compare reactions. Co-write a paragraph reporting your findings.

Writing Ideas

1. Think of a song that has an emotional impact on you—or simply a song you like. Listen to it several times and try to identify why the music moves you. Is it the tone? The rhythm? The way a particular instrument sounds? Try to describe the music for your reader. Study the lyrics. Does the song contain metaphor? Hidden meanings or allusions like a poem? Write an essay analyzing the song's impact through its music and message. Use at least one metaphor and one word from the vocabulary list.

2. Some music performers take on almost mythic status in our culture— the Beatles, Elvis, Tupac Shakur—while others burst onto the music scene and quickly fade. The Grateful Dead—while not exactly mythic—has quite a cult following. There are Dead Head clubs, Web sites—even the death of Jerry Garcia hasn't squashed the group's allure. Write an essay that attempts to explain the cult phenomenon that surrounds certain music groups, movies, or TV shows. Focus on one such group like the Grateful Dead's Dead Heads, *Star Trek* Trekkies, *Rocky Horror Picture Show* groupies. Try to find a photo to generate accurate description. Use at least one metaphor or personification in your essay.

3. Do some research on another area of unconventional medicine: acupuncture, chiropractic, herbal remedies, laugh therapy, meditation. Look at arguments from both sides of the issue. Your library should have books in the reference section (or perhaps online) that have articles on both sides of various arguments. Decide whether or not you think the therapy is credible. Provide numerous examples—as Collins does—to support your view. For tips on researching, see the Research section of this book.

Essay Connections

"A Voice for the Lonely" by Stephen Corey also explores music's impact on mood and memory. "Monster Mash" by Jack Kroll and "Prince" by Chuck Klosterman argue particular musicians' influence on culture.

DISPOSABLE ROCKET

John Updike

John Updike was an American author of novels, poems, plays, essays, and frequent contributions to The New Yorker magazine. In "Disposable Rocket," Updike reflects on the male body, traveling through several stages in a man's life from boyhood to old age, comparing the male and female body, writing, "Inhabiting a male body is much like having a bank account; as long as it's healthy, you don't think much about it. Compared to the female body, it is a low-maintenance proposition." John Updike died in January, 2009.

DUSTBIN OF HISTORY AND CULTURE

BYRON: Lord George Gordon Byron (1788–1824). A prominent writer of the English Romantic Period.

DIANA: Roman goddess of the moon and hunting, also the protector of women.

DIONYSUS: Greek god—known by the Romans as Bacchus—of wine and revelry.

DON JUAN: An epic satirical poem by Lord Byron chronicling the adventures of the hero—Don Juan—who becomes Byron's mouthpiece for his views on wealth, power, society, sex, poets, and politicians in England. In the dedication of the work, Byron insults Coleridge and Wordsworth, two of his contemporaries, also renowned poets.

MARS: The Roman god of war. The Greeks identified him with their god Ares.

VENUS: Roman goddess of love and beauty. The Greeks identified her with their goddess Aphrodite.

1   Inhabiting a male body is much like having a bank account; as long as it's healthy, you don't think much about it. Compared to the female body, it is a low-maintenance proposition: a shower now and then, trim the fingernails every ten days, a haircut once a month. Oh yes, shaving—scraping or buzzing away at your face every morning. Byron, in *Don Juan*, thought the repeated nuisance of shaving balanced out the periodic agony, for females, of childbirth. Women are, his lines tell us,

> *Condemn'd to child-bed, as men for their sins*
> *Have shaving too entail'd upon their chins, —*

A daily plague, which in the aggregate
May average on the whole with parturition.

From the standpoint of reproduction, the male body is a delivery system, as the female is a mazy device for retention. Once the delivery is made, men feel a faint but distinct falling-off of interest. Yet against the enduring female heroics of birth and nurture should be set the male's superhuman frenzy to deliver his goods: he vaults walls, skips sleep, risks wallet, health, and his political future all to ram home his seed into the gut of the chosen woman. The sense of the chase lives in him as the key to life. His body is, like a delivery rocket that falls away in space, a disposable means. Men put their bodies at risk to experience the release from gravity.

2   When my tenancy of a male body was fairly new—of six or so years' duration—I used to jump and fall just for the joy of it. Falling—backwards, downstairs—became a specialty of mine, an attention-getting stunt I was practicing into my thirties, at suburban parties. Falling is, after all, a kind of flying, though of briefer duration than would be ideal. My impulse to hurl myself from high windows and the edges of cliffs belongs to my body, not my mind, which resists the siren call of the chasm with all its might; the interior struggle knocks the wind from my lungs and tightens my scrotum and gives any trip to Europe, with its Alps, castle parapets, and gargoyled cathedral lookouts, a flavor of nightmare. Falling, strangely, no longer figures in my dreams, as it often did when I was a boy and my subconscious was more honest with me. An airplane, that necessary evil, turns the earth into a map so quickly the brain turns aloof and calm; still, I marvel that there is no end of young men willing to become jet pilots.

3   Any accounting of male-female differences must include the male's superior recklessness, a drive not, I think, toward death, as the darker feminist cosmogonies would have it, but to test the limits, to see what the traffic will bear—a kind of mechanic's curiosity. The number of men who do lasting damage to their young bodies is striking; war and car accidents aside, secondary-school sports, with the approval of parents and the encouragement of brutish coaches, take a fearful toll of skulls and knees. We were made for combat, back in the post-simian, East African days, and the bumping, the whacking, the breathlessness, the pain-smothering adrenaline rush, form a cumbersome and unfashionable bliss, but bliss nevertheless. Take your body to the edge, and see if it flies.

4   The male sense of space must differ from that of the female, who has such interesting, active, and significant inner space. The space that interests men is outer. The fly ball high against the sky, the long pass spiraling overhead, the jet fighter like a scarcely visible pinpoint nozzle laying down its vapor trail at forty thousand feet, the gazelle haunch flickering just beyond arrow-reach, the uncountable stars sprinkled on their great black wheel, the horizon, the mountaintop, the quasar—these bring portents with them, and awaken a sense of relation with the invisible, with the empty. The ideal male body is taut with lines of potential force, a diagram extending outward; the ideal female body curves around centers of repose. Of course, no one is ideal, and the sexes are somewhat androgynous subdivisions of a species: Diana the huntress is a more trendy body-type nowadays than languid, overweight Venus, and polymorphous Dionysus poses for more underwear ads than Mars. Relatively, though, men's bodies, however elegant, are designed for covering territory, for moving on.

5   An erection, too, defies gravity, flirts with it precariously. It extends the diagram of outward direction into downright detachability—objective in the case of the sperm, subjective in the case of the testicles and penis. Men's bodies, at this juncture, feel only partly theirs; a demon of sorts has been attached to their lower torsos, whose performance is erratic and whose errands seem, at times, ridiculous. It is like having a (much) smaller brother toward whom you feel both fond and impatient; if he is you, it is you in curiously simplified and ignoble form. This sense, of the male body being two of them, is acknowledged in verbal love play and erotic writing, where the penis is playfully given its own name, an individuation not even the rarest rapture grants a vagina. Here, where maleness gathers to a quintessence of itself, there can be no insincerity, there can be no hiding; for sheer nakedness, there is nothing like a hopeful phallus; its aggressive shape is indivisible from its tender-skinned vulnerability. The act of intercourse, from the point of view of a consenting female, has an element of mothering, of enwrapment, of merciful concealment, even. The male body, for this interval, is tucked out of harm's way.

6   To inhabit a male body, then, is to feel somewhat detached from it. It is not an enemy, but not entirely a friend. Our essence seems to lie not in cells and muscles but in the traces our thoughts and actions inscribe on the air. The male body skims the surface of nature's deep, wherein the blood and pain and mysterious cravings

of women perpetuate the species. Participating less in nature's processes than the female body, the male body gives the impression—false—of being exempt from time. Its powers of strength and reach descend in early adolescence, along with acne and sweaty feet, and depart, in imperceptible increments, after thirty or so. It surprises me to discover, when I remove my shoes and socks, the same paper-white hairless ankles that struck me as pathetic when observed them on my father. I felt betrayed when, in some tumble of touch football twenty years ago, I heard my tibia snap; and when, between two reading engagements in Cleveland, my appendix tried to burst; and when, the other day, not for the first time, there arose to my nostrils out of my own body the musty attic smell my grandfather's body had.

7   A man's body does not betray its tenant as rapidly as a woman's. Never as fine and lovely, it has less distance to fall; what rugged beauty it has is wrinkle-proof. It keeps its capability of procreation indecently long. Unless intense athletic demands are made on it, the thing serves well enough to sixty, which is my age now. From here on, it's chancy. There are no breasts or ovaries to admit cancer to the male body, but the prostate, that awkwardly located little source of seminal fluid, shows the strain of sexual function with fits of hysterical cell replication, and all that beer and potato chips add up in the coronary arteries. A writer, whose physical equipment can be minimal, as long as it gets him to the desk, the lectern, and New York City once in a while, cannot but be grateful to his body, especially to his eyes, those tender and intricate sites where the brain extrudes from the skull, and to his hands, which hold the pen or tap the keyboard. His body has been, not himself exactly, but a close pal, pot-bellied and balding like most of his other pals now. A man and his body are like a boy and the buddy who has a driver's license and the use of his father's car for the evening; he goes along, gratefully, for the ride.

DISPOSABLE ROCKET

Exploring Language

aggregate: on the whole, or combined. Byron means that shaving for men—because it's a daily nuisance—on the whole may equal the agony of childbirth for women, which occurs less frequently.

androgynous: appearing partly male, partly female; of unclear gender.

chasm: a deep opening in the earth; sometimes refers to a wide difference in feelings, thoughts, or interests.

cosmogonies: theories about the origin of the universe.

frenzy: wild excitement or derangement; extreme agitation.

ignoble: common, of low birth or origin; second rate; coarse; lacking refinement.

increments: stages of increasing number or value.

imperceptible: undetectable or unnoticeable; slight or minimal.

parturition: childbirth.

parapet: a balcony or low wall along the edge of a roof.

polymorphous: assuming or having many forms (*poly* means many or several).

portents: a sign of the future; an omen.

post-simian: after the apes (the prefix *post* means after).

tenancy: a tenant is someone who rents or occupies land or property, so tenancy means possession or status as a tenant.

quintessence: the most typical example or epitome; the purest or most perfect form.

Note: For pronunciation, go to dictionary.com, search the word, and click on the speaker icon.

USAGE Examine the passage where Updike uses the word *cosmogonies.* Why would he use this word in the same context with feminism?

Thinking and Talking Points

1. Updike writes, "The space that interests men is outer." How does he think it differs from female space? Do you agree or disagree? Why?
2. What other comparisons or contrasts—other than space—does Updike

make between males and females? Do you agree with him? Explain.

3. Updike claims that "To inhabit a male body, then, is to feel somewhat detached from it." Are males detached from their bodies? How is that different from females' relationship with their bodies?

4. Look up information on the gods and goddess—Diana, Dionysus, Mars, and Venus—that Updike mentions, either on the Internet or in a dictionary of mythology. What point is he trying to make about our view of the human body? Think of the types of ads Updike mentions. Do you agree with his assertions? You might also search for images to help form a conclusion.

5. In what way is a rocket "disposable"? What qualities does the male body share with a disposable rocket? What other metaphors does Updike use? Do they tie together a common theme or idea in the essay?

6. Updike writes that his subconscious was "more honest" with him as a child. What do you think he means? Is your subconscious less honest now than when you were younger?

Styling

Many writers use lists of specific examples beaded together in one long sentence to give a feeling of continuity or chaos, excitement or enormity. In "Disposable Rocket," Updike creates a vivid list to illustrate what he calls male "space":

> The space that interests men is outer. The fly ball high against the sky, the long pass spiraling overhead, the jet fighter like a scarcely visible pinpoint nozzle laying down its vapor trail at forty thousand feet, the gazelle haunch flickering just beyond arrow-reach, the uncountable stars sprinkled on their great black wheel, the horizon, the mountaintop, the quasar—these bring portents with them, and awaken a sense of relation with the invisible, with the empty.

Notice the structure of this sentence. Updike first makes his list—each item in the series separated with a comma—followed by a dash, followed by a complete sentence.

PRACTICE Fill in the blanks below with a list to go with each sentence. Don't resort to using all one-word objects. Notice that Updike sometimes describes or uses simile, "the jet fighter like a scarcely visible pin-point nozzle laying down its vapor trail at forty thousand feet."

_____ , _____ , _____ ,
_____ , _____ , _____ ,
_____ —these are a few of my favorite things.
_____ , _____ , _____ ,
_____ , _____ , _____ ,
_____ —all annoyances I've learned to live with.

_____ , _____ , _____ ,
_____ , _____ , _____ ,
_____ —that was the best summer of my life.

YOU TRY IT Based on the Updike model, write five sentences of your own containing long lists. Use this sentence style in your next writing assignment.

Teaming Up

1. **Warm-up for Writing Idea #1.** Before class, do a quick freewrite or journal entry about a dream you had and what you think the dream means. You might consult a dream dictionary if you're stuck. In your group, describe your dream, and ask the other team members for their interpretations. Discuss whether your analysis matches your class-mates'. What did you learn about yourself or other group members?

2. **Warm-up for Writing Idea #2.** Have each member of the group research the painting by Botticelli, *Birth of Venus* (available on the Internet), and do a freewrite describing her body type; then, write about what you think society considers the ideal female body type today. Compare your responses. Discuss how Botticelli's depiction of the ideal woman might differ from today's view. Who would be today's Venus?

Writing Ideas

1. Updike writes about the act of falling being prominent in his dreams when he was a boy. Think about a dream you had as a child—or maybe a more recent dream—and write an essay discussing what the dream meant, how it figured into events in your life. Explain in what way your subconscious might have been "more honest" with you as a child.

You might compare a dream you had as a child to an adult dream.

2. Research visual depictions of the gods and goddesses Updike mentions in his essay—Venus, Diana, Mars, Dionysus. Write an essay comparing each god and goddess to today's popular models. Is there a big change in our view of the ideal male and female image as Updike indicates? Why might we be moving toward a more androgynous ideal?

3. Think of an object that makes a good metaphor for a member of your family. Write an essay explaining how this person is like the object, but give at least three qualities that the person shares with the object, explaining in detail what they have in common. For example, if your mother is old fashioned in her views, has a tarnished halo—meaning you discovered something shocking about her—but puts on a respectable or prudish front, you might use an antique silver teapot as the metaphor, explaining how she holds old-fashioned—antiquated—notions about gender roles (girls cook, boys take out the trash, for example), but you found out she paid her way through college working in a strip joint when you thought she was above reproach (tarnished like silver), yet she seems prudish (gets offended at an off-color joke or won't let you wear a mini-skirt).

Essay Connections

Bernard Cooper's "Burl's" details his childhood epiphany concerning his sexual identity.

THE BLACK WIDOW

Gordon Grice

Professor of English and humanities, spiderololgist Gordon Grice eloquently explores the brutal world of the black widow spider, at the same time busting our misconceptions and urban legends about this misunderstood arachnid. His essays have been published in Harper's, High Plains Literary Review (the source of this essay), and Best American Essays 1996. He also has a book aptly titled The Red Hourglass.

DUSTBIN OF HISTORY AND CULTURE

BOUFFANT: A hairdo where the hair has been teased into a high, puffy dome on top of the head.
GARGOYLE: An architectural adornment that spouts water out of the rain gutters of buildings; the gargoyle, originally lion heads like those on the Parthenon in Athens, became associated with more grotesque beasts in the Middle Ages.
LYRE: A stringed instrument related to the harp, originating in ancient Greece.

1   I hunt Black Widow. When I find one, I capture it. I have found them in discarded wheels and tires and under railroad ties. I have found them in house foundations and cellars, in automotive shops and toolsheds, in water meters and rock gardens, against fences and in cinderblock walls. I have found them in a hospital and in the den of a rattlesnake, and once on the bottom of the chair I was sitting in.

2   Sometimes I raise a generation or two in captivity. The egg sacs produce a hundred or more pinpoint cannibals, each leaving a trail of gleaming light in the air, the group of them eventually producing a glimmering tangle in which most of them die, eaten by stronger sibs. Finally I separate the three or four survivors and feed them bigger game.

3   Once I let several egg sacs hatch out in a container about eighteen inches on a side, a tight wooden box with a sliding glass top. As I tried to move the box one day, the lid slid off and I fell, hands first, into the mass of young widows. Most were still translucent newborns, their bodies a swirl of brown and cream. A few of the females had eaten enough to molt; they had the beginnings of their blackness.

Their tangle of broken web clung to my forearms. They felt like trickling water in my arm hairs.

4   I walked out into the open air and raised my arms into the stiff wind. The widows answered the wind with new strands of web and drifted away, their bodies gold in the late sun. In about ten minutes my arms carried nothing but old web and the husks of spiderlings eaten by their sibs.

5   I have never been bitten.

6   The black widow has the ugliest web of any spider. The orb weavers make those seemingly delicate nets that poets have traditionally used as symbols of imagination, order, and perfection. The sheet web spiders weave crisp linens on the grass. But the widow makes messy-looking tangles in the corners and bends of things and under logs and debris. Often the web is littered with leaves. Beneath it lie the husks of insect prey, their antennae still as gargoyle horns, cut loose and dropped; on them and the surrounding ground are splashes of the spider's white urine, which looks like bird guano and smells of ammonia even at a distance of several feet. This fetid material draws scavengers—ants, sow bugs, crickets, roaches, and so on—which become tangled in vertical strands of silk reaching from the ground up into the web. The widow comes down and, with a bicycling of the hind pair of legs, throws gummy silk onto this new prey.

7   When the prey is seriously tangled but still struggling, the widow cautiously descends and bites the creature, usually on a leg joint. This is a killing bite; it pumps neurotoxin into the victim. The widow will deliver a series of bites as the creature dies, injecting substances that liquefy the organs. Finally it will settle down to suck the liquefied innards out of the prey, changing position two or three times to get it all.

8   Before the eating begins, and sometimes before the victim dies from the slow venom, the widow usually moves it higher into the web. It attaches some line to the prey with a leg-bicycling toss, moves up the vertical web strand that originally snagged the prey, crosses a diagonal strand upward to a higher point on a different vertical strand, and here secures the line. It has thus dragged the prey's body up off the ground. The whole operation is like that of a person moving a load with block and tackle. It occurs in three dimensions—as opposed to the essentially two-dimensional operations of orb weavers and sheet weavers.

9   You can't watch the widow in this activity very long without realizing that its web is not a mess at all but an efficient machine. It allows

complicated uses of leverage and also, because of its complexity of connections, lets the spider feel a disturbance anywhere in the web—usually with enough accuracy to tell the difference at a distance between a raindrop or leaf and viable prey.

10   The web is also constructed in a certain relationship to movements of air so that flying insects are drawn into it. This fact partly explains why widow webs are so often found in the face-down side of discarded car wheels—the wheel is essentially a vault of still air that protects the web, but the central hole at the top allows airborne insects to fall in. An insect that is clumsy and flies in random hops, such as a June beetle, is especially vulnerable to this trap. The widow often seems to choose her building sites according to indigenous smells rather than creating her own stinking waste pile from scratch. The webs turn up, for example, in piles of trash and rotting wood. A few decades ago, the widow was notorious for building its home inside the works of outdoor toilets. Scraping around with a stick before using the toilet was a common practice.

11   The architectural complexities of the widow web do not particularly impress the widows. They move around in these webs almost blind, yet they never misstep or get lost. In fact, a widow forcibly removed from its web and put back at a different point does not seem confused; it will quickly return to its habitual resting place. Furthermore, widows never snare themselves, even though every strand of the web is a potential trap. A widow will spend a few minutes every day coating the clawed tips of its legs with the oil that lets it walk the sticky strands. It secretes the oil from its mouth, coating its legs like a cat cleaning its paws.

12   The human mind cannot grasp the complex functions of the web but must infer them. The widow constructs it by instinct. A brain smaller than a pinhead contains the blueprints, precognitive memories the widow unfolds out of itself into actuality. I have never dissected with enough precision or delicacy to get a good specimen of the black widow brain, but I did glimpse one once. A widow was struggling to wrap a praying mantis when the insect's forelegs, like scalpels mounted on lightning, sliced away the spider's carapace and left exposed the clear droplet of bloody brain.

13   Widows reportedly eat mice, toads, tarantulas—anything that wanders into that remarkable web. I have never witnessed a widow performing a gustatory act of that magnitude, but I have seen them eat scarab beetles heavy as pecans; carabid beetles strong enough to

prey on wolf spiders; cockroaches more than an inch long; and hundreds of other arthropods of various sizes. Widows begin life by eating their siblings. An adult female will fight any other female; the winner often eats the loser. A popular game among Mexican children is to stage such fights and bet on the outcome. The children put the widows on a stick and pass it around so that everyone can see. Sometimes one female ties another up and leaves without killing her. I have come across such black pearls wrapped in silk and, upon peeling off the skin, seen the pearls unfold their legs and rush away.

14   The widow gets her name by eating her lover, though this does not always happen. He distinguishes himself from ordinary prey by playing her web like a lyre. Sometimes she eats him without first copulating; sometimes she snags him as he withdraws his palp from her genital pore. Sometimes he leaves unharmed after mating; in this case, he soon withers and dies on his own. I have witnessed male and female living in platonic relationships in one web. The males' palps, still swollen with sperm, proved that these relationships had not been sexual.

15   Many widows will eat as much as opportunity gives. One aggressive female had an abdomen a little bigger than an English pea. She snared a huge cockroach and spent several hours subduing it, then three days consuming it. Her abdomen swelled to the size of a largish marble, its glossy black stretching to a tight red-brown. With a different widow, I decided to see whether that appetite was really insatiable. I collected dozens of large crickets and grasshoppers and began to drop them into her web at a rate of one every three or four hours. After catching and consuming her tenth victim, this bloated widow fell from her web, landing on her back. She remained in this position for hours, making only feeble attempts to move. Then she died.

16   The first thing people ask when they hear about my fascination with the widow is why I am not afraid. The truth is that my fascination is rooted in fear.

17   I have childhood memories that partly account for my fear. When I was six my mother took my sister and me to the cellar of our farmhouse and told us to watch as she killed a widow. With great ceremony she produced a long stick (I am tempted to say a ten-foot pole) and, narrating her technique in exactly the hushed voice she used for discussing religion or sex, went to work. Her flashlight beam found a point halfway up the cement wall where two marbles hung together— one crisp white, the other a glossy black. My mother ran her stick

through the dirty silver web around them, and as it tore it sounded like the crackling of paper in fire. This sound is unique to the widow's powerful web—anybody with a little experience can tell a widow's work from another spider's by ear. The black marble rose on thin legs to fight off the intruder. As the plump abdomen wobbled across the wall, it seemed to be constantly throwing those legs out of its path. The impression it gave was of speed and frantic anger, but actually a widow's movements outside the web are slow and inefficient. My mother smashed the widow onto the stick and carried it up into the light. It was still kicking its remaining legs. Mom scraped it against the sidewalk, grinding it to a paste. Then she returned for the white marble—the widow's egg sac. This, too, came to an abrasive end.

18   My mother's stated purpose was to teach us how to recognize and deal with a dangerous creature we would probably encounter on the farm. But of course we also took the understanding that widows were actively malevolent, that they waited in dark places to ambush us, that they were worthy of ritual disposition, like an enemy whose death is not sufficient but must be followed with the murder of his children and the salting of his land and whose unclean remains must not touch our hands.

19   The odd thing is that so many people, some of whom presumably did not first encounter the widow in such an atmosphere of mystic reverence, hold the widow in awe. Various friends have told me that the widow always devours her mate, or that her bite is always fatal to humans—in fact, it almost never is. I have heard told for truth that goods imported from the Orient are likely infested with widows and that women with bouffant hairdos have died of widow infestation. Any contradiction of such tales is received as if it were a proclamation of atheism.

20   The most startling contribution to the widow's mythical status I have ever encountered was *Black Widow: America's Most Poisonous Spider,* a book that appeared in 1945. Between genuine scientific observations, the authors present the widow as a lurking menace with a taste for human flesh. They describe the experiments of other investigators; one involved inducing a widow to bite a laboratory rat on the penis, after which event the rat "appeared to become dejected and depressed." Perhaps the most psychologically revealing passage is the authors' quotation from another writer, who said the "deadliest Communists are like the black widow spider; they conceal their red underneath."

21   We project our archetypal terrors onto the widow. It is black; it avoids the light; it is a voracious carnivore. Its red markings suggest blood. Its name, its sleek, rounded form invite a strangely sexual discomfort; the widow becomes an emblem for a man's fear of extending himself into the blood and darkness of a woman, something like the legendary Eskimo vampire that takes the form of a fanged vagina.

22   The widow's venom is, of course, a soundly pragmatic reason for fear. The venom contains a neurotoxin that can produce sweats, vomiting, swelling, convulsions, and dozens of other symptoms. The variation in symptoms from one person to the next is remarkable. The constant is pain. A useful question for a doctor trying to diagnose an uncertain case: "Is this the worst pain you've ever felt?" A "yes" suggests a diagnosis of black widow bite. Occasionally people die from widow bites. The very young and the very old are especially vulnerable. Some people seem to die not from the venom but from the infection that may follow; because of its habitat, the widow carries dangerous microbes.

23   Some researchers hypothesized that the virulence of the venom was necessary for killing beetles of the scarab family. This family contains thousands of species, including the June beetle and the famous dung beetle the Egyptians thought immortal. All the scarabs have thick, strong bodies and unusually tough exoskeletons, and many of them are common prey for the widow. The tough hide was supposed to require a particularly nasty venom. As it turns out, the venom is thousands of times more virulent than necessary for this purpose. The whole idea is full of the widow's glamour: an emblem of eternal life killed by a creature whose most distinctive blood-colored markings people invariably describe as an hourglass.

24   No one has ever offered a sufficient explanation for the dangerous venom. It provides no evolutionary advantages: all of the widow's prey items would find lesser toxins fatal, and there is no particular benefit in killing or harming larger animals. A widow that bites a human being or other large animal is likely to be killed. Evolution does sometimes produce such flowers of natural evil—traits that are neither functional nor vestigial but utterly pointless. Natural selection favors the inheritance of useful characteristics that arise from random mutation and tends to extinguish disadvantageous traits. All other characteristics, the ones that neither help nor hinder survival, are preserved or extinguished at random as mutation links them with

useful or harmful traits. Many people—even many scientists—assume that every animal is elegantly engineered for its ecological niche, that every bit of an animal's anatomy and behavior has a functional explanation. This assumption is false. Nothing in evolutionary theory sanctions it; fact refutes it.

25   We want the world to be an ordered room, but in a corner of that room there hangs an untidy web. Here the analytical minds find an irreducible mystery, a motiveless evil in nature, and the scientist's vision of evil comes to match the vision of a God-fearing country woman with a ten-foot pole. No idea of the cosmos as elegant design accounts for the widow. No idea of a benevolent God is comfortable in a world with the widow. She hangs in her web, that marvel of design, and defies teleology.

THE BLACK WIDOW

Exploring Language

abrasive: in this context, harsh or rough. Can also refer to personality.

archetypal: an archetype is a recurrent character type, plot, symbol, or theme of seemingly universal significance; Carl Jung believed human beings have a collective subconscious and therefore have similar dreams. For example, dreams of flying or falling occur in almost every culture, as do literary archetypes like "Cinderella," which has variants in virtually every culture, going back as far as 500 B.C. China.

arthropods: a scientific term for animals with jointed limbs, segmented bodies (think ants), and exoskeletons (instead of skeletons, a hard outer shell), which includes insects, mollusks (snails), and crustaceans (lobster, shrimp).

carapace: protective shell or shell-like covering.

fetid: having a bad odor.

glamour: fascinating, attractive, or alluring; charm, enchantment.

gustatory: relating to the sense of taste.

indigenous: occurring naturally in a particular region or environment, as in "indigenous species."

insatiable: impossible to satisfy.

irreducible: cannot be made smaller or simpler.

malevolent: vicious ill-will.

neurotoxin: a toxin or poison that damages or destroys nerve tissue.

pragmatic: practical.

teleology: study of design in nature.

vestigial: body part left over from evolution that no longer has a purpose.

virulence: in this context, intensely poisonous.

voracious: eager to consume large quantities of food.

Note: For pronunciation, go to dictionary.com, search the word, and click on the speaker icon.

USAGE Look up "abrasive" for meanings other than the one in the Exploring Language list and use it in a sentence that implies one of those meanings.

Thinking and Talking Points

1. Reread the introduction to Grice's essay. Does the first sentence hook the reader? Why or why not? What is the effect of his listing all of the places where he has found black widows?
2. Find where the essay refutes our preconceived notions of the black widow. Did you hold these same ideas about the spider? How does Grice dispel these notions?
3. What is Grice's point in writing this essay? Is he trying to persuade you or merely inform? Defend your stand with evidence from the essay.
4. Hunt down the numerous **metaphors** and **similes** in this essay. How do they help convey an attitude about the black widow?
5. How does the essay provide information that helps the reader hunt for black widows (if desired)?
6. Grice writes in paragraph #23, "The whole idea is full of the widow's glamour: an emblem of eternal life killed by a creature whose most distinctive blood-colored markings people invariably describe an hourglass." What does the hourglass have to do with glamour? How is spider "glamorous"? See the definition under "Exploring Language."
7. What larger philosophical idea does Grice imply in his conclusion?

Styling

Many students—and non-students—think of punctuation as a mysterious code known only to English teachers that has very little purpose other than creating pause for the reader. While punctuation does create pause, it also helps strengthen your writer's voice, to say what you want to say, dramatically or demurely, simply or with complexity. Punctuation is style.

You might have noticed that Gordon Grice uses dashes in different ways for dramatic interruption or pause. Study the three ways he uses dashes: with a simple interruption, with a list that interrupts a sentence, and at the end of a sentence for emphasis.

Dashes with a simple interrupter:

> Many people—even many scientists—assume that every animal is elegantly engineered for its ecological niche, that every bit of an animal's anatomy and behavior has a functional explanation.

Notice that if you remove the words enclosed with dashes, the sentence still makes sense:

Many people assume that every animal is elegantly engineered for its ecological niche, that every bit of an animal's anatomy and behavior has a function explanation.

When practicing the use of dashes with an interrupter, test the sentence to see if you can remove the material within the dashes and still have a complete, coherent sentence. You might choose to use commas with an interrupter, or parentheses, but dashes draw attention to the interrupter "even many scientists," alerting the reader to the fact that even scientists—usually credited with logical thinking—make wrong assumptions.

Hint: Avoid using dashes with simple adjectives or prepositional phrases.

Dashes with an internal list that interrupts the sentence:

The fetid material draws scavengers—ants, sow bugs, crickets, roaches, and so on—which become tangled in vertical strands of silk reaching from the ground up into the web.

Again, you could take out the list and dashes and the sentence would still be grammatically correct and make sense: "The fetid material draws scavengers which become tangled in vertical strands of silk reaching from the ground up into the web."

CAUTION   In the sentence above, dashes become essential; without the dashes, the word "scavengers" crashes into "ants," wreaking havoc with the sentence's meaning. If you use commas instead of dashes here, your reader might think "scavengers" is part of the list that includes ants rather than ants being an example of a scavenger in a list of other such bugs.

Dashes at the end for emphasis:

Widows reportedly eat mice, toads, tarantulas—anything that wanders into that remarkable web.

Then she returned for the white marble—the widow's egg sac.

Various friends have told me that the widow always devours her mate, or that her bite is always fatal to humans—in fact, it almost never is.

Her flashlight beam found a point halfway up the cement wall where two marbles hung together—one crisp white, the other a glossy black.

In these examples, Grice might have chosen to use a comma at the end of his sentence to connect non-essential or extra material, but the dash creates a bit of drama, a longer pause, lingering on those set-off words, both on the page and in the reader's mind.

PRACTICE   In each of the sentences below, fill in the blanks with appropriate material.

Simple Interrupter

The bird— _____ —cautiously flitted down to the bird feeder.

List That Interrupts

Those flowers— _____ , _____ ,
_____ , and _____ —do not grow well on that side of the house.

At the End for Emphasis

Hummingbirds will attack almost anything— _____

YOU TRY IT   Write five of each type of dash sentence: five with simple interrupters, five with a list, and five with one dash at the end for emphasis.

Teaming Up

1. **Warm-up for Writing Idea #2:** Brainstorm urban legends you've heard about or read on the Internet. What fear does each legend prey on? Do you find these hoaxes helpful or harmful?

2. **Warm-up for Writing Idea #3:** Bring in a legend, fable, or story about an animal. Read all of the stories in your group and discuss what each story reveals about the culture. Choose one story to read to the rest of the class. Pick someone to read the story—or you can share the responsibility—and another member(s) to present your ideas. There are fables with "The Courage of Turtles" by Edward Hoagland. Many myths are available online.

Writing Ideas

1. Hunt another insect, perhaps one people usually think of as creepy or one that you fear: another type of spider, a preying mantis, a beetle, a centipede, or whatever you fancy. Be sure it's one that can be found in your immediate area. You might need to look up information on the creature's habits like what it eats, what habitat it likes, what time of year it can easily be located. Write an essay that attempts to persuade the reader of the creature's worthiness; maybe it's environmentally helpful or a friend to gardeners. Maybe it's simply fascinating. Use description, **figurative language**, and debunking of preconceived ideas about the critter.

2. A lot of urban legends get circulated on the Internet; you might have been victim to some of these untruths, usually sent as warnings to beware of some danger lurking around the next corner. Before the Internet, such stories circulated through word of mouth. Gather some of these stories, and write an essay that attempts to explain our fascination with these hoaxes and argues whether or not they're helpful, either warning of dangers that *could* occur or the opposite, that they incite fear and paranoia in an otherwise safe environment. Are they cautionary tales or fear-mongering?

3. Choose an animal and research myths and legends from different cultures about that animal. You might try Native American myths and legends, legends from around the world, *Aesop's Fables,* or a collection of animal myths from almost any country. Choose at least three different cultures and write an essay that explains how the culture views that creature and what that view reveals about the culture, its fears or hopes, its view about animals in general.

Essay Connections

Other animal essays in Sparks include "The Courage of Turtles" by Edward Hoagland and "Joyas Voladoras" by Brian Doyle.

Essays that Argue and Define

INTRODUCTION

Argument and definition essays provoke controversy and stir debate, hopefully causing readers to consider the road-less-traveled angle of a topic or contemplate a word's meaning. They attempt to provide answers to provocative questions and broaden readers' viewpoints by breaking down stereotypes: Is our romantic view of the American cowboy accurate? What does it mean to grow up black and middle class? Are Americans anti-child compared to other countries? Does Disney butcher the original fairytales in favor of "vapid" family entertainment? Is it "possible to stop all drug addiction in the United States within a very short time"? Is there an epidemic of celebrity in America?

An argument doesn't have to be about the beat-into-the-ground issues like gun control, the death penalty, and mercy killing. There is very little left to say about these tired standards; good writers strive for originality, at least in the angle explored if not the topic itself. Gore Vidal writes about drugs, but with a bold approach that can shock some readers. As you read, study the writers' tactics, how they support their points and refute opposition, how they use style to their advantage—how they get the reader to at least think about the side of an issue he or she may not agree with. An essay that surprises or gets the reader to think is something worth writing.

THE LITTLE MERMAID

Pauline Kael

Pauline Kael (1919–2001) wrote film reviews for the The New Yorker magazine from the 1960s until her retirement in 1991. For a collection of her reviews, see the book For Keeps. In this short review, Kael lambastes Disney for turning Hans Christian Andersen's The Little Mermaid into "a bland reworking of old Disney fairy tales, featuring a teen-age tootsie in a flirty seashell bra."

For a copy of this essay, visit the Links tab on the companion website: www.grtep.com.

THE LITTLE MERMAID

Exploring Language

aesthetic: pleasing to the senses; often refers to artistic taste.
peerlessly: peerless means unrivaled, unequaled, unmatched.
simpering: smiling in a silly way.
tootsie: slang for female, akin to cutie-pie, but can also imply a
woman of ill repute (prostitute).
vapid: dull, flat, boring, unimaginative.
Note: For pronunciation, go to dictionary.com, search the word, and
click on the speaker icon.

USAGE Use at least one of the Exploring Language words in your next
writing assignment, or look one up in a thesaurus and choose a lively
substitute.

Thinking and Talking Points

1. Kael writes that in the original version of *The Little Mermaid,* the mermaid will gain an immortal soul if she marries the prince, a detail
Disney left out. Even though you may not have read the original story
or seen the film, what do you think might be lost in the story by omitting the idea of gaining an immortal soul?
2. How convincing is Kael's review? List specific evidence in the review
that did or did not convince you.
3. Kael writes, "This is a technologically sophisticated cartoon with just
about all the simpering old Disney values in place." What are Disney
values? How are they simpering?
4. Kael asks, "Are we trying to put kids into some sort of moral-aesthetic
safe house?" Are parents "desperate for harmless family entertainment"? Do children lose out, as Kael indicates, by being shielded from
the classics in favor of blander cartoon versions?

Styling

Warm-up for Writing Idea #1. Specific examples are necessary in any
essay; if you don't support your point with specific examples, your

reader will think you don't know your subject. Kael cites several children's books and films, holding them up as standards, comparing them to Disney, illustrating Disney cartoons' inferiority. She didn't just write, "Other books and films are better." She reminds us of specific children's stories, hoping we'll remember and think, "I loved *Where the Wild Things Are* when I was a kid."

If you tell a friend, "I couldn't sleep all night because of the noises," your friend will mostly likely sympathize and ask, "What noises?" You would then proceed to give specific examples: somebody snoring, a barking dog, dripping faucet. Here's a paragraph from F. Scott Fitzgerald's *The Great Gatsby:*

> I couldn't sleep all night; a fog-horn was groaning incessantly on the Sound, and I tossed half sick between grotesque reality and savage frightening dreams. Toward dawn I heard a taxi go up Gatsby's drive and immediately I jumped out of bed and began to dress—I felt that I had something to tell him, something to warn him about and morning would be too late.

The groaning fog-horn, the frightening dreams, and the taxi breathe life into the paragraph.

PRACTICE Think of a genre of films—action/adventure, comedy, science fiction, horror, drama—and make a list of titles from that genre.

YOU TRY IT Using three or four of the items from your above list—you may have to alter the list to fit the **topic sentence**—write a paragraph with a topic sentence that makes a claim about that genre (something like "Most horror films attempt to scare the viewer with cheap gore-and-guts rather than a strong plot"). In a sentence or two, explain why each film title you chose from the list supports that topic sentence.

Teaming Up

1. In your group, discuss the children's literature and film examples Kael mentions in her essay, or other childhood favorites. What do you remember about the stories? What makes them literature rather than kitsch? If you have time, read one of these stories before discussion.

2. Kael writes, "They've been imprinted with Disney-style kitsch." In your group, make a list of all the places in our culture where you see Disney products or images and list companies you know Disney owns. Discuss in what ways a company like Disney might influence

society. Use your list and discussion to co-write a paragraph. The topic sentence should express an opinion; you might attempt to answer this question: have we been "imprinted with Disney-style kitsch"? Explain how the examples you use from the list support your opinion. If your group disagrees, it's okay to split up and write two paragraphs with different opinions.

Writing Ideas

1. Use the paragraph from the Styling section as a supporting paragraph of a larger essay.
2. Almost every culture has a version of the "Cinderella" fairy tale. Read several Cinderella versions. Choose two of the stories from different cultures and write a comparison/contrast essay. What do the differences tell us about the culture?
3. Watch another Disney fairy tale film and read the older version of the story—many of the written stories are from Grimms' fairy tales. Write an essay comparing the two, making a judgment about which story is more meaningful and why. Or read the original *The Little Mermaid* by Hans Christian Andersen and do a more in-depth comparison of it to the Disney version. (Available online.)

Essay Connections

Other essays critiquing culture include "The Culture of Celebrity" by Joseph Epstein, Preface From *The Dumbest Generation* by Mark Bauerlein, "A Dark and Stormy Knight: Why Batman?" by Travis Langley, and "Somebody's Baby" by Barbara Kingsolver.

DRUGS

Gore Vidal

Gore Vidal (1925-2012) has written essays and novels, among them Myra Breckenridge (1968), one of his most famous. More recent works include The Golden Age, a novel, and The American Presidency, Vidal's view of the history of this highest office and the men who have served in it. In this essay, Vidal argues that we should legalize all drugs and provide warning labels, as we do for cigarettes. He states, "This will require heroic honesty. Don't say that marijuana is addictive or dangerous when it is neither, as millions of people know—unlike 'speed,' which kills most unpleasantly, or heroin, which is addictive and difficult to kick."

DUSTBIN OF HISTORY AND CULTURE

FU MANCHU: A Chinese villain with a long mustache who appears in stories by Sax Rohmer, later made into films—the character was usually played by a white man.

GNP: Gross National Product.

DR. SPOCK: Benjamin Spock, child pediatrician who wrote *The Common Sense Book of Baby and Child Care* (1946), a controversial book which advocated affection and more permissiveness toward children, and is believed to have had a major impact on child rearing.

DR. LEARY: Timothy Leary, identified with the hippie subculture. In a 1967 speech, he coined the phrase "you must turn on, tune in, and drop out."

1   It is possible to stop most drug addiction in the United States within a very short time. Simply make all drugs available and sell them at cost. Label each drug with a precise description of what effect—good and bad—the drug will have on the taker. This will require heroic honesty. Don't say that marijuana is addictive or dangerous when it is neither, as millions of people know—unlike "speed," which kills most unpleasantly, or heroin, which is addictive and difficult to kick.

2   For the record, I have tried—once—almost every drug and liked none, disproving the popular Fu Manchu theory that a single sniff of opium will enslave the mind. Nevertheless, many drugs are bad for certain people to take and they should be told why in a sensible way.

3   Along with exhortation and warning, it might be good for our citizens to recall (or learn for the first time) that the United States was the creation of men who believed that each man has the right to do what he wants with his own life as long as he does not interfere with his neighbor's pursuit of happiness (that his neighbor's idea of happiness is persecuting others does confuse matters a bit).

4   This is a startling notion to the current generation of Americans. They reflect a system of public education which has made the Bill of Rights, literally, unacceptable to a majority of high school graduates (see the annual Purdue reports) who now form the "silent majority"—a phrase which that underestimated wit Richard Nixon took from Homer, who used it to describe the dead.

5   Now one can hear the warning rumble begin: if everyone is allowed to take drugs everyone will and the GNP will decrease, the Commies will stop us from making everyone free, and we shall end up a race of Zombies, passively murmuring "groovy" to one another. Alarming thought. Yet it seems most unlikely that any reasonably sane person will become a drug addict if he knows in advance what addiction is going to be like.

6   Is everyone reasonably sane? No. Some people will always become drug addicts just as some people will always become alcoholics, and it is just too bad. Every man, however, has the power (and should have the legal right) to kill himself if he chooses. But since most men don't, they won't be mainliners either. Nevertheless, forbidding people things they like or think they might enjoy only makes them want those things all the more. This psychological insight is, for some mysterious reason, perennially denied our governors.

7   It is a lucky thing for the American moralist that our country has always existed in a kind of time-vacuum: we have no public memory of anything that happened before last Tuesday. No one in Washington today recalls what happened during the years alcohol was forbidden to the people by a Congress that thought it had a divine mission to stamp out Demon Rum—launching, in the process, the greatest crime wave in the country's history, causing thousands of deaths from bad alcohol, and creating a general (and persisting) contempt among the citizenry for the laws of the United States.

8   The same thing is happening today. But the government has learned nothing from past attempts at prohibition, not to mention repression.

9   Last year when the supply of Mexican marijuana was slightly curtailed by the Feds, the pushers got the kids hooked on heroin

and deaths increased dramatically, particularly in New York. Whose fault? Evil men like the Mafiosi? Permissive Dr. Spock? Wild-eyed Dr. Leary? No.

10   The Government of the United States was responsible for those deaths. The bureaucratic machine has a vested interest in playing cops and robbers. Both the Bureau of Narcotics and the Mafia want strong laws against the sale and use of drugs because if drugs are sold at cost there would be no money in it for anyone.

11   If there was no money in it for the Mafia, there would be no friendly playground pushers, and addicts would not commit crimes to pay for the next fix. Finally, if there was no money in it, the Bureau of Narcotics would wither away, something they are not about to do without a struggle.

12   Will anything sensible be done? Of course not. The American people are as devoted to the idea of sin and its punishment as they are to making money—and fighting drugs is nearly as big a business as pushing them. Since the combination of sin and money is irresistible (particularly to the professional politician), the situation will only grow worse.

FOLLOW UP

DRUGS

Exploring Language

exhortation: language intended to encourage, excite, or provoke.
perennially: permanently, enduringly, constantly.
Note: For pronunciation, go to dictionary.com, search the word, and click on the speaker icon.

USAGE Locate *exhortation* in the essay and then look up synonyms. In what context does Vidal use the word? Now use the word in another context.

Thinking and Talking Points

1. Where in the essay does Vidal address and refute his opponents' views (those against drug legalization)? How well does he support his argument? Are there arguments from the other side he hasn't considered?
2. Reread paragraph #6. Do you think "forbidding people things they like or think they might enjoy only makes them want those things all the more"? Think of examples other than drugs.
3. Reread paragraphs #9 and #10. Explain what Vidal means by his statement, "The Government of the United States was responsible for those deaths." Do you agree or disagree with his reasoning? How does comparing the Bureau of Narcotics and the Mafia work in his favor?
4. Vidal writes, "The American people are as devoted to the idea of sin and its punishment as they are to making money—and fighting drugs is nearly as big a business as pushing them." Where in the essay does he support these statements? Do you agree or disagree with these ideas? Can you think of other examples that illustrate Americans are devoted to sin and its punishment?
5. Explain what Vidal means by his statement "we have no public memory of anything that happened before last Tuesday"? What examples does he use to support this statement?

Styling

You can use a colon to list items following a complete sentence or to give an explanation. Vidal writes:

> It's a lucky thing for the American moralist that our country has always existed in a kind of time-vacuum: we have no public memory of anything that happened before last Tuesday.

Notice that the phrase before the colon is a **complete sentence.** The phrase after the colon explains something in the complete sentence, in this instance, the time-vacuum. Although the sentence before the colon must be complete, what follows the colon can be either a complete or **incomplete sentence**. Here's another example of a sentence that uses a colon with an explanation; this is from Jamaica Kincaid's essay "On Seeing England for the First Time" (not in this book):

> I did not know then that this statement was meant to make me feel awe and small whenever I heard the word "England": awe at its existence, small because I was not from it.

Although the part before the colon forms a complete sentence, the phrase after the colon is incomplete, explaining "awe" and "small."

PRACTICE   After the colon in the following sentences, add a phrase or sentence that explains something in the main sentence.

Gore Vidal claims the government could end most drug addiction in the United States: _____

Some critics claim that *The Hunger Games* is not too far from current reality television shows: _____

YOU TRY IT   Create five sentences about your life—family members, hobbies, job—that use the colon with an explanation. Use this technique in your next writing assignment.

Teaming Up

1. Before coming to class, have each group member look up information on the Volstead Act. Share your information, and then compare what you've learned with the argument Vidal makes for legalizing drugs. Does he have a valid point? Can your group think of ways to refute him?

2. **Warm-up for Writing Idea #1.** Divide your group into two teams: one for legalizing drugs and one against. Don't worry about what side you really agree with. For critical thinking, you should be able to argue either side whether or not you agree. Do some research and prepare a debate. In class, debate the issue. Have an impartial judge—the teacher or another classmate—judge which side presents the strongest argument.

Writing Ideas

1. Gather information on the cost of the drug war—both economic and human—and write an essay that argues whether or not the Drug War is worth it. (See the Writing Strategies for Arguing section in this book.)

2. Throughout his essay, Vidal blames the government for the drug problem in America. Since this essay was written—1970—the drug war has raged on. Do some research to determine whether or not the drug problem has improved. Also gather information on the Iran-Contra affair. Write an essay that argues whether or not the drug situation in America has improved and to what degree the Iran-Contra affair supports Vidal's blaming the government.

Essay Connections

P. J. O'Rourke's "How to Drive Fast" satirizes drinking and driving. "The Chemist's War" by Deborah Blum recounts the government's poisoning of alcohol during Prohibition.

P. J. O'Rourke

P. J. O'Rourke is a humorist and former foreign correspondent for Rolling Stone. The following is an excerpt from an essay in his book Republican Party Reptiles. O'Rourke satirizes young people who insist on drinking or taking drugs and then driving a car.

DUSTBIN OF HISTORY AND CULTURE

CHIVAS: A type of whiskey.

SIGMUND FREUD: A 19th-century doctor who founded psychoanalysis and the theory called the Oedipus Complex, which says that children will have an erotic attachment to the parent of the opposite sex.

CHERYL TIEGS: A supermodel in the 1970s and 1980s (O'Rourke's age is showing).

ALBERTO ASCARI: An Italian race-car driver who was killed in the 1950s during a race.

THE ILIAD: Epic poem by Homer written sometime around the 9th century B.C., set in the final year of the Trojan War.

ADIRONDACKS: Mountains in New York State.

1   When it comes to taking chances, some people like to play poker or shoot dice; other people prefer to parachute jump, go rhino hunting, or climb ice floes, while still others engage in crime or marriage. But I like to get drunk and drive like a fool. Name me, if you can, a better feeling than the one you get when you're half a bottle of Chivas in the bag with a gram of coke up your nose and a teenage lovely pulling off her tube top in the next seat over while you're going a hundred miles an hour down a suburban side street. You'd have to watch the entire Mexican air force crash-land in a liquid petroleum gas storage facility to match this kind of thrill. If you ever have much more fun than that, you'll die of pure sensory overload, I'm here to tell you.

2   But wait. Let's pause and analyze *why* this particular matrix of activities is perceived as so highly enjoyable. I mean, aside from the teenage lovely pulling off her tube top in the next seat over. Ignoring that for a moment, let's look at the psychological factors conducive to placing positive emotional values on the sensory-end product of expe-

rientially produced excitation of the central nervous system and smacking into a lamppost. Is that any way to have fun? How would your mother feel if she knew you were doing this? She'd cry. She really would. And that's how you know it's fun. Anything that makes your mother cry is fun. Sigmund Freud wrote all about this. It's a well-known fact.

3   Of course, it's a shame to waste young lives behaving this way— speeding around all tanked up with your feet hooked in the steering wheel while your date crawls around on the floor mats opening zippers with her teeth and pounding on the accelerator with an empty liquor bottle. But it wouldn't be taking a chance if you weren't risking *something*. And even if it is a shame to waste young lives behaving this way, it is definitely cooler than risking old lives behaving this way. I mean, so what if some fifty-eight-year-old butthead gets a load on and starts playing Death Race 2000 in the rush-hour traffic jam? What kind of chance is he taking? He's just waiting around to see what kind of cancer he gets anyway. But if young, talented *you*, with all of life's possibilities at your fingertips, you and the future Cheryl Tiegs there, so fresh, so beautiful—if the two of *you* stake your handsome heads on a single roll of the dice in life's game of stop-the-semi— now *that's* taking chances! Which is why old people rarely risk their lives. It's not because they're chicken—they just have too much dignity to play for small stakes.

4   Now a lot of people say to me, "Hey, P.J., you like to drive fast. Why not join a responsible organization, such as the Sports Car Club of America, and enjoy participation in sports car racing? That way you could drive as fast as you wish while still engaging in a well-regulated spectator sport that is becoming more popular each year." No thanks. In the first place, if you ask me, those guys are a bunch of tweedy old barf mats who like to talk about things like what necktie they wore to Alberto Ascari's funeral. And in the second place, they won't let me drive drunk. They expect me to go out there and smash into things and roll over on the roof and catch fire and burn to death when I'm sober. They must think I'm crazy. That stuff scares me. I have to get completely shit-faced to even think about driving fast. How can you have a lot of exciting thrills when you're so terrified that you wet yourself all the time? That's not fun. It's just *not fun* to have exciting thrills when you're scared. Take the heroes of the *Iliad*, for instance—they really had some exciting thrills, and were they scared? No. They were drunk. Every chance they could get. And so

am I, and I'm not going out there and have a horrible car wreck until somebody brings me a cocktail.

5   Also, it's important to be drunk because being drunk keeps your body all loose, and that way, if you have an accident or anything, you'll sort of roll with the punches and not get banged up so bad. For example, there was this guy I heard about who was really drunk and was driving through the Adirondacks. He got sideswiped by a bus and went head-on into another car, which knocked him off a bridge, and he plummeted 150 feet into a ravine. I mean, it killed him and everything, but if he hadn't been so drunk and loose, his body probably would have been banged up a lot worse—and you can imagine how much more upset his wife would have been when she went down to the morgue to identify him.

FOLLOW

HOW TO DRIVE FAST

Exploring Language

conducive: helping or contributing.
experientially: relating to experience.
matrix: a mold or pattern from which something else originates or develops.
Note: For pronunciation, go to dictionary.com, search the word, and click on the speaker icon.

USAGE   If you look matrix up in the dictionary, you'll see a collection of meanings. Try to explain in a sentence or two how the meaning given above applies to O'Rourke's phrase "matrix of activities."

Examine the sentence in which *conducive* appears (paragraph #2). O'Rourke does something English teachers call a "shift in diction," meaning the writer mixes formal words with casual ones. Usually writers avoid this shift. Why does O'Rourke purposely mingle dressed up words like *conducive* with the phrase "smacking into a lamppost"?

Rewrite the sentence where *experientially* appears (paragraph #2) using slang or casual language. Does the sentence lose some of its impact?

Thinking and Talking Points

1. This type of satire is tongue-in-cheek irony, which means the writer says the opposite of what he or she means. O'Rourke *says* he's in favor of drinking and driving, but he *means* just the opposite—drinking or taking drugs and driving are stupid activities that can get you killed. But how does he accomplish his goal? How do we know he's not serious? Look through the essay and find several (four or five) word choices and phrases that clearly tell the reader O'Rourke isn't in favor of drunk driving. Explain why you think these phrases show that O'Rourke isn't serious.

2. Some critics argue that satirical essays—while entertaining—are not "real" argument. Refute these critics by writing a paragraph arguing in favor of "How to Drive Fast" as a more effective argument for its intended audience (teens) than a finger-wagging straight lecture. Be

specific. Use examples and quotes from O'Rourke's essay and your own experience to support your stand. Even if you disagree, it's good critical thinking to take an opposing view.

3. Notice that O'Rourke organizes his essay in traditional structure: introduction with a **thesis**, body paragraphs with **transitions**, and a conclusion that slaps reality in the reader's face with the consequence of this type of behavior—death. Identify his thesis and transitions; find other areas where he uses *real* consequences of foolish behavior to keep the reader aware that drinking and driving is stupid.

4. Some readers object to O'Rourke's style of humor. What makes his essay controversial? Does the shock value of the essay work for or against him?

5. What is ironic about the Alberto Ascari example?

Styling

While satire is a style all its own, O'Rourke does use a variety of sentence patterns to add flow to his essay. Here's one example:

> Of course, it's a shame to waste young lives behaving this way— *speeding* around all tanked up *with* your feet hooked in the steering wheel *while* your date crawls around *on* the floor mats opening zippers *with* her teeth *and* pounding *on* the accelerator *with* an empty liquor bottle.

This pattern begins with a lead-in, "Of course," with a complete sentence followed by a dash with a series of add-ons that explain the behavior mentioned in the simple sentence. The first add-on begins with an "ing" word, *speeding*; the rest begin with prepositions and other connecting words (in italics in the example).

Note: For more discussion and practice on this sentence style (without the dash) see the "Styling" exercise with "A Voice for the Lonely" and consult the "Commas with Add-Ons" in the "Punctuation is Style" section.

PRACTICE Complete the sentence below with at least three incomplete sentences. Start each with one of the connecting words or prepositions italicized above.

Fly fishing is a relaxing way to spend a vacation—_____,

_____, _____.

YOU TRY IT   Create your own sentence. Start with a complete sentence followed by a dash. Next, write at least three that explain or describe the complete sentence.

The first incomplete sentence does not have to start with *ing*—you can use any of the linking words or prepositions.

CAUTION   Edit and revise for **run-on sentences** and **fragments**. A **run-on sentence** consists of two or more sentences run together when instead they should be separated by a period, a semicolon, or a comma with a conjunction. For example, in paragraph #1, if O'Rourke had written "Some people like to play poker or shoot dice other people prefer to parachute jump," he would be guilty of creating a run-on sentence. Instead, he uses a semicolon to separate the statements.

O'Rourke does use several **fragments (incomplete sentences)** in his essay. Near the end of paragraph #4, for example, he writes: "Every chance they could get." While writers often use fragments for a particular effect, I caution beginning writers against using them until they have mastered **complete sentences**.

Teaming Up

1. In groups of three to five members, brainstorm a list of harmful or simply rebellious teen behavior. For the next class meeting, have each person bring in an article about one of these behaviors. Before coming to class, each person should prepare a summary of the article to present to the group. After discussing the articles, highlight passages from each that you all agree would be useful in writing an essay on that type of behavior. Practice incorporating these passages into writing by introducing them with the writer's name and words such as *states, shows, disagrees, agrees, argues, claims, according to.*

    EXAMPLE: Joe Brown states . . .

    Note: For the proper documentation of quotes, see the Basic Documentation section.

2. This activity works best with three people but can be adapted to larger groups. Read Writing Idea #2. Decide on a topic to satirize. Brainstorm a thesis and at least three paragraph ideas for support. Have each member of the group develop one idea into a satirical paragraph. Co-write an introduction and conclusion. Then decide how to organize the body paragraphs. Use transitions between paragraphs.

Writing Ideas

1. Find a copy of *The Onion*—a satirical newspaper (available at www.theonion.com)—and read one of the satirical news articles. Find a nonsatirical article on the same topic in a newspaper. Write an essay that analyzes the two pieces, explaining what's being satirized, why, and whether you agree that the topic deserves to be satirized.

2. Write a five-paragraph satirical essay using O'Rourke's strategy. Your target should be a behavior that you think is stupid, one where people usually ignore sensible arguments: steroid use, breast implants, political issues, drugs (narrow to a specific one like cocaine or amphetamines). Use the techniques explored in Thinking and Talking Points #1. This strategy is key to making the essay work.

Essay Connections

"Advice to Youth" by Mark Twain also satirizes the behavior of teens and adults. Jonathan Swift's "A Modest Proposal," one of the best satires in the English language, is easy to find on the Web.

PRINCE

The Fargodome
Fargo, North Dakota
December 8, 1997

Chuck Klosterman

Chuck Klosterman's work has appeared in Esquire, GQ, Spin, New York Times Magazine, and The Washington Post. He's the author of several essay collections, including Fargo Rock City, Sex, Drugs, and Cocoa Puffs, and Killing Yourself to Live. The essay "Prince" appears in "The Show I'll Never Forget: 50 Writers Relive Their Most Memorable Concertgoing Experience," where he expresses his admiration of Prince as a genius, which he defines as "considerably more gifted and creative than almost everyone else who aspires to do the things he does best."

DUSTBIN OF HISTORY AND CULTURE

BYZANTINE: Eastern half of the Roman empire, which survived after the rest of Rome fell; it was eventually overrun by the Ottomans in 1453.

CORINTHIANS (Paul's first letter to): Also known as the Epistle of St. Paul (first and second letters are now the seventh and eighth books of the New Testament). The first letter was written about 53 or 54 CE, addressed to the Christian community of Corinth, Greece, which he had founded; it deals with the problems of the early church.

BIOSPHERE II: A self-contained ecological system in Arizona; Biosphere I is the earth.

TAFKAP: acronym for "The Artist Formerly Known as Prince."

1   I loved Prince when I was thirteen, and that was humiliating. It was among my darkest secrets. Seven hours before the first day of junior high, I laid in bed and listened to my sister's *Purple Rain* cassette, mortified by my own womanliness. "This will destroy me," I privately thought. "People will see right through me. I am a pussy." At the time, the only other artists I loved were Mötley Crüe, Ratt, KISS, and Ozzy. As far as I could tell, these were the only artists any intelligent, heterosexual male could (or would) love. While much of

"Prince, The Fargodome, Fargo, North Dakota, December 8, 1997" by Chuck Klosterman excerpted from *The Show I'll Never Forget: 50 Writers Relive Their Most Memorable Concertgoing Experience,* edited by Sean Manning, (Da Capo, 2007). Reprinted by permission of Chuck Klosterman.

1985 America may have secretly appreciated "Round and Round," I was a deeply closeted Prince fanatic, unwilling to tell even my friends and family. I listened to the solo on "Let's Go Crazy," and my creeping fears were instantaneously validated: Prince was a better guitar player than Warren DeMartini. It was true, and I could not deny it. When I watch *Before Stonewall,* this is the experience I relate to.

2   Twelve years later, I had to review a Prince concert for the *Forum* newspaper in Fargo, North Dakota. By then, I had been "out" as a Prince person for seven or eight years. The only problem was that I didn't really care anymore: Prince was working through his preposterous TAFKAP period and was slowly releasing long-awaited records that mostly sucked. Oddly, I found myself lying about Prince again, but now the context was reversed: I kept finding myself saying things like, "A bad record by Prince is still better than 90 percent of the albums that will come out this year, because he is a genius. A bad Prince record is still better than anything by the Crystal Method." Which was true, I suppose, but really only proved that MTV's *Amp* appeared to be inventing a dystopic future.

3   So ANYWAY, I went to this show cautiously pessimistic. I suspected it might be embarrassing, or devoid of familiar material, or punctuated by Prince walking onto the stage and wordlessly holding up four inexplicable fingers for the duration of the evening. However, my main trepidation involved time: I had to file my review by 11:10 P.M. that night, and that deadline was inflexible. The site of the concert (the Fargodome!) was a ten-minute drive from the *Forum* office, and this was the pre-laptop era. All the radio stations claimed the show would begin at eight, but everybody knew Prince usually played long and never played on time; at his club in Minneapolis, he would (supposedly) begin impromptu rock sets at 3:45 A.M. in the middle of the week. Nonetheless, I would need to exit the Dome parking lot by 10:15—this would give me fifty minutes to write a fifteen-inch, seven hundred-word review (plus or minus five minutes to self-edit the copy before sending it to the Night Desk). If Prince played two hours, I would almost certainly miss the encore; this is a common problem for anyone who has ever covered music for a daily newspaper. I think I saw three encores in eight years.

4   I arrived at the Dome around 7:30, pleasantly surprised to find I was directly in front of the stage (reviewers are usually relegated to the side of the arena, but not tonight). My friend Ross and I idly chatted about which songs might or might not be performed. (Ross was pulling

hard for "Housequake" and "Pussy Control," if I recall correctly.) We also snickered about the smallness of the crowd; while more than twenty thousand people had showed up to the Dome for Elton John, there were only 7,114 people in the building for TAFKAP. Prince had implemented a Byzantine anti-scalping policy where he would only announce a show two weeks before the actual date, and then everyone had to purchase vouchers that could only be exchanged for tickets at the door; I believe it was modeled after the method in which citizens of communist Russia were able to attain bread. Prince has been a goofball his entire life, but the middle nineties were truly the apex of his insanity. He was so crazy in 1997 that most people didn't even notice.

5   So . . . 7,114 of us sat there and waited. And waited. I was not surprised Prince didn't go on at eight, but I grew a little irritated at 8:30. And then—off in the distance, at the rear of the auditorium—there emerged the sound of a bass drum. "Aha!" we collectively thought. "This is it. Prepare for Prince!" The drum grew louder as it moved toward the stage; the beat emanated from (what looked like) a substantial marching band (the kind of band that might perform at halftime during the annual Grambling/Southern football game). We all searched for rock's purple elf within the melee. Was he leading the pack? No. Was he hidden among their broad shoulders and flamboyant outfits? No. Was he inside the bass drum, like the Lucky Charms leprechaun? Nay.

6   He was not there.

7   He was not there, because this was actually Larry Graham and Graham Central Station. Now, I have attended many shows where the audience was unfamiliar with the opening act. However, this was the only major concert I've ever attended where every single member of the audience was completely unaware that an opening act was appearing. There had been no publicity about this whatsoever. Everybody—including myself—immediately assumed this had to be Prince's entourage. I mean, I had no fucking idea what Larry Graham looked like; I hadn't seen a picture of him since the seventies. They took the stage and tried to bury us with funk, but we all kept waiting for Prince to come out. "This is rather curious," I thought. "Why is the backing band performing 'Thank You (Falettin Me Be Mice Elf Agin)' in its *totality*?" Twenty minutes passed before we finally concluded that this was, in fact, a group relatively unrelated to Prince. And they were excellent, but they played a long time; their set was over an hour. It was now 9:45, and—for all I knew—Prince wasn't even in

Fargo. He was probably sitting inside Biosphere II, talking to a puppet and thinking about Paul's First Letter to the Corinthians.

8   It now seemed plausible that this concert might not begin before eleven, which would turn my seven hundred–word review into a less-nuanced four-word review: "Prince is a jerk." This was a real problem; there are no journalistic alternatives for covering an event that doesn't exist. Ross found this scenario increasingly comical. But then—at 9:59—a certain kind of existence began; this tiny, capricious freak walked onstage and started making rock music. And it was so goddamn mesmerizing that I remember almost none of it.

9   I initially recall thinking, "Okay, I can maybe watch five songs, and then I have to go write this stupid story." But I have no idea how many songs I experienced, or what most of these songs were, or if any of them were "Housequake" or "Pussy Control." I had a notebook, but I didn't take any notes. There may have been a medley that included "Little Red Corvette," "Raspberry Beret," and "I Could Never Take the Place of Your Man," but that might have actually occurred at a Prince concert I would see in Cleveland three years later. He was just so amazingly good at *everything*. There was a sixty-second span where he played a keyboard, a bass, and a guitar in immediate succession, and I think he played each individual instrument better than anyone ever had played them before, anywhere, during any historical period over the past eleven thousand years. *And Prince didn't even care.* He didn't look happy, and he didn't look bored. He didn't even look focused. It seemed completely spontaneous, yet it wouldn't have mattered if he had rehearsed those specific sixty seconds for eight or nine months; the experience would have been exactly the same. And what I learned at this concert—and what I suspect can only be learned through seeing Prince live—is that all the moronic bullshit I made up about Prince's bad records and the Crystal Method was completely true: Prince is a genius. I was completely right. I just didn't know what "being right" meant.

10   Prior to this concert, what I actually meant when I said, "Prince is a genius," was that, "Prince is considerably more gifted and creative than almost everyone else who aspires to do the things he does best." By this criteria, there are a handful of other musicians who would qualify as geniuses: John Lennon and Paul McCartney, Jimmy Page, Donald Fagan and Walter Becker, Tony Iommi, Ike Turner, Lindsey Buckingham, Kevin Shields, and probably twenty-five other very famous people I can't recall at the moment I'm writing this particular

sentence. For anecdotal purposes, this definition of "genius" is usually acceptable. But those artists are not geniuses; they are simply very, very, very good at a vocation they have selected. That difference became weirdly lucid whenever Prince did anything onstage, including his attempt to have sexual intercourse with a piano. Eddie Van Halen plays guitar like a genius, but that is something he *figured out* how to do. He *turned himself into a genius,* and that isn't the same thing.

11   I suppose it's possible that Prince has worked harder at his music than any of his peers; I know almost nothing about his life that hasn't been fictionalized for his semi-autobiographical movies. This is not an attempt to discredit his work ethic, or to suggest he's lazy. However, this singular Fargo concert forces me to believe that the degree to which he has (or hasn't) worked on his craft is almost completely irrelevant. Prince doesn't really deserve credit for being a genius because he is not a normal human. His ability to create and perform music is so inherent and instinctual that it cannot really be measured against normal criteria; the only other rock musicians in this class are Jimi Hendrix and (maybe) Bob Dylan. And I only realized this by *seeing* Prince from a distance of twenty-five feet. His transcendence is not accurately felt through his songs or his albums, because a lot of those songs and records aren't especially good. Some of them are semi-terrible. But bad Prince records are still valuable because *he made them.* They are like triptychs from Stonehenge.

12   I do not know what time I exited the show, but it was not even half over. I know I arrived at the *Forum* office at 10:50 and wrote 492 bland words that did not reflect the experience in any meaningful way (and this review does not mention any specific song Prince played). According to my best calculations, I probably saw forty minutes of that concert. Which were thirty-nine more than I needed.

PRINCE

Exploring Language

apex: top or highest point.

capricious: given to sudden and/or unpredictable changes in mood or behavior.

dystopic: imaginary place or society where everything is bad; opposite of utopia.

emanate: radiate or spread out from.

entourage: a group of people who follow around and/or assist an important or famous person.

inexplicable: unexplainable.

melee: a mass of disorderly or unruly people; a group of people in a confused fight.

nuance: a slight difference, especially in sound or meaning.

transcendence: rising above the ordinary, often associated with a spiritual experience.

trepidation: fear or nervousness.

triptychs: three paintings or carved panels hinged together; or hinged tablet made of three leaves, used in ancient Rome.

Note: For pronunciation, go to dictionary.com, search the word, and click on the speaker icon.

USAGE Write a sentence containing three of the above words.

Thinking and Talking Points

1. What is Klosterman's main point or thesis? What evidence does he use to support his view?

2. Usually, students are taught to avoid repetition, but sometimes repetition creates style. Notice at the end of paragraph #5, "He was not there," is set off as its own paragraph, and then repeated in the first line of the next paragraph. What effect is Klosterman trying to achieve?

3. The essay contains so-called "cuss" words and slang. Why might this language be appropriate in the context of this piece of writing? Can

you think of other writing situations where it might be necessary and acceptable? In what writing situations would it not be appropriate?

4. Find areas in the essay where the writer uses exaggeration. How is this technique used to his advantage?

5. Klosterman makes a distinction between being a genius and turning yourself into one. What is that distinction? What is his definition of a genius?

Styling

One style technique you might be familiar with is **alliteration**, the repetition of sounds close to one another, creating rhythm. Some examples from Klosterman's essay include "specific sixty seconds" (s), "Prepare for Prince" (p), and "preposterous period" (p).

PRACTICE   Find at least three other pairs of words close together that create alliteration in Klosterman's essay.

YOU TRY IT   Choose a topic and brainstorm five pairs of words that contain alliteration. Some ideas for topics might be candy (jelly beans and juju bees), descriptions of your favorite meal (simply sublime salmon), your pet (perky poodle) or favorite song or poet (melancholy musician). Using your brainstorming list, write five sentences containing alliterations.

Teaming Up

1. The "You Try It" in the "Styling" section easily adapts to a group activity. It can be done as a round robin exercise, where each person writes down an object (like the ones above), passes it to the right, and then the next person must tag on another word, perhaps an adjective, that contains alliteration. If done in groups of three, then each word winds up with two tagged on alliterations. The best of the bunch can be made into sentences.

2. **Warm-up for Writing Idea #3.** Bring in lyrics to a song you think stands up to the elements of poetry: imagery, tone and rhythm (for example **alliteration** and **assonance**), **symbol** and/or **allegory**, figurative language (**metaphor, simile, personification**). Read each set of lyrics and choose the one that best exemplifies poetry. (See the glossary for words in bold.)

Writing Ideas

1. Write an essay about the best (or worst) live show you've ever attended. It can be a concert, play, musical—as long as it was live. Describe when and where it took place and what was going on in your life during that time. Use sensory detail to describe the surroundings, the crowd, the music. Your essay should reflect the tone of the show being the best or worst in your experience.

2. Compare and/or contrast two music concerts in the same **genre** (either ones you have attended or seen on DVD). Examples of genres might be country western, classical, rock, hip-hop, or rap. Argue for one artist being superior to the other in that genre. Be specific about what areas the artist excels. Reread Klosterman's essay for ideas.

3. Compare the theme in a song that you think qualifies as poetry to a poem of the same theme. Consider researching a literature data base in your school library (if available or try your public library) and type in search terms like "poetry themes." Write an essay comparing the themes as well as other literary devices, illustrating the universality of such themes. Some themes to consider might be teen depression, anger, war, suffering, guilt, betrayal, love, philosophy, politics, jealousy, solitude, nature. For comparing elements of poetry, here is a list to consider: imagery, tone and rhythm (alliteration, assonance), symbol and/or allegory, figurative language (metaphor, simile, personification).

Essay Connections

Other essays in this book with music themes include "Monster Mash" by Jack Kroll and "A Voice for the Lonely" by Stephen Corey. Clayton Collins discusses the impact of music on the brain, in "Musical Awakenings."

ROLL OVER BACH, TOO!

Jack Kroll

Jack Kroll was an award-winning journalist and drama critic for Newsweek. He died at age 74 on June 8, 2000. This essay on the Beatles attempts to explain the group's special appeal, claiming, "For many, Sgt. Pepper was an epochal event, the matriculation of rock into high art though some may not be fans of the music, most should find a connection with his enthusiasm for this group of music icons."

DUSTBIN OF HISTORY AND CULTURE

BUSTER KEATON: (1895–1966) An American silent film star and popular comic actor.

CHARLIE CHAPLIN: (1889–1977) Actor, director, producer, mostly of silent films. Though English, he moved to America, where he got his start in film.

DUKE ELLINGTON: (1899–1974) American jazz musician, credited with bringing jazz into concert halls.

LOUIS ARMSTRONG: (1900–1971) Also known as Satchmo. American jazz musician who often performed in films and was an international celebrity.

T. S. ELIOT: (1888–1965) One of the most influential poets of the 20th century; his most famous and controversial work is "The Waste Land."

1   Were you there? If not, you really can never know. Amazement must be experienced first-hand, and the coming of the Beatles was an amazement. Girls screamed; the captions in *Newsweek*'s Feb. 24, 1964, cover story read: "eeeeeeeeeeeee . . . E E E E E E E E E E E E . . . *EEEEEEEEEEEE!*" and the London *Times* music critic praised the Beatles' "pandiatonic clusters" and "flat-submediant key-switches." Both reactions were perfectly appropriate; the Beatles were blowing minds and nervous systems. And cash registers. On their first U.S. tour, two entrepreneurial types bought the pillowcases on which the four mop-tops had reposed in a Kansas City hotel and sliced them into 160,000 tiny squares, which they sold for a dollar each.

2   The girls were screaming not at key-switches (which the Beatles, who could not read music, arrived at instinctively) but at things like the

"Yeah, yeah, yeahs," in "She Loves You," delivered by Paul McCartney and George Harrison. But what linked the screechers and the scholars was a sense of something new, an absolute freshness that the Beatles manifested musically and personally. Those early songs—"I Want to Hold Your Hand," "Please Please Me"—were both sexy and innocent. Like those two "pleases," the first a polite supplication, the second a verb vibrating with sexual possibility. A British writer described the band as "beat-up and depraved in the nicest possible way."

3   That's a perfect description of rock-and-roll charisma. But what made the Beatles the key pop artists of the '60s was the synthesis that they made out of almost every conceivable pop element. Both John Lennon and Ringo Starr hailed their hometown of Liverpool as a crucible, a port city that brought together Irish, blacks, Chinese and sailors coming from America with blues records. Clubs and pubs jumped with the sounds of country and Western, British music-hall songs and rural folk tunes. The classical composer and critic Wilfrid Mellers said that the Beatles, like "other geniuses such as Bach, Mozart and Beethoven, knew the right time and place to be born."

4   Out of all these elements, plus the influence of pioneer rockers like Chuck Berry and Little Richard, the Beatles created a unique multi-faceted music. It rocked hard, it glinted with irony, it sang with poignant melancholy, as in "Yesterday," McCartney's anthem of loss, in which he sings solo and turns his guitar into the heart-strings of loneliness. The Lennon-McCartney songs were minidramas that evoked a wide spectrum of emotion. McCartney's "Penny Lane" and Lennon's "Strawberry Fields Forever" (coupled on one amazing single) conjured up their lost worlds of childhood, Paul's a "very strange" Utopia, John's a place where "nothing is real / and nothing to get hungabout."

5   In less than five years the Beatles produced a series of albums of increasing complexity, notably *A Hard Day's Night, Rubber Soul, Revolver* and *Sgt. Pepper's Lonely Hearts Club Band*. The album's climactic number, "A Day in the Life," is the Beatles' peak achievement. "I read the news today oh boy," sings Lennon, with a sweet hopelessness. Recounting news items of death, war and absurdity, John's refrain, "I'd love to turn you on," fuses the Beatles' drug experience with the desire to transcend the horrors of a foundering civilization. The number ends with the now legendary gigantic crescendo, played by a 41-piece orchestra, that wells up like a groan from the anguished heart of the city.

6   For many, *Sgt. Pepper* was an epochal event, the matriculation of rock into high art. Kenneth Tynan called it a decisive moment in the

history of Western civilization. But some critics thought that high art was exactly what rock shouldn't be. "What's so great about Art?" demanded critic Nik Cohn, insisting that the Beatles "have flown away into limbo." In a review I compared "A Day in the Life" to T. S. Eliot's apocalyptic poem "The Waste Land." In his illuminating survey of the Beatles' career, *Revolution in the Head,* Ian MacDonald rejects the comparison. He says of "A Day in the Life": "The fact that it achieves its transcendent goal via a potentially disillusioning confrontation with the 'real' world is precisely what makes it so moving." But that splendid sentence is also a succinct summation of "The Waste Land."

7   What the Beatles did in the '60s remains the most thrilling surge of creativity in the history of pop culture. They obliterated distinctions of high and low, like Chaplin, like Buster Keaton, like Louis Armstrong and Duke Ellington. They made it clear that if art is to survive in the techno-millennium that looms ahead, it must be hooked into the realities and redemptions in the days of our lives.

ROLL OVER BACH, TOO!

Exploring Language

apocalyptic: prophetic of the world's future, usually a doomed or threatened vision.

crucible: a melting pot; in this context, a place where those of different backgrounds and styles meet, influencing change.

entrepreneurial: striking out on one's own in business or other ventures.

epochal: memorable or very significant.

matriculation: enrollment or signing up; admission to a group.

multifaceted: having many sides or appearances.

poignant: touching or moving.

redemption: atonement or making up for something.

succinct: brief, compact.

supplication: a plea or request.

synthesis: a blend or fusion.

transcend: to rise above, often used in a spiritual context.

Note: For pronunciation, go to dictionary.com, search the word, and click on the speaker icon.

USAGE Look up *crucible* in the dictionary and notice its different meanings. Use the word in at least two sentences, each with a different meaning.

Thinking and Talking Points

1. What is Kroll's thesis? Examine the examples Kroll uses to support each of his paragraphs. How well does he support his point? How does he explain his examples and tie them back to his thesis?

2. Kroll, in paragraph #6, quotes critics who disagree with his comparison of the Beatles' work to high art and comparison of "A Day in the Life" to a famous poem by T.S. Eliot, "The Waste Land." Why does he bring in critics who disagree with him? How does he turn it to his advantage?

3. Read the section in paragraph #3 where Kroll quotes critic Mellers comparing the Beatles to famous classical composers. Do you agree with this assessment? Can you think of other music groups that might be compared to classical "geniuses"?

4. Kroll writes in paragraph #4, "The Lennon-McCartney songs were minidramas that evoked a wide spectrum of emotion." Listen to one of the songs he discusses—or find the lyrics—and explain how the song is a minidrama.

Styling

An opening that hooks the reader is an important ingredient in any writing. Jack Kroll opens his essay with a simple question, "Were you there?" Asking a question arouses the reader's curiosity. He or she usually wants an answer. In her essay "No Wonder They Call Me a Bitch," Ann Hodgman spends the entire introduction—with the exception of the first line—asking questions. When you're stuck for a good opening line, think about your essay, what questions you address, and try to come up with a short question.

PRACTICE   Write a short question for each of these topics: hockey, hunting, jazz, snakes, art.

YOU TRY IT   Open your next essay with a question or series of questions.

Note: See the titles section for more introduction ideas.

Teaming Up

1. **Warm-up for Writing Idea #1.** Have someone in the group bring in the lyrics to "A Day in the Life" by the Beatles (available with the CD *Sgt. Peppers Lonely Hearts Club Band*). Now compare the verses from "The Waste Land" (the entire poem is too long to reprint here). What similarities in theme do you notice? What makes both of these pieces "apocalyptic"? How are they "hooked into the realities and redemptions in the days of our lives"?

2. **Warm-up for Writing Idea #2.** Bring in lyrics to a song you think is "hooked into the realities and redemptions in the days of our lives." Compare in your group, explaining why your choice is a mini-drama, how it fits Kroll's quote above. Now you have a start on Writing Idea #2.

Writing Ideas

1. Find the lyrics to another Beatles' song Kroll mentions in paragraph #4. Analyze the lyrics, and write an essay explaining how the song is a mini-drama, how it's "hooked into the realities and redemptions in the days of our lives."
2. Analyze a song of your own choice, possibly from Teaming Up #2, and write an essay comparing it to one of the Beatles' songs, explaining how both are "apocalyptic."
3. Research photos of the Beatles, one from their early days when Kroll says their music was "both sexy and innocent" and the other from the later years when Kroll says "the Beatles produced a series of albums of increasing complexity." Now listen to songs from both periods. Compare. Write an essay that attempts to answer this question: what does the change in appearance and the change in tone of the lyrics and music say about changes in our culture?

Essay Connections

The essay "Musical Awakenings" by Clayton S. Collins examines music's ability to heal; in "A Voice for the Lonely," Stephen Corey writes a memoir about music's impact on the senses while paying a tribute to singer Roy Orbison of "Pretty Woman" fame. The essay "Prince" by Chuck Klosterman praises him as a genius.

From "The Waste Land" by T. S. Eliot

April is the cruelest month,
breeding Lilacs out of the dead land, mixing
Memory and desire, stirring
Dull roots with spring rain.
Winter kept us warm, covering
Earth in forgetful snow, feeding
A little life with dried tubers.

* * *

Unreal City,
Under the brown fog of a winter dawn,
A crowd flowed over London Bridge, so many,
I had not thought death had undone so many.
Sighs, short and infrequent, were exhaled,
And each man fixed his eyes before his feet.
Flowed up the hill and down King William Street,
To where Saint Mary Woolnoth kept the hours

With a dead sound on the final stroke of nine.
There I saw one I knew, and stopped him, crying: "Stetson!
"You who were with me in the ships at Mylae!
"That corpse you planted last year in your garden,
"Has it begun to sprout? Will it bloom this year?
"Or has the sudden frost disturbed its bed?
"O keep the Dog far hence, that's friend to men,
"Or with his nails he'll dig it up again!"

MYLAE: where a battle was fought between Rome and Carthage in 260 B.C. Rome won.

SAINT MARY WOOLNOTH: a church in London.

Questions for Interpretation

1. April is springtime, a time of rebirth and resurrection. Why, then, does Eliot call it the "cruelest month"?
2. What does the brown fog represent?
3. People are walking across the London Bridge like the living dead, eyes fixed and staring, uttering sighs. Why does Eliot present such a picture of humans?
4. What commentary is Eliot making about war?

SOMEBODY'S BABY

Barbara Kingsolver

Born in 1955 in Kentucky, Barbara Kingsolver has won numerous awards for her novels, short stories, and essays: The Poisonwood Bible was a finalist for the Pulitzer Prize, and The Lacuna won Britain's coveted Orange Prize for Fiction in 2010. Other works include Animal Dreams, The Bean Trees, and High Tide in Tucson: Essays from Now or Never, where "Somebody's Baby" appears; Kingsolver points out the difference in cultural attitudes concerning children, contrasting her experiences in Spain to America.

DUSTBIN OF HISTORY AND CULTURE

SUBJUNCTIVE TENSE: a grammar term referring to the "mood" of a verb when used in conditional or hypothetical statements or questions, like "I wish I were taller" rather than "I wish I was taller." Though not used as extensively as in the past, the subjunctive still persists.

GUAPA: pretty; guapo means handsome.

1   As I walked out the street entrance to my apartment, a kid in maroon high-tops and a startling haircut approached, saying "Hi gorgeous." Three weeks ago, I would have assessed the degree of malice and made ready to run or tell him to bug off, depending. Today, instead, I smile, and so does my 4-year-old daughter, because after dozens of similar encounters I understand that he doesn't mean me but *her*.

2   This is not the United States.

3   For most of the year my daughter was four we lived in Spain, in the warm southern province of the Canary Islands. I struggled with dinner at midnight and the subjunctive tense, but my only genuine culture shock has reverberated from this earthquake of a fact: people there like kids. They don't just say so, they do. Widows in black, buttoned-down c.e.o.'s, purple-sneakered teen-agers, the butcher, the baker, all have stopped on various sidewalks to have little chats with my daughter. Yesterday, a taxi driver leaned out his window to shout "Hola, guapa!" My daughter, who must have felt my conditioned

flinch, looked up at me wide-eyed and explained patiently, "I like it that people think I'm pretty." With a mother's keen myopia, I would tell you, absolutely, my daughter is beautiful enough to stop traffic. But in Santa Cruz de Tenerife, I have to confess, so is every other person under the height of one meter. Not just those who agree to be seen and not heard. When my daughter gets cranky in a restaurant (and really, what do you expect at midnight?), the waiters flirt and bring her little presents and nearby diners look on with that sweet, wistful gleam of eye that before now I have only seen aimed at the dessert tray. Children are the meringues and eclairs of this culture. Americans, it seems to me now, sometimes regard children as a sort of toxic-waste product: a necessary evil, maybe, but if it's not their own they don't want to see it or hear it or, God help us, smell it.

4   If you don't have children, you think I'm exaggerating. But if you've changed a diaper in the last decade, you know exactly the toxic-waste glare I mean. It goes far beyond diapers. In the United States, I have been told in restaurants: "We come here to get away from kids." (This for no infraction on my daughter's part that I could discern, other than being visible.) On an airplane, I heard a man tell a beleaguered woman whose infant was bawling (as loudly as I would, to clear my aching ears, if I couldn't manage chewing gum): "If you can't keep that thing quiet, you should keep it at home."

5   Air travel, like natural disasters, throws strangers together in unnaturally intimate circumstances. Think how well you got to know the bald spot on the guy who reclined in front of you on some long flight. As a consequence, I think of airplanes as a splendid cultural magnifying glass. On my family's recent voyage from New York to Madrid, we weren't assigned seats together. I shamelessly begged my neighbor—a forty-something New Yorker traveling alone—if she would take my husband's seat in another row so our air-weary and plainly miserable daughter could stretch out across our laps. My fellow traveler snapped: "No, I have to have the window seat, just like you had to have that baby."

6   As simply as that, a child with needs (and ears) became an inconvenient thing, for which I was entirely to blame. The remark left me stunned and, as always happens when someone is remarkably rude to me, momentarily guilty. Yes, she's right, conceiving this child was a rash, lunatic moment of selfishness, and now I had better be prepared to pay the price.

7   In the U.S.A., where it's said that anyone can grow up to be President, we parents are left pretty much on our own when it comes to the little Presidents-in-training. Our social programs for children are the hands-down worst in the industrialized world, but apparently that is just what we want as a nation. It took a move to another country to make me realize how thoroughly I had accepted my nation's creed of every family for itself. Whenever my daughter crash-landed in the playground, I was startled at first to see a sanguine, Spanish-speaking stranger pick her up and dust her off. And if a shrieking bundle landed at my feet, I'd furtively look around for the next of kin. But I quickly came to see this detachment as perverse when applied to children, and am wondering how it ever caught on in the first place.

8   My grandfathers on both sides lived in households that were called upon, after tragedy struck close to home, to take in orphaned children and raise them without a thought. In an era of shortage, this was commonplace. But one generation later that kind of semiperme-able household had vanished, at least among the white middle class. It's horrifying thought, but predictable enough, that the worth of children in America is tied to their dollar value. Children used to be field hands, household help, even miners and factory workers—extensions of a family's productive potential and so, in a sense, the property of an extended family. But precious property, valued and coveted. Since the advent of child-labor laws, children have come to hold an increasingly negative position in the economy. They're spoken of as a responsibility, a legal liability, an encumbrance—or, if their unwed mothers are on welfare, a mistake that should not be rewarded. The political shuffle seems to be about making sure they cost us as little as possible, and that their own parents foot the bill. Virtually every program that benefits children in this country, from Sesame Street to free school lunches, has been cut back in the last decade—in many cases, cut to nothing. If it takes a village to raise a child, our kids are knocking on a lot of doors where nobody seems to be home.

9   Taking parental responsibility to extremes, some policymakers in the U.S. have seriously debated the possibility of requiring a license for parenting. I'm dismayed by the notion of licensing an individual adult to raise an individual child, because it implies parenting is a private enterprise, like selling liquor or driving a cab (though less lucrative). I'm also dismayed by what it suggests about innate fitness

or nonfitness to rear children. Who would devise such a test? And how could it harbor anything but deep class biases? Like driving, parenting is a skill you learn by doing. You keep an eye out for oncoming disasters, and know when to stop and ask for directions. The skills you have going into it are hardly the point.

10   The first time I tried for my driver's license, I flunked. I was sixteen and rigid with panic. I rolled backward precariously while starting on a hill; I misidentified in writing the shape of a railroad crossing sign; as a final disqualifying indignity, my VW beetle—borrowed from my brother and apparently as appalled as I—went blind in the left blinker and mute in the horn. But nowadays, when it's time for a renewal, I breeze through the driver's test without thinking, usually on my way to some other errand. That test I failed twenty years ago was no prediction of my ultimate competence as a driver, anymore than my doll-care practices (I liked tying them to the back of my bike, by the hair) were predictive of my parenting skills (heavens be praised). Who really understands what it takes to raise kids? That is, until after the diaper changes, the sibling rivalries, the stitches, the tantrums, the first day of school, the overpriced-sneakers standoff, the first date, the safe-sex lecture, and the senior prom have all been negotiated and put away in the scrapbook?

11   While there are better and worse circumstances from which to launch offspring onto the planet, it's impossible to anticipate just who will fail. One of the most committed, creative parents I know plunged into her role through the trapdoor of teen pregnancy; she has made her son the center of her life, constructed a large impromptu family of reliable friends and neighbors, and absorbed knowledge like a plant taking sun. Conversely, some of the most strained, inattentive parents I know are well-heeled professionals, self-sufficient but chronically pressed for time. Life takes surprising turns. The one sure thing is that no parent, ever, has turned out to be perfectly wise and exhaustively provident, 1,440 minutes a day, for 18 years. It takes help. Children are not commodities but an incipient world. They thrive best when their upbringing is the collective joy and responsibility of families, neighborhoods, communities, and nations.

12   It's not hard to figure out what's good for kids, but amid the noise of any increasingly antichild political climate, it can be hard to remember just to go ahead and do it: for example, to vote to raise your school district's budget, even though you'll pay higher taxes. (If you're earning enough to pay taxes at all, I promise, the school needs those

few bucks more than you do.) To support legislators who care more about afterschool programs, affordable health care, and libraries than about military budgets and the Dow Jones industrial average. To volunteer time and skills at your neighborhood school and also the school across town. To decide to notice, rather than ignore it, when a neighbor is losing it with her kids, and offer to baby-sit twice a week. This is not interference. Getting between a ball player and a ball is interference. The ball is inanimate.

13   Presuming children to be their parents' sole property and responsibility is, among other things, a handy way of declaring problem children to be someone else's problem, or fault, or failure. It's a dangerous remedy; it doesn't change the fact that somebody else's kids will ultimately be in your face demanding now with interest what they didn't get when they were smaller and had simpler needs. Maybe in-your-face means breaking and entering, or maybe it means a Savings and Loan scam. Children deprived—of love, money, attention, or moral guidance—grow up to have large and powerful needs.

14   Always there will be babies made in some quarters whose parents can't quite take care of them. Reproduction is the most invincible of all human goals; like every other species, we're only here because our ancestors spent millions of years refining their act as efficient, dedicated breeders. If we hope for only sane, thoughtful people to have children, we can wish while we're at it for an end to cavities and mildew. But unlike many other species we are social, insightful, and capable of anticipating our future. We can see, if we care to look, that the way we treat children—all of them, not just our own, and especially those in great need—defines the shape of the world we'll wake up in tomorrow. The most remarkable feature of human culture is its capacity to reach beyond the self and encompass the collective good.

15   Its an inspiring thought. But in mortal fact, here in the U.S. we are blazing a bold downhill path from the high ground of "human collective," toward the tight little den of "self." The last time we voted on a school-budget override in Tucson, the newspaper printed scores of letters from readers incensed by the very possibility: "I don't have kids," a typical letter writer declared, "so why should I have to pay to educate other people's offspring?" The budget increase was voted down, the school district progressed from deficient to desperate, and I longed to ask that miserly nonfather just whose offspring he expects to doctor the maladies of his old age.

16   If we intend to cleave like stubborn barnacles to our great American ethic of every nuclear family for itself, then each of us had better raise and educate offspring enough to give us each day, in our old age, our daily bread. If we don't wish to live by bread alone, we'll need not only a farmer and a cook in the family but also a home repair specialist, an auto mechanic, an accountant, an import-export broker, a forest ranger, a therapist, an engineer, a musician, a poet, a tailor, a doctor, and at least three shifts of nurses. If that seems impractical, then we can accept other people's kids into our lives, starting now.

17   It's not so difficult. Most of the rest of the world has got this in hand. Just about any country you can name spends a larger percentage of its assets on its kids than we do. Virtually all industrialized nations have better schools and child-care policies. And while the U.S. grabs headlines by saving the occasional baby with heroic medical experiments, world health reports (from UNESCO, USAID, and other sources) show that a great many other parts of the world have lower infant mortality rates than we do—not just the conspicuously prosperous nations like Japan and Germany, but others, like Greece, Cuba, Portugal, Slovenia—simply because they attend better to all their mothers and children. Cuba, running on a budget that would hardly keep New York City's lights on, has better immunization programs and a higher literacy rate. During the long, grim haul of a thirty-year economic blockade, during which the United States has managed to starve Cuba to a ghost of its hopes, that island's child-first priorities have never altered.

18   Here in the land of plenty a child dies from poverty every fifty-three minutes, and TV talk shows exhibit teenagers who pierce their flesh with safety pins and rip off their parents every way they know how. All these punks started out as somebody's baby. How on earth, we'd like to know, did they learn to be so isolated and selfish?

19   My second afternoon in Spain, standing on a crowded bus, as we ricocheted around a corner and my daughter reached starfish-like for stability, a man in a black beret stood up and gently helped her into his seat. In his weightless bearing I caught sight of the decades-old child, treasured by the manifold mothers of his neighborhood, growing up the way leavened dough rises surely to the kindness of bread.

20   I thought then of the woman on the airplane, who was obviously within her rights to put her own comfort first, but whose withheld generosity gave my daughter what amounted to a sleepless, kicking,

squirming, miserable journey. As always happens two days after someone has spoken to me rudely, I knew exactly what I should have said: Be careful what you give children, for sooner or later you are sure to get it back.

SOMEBODY'S BABY

Exploring Language

advent: arrival, beginning.

beleaguered: harassed, pestered, bothered.

cleave: in this context, stick to, cling to.

coveted: desired or wished for.

creed: belief, system, or doctrine.

discern: to recognize as distinct or different; perceive.

encumbrance: a burden or hindrance.

flinch: to draw back or shrink from; recoil.

furtively: slyly or secretly; underhandedly.

impromptu: spontaneous, improvised; spur-of-the-moment; prepared suddenly, in haste.

incensed: made angry or provoked.

incipient: just starting to be or exist; beginning.

innate: natural, inborn; existing in a being from birth as in innate talent for art.

lucrative: profitable, moneymaking.

maladies: in this context, illness, sickness, or disease.

manifold: numerous and varied; many.

myopia: shortsighted, though not in the physical sense (in this context, Kingsolver's "mother's keen myopia" refers to mothers all thinking their children are beautiful, regardless; can also mean narrow-minded or lacking understanding, in addition to referring to the vision condition of not being able to see things that are far away).

perverse: determined to go against what is right, expected, or desired; persistent or obstinate in what is wrong.

provident: in this context, cautious or prudent; also showing foresight.

retrospect: to look on the past with thought; reflecting on the past.

reverberate: returned or echoed repeatedly.

sanguine: optimistic, confident; or a reddish complexion.

semipermeable: from the word *permeate*, meaning to saturate or pervade; permeable means capable of being saturated or pervaded; semi, meaning partially or somewhat.

wistful: yearning, longing; wishful, often in a mournful or melancholy manner.
Note: For pronunciation, go to dictionary.com, search the word, and
click on the speaker icon.

USAGE   Write one sentence using *sanguine* to mean a reddish complexion; write a second sentence using the definition confident or optimistic.

Thinking and Talking Points

1. What is Kingsolver's thesis? What evidence does she use for support
   and how convincing is it?
2. How does she use contrast to her advantage?
3. The author writes that the idea of requiring a license for parenting
   would harbor "deep class biases." Give examples of what class biases
   she might mean.
4. Kingsolver claims that the United States has an "increasingly antichild
   political climate." List her support. To what extent to you agree or
   disagree? Support your view with examples that either agree with or
   counter her point.
5. What, according to Kingsolver, accounts for this cultural difference in
   attitudes toward children?
6. To read that one child dies from poverty in the United States every
   fifty-three minutes might come as a surprise or shock—what might
   account for this grim statistic? How might the problem be solvable?

Styling

"Somebody's Baby" opens the argument with a personal illustration—a
narrative—of a larger social issue (see the "Introduction" section in this
text). Brainstorm social or political topics—perhaps neglect of the elderly, the treatment of animals, the plight of schools, etc.—and choose
one to use in a narrative introduction.

PRACTICE   Write a brief story introduction that illustrates the problem.

YOU TRY IT   Use this technique in an essay.

Teaming Up

1. Brainstorm a list of social programs for children. Divide the group, half bringing in articles in favor of the program, half researching the opposite view. Make a list of points from each side, and write a summary for each view. Discuss which side has the strongest argument (not necessarily the side you agree with).

2. List Barbara Kingsolver's points (her main reasons for her view). Next to each point list a counter-argument (a point that refutes the claim). Personal views are irrelevant for the exercise; it's good practice in critical thinking to be able to argue both sides of an issue.

Writing Ideas

1. Write an essay that contrasts another cultural or social difference between the United States and another country, or between different parts of the U.S. (East Coast versus West Coast, California and New York, Oregon and California, Louisiana and Chicago, or two counties in your area, etc.). The essay must have a point or argument. Use the narrative technique in the introduction.

2. Write an essay about another group that suffers neglect or bias; avoid the obvious stereotypes, striving for an out-of-the-ordinary topic (see Gretel Ehrlich's "About Men" for ideas).

Essay Connections

"About Men" by Gretel Ehrlich argues against the cultural stereotype of the American cowboy (and men in general); Mark Bauerlein's preface from *The Dumbest Generation* argues another aspect of American culture concerning teens and young adults. For essays that analyze society, culture, and history, see that category in the "Essays by Subject and Theme" table of contents.

THE CHEMIST'S WAR

Deborah Blum

Award-winning science writer Deborah Blum teaches journalism at the University of Wisconsin-Madison. In 1992, she won the Pulitzer Prize for her series "Monkey Wars," for the Sacramento Bee (now a book), examining the ethics and dilemmas surrounding primate research. Other books include Sex on the Brain: Biological Differences Between Men and Woman; A Field Guide for Science Writers *(2005);* Love at Goon Park: Harry Harlow and the Science of Affection *(2004);* The Poisoners Handbook *(2010), and* Ghost Hunters: William James and the Search for Scientific Proof of Life After Death. *She has also published articles in numerous magazines, newspapers, anthologies, and journals:* The Los Angeles Times, The Boston Globe, The New York Times, Discover Magazine, Psychology Today, The Utne Reader, Best American Science and Nature Writing, *including* Slate *where "The Chemist's War" first appeared.*

DUSTBIN OF HISTORY AND CULTURE

PROHIBITION: The period from 1920 (Volstead Act passed in 1919 to enforce the Eighteenth Amendment) to 1933 forbidding the sale and manufacture of alcoholic beverages. In 1933, the Twenty-first Amendment repealed the law.
BOOTLEGGED: illegally made, transported, or sold alcohol.
SPEAKEASIES: nightclubs and saloons selling illegal alcohol during Prohibition.

1   It was Christmas Eve 1926, the streets aglitter with snow and lights, when the man afraid of Santa Claus stumbled into the emergency room at New York City's Bellevue Hospital. He was flushed, gasping with fear: Santa Claus, he kept telling the nurses, was just behind him, wielding a baseball bat.

2   Before hospital staff realized how sick he was—the alcohol-induced hallucination was just a symptom—the man died. So did another holiday partygoer. And another. As dusk fell on Christmas, the hospital staff tallied up more than 60 people made desperately ill by alcohol and eight dead from it. Within the next two days, yet another 23 people died in the city from celebrating the season.

3   Doctors were accustomed to alcohol poisoning by then, the routine of life in the Prohibition era. The bootlegged whiskies and so-called gins often made people sick. The liquor produced in hidden stills frequently came tainted with metals and other impurities. But

this outbreak was bizarrely different. The deaths, as investigators would shortly realize, came courtesy of the U.S. government.

4   Frustrated that people continued to consume so much alcohol even after it was banned, federal officials had decided to try a different kind of enforcement. They ordered the poisoning of industrial alcohols manufactured in the United States, products regularly stolen by bootleggers and resold as drinkable spirits. The idea was to scare people into giving up illicit drinking. Instead, by the time Prohibition ended in 1933, the federal poisoning program, by some estimates, had killed at least 10,000 people.

5   Although mostly forgotten today, the "chemist's war of Prohibition" remains one of the strangest and most deadly decisions in American law-enforcement history. As one of its most outspoken opponents, Charles Norris, the chief medical examiner of New York City during the 1920s, liked to say, it was "our national experiment in extermination." Poisonous alcohol still kills—16 people died just this month after drinking lethal booze in Indonesia, where bootleggers make their own brews to avoid steep taxes—but that's due to unscrupulous businessmen rather than government order.

6   I learned of the federal poisoning program while researching my new book, The Poisoner's Handbook, which is set in jazz-age New York. My first reaction was that I must have gotten it wrong. "I never heard that the government poisoned people during Prohibition, did you?" I kept saying to friends, family members, colleagues.

7   I did, however, remember the U.S. government's controversial decision in the 1970s to spray Mexican marijuana fields with Paraquat, an herbicide. Its use was primarily intended to destroy crops, but government officials also insisted that awareness of the toxin would deter marijuana smokers. They echoed the official position of the 1920s—if some citizens ended up poisoned, well, they'd brought it upon themselves. Although Paraquat wasn't really all that toxic, the outcry forced the government to drop the plan. Still, the incident created an unsurprising lack of trust in government motives, which reveals itself in the occasional rumors circulating today that federal agencies, such as the CIA, mix poison into the illegal drug supply.

8   During Prohibition, however, an official sense of higher purpose kept the poisoning program in place. As the Chicago Tribune editorialized in 1927: "Normally, no American government would engage in such business. ... It is only in the curious fanaticism of Prohibition that any means, however barbarous, are considered justified." Others, however, accused lawmakers opposed to the poisoning plan of being in cahoots with criminals and argued that bootleggers and their law-breaking alcoholic customers deserved no sympathy. "Must Uncle Sam guarantee safety first for souses?" asked Nebraska's *Omaha Bee*.

9   The saga began with ratification of the 18th Amendment, which banned the manufacture, sale, or transportation of alcoholic beverages in the United States. High-minded crusaders and anti-alcohol organizations had helped push the amendment through in 1919, playing on fears of moral decay in a country just emerging from war. The Volstead Act, spelling out the rules for enforcement, passed shortly later, and Prohibition itself went into effect on Jan. 1, 1920.

10   But people continued to drink—and in large quantities. Alcoholism rates soared during the 1920s; insurance companies charted the increase at more than 300 percent. Speakeasies promptly opened for business. By the decade's end, some 30,000 existed in New York City alone. Street gangs grew into bootlegging empires built on smuggling, stealing, and manufacturing illegal alcohol. The country's defiant response to the new laws shocked those who sincerely (and naively) believed that the amendment would usher in a new era of upright behavior.

11   Rigorous enforcement had managed to slow the smuggling of alcohol from Canada and other countries. But crime syndicates responded by stealing massive quantities of industrial alcohol—used in paints and solvents, fuels and medical supplies—and redistilling it to make it potable.

12   Well, sort of. Industrial alcohol is basically grain alcohol with some unpleasant chemicals mixed in to render it undrinkable. The U.S. government started requiring this "denaturing" process in 1906 for manufacturers who wanted to avoid the taxes levied on potable spirits. The U.S. Treasury Department, charged with overseeing alcohol enforcement, estimated that by the mid-1920s, some 60 million gallons of industrial alcohol were stolen annually to supply the country's drinkers. In response, in 1926, President Calvin Coolidge's government decided to turn to chemistry as an enforcement tool. Some 70 denaturing formulas existed by the 1920s. Most simply added poisonous methyl alcohol into the mix. Others used bitter-tasting compounds that were less lethal, designed to make the alcohol taste so awful that it became undrinkable.

13   To sell the stolen industrial alcohol, the liquor syndicates employed chemists to "renature" the products, returning them to a drinkable state. The bootleggers paid their chemists a lot more than the government did, and they excelled at their job. Stolen and redistilled alcohol became the primary source of liquor in the country. So federal officials ordered manufacturers to make their products far more deadly.

14   By mid-1927, the new denaturing formulas included some notable poisons—kerosene and brucine (a plant alkaloid closely related to strychnine), gasoline, benzene, cadmium, iodine, zinc, mercury salts,

nicotine, ether, formaldehyde, chloroform, camphor, carbolic acid, quinine, and acetone. The Treasury Department also demanded more methyl alcohol be added—up to 10 percent of total product. It was the last that proved most deadly.

15   The results were immediate, starting with that horrific holiday body count in the closing days of 1926. Public health officials responded with shock. "The government knows it is not stopping drinking by putting poison in alcohol," New York City medical examiner Charles Norris said at a hastily organized press conference. "Yet it continues its poisoning processes, heedless of the fact that people determined to drink are daily absorbing that poison. Knowing this to be true, the United States government must be charged with the moral responsibility for the deaths that poisoned liquor causes, although it cannot be held legally responsible."

16   His department issued warnings to citizens, detailing the dangers in whiskey circulating in the city: "Practically all the liquor that is sold in New York today is toxic," read one 1928 alert. He publicized every death by alcohol poisoning. He assigned his toxicologist, Alexander Gettler, to analyze confiscated whiskey for poisons—that long list of toxic materials I cited came in part from studies done by the New York City medical examiner's office.

17   Norris also condemned the federal program for its disproportionate effect on the country's poorest residents. Wealthy people, he pointed out, could afford the best whiskey available. Most of those sickened and dying were those "who cannot afford expensive protection and deal in low grade stuff."

18   And the numbers were not trivial. In 1926, in New York City, 1,200 were sickened by poisonous alcohol; 400 died. The following year, deaths climbed to 700. These numbers were repeated in cities around the country as public-health officials nationwide joined in the angry clamor. Furious anti-Prohibition legislators pushed for a halt in the use of lethal chemistry. "Only one possessing the instincts of a wild beast would desire to kill or make blind the man who takes a drink of liquor, even if he purchased it from one violating the Prohibition statutes," proclaimed Sen. James Reed of Missouri.

19   Officially, the special denaturing program ended only once the 18th Amendment was repealed in December 1933. But the chemist's war itself faded away before then. Slowly, government officials quit talking about it. And when Prohibition ended and good grain whiskey reappeared, it was almost as if the craziness of Prohibition—and the poisonous measures taken to enforce it—had never quite happened.

THE CHEMIST'S WAR

Exploring Language

cahoots: "in cahoots" means to be in league, partnership, or conspiracy with one or more others, usually in a secretive manner.

clamor: an outcry, uproar, or loud noise.

denaturing: in this context, to make alcohol unfit for drinking.

disproportionate: out of proportion in size or number.

fanaticism: irrational or excessive devotion or enthusiasm.

potable: drinkable.

ratification: formal approval or consent.

rigorous: harsh, severe, demanding.

saga: the informal use refers to a story or series of events over a long period; in literature, a saga is a medieval narrative (story) that tells of the adventures or deeds of a hero.

souse: to be drenched with or immersed in liquid (in this instance alcohol); the term has come to refer to a drunk.

Note: For pronunciation, go to dictionary.com, search the word, and click on the speaker icon.

USAGE Choose three of the words from the list and write a sentence for each.

Thinking and Talking Points

1. Who is at "war" in the essay? What language does Blum use that fits with the idea of war? List specific words or sentences.

2. Does Blum have a specific thesis or is her point implied? What is her opinion about the decisions the government made during Prohibition? Examine words choices that convey her tone and list them.

3. Reread the first two paragraphs. Is this narrative opening a good hook? How does it contrast with the revelation at the end of paragraph three?

4. After hitting the reader with the surprise that the government poisoned alcohol in the 1920's, Blum reveals another plan by the government to poison marijuana with the herbicide Paraquat in the

1970's—a plan they dropped after public outcry. Why does Blum include this incident? Does it strengthen her point? What claim does she make about the incident's effect today?

5. What other details does she provide about Prohibition that might not be common knowledge? What statistics come as a surprise?

6. Despite the poisoning program and resulting deaths, people continued to drink, a phenomenon of human nature Gore Vidal attempts to explain in his essay "Drugs," written in the sixties. Read that short essay and explain his point concerning people wanting what is forbidden them. What else do these two essays have in common?

Styling

Blum uses an introduction narrative technique, almost fable-like in its tone, though she does not rely on her own experience but uses newspaper articles from the twenties, creating a factual opening that reads like a story (read more on narrative openings in the "Introductions" section of your text).

PRACTICE   Brainstorm a list of issues that concern or intrigue, either current or historical, and search your college's newspaper and periodicals data base for information and editorials on one, especially articles that have a human interest slant (ideas: Paraquat, animal shelters, the economy, marijuana clinics).

YOU TRY IT   Using the articles, **in your own words**, write a narrative introduction implying an opinion about the topic. The first line should have a story-like appeal, as Blum's does: "It was Christmas Eve 1926 . . ." or "Once there was . . ." .

Teaming Up

1. The Styling exercise works well in groups: reading the articles together, brainstorming ideas for the narrative introduction, co-writing the paragraph, and revising and editing.

2. Choose at least five words from the "Exploring Language" list and use them to co-write a paragraph, either narrative (telling a mini-story), descriptive (perhaps a character sketch), or argument. The paragraph can be humorous but must follow general paragraph guidelines, sticking to the same subject.

Writing Ideas

1. Write an opinion essay that examines a government policy, action, or law. Use the story introduction technique from the Styling, or another option from the "Introductions" section in the text. The letter format with Frederick Douglas's "Letter to His Master" is another approach to expressing an opinion of a government policy or action.
2. Compare/Contrast "The Chemist's War" to "Drugs" by Gore Vidal, examining style, content, and relevance to today's concerns over these issues; has the government gotten better or worse at controlling the war on drugs? Does one writer have a stronger point or style?

Essay Connections

"Drugs" by Gore Vidal is an obvious choice for another essay questioning government policy or human behavior; "Modern Times" by Lawrence Weschler, though dated, comments on Desert Storm, but remains relevant, questioning war fought with technology. "How to Drive Fast" by P.J. O'Rourke satirizes drugs, drinking, and driving.

LETTER TO HIS MASTER

Frederick Douglass

Frederick Douglass—an American slave known as Frederick Augustus Washington Bailey—
escaped to Massachusetts, becoming a famous writer and lecturer, speaking out against the
evils of slavery, and advising Abraham Lincoln. In this eloquent letter, Douglass writes to his
former master, demanding to know the fate of his family, still owned by Thomas Auld.

DUSTBIN OF HISTORY AND CULTURE

WILLIAM LLOYD GARRISON: (1805–1879) American abolitionist who founded *The
Liberator,* an anti-slavery newspaper.

1 Thomas Auld:

2   Sir—The long and intimate, though by no means friendly relation which unhappily subsisted between you and myself, leads me to
hope that you will easily account for the great liberty which I now
take in addressing you in this open and public manner. The same fact
may possibly remove any disagreeable surprise which you may experience on again finding your name coupled with mine, in any other
way than in an advertisement, accurately describing my person, and
offering a large sum for my arrest. In thus dragging you again before
the public, I am aware that I shall subject myself to no inconsider-
able amount of censure. I shall probably be charged with an unwarrantable, if not a wanton and reckless disregard of the rights and
proprieties of private life. There are those North as well as South who
entertain a much higher respect for rights which are merely conven-
tional, than they do for rights which are personal and essential. Not a
few there are in our country, who, while they have no scruples against
robbing the laborer of the hard earned results of his patient industry,
will be shocked by the extremely indelicate manner of bringing your
name before the public. . . .

3   I have selected this day on which to address you, because it is the
anniversary of my emancipation; and knowing of no better way I am
led to this as the best mode of celebrating that truly important event.
Just ten years ago this beautiful September morning, yon bright sun
beheld me a slave—a poor, degraded chattel—trembling at the sound
of your voice, lamenting that I was a man, and wishing myself a brute.

The hopes which I had treasured up for weeks of a safe and successful escape from your grasp, were powerfully confronted at this last hour by dark clouds of doubt and fear, making my person shake and my bosom to heave with the heavy contest between hope and fear. I have no words to describe to you the deep agony of soul which I experienced on that never to be forgotten morning—(for I left by daylight). I was making a leap in the dark. The probabilities, so far as I could by reason determine them, were stoutly against the undertaking. The preliminaries and precautions I had adopted previously, all worked badly. I was like one going to war without weapons—ten chances of defeat to one of victory. One in whom I had confided, and one who had promised me assistance, appalled by fear at the trial hour, deserted me, thus leaving the responsibility of success or failure solely with myself. You, sir, can never know my feelings. As I look back to them I can scarcely realize that I have passed through a scene so trying. Trying however as they were, and gloomy as was the prospect, thanks be to the Most High, who is ever the God of the oppressed, at the moment which was to determine my whole earthly career. His grace was sufficient, my mind was made up. I embraced the golden opportunity, took the morning tide at the flood, and a free man, young, active and strong, is the result. . . .

4   Since I left you, I have had a rich experience. I have occupied stations which I never dreamed of when a slave. Three out of the ten years since I left you, I spent as a common laborer on the wharves of New Bedford, Massachusetts. It was there I earned my first free dollar. It was mine. I could spend it as I pleased. I could buy hams or herring with it, without asking any odds of any body. That was a precious dollar to me. You remember when I used to make seven or eight, or even nine dollars a week in Baltimore, you would take every cent of it from me every Saturday night, saying that I belonged to you, and my earnings also. I never liked this conduct on your part— to say the best, I thought it a little mean. I would not have served you so. But let that pass. I was a little awkward about counting money in New England fashion when I first landed in New Bedford. I like to have betrayed myself several times. I caught myself saying phip, for fourpence; and at one time a man actually charged me with being a runaway, whereupon I was silly enough to become one by running away from him, for I was greatly afraid he might adopt measures to give me again into slavery, a condition I then dreaded more than death.

5   I soon, however, learned to count money, as well as to make it, and got on swimmingly. I married soon after leaving you: in fact, I was engaged to be married before I left you; and instead of finding my companion a burden; she was truly a helpmeet. She went to live at service and I to work on the wharf, and though we toiled hard the first winter, we never lived more happily. After remaining in New Bedford for three years, I met with Wm. Lloyd Garrison, a person of whom you have *possibly* heard, as he is pretty generally known among slaveholders. He put it into my head that I might make myself serviceable to the cause of the slave by devoting a portion of my time to telling my own sorrows, and those of other slaves which had come under my observation. This was the commencement of a higher state of existence than any to which I had ever aspired. I was thrown into society the most pure, enlightened and benevolent that the country affords. Among these I have never forgotten you, but have invariably made you the topic of conversation—thus giving you all the notoriety I could do. I need not tell you that the opinion formed of you in these circles, is far from being favorable. They have little respect for your honesty, and less for your religion.

6   But I was going on to relate something of my interesting experience. I had not long enjoyed the excellent society to which I have referred, before the light of its excellence exerted a beneficial influence on my mind and heart. Much of my early dislike of white persons was removed, and their manners, habits and customs, so entirely unlike what I had been used to in the kitchen-quarters on the plantations of the South, fairly charmed me, and gave me a strong disrelish for the coarse and degrading customs of my former condition. I therefore made an effort so to improve my mind and deportment as to be somewhat fitted to the station to which I seemed almost providentially called. The transition from degradation to respectability was indeed great, and to get from one to the other without carrying some marks of one's former condition, is truly a difficult matter. I would not have you think that I am now entirely clear of all plantation peculiarities, but my friends here, while they entertain the strongest dislike to them, regard me with that charity to which my past life somewhat entitles me, so that my condition in this respect is exceedingly pleasant. So far as my domestic affairs are concerned, I can boast of as comfortable a dwelling as your own. I have an industrious and neat companion, and four dear children—the oldest a girl of nine years and three fine boys, the oldest eight, the next six, and the

youngest four years old. The three oldest are now going regularly to school—two can read and write, and the other can spell with tolerable correctness words of two syllables. Dear fellows! they are all in comfortable beds, and are sound asleep, perfectly secure under my own roof. There are no slaveholders here to rend my heart by snatching them from my arms, or blast a mother's dearest hopes by tearing them from her bosom. These dear children are ours—not to work up into rice, sugar and tobacco, but to watch over, regard, and protect, and to rear them up in the nurture and admonition of the gospel—to train them up in the paths of wisdom and virtue, and, as far as we can to make them useful to the world and to themselves. Oh! sir, a slaveholder never appears to me so completely an agent of hell, as when I think of and look upon my dear children. It is then that my feelings rise above my control. I meant to have said more with respect to my own prosperity and happiness, but thoughts and feelings which this recital has quickened unfit me to proceed further in that direction. The grim horrors of slavery rise in all their ghastly terror before me, the wails of millions pierce my heart, and chill my blood. I remember the chain, the gag, the bloody whip, the death-like gloom overshadowing the broken spirit of the fettered bondman, the appalling liability of his being torn away from wife and children, and sold like a beast in the market. Say not that this is a picture of fancy. You well know that I wear stripes on my back inflicted by your direction; and that you, while we were brothers in the same church caused this right hand, with which I am now penning this letter, to be closely tied to my left, and my person dragged at the pistol's mouth, fifteen miles, from the Bay side to Easton to be sold like a beast in the market for the alleged crime of intending to escape from your possession. All this and more you remember, and know to be perfectly true, not only of yourself, but of nearly all of the slaveholders around you.

7   At this moment, you are probably the guilty holder of at least three of my own dear sisters, and my only brother in bondage. These you regard as your property. They are recorded on your ledger, or perhaps have been sold to human flesh mongers, with a view to filling your own ever-hungry purse. Sir, I desire to know how and where these dear sisters are. Have you sold them? or are they still in your possession? What has become of them? are they living or dead? And my dear old grandmother, whom you turned out like an old horse, to die in the woods—is she still alive? Write and let me know all about them. If my grandmother be still alive, she is of no service to you, for

by this time she must be nearly eighty years old—too old to be cared for by one to whom she has ceased to be of service, send her to me at Rochester, or bring her to Philadelphia, and it shall be the crowning happiness of my life to take care of her in her old age. Oh! she was to me a mother, and a father, so far as hard toil for my comfort could make her such. Send me my grandmother! that I may watch over and take care of her in her old age. And my sisters, let me know all about them. I would write to them, and learn all I want to know of them, without disturbing you in any way, but that, through your unrighteous conduct, they have been entirely deprived of the power to read and write. You have kept them in utter ignorance, and have therefore robbed them of the sweet enjoyments of writing or receiving letters from absent friends and relatives. Your wickedness and cruelty committed in this respect on your fellow-creatures, are greater than all the stripes you have laid upon my back, or theirs. It is an outrage upon the soul—a war upon the immortal spirit, and one for which you must give account at the bar of our common Father and Creator. . . .

8   I will now bring this letter to a close, you shall hear from me again unless you let me hear from you. I intend to make use of you as a weapon with which to assail the system of slavery—as a means of concentrating public attention on the system, and deepening their horror of trafficking in the souls and bodies of men. I shall make use of you as a means of exposing the character of the American church and clergy—and as a means of bringing this guilty nation with yourself to repentance. In doing this I entertain no malice towards you personally. There is no roof under which you would be more safe than mine, and there is nothing in my house which you might need for your comfort, which I would not readily grant. Indeed, I should esteem it a privilege, to set you an example as to how mankind ought to treat each other.

9   I am your fellow man, but not your slave.

LETTER TO HIS MASTER

Exploring Language

censure: to criticize or reprimand.

chattel: personal possession or property.

deportment: manners, conduct.

disrelish: dislike or distaste.

notoriety: fame, usually with negative implications, like a "notorious criminal."

providentially: luckily or timely opportunity, sometimes referring to divine interference.

subsist: to exist; to keep alive or provide food for.

unwarrantable: unjustifiable, indefensible.

wanton: cruel or malicious; mischievous.

Note: For pronunciation, go to dictionary.com, search the word, and click on the speaker icon.

USAGE Look up the word wanton and study its different meanings. Write two sentences that use different meanings of the word.

Thinking and Talking Points

1. What examples in the essay illustrate the effects of slavery? How do these examples evoke sympathy?

2. What tone does the letter take? Is he respectful to Auld? Does he tell him off?

3. Douglass writes that refusing to allow slaves to read and write is more cruel than "all the stripes you have laid upon my back, or theirs." Why?

4. In the opening, Douglass writes, "I shall probably be charged with an unwarrantable, if not a wanton and reckless disregard of the rights and proprieties of private life." Read the rest of the paragraph. Is he being ironic or mocking? If so, how?

5. How does the letter refute the justification made by slaveholders that slaves were less intelligent and therefore less human than the slaveholders?

Styling

Douglass, like all good writers, uses a variety of sentence styles and lengths. Short sentence: "It was mine." Medium sentence: "Since I left you, I have had a rich experience." Long sentence:

> The same fact may possibly remove any disagreeable surprise which you may experience on again finding your name coupled with mine, in any other way than in an advertisement, accurately describing my person, and offering a large sum for my arrest.

Like many of Douglass's long sentences, this one uses a **loose** structure, but it does so in a unique way: after the first statement, each clause focuses in on a detail in the clause before it. He begins with a complete sentence: "The same fact may possibly remove any disagreeable surprise which you may experience on again finding your name coupled with mine."

The next phrase is dependent (in English grammar jargon), a prepositional phrase focusing on *coupled,* giving a closer detail: "in any other way than in an advertisement."

The next dependent group of words gives a detail about the advertisement: "accurately describing my person."

The last dependent group of words gives another detail about the advertisement, linking it to the previous one with a conjunction, and: "and offering a large sum for my arrest."

Note: The conjunction *and* is an option. The sentence would be correct without it. Here's a student example based on the Douglass model:

> The lightning flashed incandescently across the storm-troubled sky, illuminating the skeletal limbs of the maple grove that whipped violently back and forth in the fierce wind, casting shadows resembling nightmarish monsters against the sodden ground.

Notice that each dependent grouping provides a detail about the clause before it, getting closer each time, moving from the sky, to the limbs of the trees, and finally to the ground.

PRACTICE   Fill in the blanks below with dependent word groups, each time focusing in closer to the object or place. I've completed the first element for you.

The fog comes in at night like an uninvited guest, *creeping through the quiet streets*, _____, _____.

A hawk bolted from the mountain, *soaring into the valley below,*

_____, _____.

YOU TRY IT Write five sentences in this structure. Use this sentence style in your next writing assignment.

Teaming Up

1. **Warm-up for Writing Idea #2.** Have each member of the group bring in a current newspaper or magazine article about someone in the public eye he or she disagrees with on moral or ethical grounds. Pick out one article you all agree would make a good target, and make a list in the following order:

   a. Explain what the person or group has done that's wrong.
   b. Explain what's wrong with the behavior.
   c. Explain how the behavior hurts others.
   d. Invite the person or group to respond to the allegations.

   Draft a letter to this person or group. Have each member of the group take a copy of the letter home to revise and edit. At the next class period, choose the best revision to read to the class.

   For more on this type of argument, see *Adios, Strunk and White* by Gary and Glynis Hoffman.

2. **Warm-up for Writing Idea #3.** Have one person research and bring in a copy of a Douglass speech. The other members of the group will bring in information on free speech and censorship. Compare the issues to those Douglass brings up. What similarities do you find in the defense of free speech? Which ones do you agree or disagree with? Have the arguments changed since Douglass wrote his speech?

Writing Ideas

1. Imagine what it would be like to be denied the right to read and write. Write an essay as if you're talking to someone who has the power to grant you this right, arguing why you should be allowed to learn.

2. Write an essay to a public figure you think has committed a moral or ethical outrage on society. Follow the format in Teaming Up activity #1.

3. Research and read a speech by Douglass on free speech, then compare it to current arguments on the topic. What principles in the Douglass speech apply today? Are there any that don't? Write an essay comparing these issues, giving your opinion on the free speech debate.

Essay Connections

Another Frederick Douglass essay in this book, "Learning to Read and Write," focuses in depth on the denial of this right to slaves. Both of these essays—and his autobiography—are important historical documents, as well as moving accounts of slavery. Shelby Steele's "The Content of Our Character" focuses on current problems in the African-American community.

ADVICE TO YOUTH

Mark Twain

Mark Twain (1835–1910), real name Samuel Longhorn Clemens, American writer and humorist, is best known for The Adventures of Huckleberry Finn and Tom Sawyer, but he wrote many other novels, short stories, and essays. In "Advice to Youth," an address to students, he satirizes the arrogance of youth who lie, manipulate parents, and think they're superior.

DUSTBIN OF HISTORY AND CULTURE

GATLING GUN: A machine gun invented by Richard J. Gatling.

INNOCENTS ABROAD: A book by Mark Twain (see Teaming Up #2).

ROBERTSON: Frederick Robertson (1816–1853), English Anglican clergyman (see Teaming Up #2).

SAINT'S REST: A work written by English Puritan clergyman Richard Baxter (1615–1691) (see Teaming Up #2).

1   Being told I would be expected to talk here, I inquired what sort of a talk I ought to make. They said it should be something suitable to youth—something didactic, instructive, or something in the nature of good advice. Very well. I have a few things in my mind which I have often longed to say for the instruction of the young: for it is in one's tender early years that such things will best take root and be most enduring and most valuable. First, then, I will say to you, my young friends—and I say it beseechingly, urgingly—

2   Always obey your parents, when they are present. This is the best policy in the long run, because if you don't they will make you. Most parents think they know better than you do, and you can generally make more by humoring that superstition than you can by acting on your own better judgment.

3   Be respectful to your superiors, if you have any, also to strangers, and sometimes to others. If a person offends you, and you are in doubt as to whether it was intentional or not, do not resort to extreme measures; simply watch your chance and hit him with a brick. That will be sufficient. If you shall find that he had not intended any offense, come out frankly and confess yourself in the wrong when you struck him; acknowledge it like a man and say you didn't mean to. Yes, always avoid violence; in this age of charity and kindliness, the time has gone by for such things. Leave dynamite to the low and unrefined.

4   Go to bed early, get up early—this is wise. Some authorities say get up with the sun; some others say get up with one thing, some with another. But a lark is really the best thing to get up with. It gives you a splendid reputation with everybody to know that you get up with the lark; and if you get the right kind of a lark, and work at him right, you can easily train him to get up at half past nine, every time—it is no trick at all.

5   Now as to the matter of lying. You want to be very careful about lying; otherwise you are nearly sure to get caught. Once caught, you can never again be, in the eyes of the good and the pure, what you were before. Many a young person has injured himself permanently through a single clumsy and ill-finished lie, the result of carelessness born of incomplete training. Some authorities hold that the young ought not to lie at all. That, of course, is putting it rather stronger than necessary; still, while I cannot go quite so far as that, I do maintain, and I believe I am right, that the young ought to be temperate in the use of this great art until practice and experience shall give them that confidence, elegance, and precision which alone can make the accomplishment graceful and profitable. Patience, diligence, painstaking attention to detail—these are the requirements; these, in time, will make the student perfect; upon these, and upon these only, may he rely as the sure foundation for future eminence. Think what tedious years of study, thought, practice, experience, went to the equipment of that peerless old master who was able to impose upon the whole world the lofty and sounding maxim that "truth is mighty and will prevail"—the most majestic compound fracture of fact which any of woman born has yet achieved. For the history of our race, and each individual's experience, are sown thick with evidence that a truth is not hard to kill and that a lie told well is immortal. There in Boston is a monument of the man who discovered anesthesia; many people are aware, in these latter days, that that man didn't discover it at all, but stole the discovery from another man. Is this truth mighty, and will it prevail? Ah no, my hearers, the monument is made of hardy material, but the lie it tells will outlast it a million years. An awkward, feeble, leaky lie is a thing which you ought to make it your unceasing study to avoid; such a lie as that has no more real permanence than an average truth. Why, you might as well tell the truth at once and be done with it. A feeble, stupid, preposterous lie will not live two years—except it be a slander upon somebody. It is indestructible, then, of course, but that is no merit of yours. A final word; begin your practice of this gracious

and beautiful art early—begin now. If I had begun earlier, I could have learned how.

6   Never handle firearms carelessly. The sorrow and suffering that have been caused through the innocent but heedless handling of firearms by the young! Only four days ago, right in the next farm-house to the one where I am spending the summer, a grandmother, old and gray and sweet, one of the loveliest spirits in the land, was sitting at her work, when her young grandson crept in and got down an old, battered, rusty gun which had not been touched for many years and was supposed not to be loaded, and pointed it at her, laugh-ing and threatening to shoot. In her fright she ran screaming and pleading toward the door on the other side of the room; but as she passed him he placed the gun almost against her very breast and pulled the trigger! He had supposed it was not loaded. And he was right—it wasn't. So there wasn't any harm done. It is the only case of that kind I ever heard of. Therefore, just the same, don't you meddle with old unloaded firearms; they are the most deadly and unerring things that have ever been created by man. You don't have to take any pains at all with them; you don't have to have a rest, you don't have to have any sights on the gun, you don't have to take aim, even. No, you just pick out a relative and bang away, and you are sure to get him. A youth who can't hit a cathedral at thirty yards with a Gatling gun in three-quarters of an hour, can take up an old empty musket and bag his grandmother every time, at a hundred. Think what Waterloo would have been if one of the armies had been boys armed with old muskets supposed not to be loaded, and the other army had been composed of their female relations. The very thought of it makes one shudder.

7   There are many sorts of books; but good ones are the sort for the young to read. Remember that. They are a great, an inestimable, an unspeakable means of improvement. Therefore be careful in your selection, my young friends; be very careful; confine yourselves exclusively to Robertson's Sermons, Baxter's *Saint's Rest, The Innocents Abroad,* and works of that kind.

8   But I have said enough. I hope you will treasure up the instruc-tions which I have given you, and make them a guide to your feet and a light to your understanding. Build your character thoughtfully and painstaking upon these precepts, and by and by, when you have got it built, you will be surprised and gratified to see how nicely and sharply it resembles everybody else's.

ADVICE TO YOUTH

Exploring Language

didactic: intended to teach, but often refers to teaching in a preachy, moralistic manner.

eminence: fame or prominence.

temperate: mild, moderate.

Note: For pronunciation, go to dictionary.com, search the word, and click on the speaker icon.

USAGE Locate the sentences where Twain uses these Exploring Language words in paragraphs #1 and #5, and study their usage. Here's a challenge: use all three of these words in one sentence.

Thinking and Talking Points

1. In this type of satirical humor, writers say one thing but mean the opposite. Find examples in the essay that illustrate that Twain isn't advocating lying, feeling superior, or shooting one's grandmother. How effective is this type of humor?

2. Why do you think Twain gives satirical advice to students in his address rather than instructive advice as he claims?

3. Why does Twain write that slander is indestructible? Do you agree? Is this type of lie worse than other lies Twain mentions?

4. What is Twain's view of youth? To what extent do you agree with his view? Is his "advice" relevant today?

5. What point does he make in the last line of the essay?

Styling

Though satire has a unique style, good humorists also use strong writing techniques such as sentence variety. Notice that Twain uses some very long sentences, some very short, others medium. Sentence variety keeps the reader alert, like a song with varying beats and tones. Because you know how to write short and medium sentences, practice modeling one of Twain's longer sentences:

Only four days ago, right in the next farmhouse to the one where I am spending the summer, a grandmother, old and gray and sweet, one of the loveliest spirits in the land, was sitting at her work, when her young grandson crept in and got down an old, battered, rusty gun which had not been touched for many years and was supposed not to be loaded, and pointed it at her, laughing and threatening to shoot.

Don't let long sentences intimidate you; they're just short sentences dressed up. If you analyze Twain's sentence, you'll find the short sentence:

Only four days ago a grandmother was sitting at her work.

The rest of the sentence consists of word groups that dress up this simple sentence, describing and giving more information. Twain could have split some of this information into separate sentences, but he knew a well-written long sentence gives what English teachers refer to as "flow" to an essay. Examine the rest of the word groups to determine their purpose. The first one is an interrupter placed between "ago" and "a grandmother," giving extra information about Twain's whereabouts: right in the next farmhouse to the one where I am spending the summer.

Notice that the word group is **dependent**—it can't stand alone as its own sentence. The next two dependent word groups come after "grandmother," describing her:

old and gray and sweet

one of the loveliest spirits in the land

The next series of dependent word groups provides action—read them again (in the complete sentence above), writing them out separately on a sheet of paper, noticing that they, too, are dependent.

PRACTICE   Fill in the blank in the simple sentence below, adding a dependent clause that describes the teller:

Last week a bank teller, _____, sat innocently at her window.

Next, replace the period after window with a comma, and add a dependent clause describing what the teller is doing:

Last week a bank teller, _____, sat innocently at her window, _____.

Now, give a series of action clauses:

Last week a bank teller, _____, sat innocently at her
    window, _____, when _____,
    _____, and _____, and _____.

YOU TRY IT Write three more sentences based on the above model. Use this structure in your next writing assignment.

    Caution: Don't get discouraged if you commit comma splices at first. Writing correct long sentences sometimes takes several practice tries.

Teaming Up

1. In groups of three or four members, decide on a topic that might lend itself to satirical advice, like cheating. Brainstorm a list of satirical reasons advocating the topic. Choose one of the reasons to develop into a paragraph, and then co-write the paragraph.

2. Have each group member do a little research on the works Twain recommends students read: *The Innocents Abroad,* Frederick Robertson's *Sermons*, and Richard Baxter's *Saint's Rest* (the latter two available on the Web). You should be able to find enough information in a good encyclopedia to give you clues. In your group, discuss the findings and why Twain suggests young people should read works like these exclusively.

    Note: Try Britannica Online rather than unreliable sites. Most college libraries subscribe to Britannica Online or other reputable encyclopedias.

Writing Ideas

1. Write an essay about an experience you had with lying or slander, either by you or aimed at you, explaining the situation and the damage caused.

2. Write an essay that gives advice, either serious or satirical. You can give moral or ethical advice, as Twain does, or write a "how to" piece, a type of essay English teachers call Process Analysis: see the 'Writing Strategies' section for instructions.

3. Visit a library that has an online periodicals database and research political campaign slander. Write an essay arguing for or against this type of campaign strategy, not only whether it works, but its moral and ethical implications. Use the research to provide examples in the essay. For more on writing research papers, see the Research Section Six.

Essay Connections

P. J. O'Rourke's "Driving Fast" satirizes teen behavior. "Turbulence" by David Sedaris is a humorous account of behavior he has encountered. Jonathon Swift's "A Modest Proposal" is easy to find on the Web.

FROM *THE DUMBEST GENERATION: HOW THE DIGITAL AGE STUPEFIES YOUNG AMERICANS AND JEOPARDIZES OUR FUTURE*

Mark Bauerlein

In this preface to the paperback edition of The Dumbest Generation, *English Professor Mark Bauerlein of Emory University discusses "the swift and judgmental" response to the hardback edition of his book. Some critics agreed with his premise; others did not. Bauerlein poses the question "Do the digital diversions of the young cut kids off from history, civics, literature, fine art?" He explains his intent--not to settle the question with a definitive answer, but simply to open discussion, to "open the issue to some sober skepticism." In addition to being an English professor and a writer, Bauerlein has worked as a director of Research and Analysis at the National Endowment for the Arts, supervising work on culture and American life.*

DUSTBIN OF HISTORY AND CULTURE

GULAG: forced labor camps or detention camps, especially in Russia.

1   When The Dumbest Generation first came out, in May 2008, response in the media was swift and judgmental. Feature articles appeared in *Newsweek, The Boston Globe,* the *Chicago Tribune, The Times of London, Haaretz* (Israel), *Superinteressante* (Brazil), and *The Weekly Telegraph* (Serbia), and reviews *in The Wall Street Journal, The New York Times,* the *Los Angeles Times,* the Toronto *Globe and Mail,* while eighty or so radio and TV hosts conducted interviews. Each effort more or less deftly outlined the topic, and many landed hard on yea or nay. A blank and broad question lay on the table: Do the digital diversions of the young cut kids off from history, civics, literature, fine art? Does mounting screen time dumb them down?

2   I think yes, others say no, but I never expected to vanquish the other side and end the debate. The realistic goal was to open the issue to some sober skepticism, to blunt the techno-zeal spreading through classrooms and libraries, shopping malls and children's bedrooms. It

was to counter the sanguine portraits of informed and agile teens at the keyboard with dismaying survey results and illustrations of youth insulation and ignorance, kids shunning books and vaunting their digital nativity. We won't know the full intellectual impact of text messaging, Web 2.0, Facebook, and the rest for many years, and it will show up in distant measures such as the money firms spend on writing coaches for employees, the number of students in remedial classes, popular demand that politicians elevate their rhetoric, and whether the vocabulary level of newspapers inches downward or upward.

3   That evidence remains to be seen, but at least we can say that the general take on digital technology has expanded and diversified. In the past year, several books have joined *The Dumbest Generation* to set the purpose and uses of the tools in a critical spotlight. They include works by Andrew Keen (*The Cult of the Amateur: How Blogs, MySpace, YouTube, and the Rest of Today's User-Generated Media Are Destroying Our Economy, Our Culture, and Our Values*), Susan Jacoby (*The Age of American Unreason*), Lee Siegel (*Against the Machine: Being Human in the Age of the Electronic Mob*), Nicholas Carr (*The Big Switch: Rewiring the World, from Edison to Google*), Maggie Jackson (*Distracted: The Erosion of Attention and the Coming Dark Age*), and Hal Abelson, Ken Ledeen, and Harry Lewis (*Blown to Bits: Your Life, Liberty, and Happiness After the Digital Explosion*), and several other popular and academic studies. Together they form an imposing countervailing force, an alliance to slow the headlong rush to technologize learning, reading, writing, and social and intellectual life. They have forced a better, more reflective attitude toward the future, an appreciation of the wondrous things gained, yes, but also a sensitivity to precious goods and practices lost.

4   *The Dumbest Generation* also postulates an attitude toward the past, however, and several commentators picked up on it with a curt objection. "Here we go again," they remarked, "an aging schoolmaster knocking the kids. The old ones did it when Elvis arrived, and now they do it because of Grand Theft Auto. We've heard the grievance many times, the lament of graying folks, so let's not take it too seriously." A fair criticism, if any easy one, and it actually points to what may be the great social consequence of the digital advent. It turns on, precisely, the relationship of generations and the duties of elders. For, we all agree, one responsibility of adults in our society is to acquaint the rising generation to a civic and cultural inheritance. They have the experience and the perspective that come with aging;

the young do not. Teenagers live in the present and the immediate. What happened long ago and far away doesn't impress them. They care about what occurred last week in the cafeteria, not what took place during the Great Depression. They heed the words of Facebook, not the Gettysburg Address. They focus on other kids in English class, not leaders in Congress.

5   Maturity follows a formula: The more kids contact one another, the less they heed the tutelage of adults. When peer consciousness grows too fixed and firm, the teacher's voice counts for nothing outside the classroom. When youth identify envelops them, parent talk at the dinner table only distracts them. The lure of school gossip, fear of ridicule, the urge to belong—they swamp the minds of the young and stunt their intellectual growth.

6   Kids need a reprieve and a retreat. For them to grow up into mindful citizens and discerning consumers, then, adolescents must break the social circuit and think beyond the clique and the schoolyard. But they can't do it themselves—peer pressure is too strong—and so adults must help draw them away. Adult content, civic and historical stuff, makes the current events of high school less commanding. Mentors can provide instruction in bigger things: the op-ed page, actions of Congress, the heroism of Martin Luther King, Jr., what transpired in the gulag, what the First Amendment says, the fate of Adam and Eve...Mentors steer young minds toward deeper wisdom and young tastes toward finer consumptions. The story of heroes and villains from history sets the eminences of senior year in bracing relief. The eloquence of Emily Dickinson nicely explodes the favored patter of the hallways.

7   Yet how can adults impart it when peer-to-peer contact extends to every minute and every space of the day and night? That's the threat digital tools pose to parents and teachers. Equipped with BlackBerry and laptop, sporting a flashy profile page and a blog, teenagers pass words and images back and forth 24/7. The bedroom is no longer a sanctuary, it's a command center. E-mails, text messages, blog postings and comments, phone calls, tweets, feeds, photos, and songs pour in every evening, and if kids don't respond, they fall behind. Even when logged off and disconnected, they sense that a buddy (or nemesis) may be talking about them, passing around an image, setting a rendezvous, amplifying gossip, or leaving a message. An edifying case happens in the 2008 film *American Teen*, a documentary tracking five kids through senior year in high school in Warsaw, Indiana. At one point, an excitable girl sends her boyfriend a

topless photo of herself, not realizing it will bounce to others in the network. Two girls grab it and with sadistic, masterful glee circulate it through every connection they know, and by the next morning when the girl comes to class, every kid in school has her image downloaded and shared. The lesson strikes home: Peer contact never ends, and digital tools are as essential and ordinary as food and air and sleep.

8   This is the new habitus of the Digital Age. Youths undergo an intense awareness of one another, a high pressure social feeling. The stakes are high—is anything worse than exclusion?—and so they have to tune in, to manage that omnipresence. They don't really enjoy it, for when they leave my class and flip open the cell, they register concern, not glee. But if they don't check in, they don't know whether something big might have happened. Peer pressure long preceded the microchip, of course, but e-mail, cell phones, and the rest have cranked it up to critical levels, fostering an all-peers-all-the-time network. Communication is horizontal, centered on a narrow age bracket, while parents and teachers hover outside the loop, baffled by the immersion.

9   If parents and teachers don't contain it, if they don't find occasional substitutions for it, it will get only worse. The natural inclinations of the young flow toward one another, and each new tool speeds them faster on their way. Late-teens and early-twenty-somethings stand at a delicate threshold that marks the most important intellectual growth of their life. They have passed the basic skills of elementary and middle school, and now they acquire the higher knowledge and understanding requisite to good citizenship and tasteful consumption. These are the years in which they read good books, discuss great ideas, judge past events, and form moral scruples. If it doesn't happen in high school, in college, and in the home at this time, it probably never will. Once in the workplace, raising kids, paying bills, and doing laundry, people don't have time, energy, or guidance to ponder the *Federalis Papers* or read *The Divine Comedy*. Every hour on MySpace, then, means an hour not practicing a musical instrument or learning a foreign language or watching C-SPAN. Every cell-phone call interrupts a chapter of Harry Potter or a look at the local paper. These are mind-maturing activities, and they don't have to involve Great Books and Big Ideas. They have only to cultivate habits of analysis and reflection, and implant knowledge of the world beyond.

10   They mark the opportunity costs of digital diversions, and as they accumulate over the months, the costs rise higher than they seem at

any one moment. *The Dumbest Generation* counts them up and sounds an alert. It doesn't invoke an ideal past of multitudes of studious kids preferring Shakespeare to cartoons and activist kids debating the size of government. That never existed and never will. What did exist, though, was a climate in which the voices of elders and the value of history and civics, books and ideas, exercised more pressure on the young. Teen social life had a limit, and in those other hours the forces of adulthood were felt, if resented. When I was sixteen, I went to school and hung out with friends, and after school I played some basketball, hung out some more, and headed home. When I crossed the threshold and sat down to dinner, social life was over. I listened to my parents converse about money, work, the household, travel plans, while Walter Cronkite reported on Vietnam and Watergate. I didn't like them and didn't want to talk to them, but I couldn't reach under the table with my handheld and connect with buddies. I couldn't go up to my room, flip open the laptop, and blog about the new biology teacher. Leisure options were fewer, and without ready access to friends, things like books, libraries, museums, and homework enjoyed a larger presence.

11   That's what has changed. The Digital Age has embroiled the young in a swirl of social groupings and contests, and it threatens their intellectual development. This is not a benign evolution of old media into new media, traditional literacy into e-literacy. It is a displacement. Digital tools have designs on the eyes and ears of the kids, and they pursue them aggressively. Once youths enter the digital realm, the race for attention begins, and it doesn't like to stop for a half-hour with a novel or a trip to the museum. Digital offerings don't like to share, the tales of Founding Fathers and ancient battles and Gothic churches can't compete with a message from a boyfriend, photos from the party, and a new device in the Apple Store window. Parents and teachers have a new rival in the lives of kids: not just a circle of friends, but a spreading glossy marketplace of communications technology with a certified youth meaning. Put them together—the e-tools and the collective will of teens—and they look invincible.

FOLLOW UP

FROM THE DUMBEST GENERATION

Exploring Language

advent: arrival.
bracing: invigorating.
countervailing: to act against with equal force.
discerning: perceiving; recognizing.
eminence: high status or rank.
lament: to feel or express sorrow or regret.
nativity: birth with reference to place or attendance (in this context).
omnipresence: present everywhere at the same time.
patter: meaningless, rapid talk (in this context).
postulate: to claim or assume.
shun: to keep away from; dislike; avoidance.
vaunting: marked by boatsful pride.

USAGE Write a sentence that uses at least two of the words in the list in the same sentence (change the form of the word if needed; for example, patter to pattering).

Thinking and Talking Points

1. What is the author's thesis? What main support does he provide?
2. What purpose do the lists in paragraphs one and three serve? How might this technique work in a college essay?
3. Bauerlein addresses the opposition (critics of his argument) in paragraph four. Summarize the opposition's views and Bauerlein's defense. How adequately does he defend his position?
4. What **cause and effect** argument does Bauerlein present? What are his solutions?
5. What point does he make concerning mentors and cultural heritage?
6. Bauerlein comments that teens have not changed; they are no more interested in their parents or global events than ever. What *has* changed that impacts the intellectual growth of the young? What might be sobering about this point?

Styling

Sentences with long lists corral examples, penning them into one place to overwhelm the reader, convincing the reader by their sheer numbers (see question two). In addition to long lists, Bauerlein uses an add-on (see "Commas with Add-ons" in the "Punctuation is Style" section) to pair up items in a short list:

> The realistic goal was to open the issue to some sober skepticism, to blunt the techno-zeal spreading through **classrooms and libraries, shopping malls and children's bedrooms.**

Notice he begins with a complete sentence:

> The realistic goal was to open the issue to some sober skepticism.

This sentence could stand alone, but the add-on using a prepositional phrase gives more information without having to break into two sentences, creating better sentence variety:

> **Prepositional phrase:** to blunt the techno-zeal spreading through
> **Pair number one:** classrooms and libraries
> **Pair number two:** shopping malls and children's bedrooms.

Notice that the pairs have something in common: *classrooms and libraries* are places of learning; *shopping malls* and *children's bedrooms* distract from learning.

PRACTICE In the sentence below, first brainstorm a list of places where bullying happens, and then pair up the ones that have something in common. Pick out the two best pairs and fill in the blanks.

Bullying has become epidemic, in _____ and _____, in _____ and _____.

Note: You might need to change a preposition for grammatical correctness (while one might be "on" Facebook, one is not "in" Facebook).

YOU TRY IT Write three sentences on a topic of your choice, following this style. If working on an essay, write at least one on that topic.

Note: For variations on this sentence style, see the "Styling" section with "A Dark and Stormy Knight: Why Batman?" by Travis Langley.

Teaming Up

1. Study the long sentences in paragraphs one and three and discuss how they strengthen Bauerlein's point in each paragraph. Brainstorm a list of potential controversial topics (stay away from the overdone topics like the death penalty, gun control, abortion). Decide on one topic from the list and co-write a statement about that topic. Brainstorm a list of examples to support the statement and write up the sentence with the list.

2. **Warm-up for Writing Idea #2:** As homework, look up cyber-bullying and teen anxiety in your college's data bases such as Opposing Viewpoints, Infotrac, or newspapers. Print out at least one article. Read and annotate the article, looking up and writing down definitions of unfamiliar words. Bring the annotated article to class. In groups, each person will present their findings. Discuss which articles most directly address the topic. Make a master list of the most useful articles, complete with source citations (often found at the bottom of the article). Put the articles in Works Cited format (see Section Five).

Writing Ideas

1. Agree or disagree (see the "Writing Strategies for Arguing" section) with Mark Bauerlein's claims that technology has dumbed down adolescents, creating an intellectual void that leaves society at a disadvantage.

2. Write an essay that argues how technology induces anxiety in young people. Explore the topic of cyber-bullying and how it contributes to the problem; cull examples from news data bases and personal experience.

Essay Connections

Other essays that analyze an aspect of popular culture include "Monster Mash" by Jack Kroll, "The Culture of Celebrity" by Joseph Epstein, "Somebody's Baby" by Barbara Kingsolver, and "A Dark and Stormy Knight: Why Batman?" by Travis Langley.

ABOUT MEN

Gretel Ehrlich

Writer, rancher, documentary film maker, Gretel Ehrlich has several books to her credit, includ-
ing This Cold Heaven, The Solace of Open Spaces, Questions of Heaven, John Muir: Nature's
Visionary, and The Future of Ice. In "About Men," from Solace of Open Spaces, Ehrlich
debunks the myth of the American cowboy, claiming that those Marlboro ads have it all wrong:
"Instead of the macho, trigger-happy man our culture perversely wants him to be, the cowboy
is more apt to be convivial, quirky, and softhearted."

DUSTBIN OF HISTORY AND CULTURE

CHISHOLM TRAIL: A cattle trail that ran between San Antonio, Texas and Abilene, Kansas (exact trail unknown); it was used for about twenty years after the Civil War (1861–1865) until the expansion of the railroad made it no longer useful.

HOBBLES: Restraints used mostly on horses (though sometimes on dogs or humans), placed on the front legs to restrict movement.

1   When I'm in New York but feeling lonely for Wyoming I look for the Marlboro ads in the subway. What I'm aching to see is horseflesh, the glint of a spur, a line of distant mountains, brimming creeks, and a reminder of the ranchers and cowboys I've ridden with for the last eight years. But the men I see in those posters with their stern, humorless looks remind me of no one I know here. In our hellbent earnestness to romanticize the cowboy we've ironically disesteemed his true character. If he's "strong and silent" it's because there's probably no one to talk to. If he "rides away into the sunset" it's because he's been on horseback since four in the morning moving cattle and he's trying, fifteen hours later, to get home to his family. If he's "a rugged individualist" he's also part of a team: ranch work is teamwork and even the glorified open-range cowboys of the 1880s rode up and down the Chisholm Trail in the company of twenty or thirty other riders. Instead of the macho, trigger-happy man our culture has perversely wanted him to be, the cowboy is more apt to be convivial, quirky, and softhearted. To be "tough" on a ranch has nothing to do with conquests

and displays of power. More often than not, circumstances—like the colt he's riding or an unexpected blizzard—are overpowering him. It's not toughness but "toughing it out" that counts. In other words, this macho, cultural artifact the cowboy has become is simply a man who possesses resilience, patience, and an instinct for survival. "Cowboys are just like a pile of rocks—everything happens to them. They get climbed on, kicked, rained and snowed on, scuffed up by wind. Their job is 'just to take it,'" one old-timer told me.

2   A cowboy is someone who loves his work. Since the hours are long—ten to fifteen hours a day—and the pay is $30 he has to. What's required of him is an odd mixture of physical vigor and maternalism. His part of the beef-raising industry is to birth and nurture calves and take care of their mothers. For the most part his work is done on horseback and in a lifetime he sees and comes to know more animals than people. The iconic myth surrounding him is built on American notions of heroism: the index of a man's value as measured in physical courage. Such ideas have perverted manliness into a self-absorbed race for cheap thrills. In a rancher's world, courage has less to do with facing danger than with acting spontaneously—usually on behalf of an animal or another rider. If a cow is stuck in a boghole he throws a loop around her neck, takes his daily (a half hitch around the saddle horn), and pulls her out with horsepower. If a calf is born sick, he may take her home, warm her in front of the kitchen fire, and massage her legs until dawn. One friend, whose favorite horse was tying to swim a lake with hobbles on, dove under water and cut her legs loose with a knife, then swam her to shore, his arm around her neck lifeguard-style, and saved her from drowning. Because these incidents are usually linked to someone or something outside himself, the westerner's courage is selfless, a form of compassion.

3   The physical punishment that goes with cowboying is greatly underplayed. Once fear is dispensed with, the threshold of pain rises to meet the demands of the job. When Jane Fonda asked Robert Redford (in the film *Electric Horseman*) if he was sick as he struggled to his feet one morning, he replied, "No, just bent." For once the movies had it right. The cowboys I was sitting with laughed in agreement. Cowboys are rarely complainers; they show their stoicism by laughing at themselves.

4   If a rancher or cowboy has been thought of as a "man's man"— laconic, hard-drinking, inscrutable—there's almost no place in which the balancing act between male and female, manliness and femininity, can be more natural. If he's gruff, handsome, and physically fit

on the outside, he's androgynous at the core. Ranchers are midwives, hunters, nurturers, providers, and conservationists all at once. What we've interpreted as toughness—weathered skin, calloused hands, a squint in the eye and a growl in the voice—only masks the tenderness inside. "Now don't go telling me these lambs are cute, one rancher warned me the first day I walked into the football-field-sized lambing sheds. The next thing I knew he was holding a black lamb. "Ain't this little rat good-lookin'?"

5   So many of the men who came to the West were southerners—men looking for work and a new life after the Civil War—that chivalrousness and strict codes of honor were soon thought of as western traits. There were very few women in Wyoming during territorial days, so when they did arrive (some as mail-order brides from places like Philadelphia) there was a stand-offishness between the sexes and a formality that persists now. Ranchers still tip their hats and say, "Howdy, ma'am" instead of shaking hands with me.

6   Even young cowboys are often evasive with women. It's not that they're Jekyll and Hyde creatures—gentle with animals and rough on women—but rather that they don't know how to bring their tenderness into the house and lack the vocabulary to express the complexity of what they feel. Dancing wildly all night becomes a metaphor for the explosive emotions pent up inside, and when these are, on occasion, released, they're so battery-charged and potent that one caress of the face or one "I love you" will peal for a long while.

7   The geographical vastness and the social isolation here make emotional evolution seem impossible. Those contradictions of the heart between respectability, logic, and convention on the one hand, and impulse, passion, and intuition on the other, played out wordlessly against the paradisical beauty of the West, give cowboys a wide-eyed but drawn look. Their lips pucker up, not with kisses but with immutability. They may want to break out, staying up all night with a lover just to talk, but they don't know how and can't imagine what the consequences will be. Those rare occasions when they do bare themselves result in confusion. "I feel as if I'd sprained my heart," one friend told me a month after such a meeting.

8   My friend Ted Hoagland wrote, "No one is as fragile as a woman but no one is as fragile as a man." For all the women here who use "fragileness" to avoid work or as a sexual ploy, there are men who try to hide theirs, all the while clinging to an adolescent dependency on women to cook their meals, wash their clothes, and keep the ranch

house warm in winter. But there is true vulnerability in evidence here. Because these men work with animals, not machines or numbers, because they live outside in landscapes of torrential beauty, because they are confined to a place and a routine embellished with awesome variables, because calves die in the arms that pulled others into life, because they go to the mountains as if on a pilgrimage to find out what makes a herd of elk tick, their strength is also a softness, their toughness, a rare delicacy.

ABOUT MEN

Exploring Language

androgynous: having both masculine and feminine characteristics.
convivial: friendly, agreeable.
disesteemed: made unfavorable.
evasive: avoiding a direct response to a verbal challenge; elusive is used when the avoidance is physical.
immutability: unchangeable.
inscrutable: not easily understood; mysterious.
laconic: using few words.
romanticize: in this context, romanticize means to make something unrealistic or idealistic; to make fanciful, fictitious, or sentimental.
stoicism: repressing emotion and physical pain.
Note: For pronunciation, go to dictionary.com, search the word, and click on the speaker icon.

USAGE   Write two sentences, one using *elusive* and the other *evasive.*

Thinking and Talking Points

1. How does Ehrlich debunk the myth of the American cowboy? Which examples best support her point? Do any weaken it? Which ones surprise you the most? How does America "romanticize" the cowboy?
2. Examine the stories and quotes about and from cowboys. How does each one support a topic sentence in the paragraph?
3. What does Ehrlich's essay imply about stereotypes in general? What other not-so-obvious stereotypes exist in our culture?
4. How does Ehrlich use contrast to her advantage? Examine each one and comment on whether or not it works.
5. In paragraph #5, she examines the origins of the cowboy's standoffishness. What is the significance of her analysis? Does it adequately explain the cowboys' relationships with women?

Styling

If you've ever been told that your essay doesn't flow, the problem might be lack of **transitions**. Though many things contribute to flow in an essay—correct grammar and punctuation, sentence variety, organization—if proper transition doesn't exist between paragraphs, the piece will sound too abrupt, as if you're changing ideas without signaling your reader. You might have been taught simple transitions like however, therefore, first of all, secondly, and so on, but to bump your writing up to a more college-level style, transitions should be more subtle than these worn-out examples.

Examine the last and first sentences of each paragraph in Ehrlich's essay. She carefully shifts ideas by using the same word in a different form (*emotions* and *emotional* in paragraphs #6 and #7); words that have similar meanings or connotations (*job* and *work* in paragraphs #1 and #2); or seeming opposites (*compassion* and *physical punishment* in paragraphs #2 and #3). Though there are more sophisticated transitions, these three should get you started.

PRACTICE   For each word in the list, think of a similar word, an opposite, or use the same word in a different form: friendly, melancholy, sincere, evil, cynical, water, writer, surfer, computer, plastic.

YOU TRY IT   Examine an essay you have written to see if you've used strong transition. If not, edit the essay, using the above styles of transition.

Note: See the transition ideas in Section Five.

Teaming Up

1. **Warm-up for Writing Idea #3.** As a group, brainstorm ideas on other topics that are often advertised, and have each person bring in at least three ads so you'll have nine to twelve ads on the same topic. Some ideas might be pet food, blue jeans, surf wear, moms, make-up, toys. Examine the ads for stereotypes and list them. Discuss how each stereotype might be untrue.

2. Using the list from Teaming Up #1, co-write a paragraph using "if" to debunk the myths in one of the stereotypes. For help, examine paragraph #2 in the essay and use it for a model.

3. **Warm-up for Writing Idea #2.** Have each group member write down a figure from popular culture that he or she admires or loathes. The icon can be from the past or present as long as it fits the definition of an icon. An icon is a representative image, in this case a body of cultural assumptions; for example, Marilyn Monroe is seen as an icon of American beauty, and with that comes a set of assumptions about beauty in America. As a group, brainstorm the assumptions you make about what each image represents. Co-write a paragraph describing the icon and the assumptions you listed.

Writing Ideas

1. Write an essay that debunks a common misconception (or misconceptions) about a personality trait such as sentimentality, altruism, shyness, loneliness, individualism. Explain how there might be more sides to this character trait than our clichéd thinking usually allows. For example how might sentimentality be a negative quality? Is an individualist hiding a selfish nature? Does an altruist have an egoist alter ego? Follow the Writing Strategies for Defining Terms in Section Five.

2. The Marlboro Man might be seen as an American icon, embodying our cultural assumptions about the American cowboy. Explore another icon and write an essay that debunks our widely held assumption about that icon. You can choose from the art world, music, television, film, cereal boxes, advertising, Disney—almost anything is open for analysis.

3. Examine ads on another topic—blue jeans, toys, make-up, pet food, anything that's often advertised—and write an essay that explores the stereotypes hidden in these ads and debunk each stereotype. Describe each ad in detail.

Essay Connections

In "Somebody's Baby," Barbara Kingsolver discusses cultural attitudes about children in different countries. Joseph Epstein lambastes America's obsession with celebrity. In the preface to *The Dumbest Generation*, Mark Bauerlein laments technology's negative impact on teens and young adults.

FROM THE CONTENT OF OUR CHARACTER

Shelby Steele

Shelby Steele is a writer and educator who has many published essays and books to his credit. In this excerpt from his book, Steele argues that despite still-existing racism, overall, there is "a remarkable range of opportunity if we are willing to pursue it." African Americans, according to Steele, need to stop focusing on a victim-based identity and take advantage of what mainstream America has to offer.

DUSTBIN OF HISTORY AND CULTURE

JEAN-PAUL SARTRE: (1905–1980) French philosopher and writer and leading proponent of existentialism.

RALPH ELLISON: (1914–1994) American novelist and essayist who wrote *The Invisible Man.*

EXISTENTIAL: See "Thinking and Talking Points" #5

1   There are many profound problems facing black America today: a swelling black underclass; a black middle class that declined slightly in size during the Eighties; a declining number of black college students; an epidemic of teenage pregnancy, drug use, and gang violence; continuing chronic unemployment; astoundingly high college and high school dropout rates; an increasing number of single-parent families; a disproportionately high infant mortality rate; and so on. Against this despair it might seem almost esoteric for me to talk about the importance of individual identity and possibility. Yet I have come to believe that despite the existing racism in today's America, opportunity is the single most constant but unexploited aspect of the black condition. The only way we will see the advancement of black people in this country is for us to focus on developing ourselves as individuals and embracing opportunity.

2   I have come to this conclusion over time. In the late Sixties, I was caught up in the new spirit of black power and pride that swept over black America like one of those storms that change the landscape. I

will always believe this storm was inevitable and, therefore, positive in many ways. What I gained from it was the power to be racially unapologetic, no mean benefit considering the long trial of patience that blacks were subjected to during the civil rights movement. But after a while, by the early Seventies, it became clear that black power did not offer much of a blueprint for how to move my life forward; it told me virtually nothing about who I was as an individual or how I might live in the world as myself. Of course, it was my mistake to think it could. But in the late Sixties, "blackness" was an invasive form of collective identity that cut so deeply into one's individual space that it seemed also to be an individual identity. It came as something of a disappointment to realize that the two were not the same, that being "black" in no way spared me the necessity of being myself.

3   In the early Seventies, without realizing it, I made a sort of bargain with the prevailing black identity—I subscribed in a general way to its point of view so that I could be free to get on with my life. Many blacks I knew did the same.

4   And what were we subscribing to? Generally, I think it was a form of black identity grounded in the spirit of black power. It carried a righteous anger at and mistrust of American society; it believed that blacks continued to be the victims of institutional racism, that we would have to maintain an adversarial stance toward society, and that a right racial unity was necessary both for survival and advancement. This identity was, and is, predicated on the notion that those who burned you once will burn you again, and it presupposes a deep racist reflex in American life that will forever try to limit black possibility.

5   I think it was the space I cleared for myself by loosely subscribing to this identity that ultimately put me in conflict with it. It is in the day-to-day struggle of living on the floor of a society, so to speak, that one gains a measure of what is possible in that society. And by simply living as an individual in America—with my racial-identity struggle suspended temporarily—I discovered that American society offered me, and blacks in general, a remarkable range of opportunity if we were willing to pursue it.

6   In my daily life I continue to experience racial indignities and slights: This morning I was told that blacks had too much musical feeling (soul, I suppose) to be good classical musicians; yesterday I passed two houses with gnomish black lawn jockeys on their front porches; my children have been called "nigger," as have I; I wear a tie and carry a briefcase so that my students on the first day of class will know I'm the professor; and so on. I also know that actual racial discrimination

persists in many areas of American life. I have been the victor in one housing-discrimination suit, as were my parents before me. My life is not immune to any of this, and I will never endure it with élan. Yet I have also come to realize that, in this same society, I have been more in charge of my fate than I ever wanted to believe and that though I have been limited by many things, my race was not foremost among them.

7   The point is that both realities exist simultaneously. There is still racial insensitivity and some racial discrimination against blacks in this society, but there is also much opportunity. What brought me into conflict with the prevailing black identity was that it was almost entirely preoccupied with the former to the exclusion of the latter. The black identity I was subscribing to in the Seventies—and that still prevails today—was essentially a "wartime" identity shaped in the confrontational Sixties. It saw blacks as victims even as new possibilities for advancement opened all around.

8   Why do we cling to an adversarial, victim-focused identity and remain preoccupied with white racism? Part of the reason, I think, is that we carry an inferiority anxiety—an unconscious fear that the notion that we are inferior may, in fact, be true—that makes the seizing of opportunity more risky for us, since setbacks and failures may seem to confirm our worst fears. To avoid this risk we hold a victim-focused identity that tells us there is less opportunity than there actually is. And, in fact, our victimization itself has been our primary source of power in society—the basis of our demands for redress. The paradoxical result of relying on this source of power is that it rewards us for continuing to see ourselves as victims of a racist society and implies that opportunity itself is something to be given instead of taken.

9   This leaves us with an identity that is at war with our own best interests, that magnifies our oppression and diminishes our sense of possibility. I think this identity is a burden for blacks, because it is built around our collective insecurity rather than a faith in our human capacity to seize opportunity as individuals. It amounts to a self-protective collectivism that focuses on black unity instead of individual initiative. To be "black" in this identity, one need only manifest the symbols, postures, and rhetoric of black unity. Not only is personal initiative unnecessary for being "black," but the successful exercise of initiative—working one's way into the middle class, becoming well-off, gaining an important position—may, in fact, jeopardize one's "blackness," make one somehow less black.

10   This sort of identity is never effective and never translates into the actual uplift of black people. Though it espouses black pride, it is actually a repressive identity that generates a victimized self-image, curbs individualism and initiative, diminishes our sense of possibility, and contributes to our demoralization and inertia. Uplift can only come when many millions of blacks seize the possibilities inside the sphere of their personal lives and use them to move themselves forward. Collectively we can resist oppression, but racial development will always be, as Ralph Ellison once put it, "the gift" of individuals.

11   There have been numerous government attempts at remedying the list of problems I mentioned earlier. Here and there a program has worked; many more have been failures. Clearly, we should find the ones that do work and have more of them. But my deepest feeling is that, in a society of increasingly limited resources, there will never be enough programs to meet the need. We black Americans will never be saved or even assisted terribly much by others, never be repaid for our suffering, and never find that symmetrical, historical justice that we cannot help but long for.

12   As Jean-Paul Sartre once said, we are the true "existential people." We have always had to create ourselves out of whole cloth and find our own means for survival. I believe that black leadership must recognize the importance of this individual initiative. They must preach it, tell it, sell it, and demand it. Our leadership has looked at government and white society very critically. Now they must help us look at ourselves. We need our real problems named and explained, otherwise we have no chance to overcome them. The impulse of our leaders is to be "political," to keep the society at large on edge, to keep them feeling as though they have not done enough for blacks. And, clearly, they have not. But the price these leaders pay for this form of "politics" is to keep blacks focused on an illusion of deliverance by others, and no illusion weakens us more. Our leaders must take a risk. They must tell us the truth, tell us of the freedom and opportunity they have discovered in their own lives. They must tell us what they tell their own children when they go home at night: to study hard, to pursue their dreams with discipline and effort, to be responsible for themselves, to have concern for others, to cherish their race and at the same time build their own lives as Americans. When our leaders put a spotlight on our victimization and seize upon our suffering to gain us ineffectual concessions, they inadvertently turn themselves into enemies of the truth, not to mention enemies of their own people.

13   I believe that black Americans are freer today than ever before. This is not a hope; this is a reality. Racial hatred has not yet left the American landscape. Who knows how or when this will occur. And yet the American black, supported by a massive body of law and, for the most part, the goodwill of his fellow citizens, is basically as free as he or she wants to be. For every white I have met who is a racist, I have met twenty more who have seen me as an individual. This, I am not ashamed to say, has been my experience. I believe it is time for blacks to begin the shift from a wartime to a peacetime identity, from fighting for opportunity to seizing it. The immutable fact of late-twentieth-century American life is that it is there for blacks to seize. Martin Luther King did not live to experience this. But then, of course, on the night before he died, he seemed to know that he would not. From the mountaintop he had looked over and seen the promised land, but he said, "I may not get there with you." I won't say we are snuggled deep in the promised valley he saw beyond the mountain; everyday things remind me that we are not. But I also know we have it better than our greatest leader. We are on the other side of his mountaintop, on the downward slope toward the valley he saw. This is something we ought to know. But what we must know even more clearly is that nothing on this earth can be promised except a chance. The promised land guarantees nothing. It is only an opportunity, not a deliverance.

FROM THE CONTENT OF OUR CHARACTER

Exploring Language

adversarial: an adversary is an opponent or enemy, so adversarial involves enemies or opponents in conflict, disagreement, or contest.

collectivism: the theory or practice of group ownership and control, especially over production, distribution, and land.

élan: spirit or enthusiasm.

esoteric: limited to or understood by a smll group.

espouse: to support or advocate.

ineffectual: not producing the intended effect.

Note: For pronunciation, go to dictionary.com, search the word, and click on the speaker icon.

USAGE Look up *élan* in a thesaurus and discover other lively words that have similar connotations.

Thinking and Talking Points

1. What is Steele's thesis?
2. What is Steele defining?
3. What strategies does Steele use to develop his definition?
4. Steele's book, *The Content of Our Character,* has been both praised and condemned. From reading this excerpt, what do you think makes it so controversial?
5. Look up the word *existential.* What does Steele mean when he uses this term?

Styling

Reread paragraph #1 and study the list Steele writes to underscore the problems facing black America. He uses a complete sentence and a colon followed by a list of problems separated by semicolons. Though semicolons usually separate complete sentences, they can be used to separate items in a series when too many commas might confuse the reader.

There are many profound problems facing black America today: a swelling black underclass; a black middle class that declined slightly in size during the Eighties; a declining number of black college students; an epidemic of teenage pregnancy, drug use, and gang violence; continuing chronic unemployment; astoundingly high college and high school dropout rates; an increasing number of single-parent families; a disproportionately high infant mortality rate; and so on.

The phrase *an epidemic of teenage pregnancy, drug use, and gang violence* contains a mini-list requiring commas; if Steele had used commas instead of semicolons after *a declining number of black college students* and after *gang violence,* the reader might be confused, not knowing which items went with which phrase.

PRACTICE Fill in the blank after the colon with a list of items separated by semicolons, one containing internal commas.

Ryota filled the stereo with his favorite CDs: _____ _____

YOU TRY IT Write three complete sentences followed by colons and lists separated by semicolons, with at least one of the phrases in each sentence containing a mini-list requiring commas.

Teaming Up

1. In your group, make a list of support Steele uses in his argument. Next, make a list of arguments and examples from an opposing view and discuss the results.

2. **Warm-up for Writing Idea #1.** Before class, brainstorm a list of qualities that define you. Type the list, but don't put your name on it. In your group, collect all the responses and shuffle them, redistributing one to each member (if you get your own, shuffle again). Read the lists aloud, trying to guess whose list you have. How accurate were your guesses? Did you learn anything new about your group members?

Writing Ideas

1. Using your list from Teaming Up activity #2, write an essay that defines you, telling what experiences shaped who you are today, and how you arrived at your list.

2. Choose a quality or personality trait and write an extended definition. Some ideas: loneliness, earnestness, depression, serenity, kindness, anger, pity, shame, indignation. See "Writing Strategies for Defining Terms." Also try the personification technique for the introduction in "Hooks, Introductions, and Conclusions."

Essay Connections

"About Men" by Gretel Ehrlich busts the stereotype of the American cowboy and men in general. Barbara Kingsolver blasts American attitudes concerning children in contrast to other cultures. Paul Solotaroff illustrates our misunderstanding of people with Asperger's syndrome, a mild form of autism.

THE CULTURE OF CELEBRITY

Joseph Epstein

Among Joseph Epstein's (former editor of American Scholar) books are Snobbery: The American Version, Friendship: an Expose, and In a Cardboard Belt!: Essays Personal, Literary, and Savage. His essays have appeared in Harper's, Atlantic Monthly, The New Yorker, and Best American Essays. This excerpt from "The Culture of Celebrity" appeared in Best American Essays 2006; it reflects on our obsession with the lives of famous people simply because they are famous.

DUSTBIN OF HISTORY AND CULTURE

FLAUBERT, GUSTAVE (1821–1880): French writer best known for *Madame Bovary;* the French government charged Flaubert with immorality because of the novel's content.

MACHIAVELLIAN: Refers to Niccolo Machiavelli (1469–1527), an Italian Renaissance statesman and writer of *The Prince,* among other works; the term *Machiavellian* has come to be associated with deception and dishonesty.

ANDY WARHOL (1928–1987): American pop artist who painted mundane objects like Campbell's soup cans and Coca-Cola bottles, as well as portraits of celebrities.

SID AND MERCEDES BASS: Wealthy oil tycoons known for lavish parties; in 2006 they donated $25 million to The Metropolitan Opera.

AHMET AND MICA ERTEGUN: Ahmet Ertegun, son of a Turkish diplomat, founder and former chairman of Atlantic records, died in 2006; Mica is his widow.

TED WILLIAMS (1918–2002): Played with the Boston Red Sox from 1939–1960.

ADONIS: In mythology, a handsome young man loved by Venus; when he is killed by a wild boar, she changes his blood into a flower.

OLIVER GOLDSMITH (1730–1774): Irish born novelist, essayist, poet, and dramatist, best known for his humorous and bawdy—and still popular—play, *She Stoops to Conquer.*

FRANK MUIR (1920–1998): British writer and broadcaster of radio and television shows like *Till Death Do Us Part* and *Steptoe and Son.*

From "The Culture of Celebrity" by John Epstein as appeared in *The Weekly Standard,* October 17, 2005, Vol. 11, Issue 5. An earlier version of this essay was published in "Celebrity Culture" the Spring 2005 issue of *The Hedgehog Review: Critical Reflections on Contemporary Culture,* published by the Institute for Advanced Studies in Culture at the University of Virginia (www.virginia.edu/iasc/). Reprinted by permission.

MARCEL PROUST (1871–1922): French novelist, his best known work being *Swann's Way.*

W. H. AUDEN (1907–1973): British born poet and critic who became a U.S. citizen in 1939; poems include "The Unknown Citizen," "Lullaby," and "In Memory of W.B. Yeats."

PHILIP LARKIN (1922–1985): British poet whose collections include *The Whitsun Weddings* and *High Windows;* a novel (*Jill* and *A Girl in Winter*); he was also a jazz critic.

LENNY BRUCE (1925–1966): Comedian whose comedy was seen as obscene and outrageous; Bruce was arrested, but his controversial comedy act is seen to have been groundbreaking, opening the way for those who followed.

SEAMUS HEANEY: A native of Northern Ireland, Heaney was born in 1939, and won the Nobel Prize in Literature in 1995. In addition to his numerous poems, he translated the Old English elegiac narrative *Beowulf.*

1   Celebrity at this moment in America is epidemic, and it's spreading fast, sometimes seeming as if nearly everyone has got it. Television provides celebrity dance contests, celebrities take part in reality shows, perfumes carry the names not merely of designers but of actors and singers. Without celebrities, whole sections of the *New York Times* and the *Washington Post* would have to close down. So pervasive has celebrity become in contemporary American life that one now begins to hear a good deal about a phenomenon known as the Culture of Celebrity.

2   The word "culture" no longer, I suspect, stands in most people's minds for that whole congeries of institutions, relations, kinship patterns, linguistic forms, and the rest for which the early anthropologists meant it to stand. Words, unlike disciplined soldiers, refuse to remain in place and take orders. They insist on being unruly, and slither and slide around, picking up all sorts of slippery and even goofy meanings. An icon, as we shall see, doesn't stay a small picture of a religious personage but usually turns out nowadays to be someone with spectacular grosses. "The language," as Flaubert once protested in his attempt to tell his mistress Louise Colet how much he loved her, "is inept."

3   Today, when people glibly refer to "the corporate culture," "the culture of poverty," "the culture of journalism," "the culture of the intelligence community"—and "community" has, of course, itself become another of those hopelessly baggy-pants words, so that one hears talk even of "the homeless community"—what I think is meant by "culture" is the general emotional atmosphere and institutional

character surrounding the word to which "culture" is attached. Thus, corporate culture is thought to breed selfishness practiced at the Machiavellian level; the culture of poverty, hopelessness and despair; the culture of journalism, a taste for the sensational combined with a short attention span; the culture of the intelligence community, covering-one's-own-behind viperishness; and so on. Culture used in this way is also brought in to explain unpleasant or at least dreary behavior. "The culture of NASA has to be changed" is a sample of its current usage. The comedian Flip Wilson, after saying something outrageous, would revert to the refrain line "The debbil made me do it." So, today, when admitting to unethical or otherwise wretched behavior, people often say, "The culture made me do it."

4   As for "celebrity," the standard definition is no longer the dictionary one but rather closer to the one that Daniel Boorstin gave in his book *The Image; or, What Happened to the American Dream:* "The celebrity," Boorstin wrote, "is a person who is well-known for his well-knownness," which is improved in its frequently misquoted form as "A celebrity is someone famous for being famous." The other standard quotation on this subject is Andy Warhol's "In the future everyone will be world-famous for fifteen minutes," which also frequently turns up in an improved misquotation as "Everyone will have his fifteen minutes of fame."

5   But to say that a celebrity is someone well known for being well known, though clever enough, doesn't quite cover it. Not that there is a shortage of such people who seem to be known only for their well-knownness. What do a couple named Sid and Mercedes Bass do, except appear in boldface in the *New York Times* Sunday Styles section and other such venues (as we now call them) of equally shimmering insignificance, often standing next to Ahmet and Mica Ertegun, also well known for being well known? Many moons ago, journalists used to refer to royalty as "face cards"; today celebrities are perhaps best thought of as bold faces, for as such do their names often appear in the press (and in a *New York Times* column with that very name, "Bold Face").

6   The distinction between celebrity and fame is one most dictionaries tend to fudge. I suspect everyone has, or prefers to make, his own. The one I like derives not from Aristotle, who didn't have to trouble with celebrities, but from the career of Ted Williams. A sportswriter once said that he, Williams, wished to be famous but had no interest in being a celebrity. What Ted Williams wanted to be famous for was his hitting. He wanted everyone who cared about baseball to

know that he was—as he believed and may well have been—the greatest pure hitter who ever lived. What he didn't want to do was to take on any of the effort off the baseball field involved in making this known. As an active player, Williams gave no interviews, signed no baseballs or photographs, chose not to be obliging in any way to journalists or fans. A rebarbative character, not to mention often a slightly menacing s.o.b., Williams, if you had asked him, would have said that it was enough that he was the last man to hit .400; he did it on the field, and therefore didn't have to sell himself off the field. As for his duty to his fans, he didn't see that he had any.

7   Whether Ted Williams was right or wrong to feel as he did is of less interest than the distinction his example provides, which suggests that fame is something one earns—through talent or achievement of one kind or another—while celebrity is something one cultivates or, possibly, has thrust upon one. The two are not, of course, entirely exclusive. One can be immensely talented and full of achievement and yet wish to broadcast one's fame further through the careful cultivation of celebrity; and one can have the thinnest of achievements and be talentless and yet be made to seem otherwise through the mechanics and dynamics of celebrity creation, in our day a whole mini- (or maybe not so mini) industry of its own.

8   Or, another possibility, one can become a celebrity with scarcely any pretense to talent or achievement whatsoever. Much modern celebrity seems the result of careful promotion or great good luck or something besides talent and achievement: Mr. Donald Trump, Ms. Paris Hilton, Mr. Regis Philbin, take a bow. The ultimate celebrity of our time may have been John F. Kennedy Jr., notable only for being his parents' very handsome son—both his birth and good looks factors beyond his control—and, alas, known for nothing else whatsoever now, except for the sad, dying-young-Adonis end to his life.

9   Fame, then, at least as I prefer to think of it, is based on true achievement; celebrity on the broadcasting of that achievement, or the inventing of something that, if not scrutinized too closely, might pass for achievement. Celebrity suggests ephemerality, while fame has a chance of lasting, a shot at reaching the happy shores of posterity.

10   Oliver Goldsmith, in his poem "The Deserted Village," refers to "good fame," which implies that there is also a bad or false fame. Bad fame is sometimes thought to be fame in the present, or fame on earth, while good fame is that bestowed by posterity—those happy shores again. (Which doesn't eliminate the desire of most of us, at

least nowadays, to have our fame here and hereafter, too.) Not false but wretched fame is covered by the word "infamy"—"Infamy, infamy, infamy," remarked the English wit Frank Muir, "they all have it in for me"—while the lower, or pejorative, order of celebrity is covered by the word "notoriety," also frequently misused to mean noteworthiness.

11   Leo Braudy's magnificent book on the history of fame, *The Frenzy of Renown*, illustrates how the means of broadcasting fame have changed over the centuries: from having one's head engraved on coins, to purchasing statuary of oneself, to (for the really high rollers— Alexander the Great, the Caesar boys) naming cities or even months after oneself, to commissioning painted portraits, to writing books or having books written about one, and so on into our day of the publicity or press agent, the media blitz, the public relations expert, and the egomaniacal blogger. One of the most successful of public relations experts, Ben Sonnenberg Sr., used to say that he saw it as his job to construct very high pedestals for very small men.

12   Which leads one to a very proper suspicion of celebrity. As George Orwell said about saints, so it seems only sensible to say about celebrities: they should all be judged guilty until proven innocent. Guilty of what, precisely? I'd say of the fraudulence (however minor) of inflating their brilliance, accomplishments, worth, of passing themselves off as something they aren't, or at least are not quite. If fraudulence is the crime, publicity is the means by which the caper is brought off.

13   Is the current heightened interest in the celebrated sufficient to form a culture—a culture of a kind worthy of study? The anthropologist Alfred Kroeber defined culture, in part, as embodying "values which may be formulated (overtly as mores) or felt (implicitly as in folkways) by the society carrying the culture, and which it is part of the business of the anthropologist to characterize and define." What are the values of celebrity culture? They are the values, almost exclusively, of publicity. Did they spell one's name right? What was the size and composition of the audience? Did you check the receipts? Was the timing right? Publicity is concerned solely with effects and does not investigate causes or intrinsic value too closely. For example, a few years ago a book of mine called *Snobbery: The American Version* received what I thought was a too greatly mixed review in the *New York Times Book Review.* I remarked on my disappointment to the publicity man at my publisher's, who promptly told me not to worry: it was a full-page review, on page 11, right-hand side. That, he said, "is

very good real estate," which was quite as important as, perhaps more important than, the reviewer's actual words and final judgment. Better to be tepidly considered on page 11 than extravagantly praised on page 27, left-hand side. Real estate, man, it's the name of the game.

14   We must have new names, Marcel Proust presciently noted—in fashion, in medicine, in art, there must always be new names. It's a very smart remark, and the fields Proust chose seem smart, too, at least for his time. (Now there must also be new names, at a minimum, among movie stars and athletes and politicians.) Implicit in Proust's remark is the notion that if the names don't really exist, if the quality isn't there to sustain them, it doesn't matter; new names we shall have in any case. And every sophisticated society somehow, more or less implicitly, contrives to supply them.

15   I happen to think that we haven't had a major poet writing in English since perhaps the death of W. H. Auden or, to lower the bar a little, Philip Larkin. But new names are put forth nevertheless—high among them in recent years has been that of Seamus Heaney—because, after all, what kind of a time could we be living in if we didn't have a major poet? And besides there are all those prizes that, year after year, must be given out, even if so many of the recipients don't seem quite worthy of them.

16   Considered as a culture, celebrity does have its institutions. We now have an elaborate celebrity-creating machinery well in place—all those short-attention-span television shows (*Entertainment Tonight, Access Hollywood, Lifestyles of the Rich and Famous*); all those magazines (beginning with *People* and far from ending with the *National Enquirer*). We have high-priced celebrity-mongers—Barbara Walters, Diane Sawyer, Jay Leno, David Letterman, Oprah—who not only live off others' celebrity but also, through their publicity-making power, confer it and have in time become very considerable celebrities each in his or her own right.

17   Without the taste for celebrity, they would have to close down the whole Style section of every newspaper in the country. Then there is the celebrity profile (in *Vanity Fair, Esquire, Gentlemen's Quarterly;* these are nowadays usually orchestrated by a press agent, with all touchy questions declared out-of-bounds), or the television talk-show interview with a star, which is beyond parody. Well, *almost* beyond: Martin Short in his parody of a talk-show host remarked to the actor Kiefer Sutherland, "You're Canadian, aren't you? What's that all about?"

18   Yet we still seem never to have enough celebrities, so we drag in
so-called It Girls (Paris Hilton, Cindy Crawford, other super-models),
tired television hacks (Regis Philbin, Ed McMahon), back-achingly
boring but somehow sacrosanct news anchors (Walter Cronkite, Tom
Brokaw). Toss in what I think of as the lower-class punditi, who await
calls from various television news and chat shows to demonstrate their
locked-in political views and meager expertise on major and cable stations alike: Pat Buchanan, Eleanor Clift, Mark Shields, Robert Novak,
Michael Beschloss, and the rest. Ah, if only Lenny Bruce were alive
today, he could do a scorchingly cruel bit about Dr. Joyce Brothers
sitting by the phone wondering why Jerry Springer never calls.

THE CULTURE OF CELEBRITY

Exploring Language

congeries: a collection or mass.

ephemerality: short-lived; lasting only a short period of time.

glibly: offhand; without thought or preparation; with ease.

inept: awkward or clumsy; without skill.

mores: accepted attitudes and customs of a culture.

notoriety: the quality of being unfavorably known; well-known for the wrong reasons; infamous.

pejorative: belittling or derogatory.

posterity: future generations.

presciently: to know things before they happen; foresight.

pundit: an authority or expert; a critic; Epstein created his own word with punditi.

rebarbative: repellent or irritating.

sacrosanct: sacred; above criticism.

Note: For pronunciation, go to dictionary.com, search the word, and click on the speaker icon.

USAGE Reread paragraph #3. Which definition of "glibly" is Epstein using? Write two sentences, one using glibly as meaning without thought or preparation and the other meaning with ease.

Thinking and Talking Points

1. What evidence does Epstein use for his comment, "Celebrity at this moment in America is epidemic . . ."? Do you agree? Why or why not?
2. How does the essay distinguish celebrity from fame?
3. How does Epstein define the word *culture,* the way it's used today versus the past?
4. What is the essay's main point? What is Epstein's view of "the culture of celebrity"? What are his objections to the use of the word *community?*
5. Epstein claims that celebrities are guilty of fraudulence. How does he support this statement? Do you agree? Why or why not?

Styling

Many good writer's create their own adjectives by hooking together words that are not always adjectives—perhaps nouns or verbs—with hyphens. You might be familiar with such words that have become standard, like deep-rooted, stay-at-home moms, or close-knit. The trick is to not rely on these standards but write fresh ones of your own.

Epstein uses this technique several times: "baggy-pants words," "covering-one's-own-behind viperishness," and "dying-young-Adonis end." **Notice that the noun being described is not connected to the new adjective.**

Until you master this technique, you might be more successful if you stick to using nouns and verbs in your hyphenated words to describe another noun. If, for example, you want to describe a cat's fur, you wouldn't hook together a string of adjectives like black-silky-shiny-gleaming fur. It doesn't quite work. Instead, write something like gleams-in-the-light fur. Here you've got the verb, (gleams), a preposition and two articles (in, the) and a noun (light).

In "Bully Pulpit," Amy Dickinson could have written "the time I vomited on my sneakers," but instead chose to hyphenate, creating vomiting-on-my-sneakers incident.

Note: Be sure when you're typing to use **hyphens**, not **dashes**. Type one short line (-) for a hyphen, two (--) for a dash. Otherwise, you'll confuse your reader.

PRACTICE   Rewrite the sentence below using new, hyphenated adjectives to describe the subject (noun).

There was one time when I slipped in the cafeteria with a tray full of food and dumped it on a popular football jock.

YOU TRY IT   Write three sentences of your own using hyphenated words to describe a subject.

Teaming Up

1. **Warm-up for Writing Idea #1.** Make a list of words you think are overused (to save time, you can use the words in Writing Idea #1). Write at least three sentences for each overused word. Be specific so that the context is clear. Give a specific incident as an example. Next, replace each overused word with a fresh one.

2. **Warm-up for Writing Idea #3.** Choose a category from Writing Idea #3 and list several examples. Next, describe three of the examples in some detail. Discuss why these shows (or the merchandise) are popular and why you think stars participate.

Writing Ideas

1. Write an essay tracing the history of a word that you think is over-used. Discuss the origin of the word, its previous meaning, and how it is used today. See Writing Strategies for Defining Terms in Section Five. Some ideas might be the words miracle, awesome, or history (as in "That's ancient history").

2. Write an essay that analyzes the difference between the words *icon* and *celebrity*. Look up the origin of each word and their definitions. Use the Writing Strategies for Defining Terms in Section Five.

3. In his introduction, Epstein complains, "Television provides celebrity dance contests, celebrities take part in reality shows, perfumes carry the names not merely of the designers but of actors and singers." Choose one of these categories—dance contests, reality shows, or designer merchandise—and analyze the content. Describe each show or type of merchandise in detail. Attempt to answer why celebrities participate and why people watch these shows or buy these products. Does your analysis end up supporting or refuting Epstein's claim that celebrity is an epidemic?

Essay Connections

Other essays that analyze culture and social issues include "About Men" by Gretel Ehrlich, "Somebody's Baby" by Barbara Kingsolver, "A Dark and Stormy Knight: Why Batman?" by Travis Langley, and the preface from *The Dumbest Generation* by Mark Bauerlein.

THE WRITING LIFE: THE POINT OF THE LONG AND WINDING SENTENCE

Pico Iyer

*Travel writer and globe trotter Pico Iyer—born in England—grew up in California, received a King's Scholarship to Eton, has two masters' degrees, writing and literature, from Harvard where he taught for two years, and lives in Japan. Published in an exhausting number of magazines—*The New York Review of Books, Salon, Time, The Conde Nast Traveler, *and* Harper's, *among them—Iyer has also written numerous books on a variety of topics, his latest* The Man within my Head, *an interior exploration of his connection to Graham Greene. Others include* The Global Soul, The Sun After Dark, Tropical Classical, *and* The Open Road: The Global Journey of the Fourteenth Dalai Lama. *"The Writing Life: the Point of the Long and Winding Sentence" appeared in January 08, 2012, edition of* The Los Angeles Times, *where he defends the beauty of the long sentence to capture nuances and battle the short sound bites of the too-much-quick-information era.*

DUSTBIN OF HISTORY AND CULTURE

SALMAN RUSHDIE (1947–): Novelist (born in Bombay, India) sentenced to die in 1989 by the Ayatollah Khomeini—political and religious leader of Iran—for having written *The Satanic Verses*. Other works include *Midnight's Children* and *Shame*. (He's alive and still writing after having gone into hiding for several years).

DON DELILLO (1936–): American author whose work includes the popular *White Noise, Americana,* and *Players*.

ANNIE DILLARD (1945–): American nature writer, novelist, artist, poet; works include *The Pilgrim at Tinker Creek* (nonfiction and winner of the Pulitzer Prize), *Teaching a Stone to Talk* (nonfiction), and *The Maytrees* (novel).

WILLIAM GASS (1925–): American novelist, short story writer, critic, teacher, and proponent of long and winding sentences in his book of essays Life Sentences; his novels include *The Tunnel, Omensetter's Luck, Middle C,* and *Eyes: Novellas and Stories*.

SIR THOMAS BROWN (1605–1682): English author, physician, and philosopher, best known for his book of reflections, *Religion Medici*.

ORHAN PAMUK (1952–): Turkish novelist, born in Istanbul, who won the Nobel Prize in literature, 2006.

RSS Feeds: an acronym for Really Simply Syndication, also known as web feeds; RSS feeds deliver content, publishing in more than one place on the web.

1   "Your sentences are so long," said a friend who teaches English at a local college, and I could tell she didn't quite mean it as a compliment. The copy editor who painstakingly went through my most recent book often put yellow dashes on-screen around my multiplying clauses, to ask if I didn't want to break up my sentences or put less material in every one. Both responses couldn't have been kinder or more considered, but what my friend and my colleague may not have sensed was this: I'm using longer and longer sentences as a small protest against—and attempt to rescue any readers I might have from—the bombardment of the moment.

2   When I began writing for a living, my feeling was that my job was to give the reader something vivid, quick and concrete that she couldn't get in any other form; a writer was an information-gathering machine, I thought, and especially as a journalist, my job was to go out into the world and gather details, moments, impressions as visual and immediate as TV. Facts were what we needed most. And if you watched the world closely enough, I believed (and still do), you could begin to see what it would do next, just as you can with a sibling or a friend; Don DeLillo or Salman Rushdie aren't mystics, but they can tell us what the world is going to do tomorrow because they follow it so attentively.

3   Yet nowadays the planet is moving too fast for even a Rushdie or DeLillo to keep up, and many of us in the privileged world have access to more information than we know what to do with. What we crave is something that will free us from the overcrowded moment and allow us to see it in a larger light. No writer can compete, for speed and urgency, with texts or CNN news flashes or RSS feeds, but any writer can try to give us the depth, the nuances—the "gaps," as Annie Dillard calls them—that don't show up on many screens. Not everyone wants to be reduced to a sound bite or a bumper sticker.

4   Enter (I hope) the long sentence: the collection of clauses that is so many-chambered and lavish and abundant in tones and suggestions, that has so much room for near-contradiction and ambiguity and those places in memory or imagination that can't be simplified, or put into easy words, that it allows the reader to keep many things in her head and heart at the same time, and to descend, as by a spiral staircase, deeper into herself and those things that won't be squeezed

into an either/or. With each clause, we're taken further and further from trite conclusions—or that at least is the hope—and away from reductionism, as if the writer were a dentist, saying "Open wider" so that he can probe the tender, neglected spaces in the reader (though in this case it's not the mouth that he's attending to but the mind).

5   "There was a little stoop of humility," Alan Hollinghurst writes in a sentence I've chosen almost at random from his recent novel "The Stranger's Child," "as she passed through the door, into the larger but darker library beyond, a hint of frailty, an affectation of bearing more than her fifty-nine years, a slight bewildered totter among the grandeur that her daughter now had to pretend to take for granted." You may notice—though you don't have to—that "humility" has rather quickly elided into "affectation," and the point of view has shifted by the end of the sentence, and the physical movement through the rooms accompanies a gradual inner movement that progresses through four parallel clauses, each of which, though legato, suggests a slightly different take on things.

6   Many a reader will have no time for this; William Gass or Sir Thomas Browne may seem long-winded, the equivalent of driving from L.A. to San Francisco by way of Death Valley, Tijuana and the Sierras. And a highly skilled writer, a Hemingway or James Salter, can get plenty of shading and suggestion into even the shortest and straightest of sentences. But too often nowadays our writing is telegraphic as a way of keeping our thinking simplistic, our feeling slogan-crude. The short sentence is the domain of uninflected talk-radio rants and shouting heads on TV who feel that qualification or subtlety is an assault on their integrity (and not, as it truly is, integrity's greatest adornment).

7   If we continue along this road, whole areas of feeling and cognition and experience will be lost to us. We will not be able to read one another very well if we can't read Proust's labyrinthine sentences, admitting us to those half-lighted realms where memory blurs into imagination, and we hide from the person we care for or punish the thing that we love. And how can we feel the layers, the sprawl, the many-sidedness of Istanbul in all its crowding amplitude without the 700-word sentence, transcribing its features, that Orhan Pamuk offered in tribute to his lifelong love?

THE WRITING LIFE

Exploring Language

affectation: pretension; attempting to appear to have a quality, trait, or manner not actually possessed.

ambiguity: without clear-cut meaning or definition.

elide: omit (usually refers to a vowel or syllable); ignore or pass over; from Latin 'to crush out.'

labyrinthine: like a labyrinth (a maze or tunnel of complicated paths).

legato: smooth and connected.

nuances: slight differences in meaning or expression; subtle.

reductionism: simplifying a complex idea, distorting it; a theory that states any complexity can be reduced to its simplest parts and understood.

subtle: in this context, hard to grasp, mysterious, as in *subtle distinction*.

trite: lacking power to evoke interest; overused.

uninflected: in this context, not modulating or changing the tone or pitch of voice.

Note: For pronunciation, go to dictionary.com, search the word, and click on the speaker icon.

Thinking and Talking Points

1. Iyer writes that his use of longer and longer sentences is a protest and a rescue; explain his meaning.

2. Throughout the essay, Iyer gives examples of what we lose when we rely on fast information bites that assault our senses. List his examples.

3. In paragraph #6, Iyer writes, "The short sentence is the domain of uninflected talk-radio rants and shouting heads on TV who feel that qualification or subtlety is an assault on their integrity (and not, as it truly is, integrity's greatest adornment)." Explain how qualification or subtlety is "integrity's greatest adornment."

4. Study some of Iyer's long sentences. How do they help support his point? Be specific by pointing out sentences and analyzing their content for complex thoughts or nuances that would be lost in shorter sentences.

5. How does the example out of Hollinghurst's work in paragraph #5 help exemplify Iyer's point about the need for long sentences?

Styling

Copy the first sentence of paragraph #4. Break it down, writing each individual clause (between the commas) on a separate line, leaving space to write your own clauses underneath.

PRACTICE First, write a sentence with a colon that will require clauses as explanation. Underneath each of Iyer's clauses, write your own material to match your sentence, modeling each of Iyer's clauses, the length and punctuation, making sure each clause is **dependent**.

YOU TRY IT Put your clauses together in one long sentence. Check it for run-ons and **parallelism**. Write three more sentences in this style.

Teaming Up

1. Have two or three peers read your sentences from the "Styling" to check for errors and logic.
2. Read and analyze the long sentence below from *A Wizard of Earthsea* by Ursula LeGuin (isolate the main sentence and the descriptive clauses). Choose a topic to describe—a lavish meal, a place, a messy room (or an overly neat room), or anything else the group agrees upon. Brainstorm the details and, modeling LeGuin's sentence, write a one-paragraph description consisting of just one sentence.

> So to Ged who had never been down from the heights of the mountain, the Port of Gont was an awesome and marvelous place, the great houses and towers of cut stone and waterfront of piers and docks and basins and moorages, the seaport where half a hundred boats and galleys rocked at quayside or lay hauled up and overturned for repairs or stood out at anchor in the roadstead with furled sails and closed oarports, the sailors shouting in strange dialects and longshoremen running heavy-laden among barrels and boxes and coils of rope and stacks of oars, the bearded merchants in furred robes conversing quietly as they picked their way along the slimy stones above the water, the fishermen unloading their catch, coopers pounding and shipmakers hammering and clamsellers singing and shipmasters bellowing, and beyond all the silent, shining bay.

Note: While writing every sentence in an essay this long might become tedious, it's good practice in grammar and punctuation, and will help make writing your own long sentences easier if you can sustain correctness throughout one of this length.

Writing Ideas

1. Find a passage from a Hemingway short story or novel and one from either Orhan Pamuk or William Gass and analyze and compare/contrast the style.
2. Watch and read some of the "news flashes or RSS feeds" and other sound bites and bumper sticker-esque language that bombard us. Analyze and argue what we lose and/or gain, using quotes from these sources and from Pico Iyer's essay.

Writing Strategies

WRITING BASIC COLLEGE ESSAYS

Most essays combine **rhetorical modes** (strategies that help organize material): a process/analysis might also be an argument; a narrative might also compare and contrast; a compare and contrast might have paragraphs of cause and effect; most essays have description, and so on. The best writers don't rely on the five-paragraph format, though it helps to know how to compose in that format before moving on to other, more complex styles. The strategies in this section have been broken down into their basic rhetorical modes for clarity. It's up to the writer to decide which strategies need combining (in college, often the prompt will indicate the required format).

Getting Started with Prewriting

Most writers have trouble getting started, but the temptress Procrastination can wreak havoc with grades, so resist the appeal of Facebook, Twitter, Instagram, and other distractions. Traditional brainstorming techniques are outlined below for those who need a reminder. The standard ideas don't work for everyone, so use a method you deem comfortable, whether it's listing, clustering, freewriting, or simply writing notes on scrap paper as ideas occur throughout the day. Sometimes, it only takes determination to get something down on paper. Ernest Hemingway, in *A Moveable Feast*, wrote, "But sometimes when I was starting a new story and I could not get it going, I would sit in front of the fire and squeeze the peel of the little oranges into the edge of the flame and watch the sputter of blue that they made. I would stand and look out over the roofs of Paris and think, 'Do not worry. You have always written before and you will write now. All you have to do is write one true sentence.'" If you write one sentence, another will usually follow.

Traditional Brainstorming

FREEWRITING   Freewriting, a simple but useful technique, can help unstick you. Write down any weird or not-so-weird ideas buzzing about in your head, without any thought to structure, grammar, or spelling. Just write nonstop. Don't even think. Just write, write, write. Though most of what comes out might look like alien messages from deep space, a brilliant idea or two might be lurking, waiting for you to discover and develop it.

CLUSTERING   Write your topic in the center of a piece of paper and draw a circle around it. Draw lines out from your topic, like spokes of a wheel, and draw bubbles, like balloons, at the end of each line. Fill in each bubble with one thing that pops into your mind about your topic. Repeat this technique for each bubble.

LISTING   If you're the type of person who likes to make daily lists, here's the brainstorming technique for you. Simply write your topic at the top of a sheet of paper and list whatever flashes into your head about that topic. A list might look like this:

Too Much Childhood Supervision

no free time to play

too many structured activities

what happened to playing baseball in the park with no adults?

need to learn independence

too much pressure

don't learn decision making

can't solve their own problems

must have some supervision and guidance, of course

Next, choose three or four interesting ideas from the list and write them at the top of a sheet of paper:

independence	*problem solving*	*decisions*
wimps	can't fix things	which college
too afraid	run to mom and dad	which major
live at home	disagreements	which job
can't grow up		

You could keep this up into infinity, but you only need to keep listing until you feel you have some solid ideas to start your essay. What you now have is an idea for a thesis and three developmental paragraphs and ideas for examples to support each idea.

Basic Try-Not-to-Rely-on-It Five-Paragraph Format

This format works well as a first draft or perhaps on an in-class essay to help keep thoughts organized under time pressure, and it's a good place to start for novice writers, though once you master this basic strategy, it's time to move on to other rhetorical modes and blending styles. Basic essays consist of an introduction with a hook and a thesis, plan of development, three body paragraphs with topic sentences, and a conclusion.

THESIS STATEMENTS

A thesis can occur anywhere in a paper: some writers lead up to their thesis at the end of an essay; others use a transition paragraph after the introduction, and occasionally a writer will sneak the thesis in somewhere in the middle of the paper, but traditional essays usually have the thesis stated at the end of the introduction. Before beginning to write an essay, it helps to have a working thesis in mind—a preliminary statement that might change as you think through ideas or research a topic.

Thesis statements control the essay; everything in the paper should relate to the thesis. It is the main point, often expressed as an opinion. Though not all papers require a thesis, most college writing does. There are a few rules to keep in mind when writing a thesis:

1. A thesis cannot be a fact. It should express a point of view or opinion. The statement "Television ads supporting presidential candidates often denigrate the opponent" is a fact, not a thesis.
2. A thesis should not be too broad: "There are many controversies surrounding televised presidential campaign ads" needs to be nar-

rowed to a specific issue. This statement also breaks the first rule: it's a fact.

3. A thesis should not announce its topic: avoid phrases like "I will discuss," "this essay will show," "this essay will analyze," or "I think, I believe, it is my opinion." The first three don't express an opinion, and the last three are generally considered weak style and a way of avoiding taking a strong stand. It's a you-can't-attack-my-opinion strategy. "This essay will analyze the controversy surrounding televised presidential campaigns" is not an appropriate thesis: it is too broad and doesn't express an opinion.

1. To build a strong thesis, start with a broad topic:
   American politics

2. Narrow the topic by carving out a special area, perhaps through brainstorming:
   Television's coverage of presidential campaigns.

3. Take a stand on the topic in a rough thesis (using a should/because construction in steps three and four will help determine if the statement has an opinion and plan of development):
   Television's coverage of presidential campaigns **should be** limited.

4. Add your plan of development—your reasons for your opinion that will be used in topic sentences: presidential campaigns **should be** limited **because** the media's bias for or against a candidate misleads the public, avoids the issues, and gives the media too much power over the outcome of elections.

   This thesis, though roughly worded, has a clear focus, makes a statement rather than announcing the topic, and expresses an opinion (an opponent could argue against it).

5. Recast the thesis, smoothing out the basic wording:
   Although many might argue that limiting television coverage of presidential campaigns violates the idea of free press and free speech, the media's bias for or against a candidate takes focus away from the issues, misleading and unfairly influencing the public's view, granting the press too much power over the outcome of elections.

Plan of Development and Topic Sentences

Like a thesis statement controls the ideas in the essay, the topic sentences control the ideas in the body paragraphs. Key words in the topic sentence can help keep the paragraph from wandering off topic. Looking at the plan of development in the above thesis—the three reasons stated at the end of the statement—**the first body paragraph** would focus on the media's ability to sway elections by taking focus away from the issues; **the second body paragraph** would discuss misleading and influencing the public's view; **the last reason** would argue the power of the press. Notice that each reason is discussed in the order it appears in the thesis.

This type of organizational strategy usually saves the strongest or most important reason for the last body paragraph, pyramiding paragraphs on top of each other, least to most important.

Example Topic Sentence: Though claiming objectivity, the mainstream media often has its own agenda, unfairly misleading the public about a candidate's views by focusing on personal rather than the political issues.

BODY PARAGRAPHS

In addition to topic sentences, body paragraphs contain evidence—specific examples, supporting facts, statistics, explanations, personal experience, and description; if it's an argument essay (like the above topic) it might also incorporate refuting the opposition (see the "Writing Strategies for Argument"). In the topic on media bias, body paragraphs might contain examples of news broadcasts, perhaps contrasting interviews with two candidates that illustrate the types of questions the interviewer asked that helped the candidate avoid the issues, or description of misleading ads, and perhaps researched facts on how much air time candidates received in the last election, or supporting quotations.

Use numerous examples to support each point. A paragraph that relies on one or two examples weakens the stand, failing to sway many readers that you have a reasonable, balanced essay.

Concluding Strategies for Body Paragraphs

Body paragraphs—and all other paragraphs—contain **concluding statements**, a last sentence that finishes off the paragraph, wrapping up the idea before transitioning into the next point. Writers use different strategies for concluding a paragraph, depending on their purpose.

1. Outrage Dressed as Statistic

Deborah Blum's essay "The Chemist's War" uses a bald, shocking statistic at the end of paragraph #4. Her essay recounts events during Prohibition when the federal government poisoned industrial alcohol manufactured in the United States to discourage people from drinking bootleg liquor. The statistic, stated matter-of-factly, outrages readers who, like Blum, were unaware that the government had gone to such lengths to enforce this law:

> Frustrated that people continued to consume so much alcohol even after it was banned, federal officials had decided to try a different kind of enforcement. They ordered the poisoning of industrial alcohols manufactured in the United States, products regularly stolen by bootleggers and resold as drinkable spirits. The idea was to scare people into giving up illicit drinking. **Instead, by the time Prohibition ended in 1933, the federal poisoning program, by some estimates, had killed at least 10,000 people.**

Calling it "the federal poisoning program" and dangling the number of deaths at the end of the paragraph, neatly concludes the point, giving the reader cause to pause at the sheer callousness of the federal government, tying to the topic sentence in her next paragraph, "Although mostly forgotten today, the 'chemist's war of Prohibition' remains one of the strangest and most deadly decisions in American law-enforcement history." (The word "deadly" transitions to "killed," and "chemist's war"' to "poisoning program".)

2. Provocative Questions

Though many handbooks and instructors advise students to avoid asking questions in an essay, professional writers use questions successfully, knowing that sometimes a provocative question can leave a reader thinking and feeling, lingering over the paragraph or anxious to move on to the next. In "The Surfing Savant" by Paul Solotaroff, an essay about a gifted surfer, Clay Marzo, with Asperger's syndrome, a form of high-functioning autism, he begins the second body paragraph describing all of the things that Marzo—though elegant, confident, and graceful on a surfboard—has trouble doing on land. Toward the end of this paragraph, he writes:

In middle school, Marzo was treated so badly that his mother, Jill, had to pull him out and teach him at home, where he wouldn't be punched for staring at wannabe thugs. His agonizing shyness has fractured his family and sparked ugly set-tos with his father, Gino, an old-school hard-hat striver who accused him of flaking off and screwing up his shot at stardom. **That charge hurts Clay more than the others combined: when your own father misconceives you so badly, how can you hope that strangers will understand?**

That question tugs at the readers' minds and hearts, hopefully evoking compassion for those afflicted with such a difficult and misunderstood disorder.

Bernard Cooper, in "Burl's," uses two questions at the end of a body paragraph that illustrate the conflict he felt as a young boy struggling with his sexual identity. In this paragraph, his parents have sent him to gymnastics class to try to "tilt" him toward the male side of his nature:

> When the first day of gymnastics class arrived, my mother gave me money and a gym bag and sent me to the corner of Hollywood and Western to wait for a bus. The sun was bright, the traffic heavy. While I sat there, an argument raged inside my head, the familiar, battering debate between the wish to be like other boys and the wish to be like myself. **Why shouldn't I simply get up and go back home, where I'd be left alone to read and think? On the other hand, wouldn't life be easier if I liked athletics, or learned to like them?**

These questions illustrate the battering debate, his struggle to reconcile his desire to be himself with what others wanted and expected him to be—indeed, a battering debate.

In "Nourishing Awareness in Each Moment," Zen monk Thich Nhat Hanh ends paragraph #2 with a series of questions that are statements in disguise:

> Do you ever find yourself watching an awful TV program, unable to turn it off? The raucous noises, explo-

sions of gunfire, are upsetting. Yet you don't get up and turn it off. Why do you torture yourself in this way? Don't you want to close your windows? **Are you frightened of solitude—the emptiness and the loneliness you may find when you face yourself alone?**

These questions accuse the reader with the words *torture* and *frightened*; most will have to admit to occasionally falling into this TV trap.

3. Concluding Quotation
Though generally you want to lead in and out of quotations, sometimes they are more affective left on their own at the end of a paragraph, with just the lead-in.

In the second paragraph of "The Culture of Celebrity," Joseph Epstein, after discussing the unruliness of words, how they seem to capriciously change meanings, their refusal to "remain in place and take orders," he ends with a famous quote, **"'The language,' as Flaubert once protested in his attempt to tell his mistress Louise Colet how much he loved her, 'is inept.'"**

4. A Short Sentence for Impact
Sometimes brevity speaks louder than a lengthy sentence or other technique. In paragraph #5 of "Joyas Voladoras," Brian Doyle writes:

Mammals and birds have hearts with four chambers. Reptiles and turtles have hearts with three chambers. Fish have hearts with two chambers. Insects and mollusks have hearts with one chamber. Worms have hearts with one chamber, although they may have as many as eleven single-chambered hearts. Unicellular bacteria have no hearts at all; but even they have fluid eternally in motion, washing from one side of the cell to the other, swirling and whirling. No living being is without interior liquid motion. **We all churn inside.**

That short, impactful sentence, loaded with meaning, shifts the seemingly scientific discussion to his real point—heartbreak, both literally and metaphorically, leading into his beautiful, specific conclusion about the joys and agonies of the human heart.

Clayton Collins, in his essay on the neurologist Oliver Sacks and his work with music, quotes Sacks:

> Sacks remembers a woman with Parkinson's who would sit perfectly still until "activated" by the music of Chopin, which she loved and knew by heart. She didn't have to hear a tune played. "It was sometimes sufficient to give her an opus number," Sacks says. "You would just say 'Opus 49,' and the F-minor *Fantasy* would start playing in her mind. **And she could move.**"

The remarkable fact that a woman frozen with Parkinson's can suddenly move upon hearing a scrap of music is best stated briefly, startling and emphatic.

Joyce Carol Oates, knowing the value of the short sentence, at the end of paragraph #3 in "On Boxing," after describing the beauty of the sport, simply writes **"All is Style."**

STRATEGIES FOR CREATING TITLES

Many titles—whether films, essays, novels, songs, or plays—often seem familiar, a where-have-I-heard-that-before refrain. Writers forage through history, literature, pop culture, music, film, almost every conceivable place, for snappy titles. A title is the first part of the essay readers see; don't bore them with one of those my-summer-vacation titles: "Animal Rights" or "Comparison Essay" or "Essay #1." Why title an essay "Animal Rights" when you can use something provocative that jumps off of a bumper sticker and gives it a little twist like "Save the Whales, Screw the Shrimp" by Joy Williams?

With electronic devices like iPhones and iPads, iPods and laptops, it's easy to have quick access to sources to pillage for titles. Scroll through the iPod for song titles to borrow; look at the Netflix list for films; google a dictionary of quotations for a famous quote and snag a few words that fit the topic; visit Amazon.com or the Barnes and Noble website for book and magazine titles; pick a favorite TV station and peruse the film show titles. *The History Channel, Animal Planet, Discovery* can also be ravaged. Much old literature—poems, plays, short stories, even novels—can be found on the web. It shouldn't take long browsing to find a title that fits your topic. Below are a few categories with examples from numerous writers who have pillaged other sources for strong titles. Writers borrow from a wide range of sources, including from each other.

Literature (novelists borrowing from poetry, essays, and the Bible).

Of Mice and Men by John Steinbeck: from a line in a poem by Robert Burns called "To a Mouse."

East of Eden by John Steinbeck from Genesis 4:16.

Tender Is the Night by F. Scott Fitzgerald from "Ode to a Nightingale" by John Keats.

For Whom the Bell Tolls by Ernest Hemingway from "Meditation" 17 by John Donne.

Brave New World by Aldous Huxley from Shakespeare's play *The Tempest.*

No Country for Old Men by Cormac McCarthy from a line in the poem "Sailing to Byzantium" by William Butler Yeats.

I Know Why the Caged Bird Sings by Maya Angelou from a line in the poem "Sympathy" by Paul Lawrence Dunbar.

Where Angels Fear to Tread by E.M. Forester from "Essay on Criticism" by Alexander Pope.

Music and Film (essayists, novelists, and filmmakers borrowing from music and film)

"Somebody's Baby" by Barbara Kingsolver, from the song "Somebody's Baby" by Jackson Browne.

"A Voice for the Lonely" essay by Stephen Corey, a twist on "Only the Lonely" by Roy Orbison.

"Roll Over Bach, Too!" essay by Jack Kroll, a twist on "Roll Over, Beethoven" by the Beatles.

"Monster Mash" essay by Jack Kroll, from the song of the same title by Bobby Pickett.

She's Come Undone by Wally Lamb, from the song of the same title by The Guess Who.

Stand by Me film, title borrowed from the song "Stand by Me" by Ben E. King.

Sweet Home Alabama film, title from the song "Sweet Home Alabama" by Lynyrd Skynrd.

"Modern Times" essay by Lawrence Weschler from the silent Charlie Chaplin film *Modern Times.*

History and Pop Culture

The Big Bang Theory TV series, borrowing from science.

One Potato, Two Potato: The Folklore of American Children a book by Mary and Herbert Knapp borrowing a line from a children's rhyme.

"Got Corn?" an essay in the April 2012 *Smithsonian* magazine from the "Got Milk?" ads.

Batteries Not Included title of a film borrowed from the disclaimer on the side of electronics boxes. Student Juan Diaz titled a paper on cereal icons "Milk Not Included."

"Fiddling While Africa Starves" an essay by P.J. O'Rourke, borrowed from history, the Emperor Nero who, it is said, fiddled while Rome burned.

"Name That Tone" by Louis Menand, the title a play on an old game show, Name That Tune. Brainstorm a list of game show titles and change a word to fit your topic. (This idea works well as a group activity.)

HOOKS, INTRODUCTIONS, AND CONCLUSIONS

Numerous standard tricks for hooking the reader work well: tell a ministory, describe a scene, ask a question, use a startling remark or statistic, a quotation—but taking these standard tips and reinventing them can generate more lively hooks and introductions. These same techniques—with a little reworking—can be used in either introductions or conclusions, with a few exceptions, noted below.

Storytelling—The Personal Anecdote

This standard often works well, depending on the topic or the experience. Barbara Kingsolver, in "Somebody's Baby," begins her essay on Americans' callous treatment of children not their own, with an anecdote that contrasts Spain's loving treatment of her four-year-old daughter with the surliness of the Americans:

> As I walked out the street entrance to my newly rented apartment, a guy in maroon high-tops and a skateboard haircut approached, making kissing noises and saying, "Hi, gorgeous." Three weeks earlier, I would have assessed the degree of malice and made ready to run or tell him to bug off, depending. But now, instead, I smiled, and so did my four-year-old daughter, because after dozens of similar encounters I understood he didn't mean me but her.

> This was not the United States.

Storytelling—The Not-So-Personal Anecdote

Often, writers will borrow stories from history, the news, or other sources. (When using excavated stories, it's best to put them in your own voice rather than quoting.) In "The Chemist's War," Deborah Blum begins her essay on the government alcohol poisoning program during Prohibition with a harrowing news story from history illustrating the results of this misguided idea.

> It was Christmas Eve, 1926, the streets aglitter with snow and lights, when the man afraid of Santa Claus stumbled into the emergency room at New York City's Bellevue Hospital. He was flushed, gasping with fear: Santa Claus, he kept telling the nurses, was just behind him, wielding a baseball bat.

> Before hospital staff realized how sick he was—the alcohol-induced hallucination was just a symptom—the man died. So did another holiday partygoer. And another. As dusk fell on Christmas, the hospital staff tallied up more than sixty people made desperately ill by alcohol and eight dead from it. Within the next two days, yet another twenty-three people died in the city from celebrating the season.

(Yes, it is acceptable to have two paragraphs for an introduction either for emphasis or to break up an otherwise too-long paragraph.)

Storytelling—Borrowing from Myth, Fable, Fairy Tale, and Legend

With so many of these stories available online (an education website is usually the best source), it's easy to forage for a story with a theme that complements a topic, and they work for either **introductions or conclusions**. Summarize and rewrite them rather than copying and quoting; also lead in and out of these stories to connect them to the thesis (see "Paraphrasing" and "Summarizing"). Libraries have numerous books like *Bullfinch's Mythology, Native American Myths and Legends, Irish Folk Tales*, and many multicultural collections of fairy tales.

These sources spark endless ideas: a psychology paper on narcissistic personality disorder with the Greek myth of Narcissus, the beautiful young man who fell in love with his own reflection, thinking it a beautiful nymph; a paper on sleep disorders paired with the god of sleep and dreams, Morpheus; an essay on too much drinking amongst college students with a story of

Bacchus or Dionysus; mothers jealous of their daughters with the Grimm's "Snow White"; a definition essay on pride with Grimm's "Godfather Death."

Aesop's Fables uses animal characters as stand-ins for humans, reflecting on human nature, so they make good fodder for a number of topics: definition papers on different human qualities like anger ("The Farmer and the Dog"), ingratitude or parental neglect ("The Cuckoo, The Hedge-Sparrow, and the Owl"), hypocrisy ("The Fox and the Cat"). These fables also work in essays on animals, for example "The Crow and the Pitcher," to illustrate the intelligence of the crow.

Making Use of Symbolism, Simile, and Metaphor

Writers often glean material from symbol dictionaries for introductions, body paragraphs, or conclusions. In "Disposable Rocket," John Updike opens with a comparison: "Inhabiting a male body is much like having a bank account; as long as it's healthy, you don't have to think about it." Reg Saner, in "Tree Beyond Imagining" uses several metaphors and similes in his introduction: "Seeing is not believing. Any tree 'acting out' in such hogwild and crazy ways—or so I used to feel—can't be truly arboreal. This one thinks it's a mad dog. Here's another trying to prove chaos might be a conifer. Yet another so riven, so warped, it looks like self-knowledge." Gordon Grice in "Black Widow" discusses the symbol of this misunderstood arachnid, how we "project our archetypal terrors" onto the spider. Edward Hoagland, in "The Courage of Turtles," opens his essay with this comparison: "A turtle is a kind of bird with the governor turned low." (At this writing, online symbolism dictionaries have not proven useful as they mostly relate to dream symbolism.)

Famous Quotations and Literary Openings

Dictionaries of quotations, another language resource to plunder, usually alphabetized by topic, are easy to navigate and contain a wide range of subjects with several quotations for each entry by people ranging from Shakespeare to politicians, scientists, and philosophers—people ancient and modern, with widely different views.

Snippets of poems can also help build an introduction. Jack Kroll opens his essay with lines from Homer's *Illiad* to illustrate our long fascination with horror:

> Then his teeth flew out; from two sides, blood came to his eyes; the blood that from lips and nostrils he was spilling, open-mouthed; death enveloped him in its black cloud.

Joyce Carol Oates opens her essay "On Boxing" (not in this edition) with a quote by Irish featherweight champion Barry McGuigan:

> Why are you a boxer, Irish featherweight champion Barry McGuigan was asked.
>
> He said, "I can't be poet. I can't tell stories."

If a dictionary of quotations doesn't turn up a perfect quote, check the internet for old poetry and lines from plays and stories (similar to the advice under the "Titles" section).

See Section Five for advice on blending quotations.

Startling Remarks A short, startling sentence in the first line of an introduction or an appropriate comparison will usually get the reader's attention:

> "A lot of hummingbirds die in their sleep." Diane Ackerman
>
> "I hunt black widow." Gordon Grice.
>
> "Oliver Sacks danced to the dead." Clayton S. Collins
>
> "I loved Prince when I was thirteen, and that was humiliating." Chuck Klosterman
>
> "Were you there?" Jack Kroll

Writers build on these remarks and comparisons to flesh out their introductions (see the essays for the complete introductions).

Riddles

Professional writers use this versatile technique for topics ranging from animals, archaeology, and icons, to fairy tale characters, television personalities, and mental disorders. This riddle by George Hollister for a bird magazine uses short sentences and metaphoric language, saving the more obvious clues—"he doesn't need to fly because he can run faster" and "eats the snake"—for the end of the paragraph: "He's half tail and half feet. The rest of him is head and beak. When he runs, he moves on blurring wheels. He can turn on a dime and leave change. He doesn't need to fly because he can run faster. He kicks dirt in a snake's face and then eats the snake." The answer, of course, is a roadrunner.

Riddles can be tricky; they need to be challenging enough to intrigue the reader but not so difficult that they're impossible to guess.

Many instructions for writing riddles appear on the web, though mostly for poetry writing. Prose riddles leave more options as they don't have to rhyme. These basic guidelines use a student riddle by Sarah Cabbell in a fundamentals of composition course to exemplify some steps for creating riddles:

1. **After deciding on a topic, list the unique and significant details**: tentacles with suckers, no skeleton, is difficult to spot because it blends in with the rocks, people think it's deadly, it squirts ink, lives in the ocean.

   If Sarah had written this list up as it is, the answer would be too obvious and spoil the riddle.

2. **Disguise obvious clues, using simile, metaphor, synonyms or antonyms**: instead of "it squirts ink" she compares it to a magician; tentacles become a skirt, and so on.

3. **Use the third person he, she, it, or they.** Sarah chose "it."

4. **Use simple or compound sentences (two sentences joined with a conjunction) to create interesting juxtapositions (the relationship of objects, perhaps ones that seem like contradictions but have enough truth to make them work):** "It has an excessive number of legs but is unable to walk."

5. **Build clues from the least obvious to the final clues that will help the reader guess, but not too easily:**
   It is found throughout the world but can be hard to spot. It lives in the largest habitat on earth but makes its home in the smallest of places. It is thought to be deadly because of its legendary reputation from tall tales, but that is a misconception. Like a magician, it can perform a disappearing act. It seems to always wear a skirt, but because of its introverted personality, it never shows it off. It has an excessive number of legs but is unable to walk. It would be safe to say it is a real sucker.

6. **Reveal the answer in a second paragraph.** Sarah began her second paragraph with this **transition** sentence: "The octopus is one of the most misunderstood and mysterious animals in the ocean."

Personification Applying human characteristics to an object challenges critical thinking, forcing the writer and the reader to think more complexly about a topic in order to find its not-so-obvious qualities. In an essay titled "It's All in the Implications" (*Los Angeles Times*, 02/13/06), Pico Iyer personifies the word implication:

Once upon a time, there was a spirit called Implication. He didn't get picked very often when the other kids were choosing teams, and he tended to live in the shadows. But he always had a sense of pride, deep down, because he knew that people would call on him in their most important moments: in bed beside someone they loved, or while on their knees whispering to what—or who—they believed in. Life wasn't black or white, he knew; Implication was a friend of all the colors.

He continues the essay, with Implication being first blacklisted, becoming an outcast, then a fugitive when he walks into the post office and finds his name on the "10 Most Wanted List" along with Subtlety, Ambiguity, Diplomacy, and Mischief, a clever but grim commentary on the demise of language, lost to a world of quick sound bites.

Personification can make an **introduction** pop; it can also be combined with the riddle style. Think of a personification as a character sketch. Below is a list of details—a brainstorming list—that Ruth Gendler might have used for her personification of the quality "truth" (complete essay in the text).

Guidelines for Personifying

1. Choose an object or human personality trait: **"Truth."**
2. Assign a gender: **Male.**
3. Decide what the object or trait would look like if it were a person. No need to be detailed, but try to give it some physical characteristics: **Tall, unconventional looking, golden hair, short beard, spacious shoulders**.
4. What other qualities or objects would it have as friends or relatives: **Certainty and Uncertainty.**
5. Consider what type of job, hobbies, or activities would fit the personality profile: **Employed as a thief stealing illusions. Fascinated with X-rays, photographs of cells, and the history of plants. Studies mime. Gentle nature, not sarcastic. Wrote film reviews but quit when he found his quotes taken out of context.**
6. Set the details up in a mini-story: **See the finished product in the text.**

Extended Comparisons or Analogies

Though this technique works anywhere in an essay, it often makes a memorable conclusion. In Mark Twain's essay "Reading the River," he details what he gained and lost by becoming a river boat pilot on the Mississippi, concluding by comparing his inability to view the river simply for its beauty to a doctor who treats beautiful women only to see the disease:

> No, the romance and beauty were all gone from the river. All the value any feature of it had for me now was the amount of usefulness it could furnish toward compassing the safe piloting of a steamboat. Since those days, I have pitied doctors from my heart. What does the lovely flush in a beauty's cheek mean to a doctor but a "break" that ripples above some deadly disease? Are not all her visible charms sown thick with what are to him the signs and symbols of hidden decay? Does he ever see her beauty at all, or doesn't he simply view her professionally and comment upon her unwholesome condition all to himself? And doesn't he sometimes wonder whether he has gained most or lost most by learning his trade?

Try breaking down a social or political system to compare: In his research problem/solution paper, freshman composition student Robert Olswang compares the emperor penguin's social structure to socialism, drawing direct parallels, "His success and survival is due to a social cohesiveness that is not besieged by a systematic hierarchy where everyone is equal: where one goes, they all go." He builds on his comparison, using tenets of the socialist system to describe the penguins' actions. For the same assignment, another student used Zen Buddhism to compare to an egret.

Over the years, students have illustrated diverse, remarkable comparisons in their conclusions: a listing of abuse to a pair of old ballet slippers, that in the end, still have worth, can still dance; a daughter's relationship with her mother to a designer bag, an accessory for her mother to show off; a thorn tree to a father's anger. With a small bit of research and some thought, writing memorable endings to essays becomes less of a struggle and banishes the tired restate-the-thesis conclusions teachers dread. With a few examples and some outside resources, imagination thrives.

TRANSITIONS

An organized, well-written essay needs transitions between paragraphs and between ideas within paragraphs. Though writers use different strategies to transition, generally, the concluding line of one paragraph should have a link to a word or phrase in the first line of the next paragraph. Avoid high school transitions such as "first of all," "secondly," "however," and "in conclusion." There are stronger ways to transition:

Using a different form of the same word to begin a new idea:

Barbara Holland uses "napper" and "napping" to transition between paragraphs #4 and #5:

"Fifteen minutes later the **napper** pops back to the surface as from time travel, bewildered to find that it's only ten of two instead of centuries later.

Like skydiving, **napping** takes practice; the first few tries are **scary**."

After this one-line paragraph, she moves into six, picking up the word "scary" and turning it into "scarier":

"The American nap is even **scarier** because it's unilateral."

Using words that mean the opposite:

In "Nourishing Awareness in Each Moment," Thich Nhat Hanh ends his first paragraph with this line:

"Then I started a fire in the fireplace, and soon the crackling logs brought warmth back to the room."

He builds on this idea of warmth in the first line of paragraph #2, steering the reader into another idea, using the opposite of warmth:

"Sometimes in a crowd we feel tired, **cold**, and lonely."

He moves from physical warmth to emotional cold.

Using words with similar meanings:

In "Meat" by Brian Doyle, at the end of paragraph three, he writes:

> ". . . Tommy was never going to be six feet tall, not in this life, and he was what even his mom called *husky*."

At the beginning of paragraph four, he ties the word husky to big guys:

> "One time I asked Tommy why he called all the *big guys* Meat and he said it was just easier that way, learning their names was pointless because they all responded to the same simple stimuli."

In "A Voice for the Lonely," Stephen Corey uses the word "dawn" at the end of paragraph #1 with "early riser" in the beginning of paragraph #2; "transistor radio" at the end of #2, linked to "music" in paragraph #3.

For more on transitions, see the "Styling" with "About Men" by Gretel Ehrlich and "Strategies for Writing the Personal Essay" for time transitions.

Once finished with the big changes, work on editing for fragments, run-on sentences, punctuation, and other errors. It helps to read the paper aloud or have someone else read it. Reading the essay in reverse—beginning with the last sentence of the essay—isolates sentences, making it easier to spot mistakes.

Revising and Editing

It's midnight the night before the paper is due. You've written a draft, so you're in good shape, right? Wrong. Most students think that having a draft means they can just hit spell check on the computer and then print. I admit that occasionally a student can pull this tactic off, but for the rest of us, we've only just begun. Writing means rewriting, rewriting, and more rewriting.

First, revise the paper. Revising means big changes, like adding or deleting information, reorganizing the essay, rewriting sentences, checking that the ideas are fully developed. Here's a list of questions to ask yourself about each developmental paragraph of your essay:

1. Can I add another example?
2. Can I add more information?
3. Can I describe something and make it more vivid for the reader?
4. Can I add a statistic or quote as evidence to strengthen my claim?
5. Can I explain a quote so the reader is clear on why I used it?
6. Have I related all of the material to my thesis statement or topic sentence?
7. Are there terms my reader may not understand (for example, surfing jargon) that I need to define?
8. Have I addressed all areas of the prompt?

All of these questions may not apply to every paper, but most of them will. You can always add an example or more information or description, and check to make sure that all of the material relates to the thesis or topic sentence.

Once revision is complete, edit for grammar, fragments, run-ons, comma splices, punctuation errors, and other mistakes. See the "Sweating the Small Stuff" for help and consult the glossary for examples of fragments, run-ons, and comma splices; review the rules in "Punctuation is Style: Basic Rules and Punctuation."

STRATEGIES FOR WRITING PERSONAL ESSAYS

Storytelling comes naturally. You tell stories almost every day. When trying to tell a story in writing, keep in mind that the reader can't ask questions. It's up to you to hold the reader's attention, make a point, keep to the story, and evoke a sense of time and place.

Purpose

Why are you writing this story, sharing this memory? Though your purpose might be implied rather than stated directly, that purpose should be clear. Are you trying to inform, explain, teach, warn? Would the topic interest a general audience? Stories about car accidents or the horror of finding a significant other cheating don't offer much to the reader, even those who might have had the same experience. What kind of point can you offer that won't sound worn out? Don't drink and drive, or watch out for deceptive boyfriends or girlfriends, husbands or wives? David Sedaris's personal story about a conflict with a woman on an airplane who wanted to change seats comments on conflict/resolution. In "Mortality" by Bailey White, her car becomes a metaphor for aging. Bernard Cooper's "Burl's" explores not only sexual identity but an epiphany he has that reality is not always what it seems. Have a thought-provoking purpose or the story falls flat.

Zooming In

Most narratives zoom in on a small time period, and most writing books advise sticking to a 24-hour time period or less. For beginning writers, that's generally very good advice. Trying to write a life's story in a three-page essay, won't leave much room for detail and description. While experienced writers do sometimes flash forward or backward in time, like Edward Hoagland does in "The Courage of Turtles," many good narratives zoom in tight, like Lawrence Weschler's "Modern Times," which takes place in a few minutes in his office at work. The idea is to focus on a slice of life, to capture a meaningful moment in time. If you go much outside the 24-hour time frame, you could get into trouble with chronological order or confuse your reader by jumping in time without the proper transition.

Time Transitions

Transitions—words or phrases that help you move smoothly from one idea to another—are crucial in narrative. When writing from memory, you make automatic adjustments in time in your head, but if you leap in time without informing your reader, confusion results. When you move your story in time, let the reader know with phrases like *later that day* or *the following morning.* If you do decide to make big leaps in time, use proper transition, time indicators like "When I was five" or "After I entered high school" to help the reader travel in time with you so the reader isn't confused, thinking a small child is doing something like driving a car.

Evoking Senses

Another crucial element in writing memories is creating a vivid picture through description and sensory detail. You want the reader to hear, smell, taste, feel, see the experience. In "A Voice for the Lonely" Stephen Corey, instead of just telling the reader that it was quiet in the early mornings when he delivered newspapers, writes, "I recall stopping my brisk walk sometimes, especially in winter when every step squeaked and crunched on the snow that nearly always covered the ground, and marveling at how there were no sounds except those of my own making." He uses sound—squeaked and crunched—to show the silence. In "Burl's," Bernard Cooper describes the "medicinal odor of mothballs" that permeated his father's closet in paragraph #20, contrasting the smell of his mother's closet, "the air ripe with perfume" in #22; the sense of touch, "But no matter how much I wanted them to fit, those shoes were as cold and hard as marble" and "I was seared by a gust of heat" in paragraph #5; sight, "In the periphery of my vision, the shelf of wigs looked like a throng of kindly bystanders"; taste, "tasted Tobasco sauce" in #4.

WRITING STRATEGIES FOR EXPLAINING AND EXPLORING IDEAS

Most essays–while relying on a clear purpose, organized paragraphs with strong examples, vivid description, sentence variety, and specific details– often blend rhetorical modes: a narrative introduction for an argument paper; a definition paragraph in a cause and effect analysis; a contrast or comparison in a definition; and so on. Any of these modes can be combined to fit the writer's style or requirements of an essay.

Comparison and Contrast

In a comparison or contrast essay, you're attempting to hold one thing up to another to make a point. In Pauline Kael's review of *The Little Mermaid,* she contrasts Disney's film version to the original story by Hans Christian Andersen to illustrate the inferiority of the Disney cartoon. Comparison shows similarities to make a point, while contrast focuses on differences. For beginning writers, it's sometimes easier to make a point by writing about differences, so the example illustrates a contrast.

There are two basic methods of organization for writing a comparison or contrast paper: one side at a time or point by point. In the one-side-at-a-time method—sometimes called the block method—the first half of the essay discusses one topic and the second half compares or contrasts the other topic. A paper like Kael's "The Little Mermaid," contrasting Disney's *Cinderella* film with the old folktale from Grimms', might be organized like this:

Paragraph 1:	I.	Introduction and Thesis
Paragraph 2:	II.	Disney Film
		a. Weak charcterization
		b. Beauty wins as a primary lesson
		c. Spiritual element reduced to ninny fairy godmother
Paragraph 3:	III.	Grimms' Story
		a. Strong characterization
		b. Beauty comes from within
		c. Spiritual element in form of dead mother's spirit
Paragraph 4:	IV.	Conclusion

Notice that the same points are covered for both versions. If you were to write in the second method, point by point, you would organize the essay this way:

Paragraph 1:   I. Introduction and Thesis
Paragraph 2:   II. Characterization
                        a. Disney: weak
                        b. Grimm: strong
Paragraph 3:   III. Beauty
                        a. Disney: beauty wins is primary lesson
                        b. Grimm: beauty comes from within
Paragraph 4:   IV. Spiritual Element
                        a. Disney spiritual element reduced to ninny fairy godmother
                        b. Grimm spiritual element in form of dead mother's spirit.
Paragraph 5:   V. Conclusion

Paragraphs don't always lay out so neatly into this formula. If paragraphs get too long, they might need broken up. For example, in the point-by-point method, break Characterization into two paragraphs: one for Disney and one for Grimm.

When comparing or contrasting, it's important to let the reader know which subject you're discussing by using transitions. Here's a list of transitions commonly used in comparison and contrast essays: *on the other hand, by contrast, similarly, by comparison.*

CAUTION Don't just show how two things are alike or different. There's no point to your essay if you fail to have an opinion. Why are you comparing? To show one's superiority over the other? To warn the reader? To promote understanding of an idea? You must have a **thesis statement**.

Cause and Effect

Why do some young girls mutilate themselves? Why did the Anasazi Indians live in the remote cliffs and resort to cannibalism? What's causing the failure of our educational system? What caused the Los Angeles riots? Does excess television cause obesity in children? Cause and effect essays attempt to explain why something happens—causes—and the results of incidents—effects.

Usually results have many causes, so you want to examine your topic closely for hidden reasons. After the Los Angeles riots, many people blamed the failure of our court system to convict the police officers involved in the Rodney King beating, and while that event certainly triggered the riots, the causes are much more complex, rooted in many years of police brutality and poverty, among other things. If you're going to blame television for obesity in children, you'd better examine the children's eating habits and social lives. It could be that children who watch television and eat excessively do so because of another problem like being picked on in school or trying to escape painful family problems or abuse. It's rare that you can say "this caused that."

There's no one organizational strategy for writing cause and effect essays, but generally writers explain the problem and then examine the causes. For example, the causes of self-mutilation are complex: pressures of adolescence, self-blame, shame, anger, feelings of abandonment. To neglect one of these causes of this serious problem would result in simplistic thinking.

Often, in a short essay on a large event, it's better to narrow to a **specific cause**, though letting the reader know that many causes contributed to the event. The economic crash of 2008 had numerous causes, but the essay might focus on one contributor, the banking industry. The paper would focus more on the **effects**, though explaining in the first couple of paragraphs the problems with the banking industry followed by paragraphs discussing the results: unemployment, foreclosures, increase in homelessness and the amount of people on welfare, adults with children moving back in with parents.

A cause and effect essay on cheating in school might be first outlined for causes and effects:

"Cheating in School"

Causes	**Effects**
Peer pressure	Not being prepared for the next level course
Parental pressure	Getting caught cheating and kicked out of school
Laziness	Difficulty getting accepted at another college
Lack of ethics	Not having the skills necessary for the job market
Belief that everyone cheats	

Explaining a Process

Process Analysis essays break down a subject into its steps and explain to the reader how to do something: watch an animal in the wild, run a marathon, grow tomatoes, tile a floor, or more serious topics like visit someone in prison. Often process essays take the command form **point of view** (see "Point of View" in "Sweating the Small Stuff"). Speech classes sometimes have students explain to the class how to do something in process analysis format.

Explaining or analyzing a process in writing isn't much different from explaining it to a friend or to a class, though in writing, friends or peers cannot ask questions. Be aware of the audience by writing clear step-by-step instructions and considering the audience's level of expertise. In an essay on how to grow orchids, a general reader—like your peers in a Speech class or an English teacher—will need more details and explanation than a gardening group that already has some experiencing tending plants.

In her essay "What Really Happened," Madge McKeithen takes the reader through the detailed process of visiting a murderer in prison (one who murdered his wife, a friend of hers), from how to find the correctional institution in which the offender is incarcerated, through speaking with the lawyer who defended him, writing the request to visit, choosing a date, renting a car, checking into the facility, talking with the offender, receiving the hundreds of letters he sends over subsequent months, but most importantly, remembering her—the victim.

WRITING STRATEGIES FOR DEFINING TERMS

Words can be slippery. They change meaning, wear disguises, take on new personas depending on who's using them. Charity wears many masks, kindness one day, an insult to pride the next, sometimes a veil for greed. What determines greed for one person constitutes ambition for another. Words are master chameleons.

Purpose

When writing a definition essay, the job is to rip off the masks, expose secrets; don't be content with worn out definitions. Don't write what everyone already knows about the word. For a more interesting paper, look at the side of the word nobody talks about. If you're writing a paper defining the word *lonely,* don't fall into the pity-all-the-lonely-people trap; you won't offer your reader anything new; if, on the other hand, you take the road less traveled, as one student did, and write, "Loneliness doesn't deserve pity or guilt. It deserves to be crushed in the street, crumpled under tires like dead leaves, crunched like a paper bag. Maybe then, like the Phoenix that goes up in flames and rises from its own ashes, the lonely will create their own lives, stop hermiting themselves, learn to paint or take a dance class, volunteer for meals-on-wheels, join a singles club, and quit tormenting the rest of us with their sorrowful lives." This thesis shocks the reader out of complacency.

Language Resources

Finding a new angle for a thesis can be a difficult task, but looking up the word in various language resources can help you find an edge. Many language resources are available online and in the library or a bookstore. While a standard dictionary might be helpful, other, more exciting sources abound: dictionaries of quotations, dictionaries of slang, a thesaurus, and *The Oxford English Dictionary.* If you do decide to use a standard dictionary like *Webster's,* avoid boring phrases like "According to *Webster's* . . ." These phrases numb the mind, and the reader will be reluctant to read further. For the paper on loneliness, the student first used a dictionary of quotations to discover what others have said about the term, finding a quote by Paul Elmer More stating that people "hold themselves aloof in chosen loneliness of passion," giving her the idea to focus on loneliness as self-pitying, self-inflicted isolation. She uses this quote in her essay as part of her conclusion.

Next, she visited a thesaurus, finding a bonanza of words to string together, creating an engaging inventory to underscore her point: "Loneliness is self-abandonment, icy isolation, me and my shadow, me-myself-and-I narcissism; single, solo, solitary, stag, I-travel-light baby; unescorted, unaccompanied, unaided, unassisted, pride run rampant." Notice the thoughtful word arrangement. Rather than repeating a list from the thesaurus, she braids them—except for the first string—with **alliteration**, chaining together words beginning with *s,* following with a string of *u* words, using a semicolon to separate the strings. Both strands end with a punch, a more-than-one-word phrase breaking the monotony of a single-word list, emphasizing her notion that most people choose their loneliness. The first strand—notice the complete sentence—contains some alliteration (*m*), but mostly establishes the cold, selfish aspect of the term.

To further defend her definition, the student investigated *The Oxford English Dictionary* (or OED), a several volume set chronicling the history of the English language. She discovered that the word *lonely* derives from *alone,* which stems from Middle English, a combination of *all* plus *one,* or all one. From there she reasoned that *all one* has a selfish, me-me-me implication, further validating her view.

Examples

In addition to a purpose for defining the word, the definition needs numerous examples. In the essay on loneliness, the student gives specific examples of sorrowful lives: the lonely business man, married to his job; the housewife stuck in an unhappy marriage; the whore on Harbor Boulevard. The student discusses each example, showing how most lonely people bring about their own loneliness, admitting that some loneliness results from mental illness, "but most lonely people wear their isolation like a crown of thorns." She also harvests examples from pop culture, using the Beatles' album *Sergeant Pepper's Lonely Heart's Club Band,* citing song lyrics that express America's frenzy of pity for the lonely. Without specific, thoroughly discussed examples, the reader wouldn't be convinced of such an unconventional point of view.

Debunking Misconceptions and Preconceived Ideas

Don't just rely on the obvious when writing a definition; be original. One strategy is to argue from negation, or what a word is not. In his essay "Charm," from *I Can't Stay Long,* Laurie Lee writes, "Certainly, charm is not a question of learning palpable tricks, like wrinkling your nose, or having a laugh in your voice, or gaily tossing your hair out of your dancing eyes and twisting your mouth into succulent love-knots." He busts the standard view of charm, following with specifics defining charm: "Charm can't withhold, but spends itself willingly on young and old alike, on the poor, the ugly, the dim, the boring, on the last fat man in the corner."

Learning to write strong extended definitions is an important writing and thinking skill. Whether writing an essay defining Romanticism for art history, existentialism for philosophy, or Puritanism for religious studies, learning to capture elusive words and make them concrete challenges your mind, your assumptions, broadening your view of the world.

WRITING STRATEGIES FOR ARGUING

Standing up to the high school bully. Wondering whether technology keeps us too much in touch. Deciding if we've lost the war on drugs. Rethinking the value of television talk shows. Opinions on these topics—and many others—form the basis for argument. The trick, though, when writing an argument essay is to support opinion with solid evidence. The goal is persuasion—don't just spout an opinion. To convince a reader—especially one who doesn't agree—state the point clearly, back it up with proof, and refute points from the other side.

Stating the Point

The point is the **thesis statement**, the writer's opinion on the topic. "Drugs should be legalized because we've already lost the war" states an opinion without using *I*. Generally, in college argument essays, avoid using *I*. First, it's redundant: if you state it, then it is your opinion, no *I* needed. Second, it's considered weak, wishy-washy to write *I think* or *I believe*. It's akin to saying, "It's only my opinion, so don't take me that seriously." Stand up for your convictions with a forceful statement. Notice, too, that the above statement contains *should* and *because*. Those two words signal your opinion—*should*—and your reasons for that opinion—*because*. As you become more practiced at writing thesis statements, you'll want to drop the obvious use of should and because, writing your statement in a more polished manner, as Gore Vidal does in "Drugs": "It is possible to stop most drug addiction in the United States within a very short time. Simply make all drugs available and sell them at cost." Of course, if Vidal doesn't support that statement with solid evidence, we'd simply ignore him.

Supporting Your Point

Support a point in an argument essay the same way as in any essay (see the section on Writing Basic College Essays), with strong examples, statistics, quotes, details. Know the topic, by researching. Explore both sides of the issue in order to refute the other side.

Refuting the Opposition

Know the other side's objections to the argument and respond, showing how they might be wrong or misguided. One approach is to bring up their objections, either in the form of a quotation or paraphrase, and then respond: "Those who oppose legalizing drugs claim that legalization will lead to more drug addiction. Not so. People who are going to take drugs will do so, legal or not. During Prohibition, when alcohol was illegal, the law didn't stop alcoholism or drinking; it just turned it into a criminal activity." This strategy states the other side's view and then refutes it. The key is to be sure the reader knows when you are presenting an opposing view. Use phrases like "Opponents believe," to avoid confusing the reader.

Organization

Though a basic organization—introduction with thesis, body paragraphs, conclusion—works for arguments, almost any mode can be used or blended with other modes for a hybrid: a contrast or comparison essay might begin with a narrative and then argue one side over another or a cause and effect might use a definition in the opening or body. It depends on the paper's purpose. For addressing the opposition, use statements from the opponent's view as topic sentences and refute them. Another strategy spends three or four paragraphs discussing the writer's views, and then presents the opposition's views in one or two paragraphs, refuting them as they're presented.

WRITING STRATEGIES FOR CLASSIFICATION

When visiting Disneyland or Disney World, visitors find their way around by looking at a map divided into different areas, classified according to time or place: Frontierland, Tomorrowland, Fantasyland, Adventureland, Main Street USA, Critter Country, and so on. These classifications orient them to the park and let them know what to expect. Even a first-time visitor will probably figure out that Space Mountain is in Tomorrowland, not Frontierland. The descriptive names make sense of an otherwise chaotic place. A divided and classified closet: summer clothes, work attire, winter wardrobe; a pantry: canned goods, spices and baking supplies, breakfast items, boxed foods; a notebook: science, English, math, history, geology. If a hardware store heaped the paint in with the garden tools, the faucets in with the tulip bulbs, shoppers would walk out.

Writers often classify to make sense of a complex topic, poke fun or satirize, explain a comparison involving more than two subjects. A student might be asked to write a paper for a sociology class discussing parenting styles; periods of art in an art history class; types of earthquakes in a geology class. Classification can be useful for many topics.

In her essay "Friends, Good Friends—and Such Good Friends" (not in this book), Judith Viorst classifies her friends into seven categories: convenience friends, special-interest friends, historical friends, crossroads friends, cross-generational friends, part-of-a-couple friends, men who are friends. Viorst follows good rules of classification to write her essay:

Purpose

1. **Make a point.** If you write an essay classifying teenagers according to high school cliques, and you just list the types, you aren't doing your reader a service. Anyone can make a list of types. The classification needs a thesis. Is it trying to warn the reader about a certain type of clique? Argue that cliques are detrimental to student learning? Illustrate that strict conformity leads to problems later in life? In Viorst's essay, she doesn't just discuss the types of friends; she makes a point:

   > I once would have said that a friend is a friend all the way, but now I believe that's a narrow point of view. For the friendships I have and the friendships I see are conducted at many levels of intensity, serve many different functions, meet different needs and range from those as all-the-way as the friendship of the soul sisters mentioned above to that of the most nonchalant and casual playmates.

   She then discusses each class of friends, pointing out how the class fits into her definition of friendship. Notice that she busts the standard view of friendship as being the no-matter-what kind.

Ruling Principle

2. **Tie each category back to the thesis.** For Viorst, it's the level of intimacy that ties the essay together. In English teacher jargon, this would be called the "Ruling Principle of Classification," how the topic is divided. Should a classification of rocks be by size, color, shape, composition? Pick one ruling principle and stick to it. If Viorst suddenly threw in a class of friends and didn't mention the intimacy factor, we would wonder why she added that category. If you classified Adventure films according to character types and then discussed a group by dialogue, the essay would be straying from the ruling principle, and would not stick together. The ruling principle is the glue of the essay.

Support

3. **Use numerous examples.** Every essay needs strong examples. In her category on Convenience friends, after defining what she means by convenience, Viorst lists the types of things these women do for each other: "Convenience friends are convenient

indeed. They'll lend us their cups and silverware for a party. They'll drive our kids to soccer when we're sick. They'll take us to pick up our car when we need a lift to the garage. They'll even take our cats when we go on vacation." Listing specific good-neighbor chores gives her point weight. She goes on to give examples of what she would and would not discuss with a convenience friend, the intimacy factor, gluing her essay back to its point.

4. Avoid simplifying. Acknowledge that the topic may be more complex than the classification covers. Admit the generalization and mention possible exceptions to the categories. In a paper on high school cliques, admit that not every student fits neatly into one of these groups. The conclusion might be a good place to write a disclaimer.

Labels

5. Label the groups. Notice that Viorst has descriptive labels that hint at the topic and give it flavor. The reader can tell by the label what to expect. When brainstorming a list of high school cliques, one class came up with the following groups: Rah Rahs (jocks and cheerleaders), Bandos (students in the band), Brains (formerly referred to as nerds), Misfits (students who dress and act in opposition to the rest of the crowd), Stoners (speaks for itself), Clubbies (students who always join clubs or run for office).

Organization

6. Organize the paper. There are many ways to organize material for classification, depending on the topic, but here are two common methods: chronological and emphatic order. If classifying historical time periods, consider organizing chronologically—time order—in the order the events occurred in time. If organizing friends, use emphatic order—least important category or shortest category first, and the most important or longest last.

SUMMARIZING

A summary is a restatement—in your own words—of another writer's work. In college, you might be asked to summarize a chapter in a textbook, summarize an article and then respond in an essay to the writer's ideas, or summarize to demonstrate understanding in a reading class. Learning to summarize helps you absorb material for tests, improve reading comprehension, and learn to identify key points. To summarize correctly, follow these steps:

1. Read the article through once to get the general idea.
2. Read a second time, highlighting key ideas—or taking notes if you don't want to defile your book.
3. Then—without looking at the text—write one-sentence summaries for each paragraph of the writer's main ideas.
4. Now write a draft of the summary from the sentences, providing examples from each paragraph that support the main ideas.
5. Check the summary against the author's work, making sure your writing is in your own words. When using any of the author's original words, put them in quotation marks. It's okay to put quotation marks around parts of a sentence to distinguish the writer's words from your own. For example, if you are summarizing Shelby's Steele's piece from his book *The Content of Our Character,* you might write a sentence like this:

> Although Steele concedes that prejudice against blacks is still a problem in America, overall, he thinks "there is also much opportunity."

Note: See the Paraphrasing section for information on how to paraphrase correctly.

TIPS FOR WRITING SUMMARIES

1. A summary should be about one-quarter the length of the article being summarized. If the summary is longer than one page, you may have to break it into paragraphs. A good rule is to change paragraphs when beginning to summarize a new idea.
2. Do not give an opinion in a summary. Save your views for critiques.
3. Always give the title of the text being summarized as well as the author's name in the introduction of the summary. Don't just write the title of the piece at the top of the page. Introduce the writer and the work:

> In the article "Drugs" by Gore Vidal, the author argues in favor of legalizing all drugs.

> Notice that this opening sentence introduces the title, the author, and the author's thesis.

4. Be sure to paraphrase correctly (see below).

PARAPHRASING

Paraphrasing—simply put—means rewording. When taking an in-class essay examination based on material from a text, you repeat the material on the test in your own words. You're not quoting from the text but writing what you remember. You might use paraphrasing in a research paper to liven up another writer's words by using your own style, replacing a style that might otherwise sound dry.

A direct quote would look like this (the number in parentheses is the page number where the original statement is found):

Joseph Verrengia reports, "Laboratory tests on some of the artifacts, including a piece of human excrement, have revealed traces of a human protein that scientists say is the first direct evidence of cannibalism among the Anasazi" (15).

A paraphrase of the above quote might look something like this:

According to Joseph Verrengia, science has proven—using tests on human waste left at the scene of the crime—that the Anasazi did, indeed, chow down on their brethren, slicing and dicing, roasting and toasting their own kind, a grisly banquet for reasons unknown (15).

Give the source in both instances. It's unnecessary to cite every line of a summary as readers know the material has been reworded, but always give credit to others' words and ideas when paraphrasing in an essay. Otherwise, you're guilty of **plagiarism**.

Be sure to *completely* reword the material or put quotation marks around partially quoted material. When using any of the writer's original words, put quotation marks around them. If in the Verrengia example above the writer had written "piece of human excrement" instead of "human waste" and didn't put quotation marks around Verrengia's words, it would be considered plagiarism. See #5 under Summarizing.

PLAGIARISM AND GENERAL ADVICE FOR USING SOURCES

"This above all: To thine own self be true."

—William Shakespeare

Many students come to college with mistaken or vague definitions of **plagiarism**. Most know that it's wrong to download a paper off the Internet or borrow another student's work and present it as their own—a revolting practice—but knowing when to document a source can some-times be confusing. Though most students have integrity and wouldn't plagiarize on purpose, some students pillage sources unintentionally, unaware that they are plagiarizing. You must give credit to every source. This is tricky business. However, if you remember some general guide-lines, you'll be safe.

1. Always give an in-text citation showing the source of the mate-rial. See the research section for information on how to correctly cite material within an essay.

2. If information is common knowledge, or something you already know, you do not have to cite a source because *you* are the source. In a paper on AIDS, it's not necessary to cite a source on the trans-mission of the virus. For most people, that's common knowledge. If you're a saltwater aquarium hobbyist writing an essay on how to start an aquarium, then you're probably an expert on many aspects of this exotic pastime, so you don't have to cite that infor-mation unless it's something you have to look up.

3. Avoid overquoting or overparaphrasing—stringing material together with little of your own writing. Instead, comment on material, giving your own opinion. Ask yourself, "Do I agree with this writer? What do I think? How does the quote or paraphrase support or refute my own opinion? Is the material logical? Help-ful to the reader?"

4. Blend quotations smoothly. Don't just leave them dangling. See the research section for how to blend quotes. The Summarizing section, above, also has ideas for blending quotes.

5. Make sure you've interpreted the quote correctly and that it's relevant to your point.

6. Be fair to the writer when quoting or paraphrasing. Partial quota-tions are acceptable as long as they don't change the meaning of the original work. Always use quotation marks around another's words.

Research

When writing college essays, you will probably be required to do some research and incorporate it into your own writing. If you use researched material, you must document it correctly. Remember that any words or ideas that are not your own must be documented (see Plagiarism). This section illustrates how to find materials, site information within an essay, and assemble Works Cited pages using the MLA (Modern Language Association) style of documentation. Not every school or department uses MLA format, but most English Departments do. Other styles include APA (American Psychological Association) and Chicago Manual of Style. If a teacher requires a style other than the MLA, visit the library or search the reference section of a reliable web site. One site that can help you with your works cited page is EasyBib.com.

BASIC SOURCES

The library is king of information. Libraries pay for services and databases that you cannot get for free on the Web. Infotrac, for example, contains articles from periodicals like magazines and journals and specific newspaper databases. You can search for hours on the Web and find nothing reliable on a topic or spend ten minutes in your library databases and find a bonanza of materials. And the library has librarians to help. You won't find that kind of service on the Web (see "The Web" below).

The library has a book catalogue, usually on computer, where you can instantly find books on any topic. They also have reference materials like dictionaries and encyclopedias specific to a subject: art dictionaries, symbol dictionaries, reptile dictionaries. They have copy machines, computers, and access to other libraries.

Don't limit a search to books or the Web. Use a variety of sources to ensure you've found the best information on your topic. Interview people, experts in the field. For example, if you're writing an essay on reptiles, phone the local zoo and speak to the keeper of the reptile house. If writing about a social or community issue, write to or call city officials like parole officers and social workers. Talk to professors in colleges who are experts in their fields.

Don't forget that grab bag, the television. Proceed with caution, as with the Web. Avoid talk shows—unless you're writing a paper on the intellectual deterioration of America and want to use talk shows for examples. Rely on PBS stations that show quality programs. Stations with a focus on history, animals, and science generally have reliable information, but again, be cautious: these shows might also have a bias.

THE WEB

While the Web is a great tool that has quick access to information, it also contains a lot of false or biased material. Junk clutters the information superhighway. Anyone can put up a Web page, so be certain to use valid sites. In general, *only use databases that the school library subscribes to.* College libraries pay a lot of money to provide students access to academic, valid research. Take advantage of that privilege. Most databases can be accessed from home, even when the library is closed. Ask your school's librarian for help if you're not familiar with these services. Keep in mind this simple rule: if it's not paid for by a college library, proceed with caution. Even if it's an online encyclopedia, it can contain wrong information. Legitimate online encyclopedias—like Britannica Online—charge for the service.

Evaluating Web Sites and Other Sources

There's a T-shirt/bumper sticker slogan that states, "Question Authority, But Raise Your Hand First." Use this as your **mantra** when evaluating sources, whether from a library, periodical database, interview, television program, film, radio, or the Web. Again, be especially cautious using the Web. It's not considered academic to rely on the Internet instead of books or periodicals. But if you do use an Web site, evaluate sources critically and respectfully. Here are a few guidelines:

1. Is the source trustworthy? Can the site be counted on for accurate, up-to-date information? Find out what organization or individual runs the site. Consider asking the school's librarian.

2. Does the site contain a **bias**? Most do, so don't necessarily rule out a Web source for this reason, but try to determine whether the information is too far out of the mainstream to be credible. A source that claims the Holocaust didn't happen would not be considered dependable. A website maintained by a political group—Republican, Democratic, Libertarian—will have a distinct bias.

3. Don't rely on only one source. If you're writing a paper on the medical use of marijuana and only rely on a Web page sponsored by medical marijuana advocates, your essay will not be thoroughly researched. Use a variety of sources on both sides of the issue.

4. Always cite the Web source correctly. See the Basic Documentation section.

5. Does the source provide new, interesting information you hadn't considered that will add to your essay?

6. What is the writer's style? Is the **tone** too emotional? Does the writer rely on **jargon**? Are the ideas clear?

BASIC DOCUMENTATION

This section provides the basics of MLA documentation, covering the most commonly used sources, so if a source documentation problem is not discussed here, the library should have a copy of *The MLA Handbook,* which provides more in-depth documentation information.

Format

Do not use a title page for your research paper unless specifically requested to by your teacher. Instead, in the upper left corner of the page, put your name, the teacher's name, the class, and the date. In the upper right corner, put your last name and the page number. Put your last name and page number on every page of your document, but the left corner information goes only on the first page. (See the sample at the end of the documentation section.)

Double space the entire document. Do not put extra spaces between paragraphs. Indent the first line of each paragraph.

Use one-inch margins all around your paper, and use a standard type size like 12 point. If you use huge type, it will look like you've run out of things to say and are trying to take up space by using big type.

In-Text Citation

Within an essay, an in-text citation is brief information about a source provided in parentheses. When writing a paper using information and quotes from books, magazines, journals, newspapers, interviews, the Web, or other sources, give an in-text citation next to the quote or information. Generally, use the writer's last name and the page number.

Do not use a comma to separate the author's name from the page number, nor should you write *p.* for page. Cite the source just like the examples below. If using the writer's name to introduce the quote, then only the page number is required in parentheses. Keep in-text citations as brief as possible, saving detailed information for the Works Cited pages. Here's an example of blending a quote with your own writing:

```
Fairy tales teach children about the real world.
We grow up to find out, "As we had suspected, the fairy
tales had been right all along—the world was full of
hostile, stupid giants and perilous castles and people
who abandoned their children in the nearest forest"
(Lurie 18).
```

Notice that the period goes outside the parentheses. The following example uses the writer's name to introduce the quote:

```
Fairy tales teach children about the real world.
According to Alison Lurie, we grow up to find out, "As
we had suspected, the fairy tales had been right all
along—the world was full of hostile, stupid giants and
perilous castles and people who abandoned their chil-
dren in the nearest forest" (18).
```

Because the writer's name introduces the quote, there's no need to repeat it in the in-text citation, only the page number.

If two people wrote the work, use both names in parentheses: (Brown and Smith 44). For three authors, follow the same strategy: (Brown, Smith, and Diaz 44). When a source has three or more authors, use the last name of the first author listed followed by *et al.* (and others): (Brown et al. 44).

If the source doesn't list an author, then abbreviate the title instead. A book titled *Medicines of the Rain Forest* with no author would be cited like this: (*Medicines* 32).

When using a quote of more than three typed lines, set the quote off by indenting *two* tab spaces, eliminating the quotation marks, and putting the period before the in-text citation:

```
Fairy tales teach children about the real world,

how to cope with problems, be kind, and have hope. We

grow up to find out:

          As we had suspected, the fairy tales had been right

          all along—the world was full of hostile, stupid

          giants and perilous castles and people who aban-

          doned their children in the nearest forest. To suc-

          ceed in this world you needed some special skill

          or patronage, plus remarkable luck; and it didn't

          hurt to be very good-looking. (Lurie 18)
```

Warning: Keep long quotations to a minimum or it looks like you're not doing your own thinking and writing, stringing together others' ideas instead.

Citing Online Sources within an Essay

When citing online sources—whether web pages or online data bases—within an essay, treat them the same as print sources if they have authors and page numbers. Without the author or page number, sometimes it's better to mention the article title, web page creator, or web site in the text and not use an in-text citation. **Do not** use a web address in the essay or in an in-text citation; it clutters the text. That information belongs on the works cited page. Keep the essay clean, only giving brief information in parentheses. When using a parenthetical reference for an online source with no author or page number, cite the article title in quotation marks, if available, or an abbreviated title of the web page in italics, but provide enough information to clearly identify the source on the works cited page.

An article cited: ("Killdeer").

When two articles share a title, identify the source as well in italics:

("Killdeer" *Britannica*).

("Killdeer" *Science Resource Center*).

Works Cited

The eighth edition of the MLA now refers to the main source (a source that contains another source within it, like an article or chapter), as a "container." Book titles, magazine titles, newspaper titles, television programs, journal titles, films, Netflix, Hulu, web page titles, and other main sources are considered containers. They've simplified the formula for all sources in this order: author, title of source, container, other contributors, version, number, publisher, publication date, and location. Obviously, not all of these designations will apply to all sources.

The works cited section at the end of the paper lists in alphabetical order— by author, article title, or source title, in that order—information about the sources cited in the essay, corresponding to the in-text citations within the text, making it easy for the reader to find.　When available, always use the author's last name.　A works cited page begins on a **separate sheet of paper** but is numbered in sequence with the rest of the essay.　If the paper is five pages long, then page six would become the works cited page.　The writer's last name and page six go at the top of the page in the right hand corner (see the example works cited page).

BOOKS　To cite a book, use the following information in this order: author's last name, followed by the first name; the title of the book, in italics; publisher and the publication year.

> Bettelheim, Bruno. *The Uses of Enchantment*. Random
> 　　House Publishers, 1975.

When an entry takes up more than one line, use one tab space to indent the second line of the entry.　Use a period after each section and space twice, as indicated in the example; add a comma after the publisher, and a period after the year.

> Tomlinson, Carl M. and Carol Lynch-Brown. *The*
> 　　*Essentials of Children's Literature*. 2nd ed.
> 　　Allyn and Bacon Publishers, 1996.

The first name on the list is alphabetized with last name first, while the other authors' names are listed with first name followed by last name. If an edition number is listed on the book, place it after the book title.

For books with **three authors**, cite all three:

> Darigan, Daniel L., Michael O. Tunnell, and James S.
>
> Jacobs. *Children's Literature: Engaging Teachers and*
>
> *Children in Good Books*. Pearson Publishers, 2002.

When more than three authors are listed, use the first author listed followed by the abbreviation et al. (and others):

> Beechy, Michael et al. *1,000 Symbols*. The Ivy Press
>
> Publishers, 2002.

If a book has been translated, give the translator's name after the title:

> *Beowulf*. Trans. Seamus Heany. Farrar, Straus and
>
> Giroux Publishers, 2002.

ENCYCLOPEDIA ARTICLES   When citing articles from encyclopedias, use the author's last name (if available), the article title in quotation marks, the encyclopedia title in italics, the edition, and print:

> "Killdeer." *Grizmek's Animal Encyclopedia*. 2004 ed.

MAGAZINE ARTICLES   For magazines, use the author, title of the article, title of the magazine, the day and month, the year, and the page numbers the article runs through:

> Zax, David. "The Write Stuff." *Smithsonian Magazine*,
>
> March 2014, pp. 14-15.

Notice that the day goes before the month. The article title is in quotation marks and the magazine title in italics. Multiple authors would be written the same as for books. Notice the pages the article runs through are after the year with *pp.* for page. For magazines published monthly, leave out the day.

NEWSPAPER ARTICLES   Again start with the author's last name, the title of the article in quotation marks, followed by the newspaper title in italics. If the title of the city is not part of the paper's title, add it in brackets after the newspaper title. Because newspapers have sections, give the section and page. If the newspaper has an early and late edition, specify which one the article came from.

Example with no city in the title:

> Dillow, Gordon. "'Our Kids' Really Can't Be Saved."
>
>   *Orange County Register* [Santa Ana},20 Feb. 2000.

Example of an entry specifying an edition:

> Brown, Sylvia. "Budget Crimes." *Los Angeles Times* 20
>
>   March 1997, late ed.: D1 +.

The + sign indicates the article is on more than one page; the *1* is the page number; the *D* is the section.

SCHOLARLY JOURNALS   It's important to know the difference between a magazine and a journal. Magazines are aimed at the average reader and usually come out weekly or monthly. Journals—although some are published monthly—usually come out quarterly, biannually, or annually and tend to be specific to a field of study, like the *Shakespeare Quarterly*. If you're not sure if it's a magazine or journal, check the front and inside cover; you should be able to find the term *journal.*

Treat a journal article like a magazine article, with a couple of exceptions: the volume number and possibly issue number, determined by whether or not the journal has continuous pagination. If, for example, issue 3 of a journal begins on page 232 instead of page 1, then the journal is paginated continuously and does not need the issue number. Usually this type of pagination covers a year and starts over with page 1 in the new volume in the next year. If each issue starts with page 1, then use the issue number.

Example of a journal entry without an issue number:

> Yolen, Jane. "America's Cinderella." *Children's*
>
>   *Literature in Education* vol. 8, 1977, pp. 21-29.

The *8* stands for the volume number. Put quotation marks around the article title and italicize the journal title. Here's an example of an entry with an issue number:

> Hearn, Michael Patrick. "Happily, Ever After: The
>
> Resilience of the Fairy Tale." *Tall: Teaching and*
>
> *Learning Literature with Children and Young*
>
> *Adults,* vol. 8, no. 1, 1977, pp. 48-49.

The *8* stand for the volume number and the *1* for the issue number. Notice a period separates the volume and issue.

INTERVIEWS Always begin an interview citation with the name of the person interviewed. If you're interviewing an individual in person, cite the interview like this:

> Roberts, Julia. Personal Interview. 27 July 1999.

If you interviewed the person over the phone, Phone Interview would replace Personal Interview.

If you're citing an interview published in a magazine or newspaper, it would look like this:

> Roberts, Julia. Interview. *New York Times* 18 Jan.
>
> 1999, late ed.: D22.

Cite a television or radio interview similar to the above, but give the interviewer's name when available and the title of the program, underlined or in italics:

> Roberts, Julia. Interview with Barbara Walters. *Sixty*
>
> *Minutes*. NBC. New York. 18 Jan. 1999.

FILMS Generally, cite a film by giving the title first, followed by the director, major actors, studio, and year of release:

> *Lone Star*. Dir. John Sayles. Perf. Kris
>
> Kristofferson, Matthew McConaughey, Chris Cooper,
>
> and Elizabeth Pena. Columbia Tristar, 1996.

Perf. is an abbreviation for Performers.

TELEVISION SHOWS   Usually for a television program, you will need the title of the episode (if there is one) in quotation marks, the title of the show (in italics), name of the network, call letters and city of the local station—if any—and the date the show aired:

Television Show Without an Episode Title

Pythons: A Predator's Perspective. DSC. 15 July 2008.

Television Show With an Episode Title

"The Fastest Man Alive." *The Flash.* CW 14 October 2014.

Note: If citing a DVD, place a comma after the year and add the word disc and the disc number, "disc 6."

ELECTRONIC SOURCES AND THE WEB   **Note:** Generally, electronic sources and web sites are treated like their paper counterparts with a couple of exceptions: the URL and the date of access. Copy and paste the URL straight out of the browser window but delete the http//.www. Cite the page numbers if available. If not, use the abbreviation n. pag. indicating no page. For an article in an **online data base**, use the author's name (if available), the article title in quotations marks, periodical title in italics, the data base title, URL, and date of access.

Jojola-Elverum, Susan M., and Kenneth M. Green.

"Killdeer Parasitizes Mountain Plover Nest."

Wilson Bulletin, vol. 112, no. 4, 2000, pp. 454.

Academic OneFile, Accessed 24 Sept. 2016.

Example of a blog:

Langley, Travis Phd. "Beyond Heroes and Villains."

Project Superhero: Superheroes for All Ages, 5

Dec. 2015, psychologytoday.com/blog/beyond-

heroes-and-villains/201412/project-superhero-

superheroes-all-ages, Accessed 17 Sept. 2016.

For an encyclopedia like *Britannica,* cite the author (if available), article title, the container, date of access, and URL.

> Robertson, Clinton and Charles. "Killdeer."
>
> *Encyclopedia Britannica* 2004 ed. 5 May 2012,
>
> academic.eb.com.ezproxy.occlib.nocccd.edu/levels/
>
> collegiate/article/45437, Accessed 10 Oct. 2016.

For Web sites, give the author (if any), title of the page (if it's part of a larger site), the title of the web page in italics, the publisher of the web site, date the site was last updated, the container, date of access, and the URL.

> "Cinderella." *The Cinderella Project.* Ed. Michale N.
>
> Saida. University of Southern Mississippi, October
>
> 2005. 15 May 2012, media.usm.edu/english/fairytales/
>
> cinderella/cinderella.html. Accessed 10 Oct. 2016.

Treat *Youtube* videos and other social media sites the same as you would any web page: title of the video, title of the web page, the date of publication, the date of access, and the URL.

Works Cited Example

Study the following Works Cited sample. Notice the title. It's no longer called a bibliography because that term refers to books and you use a variety of sources. Follow these guidelines:

1. Do not number the entries.
2. Double space the entire section. Resist the temptation to put extra spaces between each entry or between the title of the section and the first entry.
3. Place article titles in quotation marks and italicize book, magazine, periodical, and web page titles.
4. When the entry runs more than one line, indent one tab space for following lines.
5. Put your last name and page number in the upper right corner of the page.
6. Alphabetize by author's last name. If no author is listed for a work, alphabetize the work by title.
7. Place a period at the end of each entry.
8. Use the punctuation shown in the sample entries.

Smith 7

Works Cited

Beechy, Michael et al. *1,000 Symbols*. The Ivy Press, 2002.

"Killdeer." *Grizmek's Animal Encyclopedia.* 2004 ed.

Langley, Travis Phd. "Beyond Heroes and Villains." *Project Superhero: Superheroes for All Ages,* 5 Dec. 2015, villians/201412/project-superhero-superheroes-all-ages, Accessed 10 Oct. 2016.

Lepore, Jill. *The Secret History of Wonder Woman.* Vintage Books, 2014. *EBSCOhost Ebook Collection,* ebscohost.come. ezproxy.occlib.nocccd/ehost, Accessed 10. Oct. 2016.

Rosenberg, Robin. "The Psychology of Wolverine." *Psychology Today,* 07 Aug. 2013, psychologytoday.com/ psychologyofwolverine, Accessed 17 Sept. 2016.

Wheelwright, Jeff. "Attack of the Flying Carp." *Discover* March 2012, pp. 60-66.

Example First Page of a Research Paper

Smith 1

Jane Smith

Professor Diaz

English 100

6 Sept. 2016

Title

Begin typing the first line here. Don't forget to indent. Notice there are no extra spaces between the title and the first line or between the class information and the title. Resist the temptation to include extra spaces.

Also, notice that there are no extra spaces between para-graphs. Just indent one tab space, double space your entire document, and use one-inch margins all around.

Punctuation is Style: Basic Rules and Practice

Though learning punctuation rules may seem tedious, punctuation is style, not just correctness. Practicing basic punctuation teaches writers how to use different sentence parts to express thoughts with strong sentence variety.

Once writers learn the key components of a sentence—noun (subject), verb (action), and expressing a complete thought—they can add other sentence parts to create their own styles: lead-ins, add-ons, interrupters, colons with lists or explanations, multiple subjects and verbs, and many other words, clauses, and phrases. Knowing punctuation rules fosters sentence variety.

Dashes are the drama queens of punctuation, drawing attention; multiple lead-ins create anticipation, forcing the reader to wait for the main sentence (**periodic sentence**); multiple add-ons can stack up verbs with forcefulness, overwhelm the reader with important concrete details, or add a lilting flow with "ing" clauses or phrases (**loose sentence**); semicolons hitch together complete thoughts, building strong pause to emphasize irony, humor, bitterness, and so on.

Understanding how these various parts function and are combined improves style, clarifies meaning, and assists a writer in developing a unique voice.

COMMAS

Commas with Items or Actions in a Series

When several items or actions occur in a row, they require commas.

Example:
Blouses, jeans, t-shirts, socks, and shoes littered the bedroom.

Note: Some manuals say to leave the comma out before the "and," but for clarity's sake, put the comma before the conjunction (but, or, yet, so, for, and, nor*) when there are more than two items. Otherwise, the last two items become linked and might confuse the reader.

If there are only two items, omit the comma:

Example:
Socks and shoes littered the hallway.
*Tip: To remember conjunctions, memorize the acronym BOYSFAN.
But
Or
Yet
So
For
And
Nor

Practice: Insert commas where needed. One sentence is correct.

1. The Cocker Spaniel bolted to its feet growled and threw itself against the window at the mailman.

2. Dorothy cocked the shotgun sighted the target and pulled the trigger.

3. William Steig wrote and illustrated numerous children's picture books.

4. The Border Collie can retrieve ropes balls keys shoes and many other items on command.

5. Scones lemon bars brownies cupcakes decorated for Halloween and a variety of over-sized cookies filled the bakery shop window.

6. The Volkswagon careened down the hill hit a boulder flipped over rolled several times and landed in the ditch.

7. Scientists now know that animals have better memories can reason more complexly live more socially complex lives have more complex understanding of others and have more self-awareness than was previously thought.

8. Maria competed in the long jump the 500 meter race the pole vault and the relay.

9. Her favorite hobbies include raising turtles painting landscapes decorating cakes growing orchids surfing with her friends and watching black and white movies.

10. The coffee shop owner worked the breakfast rush helped clean up the aftermath interviewed a perspective employee and chatted with customers in the lull of the afternoon.

Commas with Lead-in (or Introductory) Material

When an incomplete word group (dependent clause, phrase, or single word) introduces a subject, the introduction takes a comma before the subject. Some words signal that there might be a comma needed before the subject. Watch for words like while, since, when, because, words ending in "ing," and prepositions (above, around, beneath, beyond, below, over, under, in, into, upon, and many others).

Example:
While driving down the highway in her new Volkswagen convertible, she felt completely free from the stress of her first college semester.

"While driving down the highway in her new Volkswagen convertible" leads into (or introduces) the subject "she."

Warning: To avoid modifier errors, check that the lead-in material refers directly to the subject. For example, in the following sentence, the introductory material refers to a subject not stated in the sentence, momentarily confusing the reader:

Aiming the rifle, the quail flew into the tree.

Is the quail aiming the rifle?

Note: Check that lead-in clauses or phrases beginning with "ing" are not the subjects of sentences. If they function as the subject, don't use the comma.

Example:
Painting landscapes is her favorite hobby.

"Painting" is the subject of the sentence, not part of a lead-in. The following sentence requires the comma because the "ing" word group introduces the subject, Juan.

Example:
Carrying his fishing rod, Juan headed for the lake.

Another common error is using a comma after words like "although" and "because." Be sure the comma goes at the end of the lead-in.

Wrong:
Although, the injured player was never able to play hockey again he became a famous sportscaster.

Correct:
Although the injured player was never able to play hockey again, he became a famous sportscaster.

Reminder: The subject of the sentence, or noun, is a person, place, or thing.

Practice: Insert commas where needed.

1. To protect your skin from skin cancer you should wear sunscreen of SPF 50 or higher.

2. If you're allergic to milk you can try dairy products like ice cream and cheese made of soy.

3. During the holidays students often forget many of the punctuation rules they learned in English class.

4. With strong winds over 50 miles per hour the storm blew debris all over the road.

5. In an ice storm power lines often break under the weight of the ice.

6. To justify his decision the president went on national TV to argue that his plan would create new jobs.

7. Because the electricity went out during the storm several students were unable to finish their term papers.

8. While doing her usual Monday morning online banking she noticed suspicious activity and immediately called the bank.

9. When running a marathon it is important to stay hydrated.

10. Since the robbery the bank has increased security.

Commas with Add-Ons (Non-essential Elements)

Add-ons provide extra information following a complete sentence and require a comma.

Incorrect:
She drove down the coast highway in her red Mustang convertible **wondering how her life had become so complicated.**

Correct:
She drove down the coast highway in her red Mustang convertible**, wondering how her life had become so complicated.**

The main sentence ends after the word convertible, but adding on the extra information—not essential to the meaning of the main clause—requires the comma.

A dash can also replace the comma with add-ons (see the section on dashes).

Directions: Insert a comma or a dash after the main clause to set off the add-on.

1. Gastric bypass surgery can put early diabetes into remission in obese patients sometimes within a few days.

2. Personal jet packs still fascinate adventurous people despite the obvious dangers.

3. Newly discovered dinosaur fossils have revealed the diversity of the family known as tyrannosaurs some with surprisingly outlandish features like extremely long snouts and Mohawk-like crests.

4. Many animals are on the brink of extinction especially the northern white rhinoceros.

5. Scientists have not yet given up on the northern white rhinoceros preserving sperm by cryopreservation in hopes of somehow reviving the species.

6. Biologists at the San Diego Safari Park have been successful preserving some almost-extinct species even returning the California Condor to the wild.

7. Conservationists have also repopulated the Arabian Oryx an antelope-like animal that some believe started the unicorn myth.

8. Whale sharks pose no threat to humans though their huge size might be intimidating

9. Some biologists hope to resurrect—through cloning—the passenger pigeon a beautiful bird that once numbered in the billions.

10. Ants are known as extremely clean insects building toilets for their waste and carrying their dead outside of the nest.

Commas with Interrupters

Often writers use material that is not necessary to the meaning of the sentence but provides additional information or description. If you removed the material from the sentence, it would still make sentence sense:

Example:
The vinyl seat, sticky from the heat, clung to her skin.

The word group "sticky from the heat" interrupts the sentence "The vinyl seat clung to her skin." Don't put commas around elements in a sentence unless they interrupt.

Example:
Her job at the bank provided a good income.

The word group "at the bank" is a prepositional phrase, not an interrupter. Interrupters often go between the subject and verb.

With Appositives

Appositives rename or give more information about a noun right next to them. Treat them as interrupters and put commas on **both** sides of them.

Example:
Jerry, her acupuncturist, moved to Thailand.
"Her acupuncturist" renames the noun Jerry.

Example:
The dog, a small terrier, slept in the corner of his pen at the rescue center.

"A small terrier" renames the dog.

Dashes can be used with appositives, though it isn't usually necessary and can seem overdone. Commas are often the best choice.

Practice: Insert commas around interrupting material.

1. Marilyn Monroe even with all of the adulation she received was unhappy.

2. Tommy's ex-girlfriend the one who relentlessly stalked him was finally arrested.

3. Sarah who has red hair brought her pet bearded dragon to class.

4. Barry an excellent musician played the bass guitar in a rock band.

5. Jose's brother the competitive one always burst into a rage if Jose beat him at basketball.

6. Orangutans thought by some to be smarter than chimpanzees have a complex social structure with cultural traditions.

7. Alex a smart African gray parrot helped prove that animals can grasp abstract concepts.

8. Many paintings by the artist Jan Lievens a contemporary of Rembrandt's are often attributed to Rembrandt.

9. The two great painters studying under the same master knew each other and even modeled for one another.

10. Mansfield Correctional Facility now an historical site in Ohio was used in the film *The Shawshank Redemption*.

Commas Between Two Complete Sentences Joined with a Conjunction

See the tip with comma rule number one, items in a series. When two complete sentences are joined together with a conjunction creating a compound sentence, a comma is required.

Example:
Mai wanted to study creative writing, but her parents wanted her to study medicine and become a doctor.

Note: A comma is required after "writing" because there is a complete sentence after "but": "Her parents wanted her to study medicine" can stand on its own as a sentence. No comma comes after "medicine" even though there is a conjunction because "become a doctor" is not a complete sentence.

Exception: When two sentences joined with a conjunction are short, a comma is not necessary:

Example:
Go to work and don't be late. (These short commands–though complete sentences–don't require commas.)

Note: Don't mistake "then" for a conjunction. Two complete sentences joined with "then" need a semicolon, a period, or a conjunction with a comma. A comma alone won't do the job and creates an error called a comma splice.

Wrong:
She ran in the marathon, **then** she won the pole vault.

Correct:
She ran in the marathon, **and then** she won the pole vault.
She ran in the marathon; **then** she won the pole vault.
She ran in the marathon. **Then** she won the pole vault.

Tip: Check the word groups on both sides of the conjunction for a complete sentence before adding a comma.

Practice: If the conjunction joins two sentences, add a comma. Two are correct.

1. Miranda earned a 4.0 GPA in high school but she could not get into the college of her choice.

2. The refrigerator needed cleaning and the garbage reeked of an unpleasant odor.

3. Joshua passed his final exam in history with an A but he still failed the class because he didn't turn in his research essay.

4. Numerous children's films have been based on quality picture books but the films lack the literary and artistic value of the originals.

5. The picture book *Jumanji* by Chris Van Allsburg has stunning drawings but the movie added silly scenes and dialogue.

6. She turned on the radio and listened to a football game to keep from falling asleep at the wheel.

7. Writer David Sedaris finds humor in odd situations and his newest book, *When You Are Engulfed in Flames,* is sure to be a hit.

8. Plastic is a marvelous invention but it may cause cancer as well as problems in landfills.

9. You should never use plastic to cook food in the microwave nor put hot beverages in plastic cups.

10. Many people think they eat healthy yet most don't get the recommended five servings of fruits and vegetables.

Commas Between Two or More Words that Describe (Adjectives)

When two or more adjectives describe the same subject (noun), they require commas.

Example:
Sylvester collects smooth**,** shiny pebbles which he thinks have magical powers.

"Shiny" and "smooth" both describe the pebble. A simple test to see if adjectives require commas is to switch their places in the sentence and see if it still makes sense. If it does, then add a comma; if not, leave the comma out.

Sylvester collects shiny, smooth pebbles which he thinks have magical powers.

For a second test, put "and" between them. If it makes sense, use the comma; if it doesn't, then leave the comma out.

Sylvester collects **smooth and shiny** pebbles which he thinks have magical powers.

Note: Don't use a comma between the adjective and the subject.

Wrong:
Sylvester collects smooth, shiny, pebbles.

Practice: Place commas between two or more adjectives that describe the same subject.

1. Her tattered dirty coat could not keep out the piercing cold.
2. The sultry record-breaking heat sent thousands of people to California's southland beaches.
3. Cobwebs blanketed the musty damp rotting cellar.
4. Brutal windy weather kept shivering Missourians indoors.
5. The orchids grew in an orchestra of exotic colorful shapes.
6. Ramon ran through the quiet fog-shrouded streets of San Francisco.
7. The sunset looked eerie through the dark smoky atmosphere caused by the wildfire.
8. Black widow spiders construct messy tangled webs that are surprisingly efficient.
9. Tantalizing sweet nectar attracted orioles as well as hummingbirds.
10. Nutritious tasty meals can be made in thirty minutes or less.

Commas with Dates

Set off the year with commas on both sides with a month *and* a date: January 1, 2000, scared many people who thought the millennium would bring a catastrophe.

Don't use commas with the month and the year:
Many people celebrated the millennium in January 2001.

COLONS

There are two basic ways to use colons: with a list or an explanation.
One rule to remember is to always use a complete sentence before you
use a colon.

Example with a list:
The many foods that triggered her allergies flitted through her mind as
she looked at the restaurant menu: peanuts, shrimp, crab, wheat, milk,
eggs, and soy.

Example with an explanation:
Virginia couldn't decide which pet in the animal shelter she wanted
most: the white kitten with the big blue eyes or the sad mutt with the
oversized ears that no one seemed to want.

The puppy and kitten examples explain her decision.
Tip: Never use a colon after such as, like, or for example. A colon
replaces these overused phrases. Notice that using a colon with such as
or for example breaks the use-a-complete-sentence-first rule.

Practice: Add a colon where needed with a list or an explanation. One
sentence is correct.

1. Orchids come in many varieties lady slippers, butterfly orchids,
   cymbidiums, cattelyas, and many other species.

2. Both jobs had advantages one providing great health coverage
   but the other with more opportunities for advancement.

3. Regina mulled over her opportunities stay in school and finish
   her education or take the acting job that might lead to fame and
   fortune.

4. There are three types of drivers that irritate me the most parking
   spot hogs who steal spaces or park across two spots, impatient
   people who honk at the elderly, and those with road rage who
   weave in and out of traffic, screaming and making rude gestures
   to other drivers.

5. Many types of seashells washed up on the beach scallops, mussels, conch shells, clams, sea urchins, and others I couldn't identify.

6. Science can now accomplish many things that were once considered science fiction cloning, regenerating tissue, replacing joints, and using DNA to diagnose genetic disorders, among others.

7. Many new drugs have been invented to improve brain functions like memory, alertness, attention span, and mental illness.

8. Researchers think they have solved the puzzle as to why we need to sleep maintaining the immune system.

9. Many bird species are disappearing from North America nighthawks, whip-poor-wills, barn swallows, flycatchers, and many others.

10. Some spices not only enhance the flavor of food but also provide antioxidants for better health cinnamon, ginger, red pepper, and curry belong on the top of the list of antioxidant rich spices.

RUN-ONS, COMMA SPLICES, AND SEMICOLONS

There are two basic ways to use the semicolon: to connect two complete sentences in place of a comma and conjunction and to separate items in a list when commas would create confusion.

The sentences should illustrate a close connection in thought, contrast, or comparison. In this instance, the semicolon acts as a stop sign signaling the reader to apply the brakes rather than slow down and yield like a comma.

Example
She loved her boyfriend; his mother was another matter.

The semi-colon is a good choice, more dramatic than a comma and a conjunction, creating tone, emphasizing the relationship friction between the mother and the girl.

Run-on Sentences
Two sentences put together without the proper connection are called run-ons. Semicolons provide one way to fix a run-on or a fused sentence. Many people think any long sentence qualifies as a run-on, but

in college, most teachers want varied structure with some long sentences—if they're correct. A run-on can occur in short sentences:

Example:
She loved her boyfriend his mother was another matter.

Though short, without a period and a capital, a semicolon, or comma with a conjunction, it's a run-on sentence. Writers sometimes attempt to connect two sentences with a comma, creating another error called a **comma splice.** A comma alone doesn't fix a run-on. To correct run-ons and comma splices, use either a semicolon, a comma with a conjunction, a period and a capital, or recast the sentence to make one clause dependent:

She loved her boyfriend; his mother was another matter.
She loved her boyfriend, **but** his mother was another matter.
She loved her boyfriend. **H**is mother was another matter.
Though she loved her boyfriend, his mother was another matter.

Semicolons also connect complete sentences joined by the words however, moreover, nevertheless, nonetheless, therefore, and other transitional words (called conjunctive adverbs or adverbial conjunctions). When these words interrupt a sentence rather than join two, put commas around them.

Example connecting two sentences:
The coyotes harassed the alley cat for over an hour as it hid under the truck; however, they finally gave up and went to look for easier prey.

Note that a comma goes after the however.

Example interrupting one sentence:
The coyotes, however, did not give up easily.

Tips: Check both sides of the word for a complete sentence. If there is a complete sentence on either side, then you need the semicolon and the comma. "The coyotes" is not a complete sentence; it's only a subject. Don't use the semicolon. Treat it as an interrupter. When you take out the however, there is one sentence, not two: The coyotes did not give up easily.

Practice: Use a semicolon, a comma with a conjunction, a period and a capital, or recast to correct the following run-on sentences. Use a variety of these methods.

1. Gardening can be an enjoyable and profitable hobby however you shouldn't garden if you're allergic to bees.

2. Taking precautions however can allow you to enjoy the outdoors despite this deadly allergy.

3. Vincent Van Gogh painted sunlit landscapes in the south of France he also painted lively nighttime scenes that some critics say merge fantasy and reality.

4. Spotted owls in Oregon have struggled to survive now they're being bullied by a new neighbor, the barred owl.

5. She enjoys making homemade lasagna her favorite thing to cook is salmon in salsa verde.

6. The band gave a performance almost identical to the one several years ago fans still felt they got their money's worth.

7. Jamal became an artist despite his father's protests now Jamal has his own art studio and earns a six figure income.

8. Hurley is shy and overweight nevertheless he finally got up the nerve to ask the blond psychologist on a picnic.

9. Joel dribbled the ball down the court he slipped past players twice his size to make the basket.

10. Jonah earned a 4.0 GPA he still couldn't get into the college of his choice.

11. Most people think orchids are difficult to grow however they thrive quite nicely with minimal care.

12. Internet hackers are almost impossible to stop banks won't prosecute because it's too expensive.

13. People usually think of illegal drugs when they hear about drug abuse prescription drug abuse, though, is on the rise among teens.

Practice:

Fix any run-on or comma splice errors in the following paragraph with one of the four methods discussed.

In Victorian England, people were obsessed with rare, difficult-to-find orchids. Orchid hunters, men paid by nurseries to find these exotic flowers, faced danger and death in places like Panama, Madagascar, India, and Peru. The men were tough and smart they were willing to risk their lives for the large sums of money nurseries paid them to find these rare plants. Some died of disease, some died of accidents. They even murdered each other. Owning wild orchids was outlawed in 1975 however thieves still smuggle and steal orchids from backyards and poach them from the wild in places like Florida. Orchid thieves walk for miles through swamps for orchids like the ghost orchid, an endangered species that may soon be gone, orchid mania thrives despite the laws, which thieves know are difficult to enforce.

Semicolons: separate items in a list when commas would create confusion. Objects and their details can crash into each other in a sentence if not properly distinguished from one another:

Example:
The art teacher posted a list of supplies to bring to the next class meeting: one set of graphie pencils, preferably the turquoise ones; a set of Prismacolor pencils; two types of charcoal, vine and compressed; two stomps for blending, one for charcoal and one for graphite; a pad of 400 series drawing paper, size 18 X 24; a drawing board to hold the pad of paper; an Exacto knife; and an artist's box to keep all of the materials organized.

Without a semicolon, the reader—unless familiar with art supplies—would have difficulty knowing which detail goes with which object. For consistency, use a semicolon before each new object as well as before the conjunction (and). Usually a semicolon replaces a conjunction between two sentences, but in this instance, the semicolon makes it clear the Exacto knife is a separate item, not connected to the artist's box.
Note: Also see the "Styling" with Shelby Steele's "On the Content of Our Character."

DASHES

Dashes can be used three ways: Replace commas with dashes to set off an interrupter. Dashes draw attention; only use them to emphasize an interrupter. They're also used to set off elements at the end of a sentence for emphasis and for a list that interrupts a sentence because the commas would be confusing **(see the "Styling" accompanying Gordon Grice's "Black Widow" for more instruction)**. Dashes— visually shouting at the reader for attention—can help create a tone or make the reader more carefully consider something in the sentence that would be toned down by commas or parentheses.

Examples:
At the end of the sentence with add-on material (nonessential elements):
In "A Voice for the Lonely," Stephen Corey writes about music's emotional impact on the listener:

"And in an even more strange way, a song we love goes silent as we 'listen' to it, leaving us in that rather primitive place where all the sounds are interior ones—sounds which can't be distinguished from feelings, from pulsings and shiverings, from that gut need to make life stronger than death for a least a few moments."

Corey could have used a comma after "interior ones," but he chose the dash so the reader will pay more attention to his explanation of the sounds.

Sometimes writers will reverse this strategy, placing the complete sentence after the dash rather than before it, as Lawrence Weschler does in "Modern Times":

"On the ground, the carnage of war, the gore, the frantically desperate attempts at rescue, the bitterly expiring hopes—**they're all the same as they've ever been.**"

This strategy creates a sense of anticipation leading up to the main idea.

A dash can also be used to set off a list at the end of a sentence in place of a colon.

With an interrupter:
In "Burl's" by Bernard Cooper, he describes what he thinks, at first, are two women walking toward him on the hot sidewalk outside a restaurant when he was a child:

"The silky fabric—one dress was purple, the other pink—accentuated their breasts and hips and rippled with insolent highlights."

The colors highlight the men's attempts at femininity.

With a list that interrupts a sentence:
Edward Hoagland, in "The Courage of Turtles," describes how turtles cope with their plight:

"They don't feel that the contest is unfair; they keep plugging, rolling like sailorly souls—a bobbing, infirm gait, a brave sealegged momentum—stopping occasionally to study the lay of the land."

And the tough role of frogs in the food chain:

"Frogs' tasty legs are the staff of life to many animals—herons, raccoons, ribbon snakes—though they themselves are hard to feed."
The commas might confuse a reader if the dashes didn't enclose the entire interrupter. When using this technique, check to see the sentence would be grammatically correct without the list.

Practice:
Use the practice exercise under "Commas with Interrupters," but replace the commas with dashes.

FRAGMENTS

The word fragment means "piece," so a sentence fragment is a piece of a sentence, a job left undone by the writer who has either left out a subject, a verb, or not expressed a complete thought. Often, fragments can be attached to a complete sentence with a comma or combined in other ways.

Example:
Wrong:
Some scientists are on the verge of creating a half-dinosaur, half chicken hybrid. By adding dinosaur DNA to a chicken egg.

The second sentence is a fragment and needs to be combined with the first sentence.

Correct:
Some scientists are on the verge of creating a half-dinosaur, half-chicken hybrid by adding dinosaur DNA to a chicken egg.

Some scientists are on the verge of creating a half-dinosaur, half-chicken hybrid—by adding dinosaur DNA to a chicken egg.

By adding dinosaur DNA to a chicken egg, some scientists are on the verge of creating a half-dinosaur, half-chicken hybrid.

Note: Fragments can be used for emphasis though with caution.

Practice:
Correct the following fragments by either attaching them to an existing sentence or completing the thought by adding missing words.

1. During WWII, women took on many roles vacated by men. Roles flying planes and working in factories on assembly lines.

2. Women were trained as pilots. In a program called WASP, an acronym for Women Airforce Service Pilots.

3. Many male pilots resented the women. Because they felt their jobs were threatened.

4. People were skeptical of women pilots. Thinking they were too high strung.

5. Working hard and persevering. The women pilots became as good or even better than men.

6. Wearing men's khaki jumpsuits they dubbed zoot suits.

7. Having no opportunity to prove themselves in combat because the war ended. Women were not considered veterans.

8. Though they had earned wings. They received no recognition for their part in the war effort.

9. Keeping in touch, launching a campaign, hoping for full military recognition.

10. Congress passed a bill in 1977. By 1979 considered women veterans.

Underline fragments in the following paragraph and then correct them.

Edgar Allan Poe, born in Boston in 1809. His parents were actors in traveling shows. His father died in 1810 and his mother in 1811. Leaving Edgar penniless. A merchant, John Allan, from Virginia took Edgar in and raised him. Though he mistreated young Edgar. When Edgar went to college, the wealthy John Allan refused to pay for tuition or support Edgar. Edgar left the University of Virginia after a short time and turned to drinking and gambling. Moving to Boston to begin his career as a writer. He published his first book, a volume of poetry, in 1827, but it didn't find many readers. Finally, in 1833, Edgar received payment for a short story, drawing the attention of a publisher who liked Edgar's work. And gave him a job as an editor. He lost the job due to his drinking. He soon married his cousin, Virginia Clemm. Who was thirteen years old. Edgar gained success publishing short stories and poems, establishing his brilliance as a writer with his poem "The Raven." He died of alcoholism in 1849 at the age of forty. Three years after the death of his wife, Virginia, who died of tuberculosis in 1846.

COMPREHENSIVE QUIZ

Add punctuation and fix fragments, run-ons, or comma splices where needed. Some sentences will need more than one type of punctuation.

1. Ben and Jerry's ice cream comes in many flavors Chunky Monkey Cherry Garcia Peppermint Stick and plain vanilla to name a few.

2. Her cat Mo serenely watches fish in the aquarium, her other cat Picasso likes to pry open the lid and try to catch the fish.

3. Geoffrey the goldfish swims luxuriously in his big tank however he darts with agitation when Picasso decides to use Geoffrey's home as a kitty entertainment center.

4. Most days however Picasso sleeps in his cat tower in the window.

5. Scholars once thought of the Anasazi Indians as peaceful hunters and gatherers evidence has proven that they participated in cannibalism.

6. Running down the quiet foggy trail startled by two deer that appeared out of the mist.

7. Walking down the street in her new glasses Rose says that she loves Wonder Woman and her grandmother she doesn't mention the rest of her family.

8. When the school bell rang for the last day of the year happy students streamed out of classrooms and into the beginning of summer vacation.

9. Those flowers tulips daisies snapdragons and marigolds won't grow in that soil.

10. An abundance of shoes cluttered the hallway sneakers Uggs sandals flip flops strappy heels and cowgirl boots.

11. The television show Gilmore Girls her daughter's favorite finally ended after seven years.

12. Her favorite episodes are Cinnamon's Wake, That Damned Donna Reed, and They Shoot Gilmores, Don't They?

13. The whale shark is a slow-moving polka-dotted deep-diving shark.

14. Weighing up to several tons whale sharks are also notable for their markings unique spots that help scientists identify individual fish.

15. Whale sharks feeding mostly on plankton are named for their great size and diet.

16. Snorkeling with whale sharks a popular tourist pastime.

17. There are a few rules to remember when swimming with whale sharks only two divers at one time in the water no flash photography and no physical contact with the fish.

18. The red-tailed hawk a magnificent bird is abundant in Missouri

19. Neil LaBute is a witty playwright and screenwriter but some people call him a misogynist jerk.

20. When you finish reading Harry Potter you should read Ursula LeGuin's A Wizard of Earthsea, it's a better book.

Basic Sentence Modeling

Punctuate the following sentences; then create your own sentences by modeling each structure. For loose and periodic sentence styles, check the "Style Guide" in the front of the text for essays with exercises and explanations. Check the answers (yes, they are in the book) before modeling.

Note: Practice these styles *after* completing the punctuation exercises in the "Punctuation is Style" section. If you have difficulty, review the problem in the punctuation practice.

1. Larry believes in being prepared for each boxing match therefore he practices his technique every day at the gym. (Two sentences joined with a conjunctive adverb).

2. Good boxing technique does not however ensure that Larry will develop enough power to compete as a professional boxer. (Conjunctive adverb serving as an interrupter).

3. Women some scientists believe may see 99 million colors unknown to men. (Simple interrupter).

4. Contrary to popular belief a black widow spider's bite is rarely fatal usually resulting in death only when the victim is an infant elderly or has a compromised immune system. (Lead-in with add-on that includes items in a list).

5. As many people know meditation can reduce stress it can also help ease mild depression. (Lead-in and run-on; correct the run-on in addition to adding the comma after the lead-in).

6. Dogs have an expression similar to smiling that is usually seen when the dog is relaxed playing or socially interacting. (Simple items or actions in a series)

7. Scientists have determined that small dogs have more dreams than big dogs and the smallest dogs dream five or six times in an hour. (Compound sentence or two complete sentences joined with a conjunction).

8. A dog has the basic emotions of a two-year old human happiness fear anger excitement contentment distress and love. (List following a complete sentence).

9. Swimming at a leisurely pace moving gracefully through the water tolerating snorkelers eating only small prey posing no

threat to humans the whale shark is a growing attraction world-wide. (Periodic Sentence).

10. The boxer fiercely fought his opponent dodging a left hook jabbing quickly with his left hand stepping back to evade a punishing blow to the head lunging forward and throwing an uppercut to the chin swinging an unsuccessful right hook sliding left to avoid a jab and finishing with a right-handed uppercut to the jaw for a knockout. (Loose Sentence).

ANSWERS

Commas with Items or Actions in a Series

1. The Cocker Spaniel bolted to its feet, growled, and threw itself against the window at the mailman.

2. Dorothy cocked the shotgun, sighted the target, and pulled the trigger.

3. William Steig wrote and illustrated numerous children's picture books. **Correct**

4. The Border Collie can retrieve ropes, balls, keys, shoes, and many other items on command.

5. Scones, lemon bars, brownies, cupcakes decorated for Halloween, and a variety of over-sized cookies filled the bakery shop window.

6. The Volkswagon careened down the hill, hit a boulder, flipped over, rolled several times, and landed in the ditch.

7. Scientists now know that animals have better memories, can reason more complexly, live more socially complex lives, have more complex understanding of others, and have more self-awareness than was previously thought.

8. Maria competed in the long jump, the 500 meter race, the pole vault, and the relay.

9. Her favorite hobbies include raising turtles, painting landscapes, decorating cakes, growing orchids, surfing with her friends, and watching black and white movies.

10. The coffee shop owner worked the breakfast rush, helped clean up the aftermath, interviewed a perspective employee, and chatted with customers in the lull of the afternoon.

Commas with lead-in (or introductory) material:

1. To protect your skin from skin cancer, you should wear sunscreen of SPF 50 or higher.

2. If you're allergic to milk, you can try dairy products like ice cream and cheese made of soy.

3. During the holidays, students often forget many of the punctuation rules they learned in English class.

4. With strong winds over 50 miles per hour, the storm blew debris all over the road.

5. In an ice storm, power lines often break under the weight of the ice.

6. To justify his decision, the president went on national TV to argue that his plan would create new jobs.

7. Because the electricity went out during the storm, several students were unable to finish their term papers.

8. While doing her usual Monday morning online banking, she noticed suspicious activity and immediately called the bank.

9. When running a marathon, it is important to stay hydrated.

10. Since the robbery, the bank has increased security.

Commas with Add-Ons (A dash might also be used in place of the comma in each sentence)

1. Gastric bypass surgery can put early diabetes into remission in obese patients, sometimes within a few days.

2. Personal jet packs still fascinate adventurous people, despite the obvious dangers.

3. Newly discovered dinosaur fossils have revealed the diversity of the family known as tyrannosaurs, some with surprisingly outlandish features like extremely long snouts and Mohawk-like crests.

4. Many animals are on the brink of extinction, especially the northern white rhinoceros.

5. Scientists have taken steps to try to save these animals, preserving sperm by cryopreservation in hopes of somehow reviving these species.

6. Biologists at the San Diego Safari Park have been successful preserving some almost-extinct species, even returning the California condor to the wild.

7. Conservationists have also repopulated the Arabian Oryx, an antelope-like animal that some believe started the unicorn myth.

8. Whale sharks pose no threat to humans, though their huge size might be intimidating

9. Some biologists hope to resurrect—through cloning—the passenger pigeon, a beautiful bird that once numbered in the billions.

10. Ants are known as extremely clean insects, building toilets for their waste and carrying their dead outside of the nest.

Commas with Interrupters

1. Marilyn Monroe, even with all of the adulation she received, was unhappy.

2. Tommy's ex-girlfriend, the one who relentlessly stalked him, was finally arrested.

3. Sarah, who has red hair, brought her pet bearded dragon to class.

4. Barry, an excellent musician, played the bass guitar in a rock band.

5. Jose's brother, the competitive one, always burst into a rage if Jose beat him at basketball.

6. Orangutans, thought by some to be smarter than chimpanzees, have a complex social structural with cultural traditions.

7. Alex, a smart African gray parrot, helped prove that animals can grasp abstract concepts.

8. Many paintings by the artist Jan Lievens, a contemporary of Rembrandt's, are often attributed to Rembrandt.

9. The two great painters, studying under the same master, knew each other and even modeled for one another.

10. Mansfield Correctional Facility, now an historical site in Ohio, was used in the film *The Shawshank Redemption*.

Commas with Two Sentences Joined by a Conjunction

1. Miranda earned a 4.0 GPA in high school, but she could not get into the college of her choice.

2. The refrigerator needed cleaning, and the garbage reeked of an unpleasant odor.

3. Joshua passed his final exam in history with an A, but he still failed the class because he didn't turn in his research essay.

4. Numerous children's films have been based on quality picture books, but the films lack the literary and artistic value of the originals.

5. The picture book *Jumanji* by Chris Van Allsburg has stunning drawings, but the movie added silly scenes and dialogue.

6. She turned on the radio and listened to a football game to keep from falling asleep at the wheel. **Correct**

7. Writer David Sedaris finds humor in odd situations, and his newest book, *When You Are Engulfed in Flames,* is sure to be a hit.

8. Plastic is a marvelous invention, but it may cause cancer as well as problems in landfills.

9. You should never use plastic to cook food in the microwave nor put hot beverages in plastic cups. **Correct**

10. Many people think they eat healthy, yet most don't get the recommended five servings of fruits and vegetables.

Commas Between Words that Describe (Adjectives)

1. Her tattered, dirty coat could not keep out the piercing cold.

2. The sultry, record-breaking heat sent thousands of people to California's southland beaches.

3. Cobwebs blanketed the musty, damp, rotting cellar.

4. Brutal, windy weather kept shivering Missourians indoors.

5. The orchids grew in an orchestra of exotic, colorful shapes.

6. Ramon ran through the quiet, fog-shrouded streets of San Francisco.

7. The sunset looked eerie through the dark, smoky atmosphere caused by the wildfire.

8. Black widow spiders construct messy, tangled webs that are surprisingly efficient.

9. Tantalizing, sweet nectar attracted orioles as well as hummingbirds.

10. Nutritious, tasty meals can be made in thirty minutes or less.

Colons

1. Orchids come in many varieties: lady slippers, butterfly orchids, cymbidiums, cattelyas, and many other species.

2. Both jobs had advantages: one providing great health coverage but the other with more opportunities for advancement.

3. Regina mulled over her opportunities: stay in school and finish her education or take the acting job that might lead to fame and fortune.

4. There are three types of drivers that irritate me the most: parking spot hogs who steal spaces or park across two spots, impatient people who honk at the elderly, and those with road rage who weave in and out of traffic, screaming and making rude gestures to other drivers.

5. Many types of seashells washed up on the beach: scallops, mussels, conch shells, clams, sea urchins, and others I couldn't identify.

6. Science can now accomplish many things that were once considered science fiction: cloning, regenerating tissue, replacing joints, and using DNA to diagnose genetic disorders, among others.

7. Many new drugs have been invented to improve brain functions like memory, alertness, attention span, and mental illness. **Correct**

8. Researchers think they have solved the puzzle as to why we need to sleep: maintaining the immune system.

9. Many bird species are disappearing from North America: nighthawks, whip-poor-wills, barn swallows, flycatchers, and many others.

10. Some spices not only enhance the flavor of food but also provide antioxidants for better health: cinnamon, ginger, red pepper, and curry belong on the top of the list of antioxidant rich spices.

Run-ons, Comma Splices, and Semicolons: Answers will vary.

1. Gardening can be an enjoyable and profitable hobby; however, you shouldn't garden if you're allergic to bees. (Or period and a capital)

2. Taking precautions, however, can allow you to enjoy the outdoors despite this deadly allergy.

3. Vincent Van Gogh painted sunlit landscapes in the south of France; he also painted lively nighttime scenes that some critics say merge fantasy and reality. (Or period and a capital)

4. Spotted owls in Oregon have struggled to survive; now they're being bullied by a new neighbor, the barred owl. (Or period and capital or comma with conjunction "and")

5. She enjoys making homemade lasagna, **but** her favorite thing to cook is salmon in salsa verde. (Or semicolon or period and capital)

6. The band gave a performance almost identical to the one several years ago, **but** fans still felt they got their money's worth. (Or period and capital or semicolon)

7. Jamal became an artist despite his father's protests; now Jamal has his own art studio and a six figure income. (Or comma with conjunction or period and capital)

8. Hurley is shy and overweight; nevertheless, he finally got up the nerve to ask the blond psychologist on a picnic. (Or comma with conjunction or period and capital)

9. Joel dribbled the ball down the court. **H**e slipped past players twice his size to make the basket. (Or comma with conjunction or semicolon)

10. **Although** Jonah earned a 4.0 GPA, he still couldn't get into the college of his choice. (Or period with capital or semicolon)

11. Most people think orchids are difficult to grow**;** however**,** they thrive quite nicely with minimal care. (Or period with capital)

12. Internet hackers are almost impossible to stop**.** **B**anks won't prosecute because it's too expensive. (Or semicolon)

13. People usually think of illegal drugs when they hear about drug abuse **though** prescription drug abuse is on the rise among teens. (Or semicolon, period with capital, or comma with conjunction)

One possible solution (answers will vary).

In Victorian England, people were obsessed with rare, difficult-to-find orchids. Orchid hunters, men paid by nurseries to find these exotic flowers, faced danger and death in places like Panama, Madagascar, India, and Peru. The men were tough and smart; they were willing to risk their lives for the large sums of money nurseries paid them to find these rare plants. Some died of disease. Some died of accidents. They even murdered each other. Owning wild orchids was outlawed in 1975; however, thieves still smuggle and steal orchids from backyards and poach them from the wild in places like Florida. Orchid thieves walk for miles through swamps for orchids like the ghost orchid, an endangered species that may soon be gone. Orchid mania thrives despite the laws, which thieves know are difficult to enforce.

Dashes

1. Marilyn Monroe—even with all of the adulation she received—was unhappy.

2. Tommy's ex-girlfriend—the one who relentlessly stalked him—was finally arrested.

3. Sarah—who has red hair—brought her pet bearded dragon to class.

4. Barry—an excellent musician—played the bass guitar in a rock band.

5. Jose's brother—the competitive one—always burst into a rage if Jose beat him at basketball.

6. Orangutans—thought by some to be smarter than chimpanzees—have a complex social structural with cultural traditions.

7. Alex—a smart African gray parrot—helped prove that animals can grasp abstract concepts.

8. Many paintings by the artist Jan Lievens—a contemporary of Rembrandt's—are often attributed to Rembrandt.

9. The two great painters—studying under the same master—knew each other and even modeled for one another.

10. Mansfield Correctional Facility—now an historical site in Ohio—was used in the film *The Shawshank Redemption*.

One possible solution (answers may vary)

1. During WWII, women took on many roles vacated by men, <u>roles flying planes and working in factories on assembly lines.</u>

2. Women were trained as pilots <u>in a program called WASP, an acronym for Women Airforce Service Pilots.</u>

3. Many male pilots resented the women <u>because they felt their jobs were threatened.</u>

4. People were skeptical of women pilots, <u>thinking they were too high strung.</u>

5. <u>Working hard and persevering</u>, the women pilots became as good as or even better than men.

6. <u>The women wore</u> men's khaki jumpsuits they dubbed zoot suits.

7. <u>Having no opportunity to prove themselves in combat because the war ended</u>, women were not considered veterans.

8. <u>Though they had earned wings</u>, they received no recognition for their part in the war effort.

9. <u>They kept</u> in touch, launching a campaign, hoping for full military recognition.

10. Congress passed a bill in 1977, and by 1979, they <u>considered women veterans.</u>

One possible solution (answers may vary).

<u>Edgar Allan Poe was born in Boston in 1809.</u> His parents were actors in traveling shows. His father died in 1810 and his mother in 1811, <u>leaving Edgar penniless.</u> A merchant, John Allan from Virginia, took Edgar in and raised him, <u>though he mistreated young Edgar.</u> When Edgar went to college, the wealthy John Allan refused to pay for tuition or support Edgar. Edgar left the University of Virginia after a short time and turned

to drinking and gambling. He moved to Boston to begin his career as a writer. He published his first book, a volume of poetry, in 1827, but it didn't find many readers. Finally, in 1833, Edgar received payment for a short story, drawing the attention of a publisher who liked Edgar's work and gave him a job as an editor. He lost the job due to his drinking. He soon married his cousin, Virginia Clemm, who was thirteen years old. Edgar gained success publishing short stories and poems, establishing his brilliance as a writer with his poem "The Raven." He died of alcoholism in 1849 at the age of forty, three years after the death of his wife, Virginia, who died of tuberculosis in 1846.

Comprehensive Quiz (Answers may vary)

1. Ben and Jerry's ice cream comes in many flavors: Chunky Monkey, Cherry Garcia, Peppermint Stick, and plain vanilla, to name a few.

2. Her cat, Mo, serenely watches fish in the aquarium; her other cat, Picasso, likes to pry open the lid and try to catch the fish. (Or period and capital or comma with conjunction; or make a dependent clause with the world "while" after aquarium)

3. Geoffrey, my goldfish, swims luxuriously in his big tank; however, he darts with agitation when Picasso decides to use Geoffrey's home as a kitty entertainment center. (Or period and capital)

4. Most days, however, Picasso sleeps in his cat tower in the window.

5. Scholars once thought of the Anasazi Indians as peaceful hunters and gatherers. Evidence has proven that they participated in cannibalism. (Or semicolon or comma with conjunction; or make the first clause dependent by adding "Although" before scholars with a comma after "gatherers")

6. Running down the quiet, foggy trail, **she was** startled by two deer that appeared out of the mist.

7. Walking down the street in her new glasses, Rose says that she loves Wonder Woman and her grandmother, but she doesn't mention the rest of her family. (Or semicolon or period with capital)

8. When the school bell rang for the last day of the year, happy students streamed out of classrooms and into the beginning of summer vacation.

9. Those flowers—tulips, daisies, snapdragons, and marigolds—won't grow in that soil.

10. An abundance of shoes cluttered the hallway: sneakers, Uggs, sandals, flip flops, strappy heels, and cowgirl boots.

11. The show *Gilmore Girls,* her daughter's favorite, finally ended after seven years.

12. Her favorite episodes are "Cinnamon's Wake," "That Damned Donna Reed," and "They Shoot Gilmores, Don't They?"

13. The whale shark is a slow-moving, polka-dotted, deep-diving shark.

14. Weighing up to several tons, whale sharks are also notable for their markings, unique spots that help scientists identify individual fish.

15. Whale sharks, feeding mostly on plankton, are named for their great size and diet.

16. Snorkeling with whale sharks **is** a popular tourist pastime.

17. There are a few rules to remember when swimming with whale sharks: only two divers at one time in the water, no flash photography, and no physical contact with the fish.

18. The red-tailed hawk, a magnificent bird, is abundant in Missouri. (or dashes)

19. Neil LaBute is a witty playwright and screenwriter, but some people call him a misogynist jerk.

20. When you finish reading *Harry Potter,* you should read Ursula LeGuin's *A Wizard of Earthsea.* It's a better book. (Or semicolon after the book title)

Basic Sentence Modeling (modeling answers will obviously vary).

1. Larry believes in being prepared for each boxing match; therefore, he practices his technique every day at the gym. (Two sentences joined with a conjunctive adverb). (Or use a period and a capital after "match")

2. Good boxing technique does not, however, ensure that Larry will develop enough power to compete as a professional boxer. (Conjunctive adverb serving as an interrupter).

3. Women, some scientists believe, may see 99 million colors unknown to men. (Simple interrupter). (Or replace the two commas with dashes or parentheses).

4. Contrary to popular belief, a black widow spider's bite is rarely fatal, usually resulting in death only when the victim is an infant, elderly, or has a compromised immune system. (Lead-in with add-on that includes items in a list).

5. As many people know, meditation can reduce stress; it can also help ease mild depression. (Lead-in and run-on; correct the run-on. Or use a period and a capital or a comma with a conjunction in place of the semi-colon).

6. Dogs have an expression similar to smiling that is usually seen when the dog is relaxing, playing, or socially interacting. (Simple items or actions in a series)

7. Scientists have determined that small dogs have more dreams than big dogs, and the smallest dogs dream about six or seven times in an hour. (Compound sentence).

8. A dog has the basic emotions of a two-year old human: happiness, fear, anger, excitement, contentment, distress, and love. (List following a complete sentence requiring a colon or a dash).

9. Swimming at a leisurely pace, moving gracefully through the water, tolerating snorkelers, eating only small prey, posing no threat to humans, the whale shark is a growing attraction worldwide. (Periodic Sentence).

10. The boxer fiercely fought his opponent, dodging a left hook, jabbing quickly with his left hand, stepping back to evade a punishing blow to the head, lunging forward and throwing an uppercut to the chin, swinging an unsuccessful right hook, sliding left to avoid a jab, and finishing with a right-handed uppercut to the jaw for a knockout. (Loose Sentence).

Sweating the Small Stuff

Many common errors trip-up writers if they neglect to edit and revise their work. Though not sweating the small stuff might be a nice life philosophy, it won't pass muster in a college course or in a work environment. A few of these sweat-it-out errors include shifts in point of view and mixing plural and singular pronouns, shifts in tense, *I* versus *me*, writing out numbers, confused words, apostrophes and contractions, and made up words.

SHIFTY SHIFTS

Shifting point of view can be a puzzling problem for some, but practice and diligent editing can help eliminate this troublesome mistake. There are three points of view to write from:

First Person (I, we)
Second Person (you)
Third Person (he, she, it, or they)

Most narratives use **first** person point of view, but writers also use it to create an I-was-there account or as a personal example in a larger essay. An argument introduction, for example, might use a first person **anecdote** (a short personal story) to hook the reader. In "Somebody's Baby," Barbara Kingsolver uses this technique to open her essay that argues Americans treat children like "toxic waste":

As I walked out the street entrance to my apartment, a kid in maroon high tops and a startling haircut approached, saying "Hi gorgeous." Three weeks ago, I would have assessed the degree of malice and made ready to run or tell him to bug off, depending. Today, instead, I smile, and so does my 4-year-old daughter, because after dozens of similar encounters I understand that he doesn't men me but *her.*

This is not the United States.

Second person is used in process/analysis essays or **command form** style, or any time the writer wants to create intimacy with the reader. David Huddle uses the second person in "Museum Piece":

Jan Vermeer's *Girl with the Red Hat* always appealed to you because of that hat.

Huddle's use of second person startles with its assumption that the reader is standing next to Huddle, viewing the painting. It pulls the reader in, creating a conversational atmosphere, an intimacy that invites closer inspection of the writing and the artwork.

Sometimes writers use the command form, dropping the obvious use of "you," implying it by giving commands. In "What Really Happened," Madge McKeithen writes a personal essay about confronting a friend's killer in prison, using second person, relying mostly on commands. She brutally takes the reader through the painful step-by-step process from getting permission from a judge to visit the murderer, confronting this criminal, grieving and trying to understand her friend's murder, and finally seeing her dead friend's now-grown son at a wedding:

Receive the hundreds of pages of letters he sends over the next few years. Keep thinking of her. (That part is not hard.) Write from her son's perspective. Write it as fiction. Write from her perspective. Listen.

Ask. *Where are her words?*

Shred his.

Wait several years. Attend a wedding. Be sociable. Hear the charming man next to you talk about his four children, his wife,

that his father killed his mother when he was small,
his career, his hopes for his children, his love for the grandmother who raised him.

Her chilling account in second person demands attention, rousing
the reader's empathy.

Third person, though often presented as the objective point of view,
still contains the writer's opinion and is no more objective than first or
second. Many college essays, though, require third person because of its
perceived formality.

Some psychologists and sociologists believe that Facebook
makes **people** more lonely and isolated from the real world.

Note: Whether using first, second, or third person, stay consistent.
Unnecessary shifting is grammatically incorrect:

Incorrect:
Students in the tutoring center can practice their writing skills.
You can get help on an essay or work on grammar at a computer.

The point of view shifts from the plural, third person in the first sentence to second person in the second sentence.

Correct:
Students in the tutoring center can practice **their** writing skills.
They can get help on an essay or work on grammar at a computer.

Or
In the tutoring center, **you** can practice **your** writing skills. **You**
can get help with an essay or work on grammar at a computer.

PRACTICE: Correct the shifts in point of view in the following paragraph,
changing it all to **third** person.

Some psychologists and sociologists believe that Facebook makes
people more lonely and isolated from the real world. We are spending
less time talking to each other face-to-face as we obsess over what's happening online. Students no longer talk to classmates during a break but
whip out your phones to text, play games, or check Facebook. Studies
show that we can also become more narcissistic if you spend too much
time on social media sites. A June 6, 2015, article in the newspaper *The
Orange County Register* claims, "Narcissistic people feel superior to oth-

ers and believe they deserve special treatment. When they feel humiliated they often lash out aggressively or even violently." The article goes on to say how all of your postings on Facebook are attention grabbers that "reinforce narcissistic tendencies." It is easy for me to believe when I see people posting pictures of their fancy dinners, every place they go, and constantly updating your status. Social media also feeds anxiety as people worry about what's being said about them or how many people like our posts. Though social media can help people stay more connected, it also breeds problems. Relationships suffer when your spouse or significant other ignores you at dinner to check their status or post a picture of his or her huge plate of mushroom ravioli. A child who constantly plays games on the Ipad is not learning social skills. It is a positive step that researchers are finally studying the negative effects of social media.

SHIFTS IN TENSE

Most writers—beginners or seasoned—mistakenly shift tense on a first draft but edit out the problem:

Incorrect:
Many psychologists **study** our fascination with superheroes. They **saw** many parallels between these icons and human mental disorders.

Correct:
Many psychologists **study** our fascination with superheroes. They **see** many parallels between these icons and human mental disorders.

PRACTICE: Correct any shifts in tense in the following paragraph.

Psychologists disagree over the value of superheroes in modern culture. Some believe today's violent superheroes encouraged aggressive behavior, selfishness (Iron Man and his playboy lifestyle), and rarely display the virtues of the superheroes of the forties and fifties; others view them as inspiring role models because of their flaws, how they grappled with human issues like relationship problems, financial troubles, identity crisis, and discrimination. Batman overcoming his traumatic childhood illustrated that overcoming adversity to help others can promote psychological healing. Spiderman struggles with personal loss, relationship problems, bullying at school, and financial issues. The Avengers had to learn to work as a team, despite their disputes, just like in the real-world work environment. The X-Men battled discrimination and identity crisis, Thor deals with sibling rivalry, and Wonder Woman was a strong role model for women. Pro-superhero advocates also believe modern superheroes depicted moral dilemmas like justice and the death penalty. Should superheroes simply kill villains like the Joker or try to rehabilitate them? Regardless of whether they promote negative behavior or provide psychological insight, superheroes' popularity does not appear to be waning any time soon.

Note: Always write about fictional characters—whether in literature, film, or television—in the **present** tense.

SHIFTS IN NUMBERS

Shifts in numbers occur when the writer begins a sentence either singular or plural but shifts:

Incorrect:
A student should visit the writing center to get help with **their** essays.

"A student" refers to one (singular); "their" is plural, meaning more than one.

Correct:
Students should visit the writing center to get help with **their** essays.

PRACTICE: Fix the following sentences for shifts in numbers. Check to make sure the changes are grammatically correct as subjects or verbs may need to shift tense to stay consistent.

1. German Shepherds make a good guard dog.

2. When applying for a student loan, the applicant should make certain that they will be able to pay back the money. Some students end up paying hundreds of thousands of dollars in school loans, financially burdening an individual for the rest of their lives.

3. In the 1990s, researchers discovered that a dolphin could recognize themselves in the mirror.

4. Human children react the same way to mirrors as a dolphin. A child begins this behavior at around the age of two.

5. Crows exhibit intelligence equal to that of the chimpanzee; a crow can use tools to forage for food to feed themselves and its young.

WRITING OUT NUMBERS

Rules for writing numbers vary, but there are some simple guidelines for using numbers in essays. If your essay contains just a few numbers, write them out (especially numbers 1-9 or numbers consisting of one or two words); for essays with frequent numbers, spell out 1-9 and use numerals for the rest.

Example:
Crysti bought **three** turtles at the rescue center.

Exception:
If a number begins a sentence, **always** write it out: **Five hundred and fifty-six** people were injured in the train collision.

QUOTATION MARKS AND UNDERLINING/ITALICS

Note: Quotation marks used when citing sources in a research paper or on a works cited page are covered in section five.

Quotation marks are used to set off dialogue in writing, signaling when a new speaker is speaking (see the "Styling" exercise with David Sedaris's "Turbulence").

As a general rule, use italics (most writers consider underlining outdated but underline if italicizing is impossible, like when handwriting) when referring to a large work that contains essays, articles, chapters, poems, episodes, or songs within it. A book title, for example, always takes italics while a chapter *within* a book needs quotation marks.

Examples

Major Works in Italics	Items within the Major Works in QuotationMarks
New York Times Magazine	"The Global-Warming Heretic" (magazine article).
The Smithsonian Magazine	"Dinosaur Wars: Who Owns America's Fossils? (magazine article).
The Orange County Register (Newspaper)	"It's all about Me! Teens, Fueled by Social Media, Have a Healthy Dose of Narcissism" (Newspaper Article).

Best American Science and Nature Writing 2013 (Book)	"Is Facebook making us Lonely?" (Book Chapter).
A Midsummer Night's Dream (Play)	"Lord, what fools these mortals be!" (Lines in a play)
The Big Bang Theory (TV Show)	"The Bad Fish Paradigm" (Episode title of a TV show).
Tragic Kingdom (CD title)	"Just a Girl" (Song on a CD).

Note: Place semi-colons or colons **outside** the quotations marks, commas and periods **inside.**

OTHER STICKY WICKETS

Is it *I* or *Me?*

This little grammar goblin frustrates many writers, but an easy way to determine the correct use is simply remove the other subject.

The sentence "Maria and I love to go shopping at unusual boutiques," would read "I love to go shopping at unusual boutiques." It sounds correct.

In the following sentence, try removing the other subject and see what happens:

Maria and me went shopping yesterday at an unusual boutique.

You would never write "Me went shopping yesterday at an unusual boutique." But situations do exist where *me* instead of *I* is correct:

Incorrect:
A nice cold Coca-Cola refreshes Maria and I after a long shopping day.

It's clear to most readers that "A nice cold Coca-Cola refreshes I after a long shopping day" is incorrect. In this situation, use *me* instead of *I*.

Correct:
A nice cold Coca-Cola refreshes *Maria and me* after a long shopping day.

Note: Always write the other person first, not me and Maria, but Maria and me.

In the following sentences, fill in the blank with the correct pronoun *I* or *me*.

1. My best friend, Carlos, and _____ love superhero movies and TV shows.

2. An *Avengers* movie can make Carlos and _____ happy for an entire summer afternoon.

3. Carlos's mom gave Carlos and _____ the entire DVD set of *The Flash* TV show.

4. Carlos and _____ binge-watched the show all in one day.

Already Versus All Ready:
Already is an adverb and refers to something that has been done or a specified time:

> When Joe arrived at the party, it had **already** begun.

All ready refers to a prepared group:

> We are all ready to leave for the party.

Fill in the blanks with either *already* or *all ready*

1. Science has _____ made great strides in recreating extinct species.

2. One extinct species science has _____ cloned is the Pyrenan ibex, though the animal only lived a short time after birth.

3. We are _____ to leave for the airport.

4. The sheep stood in the pen, _____ for the shearing to begin.

COMMON CONFUSED WORDS

To, too, two
> to = a preposition that indicates motion or direction.
> too = also, in addition, or excessively; extremely as in *too* easily persuaded;
> two = the number 2

Its, it's
> it's = a contraction for it is (this one is easy to check; if you don't mean "it is" then use its)
> its = belonging to it

Your, you're

> your = it belongs to you
> you're = a contraction for you are.

They're, there, their

> they're = a contraction for they are.
> there = a place
> their = belonging to them

We're, were, where

> we're = a contraction for we are
> were = the past tense of are
> where = a place

Then, than

> then = a point in time
> than = comparison

PRACTICE: As a reminder to proofread for these mistaken words, write one sentence for each; more than one word might be used in the same sentence:

> **Example:** If you're taking Allison *to* the fair, take me, *too.*

APOSTROPHES

Though most students understand the basics of apostrophe use, the barrage of short sound bites now used to communicate have created a shorthand for texting and twittering that doesn't translate to academic writing. To break this bad habit, study the use of apostrophes as a gentle reminder. Though cell phones sometimes put in missing apostrophes, the computer programs do not (as of this writing). Ultimately, it is the writer's responsibility to proofread work for these mistakes.

Use apostrophes to show possession or contraction.

Possession

If a noun does not already end in "s," use an apostrophe plus and s:

> Billy**'s** bike leans against the car, leaving a scratch on the fender.
> (The bike belonging to Billy)

If a noun is *singular* (only one) but ends with an "s," like some people's names, then add apostrophe and "s."

Luis**'s** bicycle sat in the garage, dusty from misuse.

Note: It's acceptable to leave off the "s" in this situation and just use the apostrophe.

If a noun is plural and ends in "s," use just the apostrophe (plural possession):

The boys**'** bicycles littered the front yard.

When two or more people claim ownership of the same object, use the apostrophe with the last noun only:

Anita, Reese, and Maria**'s** sailboat won the Newport/Ensenda race last spring.

When two or more people have *individual* possession, make all the nouns possessive:

John Lennon's and Paul McCartney's music became popular after the Beatles group split up.

Contractions

In contractions, apostrophes take the place of letters. Below are common words needing the apostrophe in their contracted forms.

cannot = can't (cant is *incorrect*)
do not = don't (dont is *incorrect*)
will not = won't (wont is *incorrect*)
are not = aren't (arent is *incorrect*)
shall not = shan't (shall'nt is *incorrect*)
could have = could've (*never* could of or couldve)
should have = should've (*never* should of or shouldve)
would have = would've (*never* would of or wouldve)

Note: for *its* verses *it's*, *you're* verses *your*, and other common misused contractions, see the "Confused Words" section.

PRACTICE: Write at least one sentence for each of the above possessive and contracted forms.

EVERYDAY VERSUS EVERY DAY

Everyday, when written as one word, means ordinary or usual:
>   I wear my everyday shoes to work in the garden.

Every day, written as two words, refers to something that occurs each day:
>   Every day, I check the plants in my garden for insects and other pests.

Test: Place the word *single* between every and day to see if it's correct:

>   **Incorrect:** I wear my every single day shoes to work in the garden.

>   **Correct:** Every single day, I check the plants in my garden for insects and other pests.

Though placing the word *single* in the sentence would be redundant, it can help to check the usage.

MADE UP WORDS

Alot is one made-up word that many people use in writing. **Always** write it as two words, or even better, replace it with *numerous* or *many*.

Nowadays is the correct way to write this word. Frequently, students will write *now-a-days, now in days,* or some other creative twist. Write *nowadays*.

Alright, though gaining popularity, is still considered incorrect by most grammar mavens, so write it as two words, *all right*.

Passersby is the plural form of this word, not *passerbys*.

Themselves, ourselves are the correct plural forms, not "ourselfs" and "themselfs."

PRACTICE: Write one sentence using the correct version of each of the made up words.

WORDINESS

Unnecessary repetition or redundancy—obvious statements, use of flat, worn out phrases, or excessive use of "to be" verbs (is, are, was, were, be, being, been, am)—contributes to wordiness. Don't use five words where one will do the job. Careful revision will help reduce or eliminate this problem. Sentences are like unruly plants: they need to be trimmed and shaped. Neglecting to edit and revise for space-gobbling words and phrases, gives the impression of an immature or careless writer.

Redundancy

Don't use synonyms (words that have the same or similar meanings).
  Examples of Redundancy:
  The tree frog's eyes are gigantic and huge.
  She used the moist, wet towel to clean up the spilled milk.

If something is gigantic, it is huge; moist is wet. Use one or the other, not both. Also eliminate redundancies like "**in my opinion**" and "**I believe**." If you state it, it is your opinion (for more on these phrases, see the thesis statement section).

Other redundancies or stating the obvious:

He had a smile on his face. (Where else would a smile be? Granted, the eyes might also "smile," as in "Her eyes smiled with delight while her mouth struggled to remain neutral," but generally, keep it simple: He smiled).

Her hat was pink in color. (Pink is a color).

Robin Williams was sad and depressed. (Synonyms).

Each and every child received a new pair of shoes.
(Each is every; only use one of these words).

He rose each day at 3:00 A.M. in the early morning. (A.M. means morning, and 3:00 is early by most people's standards; the same rule applies for P.M.)

Many other wordy phrases clutter writing:

Flat, Worn out Phrases and Clauses:
Though the phrase "due to the fact that" may sound lofty to some individuals, it's wordy and what some label "pompous diction." Replace it with the cleaner "because."

Wordy: **Due to the fact** that our flight was cancelled, we will not be attending the conference.

Better: Because our flight was cancelled, we'll not be attending the conference.

Avoid phrases like **"In today's society," "In this day and age," "Back in the day," "In this point in time"** and other vague, cliché statements. Many people love these word locusts, but stop using them; they serve no purpose except to tangle writing. Replace with "Today" or even better, a declarative statement that eliminates wordy leads-ins.

Wordy: **In today's society**, social media has caused many people to become increasingly isolated from their friends and families.

Better: Social media has caused many people to become increasingly isolated from their friends and families.

Follow the same advice for *at the present time* and *on a frequent basis.* Replace with *now* and *frequently.*

Edit for unnecessary use of the adverbs **really, very, totally.**

Wordy: His rude comment totally upset her.
Better: His rude comment upset her.

Excess use of "To Be" Verbs (is, are, was, were, be, being, been, am)

Though sometimes necessary, excessive use of "to be" verbs creates a sing-song, lulling-to-sleep rhythm. Sentence variety keeps the reader awake with anticipation, and pruning out "to be" verbs helps liven style. On every draft of an essay, ruthlessly take a highlighter to "to be" verbs; if the paper is scatter-shot with highlights, edit out as many as possible, replacing with stronger verbs.

Edit for *there are, there is, there were, there was,* especially when they begin a sentence. Instead, make the *real* subject take the place of these space eaters.

> **Wordy:** There was a stranger pounding on the door.
> **Better:** A stranger pounded on the door.

> **Wordy:** There was a dog barking at the mailman.
> **Better:** A dog barked at the mailman.

Revise for phrases that use "who" and "which" attached to a "to be" verb:

> **Wordy:** Sean, who is an A student, applied to the University of Florida.
> **Better:** Sean, an A student, applied to the University of Florida.

> **Wordy:** The concert, which is in the park, begins at 6:00.
> **Better:** The park concert begins at 6:00.

> **Wordy:** The dog, who was barking at the cat, is a German shepherd.
> **Better:** The German shepherd barked at the cat.

PRACTICE: Revise the following paragraphs to eliminate wordiness.

The scientific community is in an uproar about Freeman Dyson, who is a scientist and a physicist. Due to the fact that he is a brilliant and intelligent math prodigy, Dyson is really admired by many other scientists. Dyson is admired for his ability to solve problems, but he is embroiled in controversy. This is because he has doubts about global warming. Dyson thinks global warming is totally exaggerated. This is the reason why he is unpopular among environmentalists and some scientists. Some environmentalists believe Dyson's claims are because of the reason that he is too old and that he is losing his mind. Oliver Sacks, who is a famous neurologist, is Dyson's friend. He says that at this point in time Dyson's mind is fine.

Dyson thinks that global warming is a distraction. This is because he believes that in today's society, the global warming issue is distracting science from more seriously disturbing problems like war, poverty, and nuclear weapons. Dyson absolutely has faith in the creative imagination of scientists to solve global warming problems. This solving of the climate would be with plants that are bio-engineered to eat carbon dioxide. Dyson also believes that environmentalists are obsessed with climate change to the point that it has become almost like a religion to them. Dyson dismisses Al Gore's film that is called *An Inconvenient Truth* because Dyson believes that Al Gore's film is based on totally bad science. This science uses models that are unreliable and are computer generated. Computer generated models, Dyson believes, are bad due to the fact that they are not able to accurately recreate the atmosphere.

Many articles have been written about this controversy that is heated and surrounds Dyson. An article that is in *The New York Times Magazine* and is dated March 29, 2009, is an interesting article that you should read.

Glossary

adjective   a word that describes or modifies a noun: "Children's dirty faces peered in the candy shop window." The word *dirty* describes *faces*.

adverb   a word that describes or modifies a verb, an adjective, or another adverb: "The girl longingly peered through the shutters." The word *longingly* describes how the girl peered.

alliteration   using words close together that begin with the same letter or sound: *feasting* and *flying* both begin with *f*.

allusion   an indirect or implied reference; don't confuse with *illusion*, meaning deceptive appearance or delusion.

annotating   adding notes or explanation; critical commentary.

anthropomorphizing   assigning human characteristics or personality traits to animals.

appositive   a word or phrase that renames, describes, or gives more information about a noun (subject) and helps eliminate clunky clauses using *who* and *which*. "The orchids, *cymbidiums,* grew splendidly in the greenhouse." *Cymbidiums* renames *orchids* and is much cleaner than writing *which are cymbidiums.*

assonance   repetition of vowel sounds; resemblance of sound between words.

bias   a tendency or preference; sometimes prejudice.

cause and effect   cause effect arguments analyze and attempt to explain why something happens--causes--and the results of the incidents--effects.

chronological order   organization by time order, or order in which events happened.

classification   organizing an essay by grouping ideas or objects according to type or characteristic; an essay classifying high school students might be organized according to the group they associate with: jocks, cheerleaders, band members, nerds, brains, etc.

cliché   worn-out phrases such as *drinks like a fish, light as a feather,* or *not playing with a full deck.* General rule: if you've heard it before, don't use it in your writing.

comma splice   a writing error in which you join two sentences with a comma. Comma splices can be fixed with a semicolon, a comma with a conjunction, or a period and a capital.

> *Incorrect:* That cat is a Persian, her name is Cleopatra.
> *Correct:* That cat is a Persian; her name is Cleopatra.
> *Correct:* That cat is a Persian, and her name is Cleopatra.
> *Correct:* That cat is a Persian. Her name is Cleopatra.

Sometimes a comma splice can be fixed by making one of the clauses dependent.

> *Incorrect:* I waited in line for tickets to the Dave Matthews Band concert, a storm broke out and it began to rain.
> *Correct:* As I waited in line for tickets to the Dave Matthews Band concert, a storm broke out and it began to rain.

The word *as* makes the first clause dependent.

command form   drops the use of "you" when writing in second person point of view, as in a process/analysis paper.

complete sentence   a statement that can stand on its own; it expresses a complete thought. See **fragment**.

conjunction   a connecting word: *for, and, nor, but, or, yet, so.* In an informal essay, you can begin a sentence or paragraph with a conjunction, but do so sparingly.

connotation   a suggestion or implication: "Her words had sinister connotations."

criticism   in the context of this book, criticism refers to essays or articles by professionals commenting on or critiquing the work of others, whether it's film, art, or literature.

definition   In the context of this book, definition refers to a type of essay called extended definition where the entire essay focuses on defining one word in depth. See "Writing Strategies for Defining."

dependent clause   a clause that cannot stand on its own as a sentence; it is depending on another complete sentence. See **independent clause**.

> *Dependent clause:* When she ice skates
> *Dependent clause introducing an independent clause:* When she ice skates, the crowd roars with applause.

emphatic order   organization according to which points are the most important or most developed, saving the strongest or most in-depth discussion for the end of the essay right before the conclusion.

figurative language   metaphor, simile, personification, analogy.

first person   the *I* point of view.

fragment, sentence fragment   the word *fragment* means a piece, so a sentence fragment is a piece of a sentence—it's missing something, either a subject or verb, or it has both of these but doesn't express a complete thought.

freewrite   a warm-up or prewriting exercise where you write on your topic without stopping to think, disregarding organization, grammar, spelling, or punctuation.

genre   the largest category for classifying the arts. Film genres would include science fiction, drama, comedy, and western.

hyphen   a punctuation symbol that joins words together to make one, like *deep-rooted.* Don't confuse hyphens with dashes: a hyphen is shorter than a dash, so when you're typing dashes, use two hyphens.

incomplete sentence   see **fragment**.

independent clause   a group of words that could stand on its own as a complete sentence; it forms a complete thought. See **dependent clause**.

interrupter   a word or phrase that interrupts a sentence, requiring commas, dashes, or parentheses: "I told you, Binh, that the essay was due today." *Binh* interrupts the sentence "I told you that the essay was due today."

interrupting clause   a group of words that interrupts a sentence, requiring commas, dashes, or parentheses: "Crystal's hair, cut Winona Ryder style, glistened with auburn highlights." The clause *cut Winona Ryder style* interrupts the sentence "Crystal's hair glistened with auburn highlights." If you want the clause to get more attention, use dashes; if you want it to be less noticeable, use parentheses.

introductory clause   a dependent clause that introduces the main sentence: "When I work in my garden, I feel serene." The main sentence is "I feel serene"; *when I work in my garden* introduces the sentence. Use a comma after introductory clauses or phrases.

jargon   language used by a particular group, often not understood by the general population: computer jargon, English teacher jargon (some of the terms in this glossary are English teacher jargon).

loose sentence   a sentence structure that begins with a complete sentence followed by a series of clauses or phrases that add description or information. See **periodic sentence**.

mantra   a word or sound you repeat to help you concentrate during meditation.

metaphor   a direct comparison between two objects not using *like* or *as.* "She is a poem." See **simile**.

narrative   an essay or work of fiction told in story form.

noun   a person, place, or thing.

opposition   in an argument essay, the opposition is the other side; the opposite view.

parallelism   when a sentence structure is out of balance, it has a parallelism problem. **Example:**

Incorrect: The girls went swimming, hiking, and to fish.

Correct: The girls went swimming, hiking, and fishing.

periodic sentence   a sentence that begins with a series of dependent clauses or phrases describing or giving more information about the main sentence, which comes at the end. See **loose sentence**.

personification   giving human qualities to inanimate objects: "The chair *sulked* in the corner."

plagiarism   presenting someone else's words or ideas as your own—a serious academic offense. Always give credit to the proper source.

point of view   (see First, second, third person).

preposition   a word that links words or phrases by showing relationship, direction, or position: *of, from, by, after, through, in,* etc.

prewriting   the process of figuring out what you want to write about and which direction your writing will take. See the Getting Started and Traditional Brainstorming sections of this book.

rationale   an explanation or reason.

refute   to deny or prove wrong. In an argument essay, you should refute your opposition by presenting the other side's views and discussing how their thinking is illogical or misguided.

run-on sentence, fused sentence   two complete sentences that are run together but should be separated with a period, semicolon, or comma with a conjunction: "That cat is a Persian her name is Cleopatra." Don't try to fix a run-on with a mere comma. That's like yielding at a stop sign and creates another error called a **comma splice**. Fix a run-on the same way you would a comma splice.

second person   you (a more intimate way to address the reader). *Caution:* Don't use "you" in the general sense, meaning "anyone."

semicolon   a mark of punctuation (;) used to join two complete sentences when the thoughts are closely related. Do not use a semicolon with conjunctions; it replaces them.

sentence variety   using many different sentence styles in your essay rather than repeating the same structure.

simile   a comparison that uses *like* or *as*. "She moves like a poem." See **metaphor**.

specific details, specific examples   details or examples that are not vague words or phrases. Instead of *flower;* write *daisy; beer* becomes *Budweiser; oak* replaces *tree.*

subtext   an underlying meaning or message in a piece of writing, not directly stated but inferred.

thesis statement   the controlling idea or argument of an essay. A thesis should be specific, contain an opinion rather than fact, and not just announce your topic.

third person   someone else, not *I* (first person) or *you* (second person): *students* are; *she* writes; *researchers* believe.

tone   your writer's voice; the emotional or intellectual attitude, style, or manner of expression in your writing: sarcastic, ironic, comic, nostalgic are examples of tone.

transitions   words or phrases that help move sentences or paragraphs smoothly from one idea to the next. Some common transitions are conjunctive adverbs like *however, moreover, nevertheless, therefore;* phrases like *in addition, on the other hand;* single words like *thus, also, first, second, third, finally.* A more sophisticated trick for transitions is to pick up a word or idea at the end of one paragraph and use it in the beginning of the next one. See the Writing Strategies section for more on transitions.

verb   a word that expresses action (*jumped, went, made, drank, ran*) or state of being (*is, are, was, were, be, being, been, am*).

Index